Ghosts of the
Colorado Plains

Ghosts of the
Colorado Plains

M. L. EGAN

Perry Eberhart

Swallow Press/
Ohio University Press
Athens

Copyright © 1986 by Perry Eberhart

Swallow Press books are published by

Ohio University Press, Athens, Ohio 45701

First paperback edition printed 1996

02   5 4 3 2

Printed in the United States of America

on recycled acid free paper

Library of Congress Cataloging in Publication Data

Eberhart, Perry
    Ghosts of the Colorado Plains

    Bibliography: p.
    Includes indexes.
        1. Cities and towns, Ruined, extinct, etc.—
Colorado—History. 2. Colorado—History, Local.
3. City and town life—Colorado—History. I Title.
F777.E238   1986
ISBN: 0-8040-0832-9   ISBN: 0-8040-0833-7 (pbk.)

To Mariah
     Toni
     Courtney
     Lindsey
     Travis
     Dominic
     Emily
     Jesse

and the wonderful gift of tomorrow

This Old Town

I was born here.
In a longago land of shadows and muted sounds
I brushed against the pages of my days,
Partially separated the shadows and sounds.
The world was hot and cold against my cheeks

Within these small structured walls I learned
While my fancies found wings
And sailed far beyond these walls.

I worshipped here.
The soaring sounds touched God
And He made me a sinner.

I loved here,
And became immortal
For a moment.

I heard the music of life
And I carried the music within me.

In the melted minutes of larger shadows and louder sounds
I sweat cold sweat
I smelled the odors of life
Tasted dirt
Felt pain
And slowly died.

I was buried here
Under the cold clay of a faraway field.
A few unheard words gave my entire life meaning,
Stirring my silent screams even more than before.

The town is gone now
And the treasure of my life is spent
Upon the night winds and the weeds,
And on eternity.

Contents

Preface

This began as an average-size book, maybe as large as my earlier *Guide to Colorado Ghost Towns and Mining Camps*. It got out of hand early on, when I found that there are many other sites in Colorado, besides the mining towns in our mountains, that are just as historical and/or colorful. I cut the material in two a couple of years ago, but there was still too much. So, finally, I have divided it all into four parts and call the whole thing "Colorado's Neglected Ghosts." If the beleaguered publisher and reading public bear with me, I plan to publish the ensuing volumes within the next three years, to give a fairly comprehensive look at all the once important sites in the state, pinpointed by detailed maps and illustrated with historical and modern photographs, many of them never published before.

In selecting the sites which appear in this first volume, I attempted to find a representative cross-section of sites in each category, as well as those I thought were the most colorful and historical. In some categories, limiting the number of sites was difficult. One thing about ghost-towning — there is always another one just down the road, one you may not even have heard of before.

There are a couple of things that might make the maps easier to understand. Most farm communities were scattered settlements. Even the basic elements — the post office, general store, church and school — were not necessarily together. For the long-gone sites that have been plowed up, paved or built over, I attempted to pinpoint locations as closely as possible, using old records, maps, etc.; but they do not always agree. That is why I hid behind the label "approximate site." Mileage on the maps is measured from the official limits of the town or city the site is measured from.

I hope that, with this book, you can follow the same trails and back roads I did, and enjoy the same excitement of discovery.

LIST OF MAPS

LIST OF ILLUSTRATIONS

CHAPTER I

THE FIRST GHOST TOWNS

The first informal settlement in what is now Colorado has been traced back nearly 20,000 years. The closest thing to permanent settlements were "kill" and "slaughter" sites (not necessarily the same), where ancient man trapped ancient animals and butchered them for their meat and hides. To date, several of these sites have been found, mostly in northeastern Colorado, in Larimer, Weld and Yuma counties.

Artifacts, petroglyphs and pictographs* throughout the state date other temporary settlements, hunting areas and passageways of the Red Man through the centuries. Some more permanent residences in caves and overhangs in far western Colorado date from before Christ; ancient corncobs and evidence of primitive irrigation facilities tell of the first agriculture.

From there they moved into pit houses, often found on top of plateaus in southwestern Colorado, then into the highly advanced Pueblo cliff dwellings, which were suddenly abandoned—because of prolonged drought it is believed—around 1275.

Between that time and the first Hispanic settlers, more modern pictographs and petroglyphs and countless areas of tepee rings tell of continuous Indian activity until modern times.

There were a few unique Indian settlements which, although short-lived, heralded modern community settlement by their paleface counterparts.

The first such settlement on the Plains was called El Quartelejo, frequently translated as "far away home" or "home away from home." This settlement was made in 1694 by a large number of Picuries Indians escaping the oppression of the Spanish in what is now northern New Mexico.

Shortly after the Picuries fled northward, a search expedition led by Juan de Archuleta combed the Plains for the tribe, to no avail. In 1706 another expedition under Juan de Uribarri (sometimes shown as "Ulibarri") eventually found the runaways and returned some 60 of them to New Spain.

About 12 miles north of Scott City, Kansas (in an area now called Scott County State Park and El Quartelejo Indian Ruins) the foundations of the only "Pueblo" Indian ruins in Kansas were found, and are now considered to be the site where the Picuries settled nearly 300 years ago.

For many years, some reputable historians believed that El Quartelejo was on the eastern Colorado Plains, more specifically north of the Arkansas River about 100 miles or so east of present Pueblo.

There is no doubt that the ruins found in Kansas were made by a most isolated Indian tribe, Pueblo in character. However, as far as this author could determine, there is no documented evidence that links this site absolutely with the runaway Picuries tribe.

Although there is now no trace of these later settlements, they were in eastern Colorado.

SAN CARLOS DE LOS JUPES

(Pueblo County)

Comanche tribes were particularly bothersome to the Spanish in the northern colonies of New Spain (New Mexico). Because these people were nomadic, the Spanish could not wreak havoc upon their tribal homes. But the Comanche tribes, at home in and knowledgeable about the land, made lightning raids upon the Spanish colonies and disappeared into the landscape.

In 1779 (three years after the Declaration of Independence) Juan Bautista de Anza, Governor of New Spain, assembled a large body of troops (as many as 800 total) and Apache Indian allies, and set out to track and destroy the most troublesome tribe and its most cunning Chief, Cuerno Verde (Green Horn). De Anza tracked Green Horn through the San Luis Valley, over the Sangre de Cristos, and onto the eastern plains of Colorado.

At a site a short distance north of Pueblo, near the present Pueblo–El Paso County line, de Anza's troops overtook the slower, following members of Cuerno Verde's tribe, mostly women and the younger and

---

*Petroglyphs are painted symbols; pictographs are figures carved or etched into rock walls.

more elderly members of the tribe. They were all slaughtered. Ironically, the site at or about where the slaughter took place was later called WIGWAM.

De Anza came upon Cuerno Verde and his braves at a point southwest of Pueblo and finished the rest of the tribe. The site of the battle was on or near the present site of Colorado City, along or near a creek later named the Green Horn and in the shadow of what is now called Greenhorn Mountain.*

There have been many reasons given for the unique experiment attempted by the Spanish nine years later: restitution to the Indians, a new "tactic," a guilty conscience, or a combination of these and some others not mentioned.

At any rate, in 1787 the Spanish offered to provide the Jupes, a still bothersome Comanche tribe, with a complete village and the provisions and know-how to begin a model agricultural community.

There were also interesting reasons given for Los Jupes accepting the offer. But it was obvious that northern New Mexico was being overrun by better supplied and stronger colonists.

Ironically (some believe it was intentional) the agricultural village was set not far from the site of the death of Green Horn and his troops—a short distance east of Pueblo on the Arkansas (see p. 70) near the mouth of the St. Charles (San Carlos) River: an idyllic and fertile region.

Spanish workers built a village, nineteen adobe houses. Horses, oxen, sheep and seeds were provided, as were plows and the other tools of the time. "Experts" instructed the Indians on how to plant and cultivate the fields and raise the animals.

It seemed a most noble experiment. And it seemed, for a very short time, that it might have been successful despite the fact that it provided a lifestyle completely foreign to the nomadic Indians. But if the Spanish had gone into tribal tradition a little more deeply, they probably would not have attempted the experiment.

Early in 1788, the village was completely abandoned. According to tribal belief the site became full of evil spirits on the death of one of the most esteemed women of the tribe, greatly admired by Chief Paruanarimuco. It was not safe for the tribe to linger here, and they moved a great distance away.

Although Spanish officials encouraged others, including their own people, to settle here in subsequent years, the Indians refused because of the evil spirits, and Mexicans would not settle because of their fear of Indians.

Any trace of the short-lived experimental village disappeared many moons ago.

POINT OF ROCKS
(Otero County)

Another attempt to "civilize" the nomadic Plains Indians was sponsored by the U.S. Government in 1863. The motive was undoubtedly more selfish than the Spanish settlement of Los Jupes. It was also more costly, but it was just as unsuccessful and even shorter-lived.

In 1860, the government inveigled some plains tribes to surrender rights of eastern plains for a reservation, as such, along the Arkansas. The new "reservation's" western boundary was six miles east of the junction of the Huerfano and Arkansas Rivers; the northern was the Big Sandy River. It was bounded on the east by Big Sandy Creek, and on the south by the Arkansas River.

Shortly thereafter the Indian agency that had been in Big Timbers west of Lamar was moved to a point along the Arkansas, at about the center of the new reservation.

There were some indications that the next move by the government was proposed to further restrict the land held by the Indians on the reservation.

However, early in 1863, the government began development of a large agricultural community near the agency. Several buildings were constructed, irrigation ditches were laid out and their construction begun, and several hundred acres were plowed up. The Indians watched all this activity with interest.

The site was named POINT OF ROCKS for a massive jut of rocks above the Arkansas, a short distance north of present La Junta.

When government "experts" moved in and attempted to show the Indians how to plant seeds and use the tools that were provided, the Indians realized that all this activity had been for their benefit. They were expected to do the work, and they balked.

One night they rounded up all the livestock and horses around the agency, and silently stole into the night. Some claim a massacre of agency people, similar to the Meeker Massacre a few years later, was discussed by the Indians but rejected at the last moment.

It was the end of another noble experiment. It was not only unsuccessful as an agricultural settlement; now the Indians would no longer be restricted to the "reservation" boundaries, and roamed the plains again as they had for generations.

_____

*A State Historical Society marker is located in Greenhorn Meadow Park, 3.4 miles west of I-25, just off Colorado 165, in Colorado City.

CHAPTER II

HISTORIC STAGE STATIONS

Stage stations were much more than just a place to board or leave the stagecoach. In most cases they were the center of civilization in a desolate area, the only lifeline to the outside world. Many early stage stations were built like miniature fortresses. During the many Indian scares, real or imagined, all the settlers from miles around would gather at the stage station to wait it out. Even "scares" became social events, rare opportunities for long-distant neighbors to get together and relieve the isolation of frontier life.

Like railroad stations a few years later, stage stations meant excitement. Settlers would make every excuse to meet a scheduled stage to hear the latest news from "the states." Stages brought the news, the latest fashions, gossip—a direct line to the exciting world that was.

Settlers picked up their mail and packages from Back East at the stage stations.

Many stage stations furnished more than just the bare necessities. Most welcomed by the traveler were the stations that offered food and drink, an almost essential respite from the dusty, bumpy, nerve-rattling ride, and insulation for the ride ahead.

As more settlers set up housekeeping within riding

A typical stage station, in a painting by Frederic Remington. (*Courtesy Denver Public Library Western History Department.*)

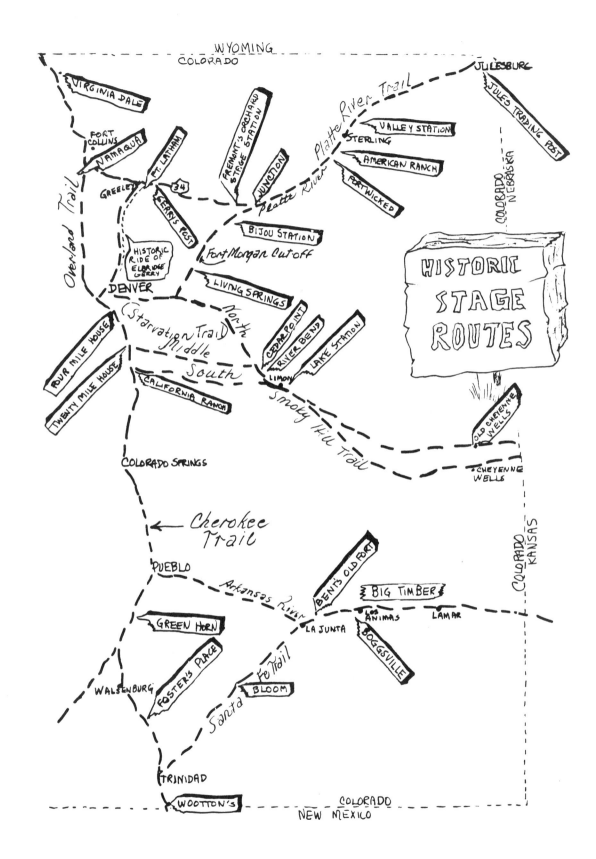

WYOMING
COLORADO

VIRGINIA DALE

JULESBURG

Platte River Trail

JULES TRADING POST

VALLEY STATION

FORT COLLINS

NAMAQUA

FT. LATHAM

FREMONT'S ORCHARD STAGE STATION

JUNCTION

STERLING

AMERICAN RANCH

FORT WICKED

GREELEY

34

KERRY'S POST

Platte River

COLORADO NEBRASKA

Overland Trail

BIJOU STATION

HISTORIC RIDE OF ELBRIDGE GERRY

Fort Morgan Cut-off

DENVER

LIVING SPRINGS

HISTORIC STAGE ROUTES

North

CEDAR POINT

RIVER BEND

Starvation Trail

Middle

LAKE STATION

FOUR MILE HOUSE

South

LIMON

TWENTY MILE HOUSE

CALIFORNIA RANCH

Smoky Hill Trail

OLD CHEYENNE WELLS

COLORADO SPRINGS

CHEYENNE WELLS

Cherokee Trail

COLORADO KANSAS

PUEBLO

Arkansas River

BENT'S OLD FORT

BIG TIMBER

LAMAR

GREEN HORN

LOS ANIMAS

LA JUNTA

BOGGSVILLE

WALSENBURG

FOSTER'S PLACE

Santa Fe Trail

BLOOM

TRINIDAD

WOOTTON'S

COLORADO
NEW MEXICO

distance of the stage station, many stations provided space—often in horse barns—for dances, meetings and other get-togethers. Some had picnic areas and a place for sporting events, such as crude arenas for racing and the earliest rodeos. (Note the Twenty Mile House, Four Mile House, and other stations along the Smoky Hill Trail.) Some Saturday nights and holidays the dances lasted all night and the social get-togethers lasted all day.

There were stage stations every 12 to 15 miles. About every 50 miles were "swing stations" where the horses were changed. Eating stations were often in the few towns along the way, but there were long stretches where the eating stops were far apart, often depending upon the whim of the line officials or station managers themselves.

As with virtually all other types of towns, most aspired to become the "city" of the future for that area. However, most stage stations disappeared quietly when the first railroads rumbled through. Some lucky ones remained as railroad stations, and some even evolved into local centers. And, believe it or not, many of today's towns and cities began as stage stations, while others were named for stage stations that had been located nearby.

But by and large there is little to remind us of the countless stage stations that dotted the frontier—although in their day they were the most exciting places there were, usually the only sites for miles in all directions.

There were literally hundreds of stage stations. The following are just a few of the more historic.

The Smoky Hill Trail

The Smoky Hill Trail was a very busy, albeit difficult, stage route from Kansas to Denver from about 1864 until the opening of the Kansas Pacific Railroad, which followed the same general route, made the stage unnecessary. The last stage over the trail arrived in Denver on August 21, 1870, six days after the Kansas Pacific made its connection at Comanche Crossing (see Chapter XVIII).

The Smoky Hill Trail was sometimes called the Butterfield Trail or Route, after David A. Butterfield, who made it his stage line from Kansas.

There were several variations in the stage route. The primary routes were Smoky Hill North, and Smoky Hill South, and a stretch that generally ran between those two routes, considered the most difficult route of the three, called the Starvation Trail or Middle Smoky Hill Trail.

The long, lonely stretches of the Smoky Hill Trail through eastern Colorado made it "easy pickin's" for marauding Indians and highwaymen. Water was also difficult to come by, and the lack of it was one of the reasons for the many sun-bleached skeletons found along the trail.

Despite the difficulty and drawbacks of this route, it was used by emigrants, sometimes on foot—attesting to their determination to reach the promised land.

FOUR MILE HOUSE
(Denver County)

The historic FOUR MILE HOUSE has been preserved and restored as a focal point of one of Denver's most interesting and unusual parks. This station, Denver's oldest existing building, is a city landmark and on the National Register of Historic Sites.

Four Mile House served as a stage station on the Butterfield Dispatch, the Denver & Overland Express and the Santa Fe Stage. It was the first station out of Denver on the Cherokee Trail and the southern branches of the Smoky Hill Trail,* and the last station before arriving in the "Big City."

Four Mile House and the other "Mile Houses" along the stage lines were named for their distance from the Denver City limits at the time, Broadway and Colfax. (Many have claimed the mileage was measured from the originating station at 15th and Larimer Streets.)

This station was most important as the last step before entering Denver after a long, dusty, bumpy, jarring ride, which was often extremely hot or extremely cold, and frequently plagued with the fear of Indians and highwaymen.

The stop enabled the passengers to freshen themselves for the grand entrance into the "Queen City of the Plains." The coach itself was cleaned of the trail dust and given fresh horses to enhance the entry. A key facet of the "freshening up" process was the well-stocked saloon that enabled passengers to wash away the memory of the recent trip and reinforce themselves for the immediate challenge to come. In the other direction, heading out of Denver, the stop was a bracer for the long perilous journey ahead—sufficient reason for the temperate to partake.

Many people have delved deeply into the history of the site in preparing for the National Register application and its park–museum status. It is probably as well-researched as any site can be, but there are still some pieces missing and information is disputed. The latest and most important material is contained in the booklet "Denver's Four Mile House" (available at Four Mile House) by Bette D. Peters, Historian and Administrative Assistant of Four Mile Historic Park, Inc.

---

*Much of the importance of Four Mile House was that it was at the crossroads of important early trails, the north–south Cherokee and Jimmy Camp Trails, and the Southern and Middle (Starvation) Smoky Hill Trails.

Four Mile Historic Park
715 FOREST ST.

The site was settled by Samuel and Jonas Brantner who arrived by covered wagon in July of 1859 (some say 1858) and built the original log building during the summer. It wasn't just one of your simple, dirt-floor temporary log cabins. The Brantners built a solid two-story building 22 feet wide and 32 feet long of thick, hand-hewn square logs of native ponderosa pine, dovetailed in the corners. Thick wood planking covered the floor, and there were heavy log rafters and wood shingles on the roof. The foundation stone was quarried from a nearby bluff. The solid strength of the original building is the primary reason the site has remained.

In this building Annie Brantner was born on October 14, 1859.

In 1860, the building was purchased by Mary Cawker, one of the most colorful ladies of the region and perhaps the most colorful resident of Four Mile House. She was not satisfied with the sturdy, handsome log building. She added much to it and the grounds around it in the four years she lived here. She lined the interior walls with floral wallpaper, and made many other improvements. She initiated the longtime tradition of hospitality, an important part of which was a well-stocked tavern.

She also added a giant corral and other outbuildings, and improved the landscape.

Mary Cawker sold the ranch–stage station to Levi Booth in 1864. The Booth family lived here for the next 60 years, adding to the original building, the outbuildings and to the family. All thrived. The Booth farm and ranch covered some 600 acres during its heyday. Booth added a large brick addition in 1883, butting it against the log wall of the original house. The new addition

followed the local architectural style of the day, with a steeply pitched roof, bay window and ornamental wood porches.

The coming of the Kansas Pacific and other railroads greatly lessened the stage activity at Four Mile House. However, it continued as a welcome way station for travelers. And its reputation as a neighboring gathering place and watering hole grew over the years.

The orchards and fields full of wildflowers surrounding the buildings were the scenes of countless family picnics and neighborhood gatherings. The Booths maintained a well-stocked tavern,* at least until the early 1870's, as long as Four Mile House functioned as a stage station.

Levi Booth died in 1912, Millie in 1926, and the Four Mile House and more than 600 acres of land that surrounded it passed into the hands of their descendants. In 1945 Mrs. Grace Booth Working, who was born in the house in 1868, sold it and some of the surrounding acreage to the Glen Boultons. Other tracts of the one-time large estate had been sold over the years, and only 12 acres remained. The Boultons, now of Mission, Texas, leased the property to others during the ensuing years and, although they attempted to keep the buildings in good repair, the old structures suffered, their future in doubt.

The historic significance of the Four Mile House was first acknowledged in 1934 when it became the first residential structure in Colorado to be recorded in the Historic American Building Survey. The Daughters of the American Revolution dedicated a historic plaque on the building in 1941.

The surrounding area was annexed to Denver in 1955. Shortly after that the Denver Parks and Recreation Foundation, better known as the "Park People," The Denver Landmark Commission, State Historical Society and other groups and private individuals were successful in acquiring the site and promoting its preservation and restoration. In 1975, the City and County of Denver took over the buildings and the 12 acres surrounding it. The Denver Parks Department did the first repairs on the buildings, and the Park People took total responsibility for the preservation, restoration, and future development of the site.

In 1977, the Four Mile Historic Park, Inc., was established to assume total responsibility for the perpetual

---

*Although some people claim that Levi Booth was a teetotaler, it apparently did not influence his business sense and he was better known for his hospitality. Some reports on Four Mile House attach to it the same festive stage station folklore given Twenty Mile House and other stations—the gala affairs and all-night dances—but Four Mile House apparently was not as prominent in this respect. For that sort of excitement, local residents could travel to Denver City. The stage station should not be confused with the nearby roadhouse on Leetsdale Drive.

Millie and Levi Booth (*above*) on the porch of Four Mile House. This brick addition to the original house was added in the 1880s.

The saloon in the historic stage station has been carefully restored to look as it did when it was a most welcome stop for travelers after a long, uncomfortable journey.

Below, Four Mile House restored, as it looked in 1980. Original station is shown at left. The photo at right, taken from a different angle, shows the brick addition.

Photos courtesy Four Mile House Historic Park

and continuing development of the house as a history museum and the land as a public historic park.

On May 1, 1978, Four Mile Historic Park was dedicated as a public park; in August of that year the house opened as a museum. A great deal of progress has been made in the restoration of the property. Ongoing plans also call for the reconstruction of early-day corrals, stables and barn, and additional landscaping to better represent the early history of the site as a pioneer oasis and gathering place.

TWENTY MILE HOUSE (Pine Grove, Parker)

(Douglas County)

TWENTY MILE HOUSE, named for its distance from Denver, was another famous and lively stage stop on the Smoky Hill Trail.

This stage stop dates from 1864 and was located just west of present Parker. Nelson Doud acquired the house in 1870. He, his wife and five daughters heralded the heyday of the site. The cuisine and the hospitality

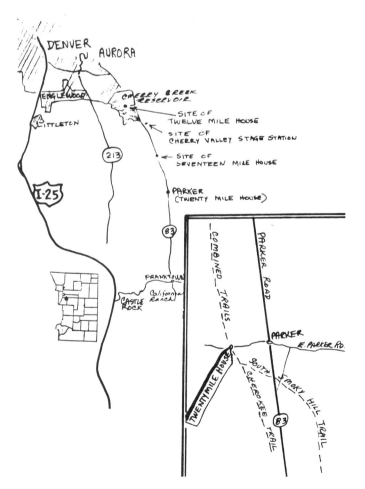

were known all along the Smoky Hill Trail. The dining room was often converted into a dance hall, and most weekends and holidays settlers and travelers came from far and wide to dance the night through.

The north end of the stage building was one-story brick housing the stage station and a little store. The south end of the building was two stories high, made of brick and adobe insulated with sawdust. This section contained the dining room and the living quarters.

The walls were at least six inches thick. As with many stage stations, it served as a welcome refuge during Indian scares, and there were many in this isolated area.

James C. Parker acquired the building in 1874. He moved the post office here from PINE GROVE (see "The Towns Before"), which was located about a mile and a half south of the stage station. Parker had previously operated stage stations at Lake and Kiowa.

In addition to the post office, Parker operated the little store and a blacksmith shop. His brother, George Parker, built a cabin near the stage station and operated a saloon, another attraction to thirsty travelers. His cabin, the first house built there, was located just across from where the depot is now situated.

The site was first known as PARKER'S.

As the Indians were not so pesky during the late 1870's and 1880's, more settlers built here. Soon the little community became a busy place. The name was shortened to PARKER.

Meanwhile, the Kansas Pacific Railroad replaced the stage line but increased the activity in the town. Very little of the original buildings remain today, and what little is left has been covered with clapboard and other materials. The stage station buildings were torn down in 1946.

The same year, an historic marker was dedicated in Parker. It read: "Due west one-half mile stood the TWENTY MILE HOUSE (20 miles from Denver). First house built in Parker, 1864. On the Smoky Hill Trail, an emigrant route that was dotted with unmarked graves of pioneers. Junction of the Smoky Hill and Santa Fe stage lines. A refuge for early settlers against Indian attacks. Hostelry kept in turn by Nelson Doud and James S. Parker (for whom the town is named)."

LAKE STATION (Hedinger's Lake Station, Hedinger's Ranch)

(Lincoln County)

LAKE STATION, 2½ to 3 miles southeast of present Limon, was one of the most historic stage stations on the old Smoky Hill Trail. It was known as "Station Number 24" on the Leavensworth and Pikes Peak Express, at the junction point of Smoky Hill South and Smoky Hill North.

The stage facilities were strongly built for protection against Indian attack. Part of the facilities were underground, including two big rooms connected by tunnel. The underground rooms were usually used for storage and for livestock. However, during one Indian scare stage passengers lived and ate in one of the underground rooms.

Despite the extreme precautions taken against Indians, the above-ground facilities were burned to the ground in 1867. Two years later, the barking of dogs warned residents of another pending attack, giving them time to set up defenses.

An early stage station manager here was James S. Parker, who was later transferred up the line to Twenty Mile House near Pine Grove, a forerunner of Parker.

LAKE STATION became a station on the Kansas Pacific Railroad in 1870. It became a shipping point for a large ranch area. The site was also known at the time as HEDINGER'S LAKE STATION or HEDINGER'S RANCH.

LAKE STATION held its own on the railroad until 1886 when the Chicago, Kansas & Nebraska Railroad (becoming the Chicago Rock Island & Pacific in 1891) crossed the Kansas Pacific tracks at Limon, about three miles northwest of Lake. Limon grew rapidly while Lake faded.

The onetime dugouts that served the stage station, later served as a potato cellar. It is said that part of the hole could be seen until a few years ago when a house was built above the site.

Elbridge Gerry. (*Courtesy Colorado Historical Society.*)

The Platte River Trail

This trail which followed the South Platte River from extreme northeastern Colorado into Denver was the most used stage and emigrant trail into Denver and the gold fields. Before 1859, it was the primary route of explorers and mountain men into Colorado.

In 1864, a shortcut was established from around Fort Morgan on the Platte River, southwestward to Box Elder Station, directly east of Denver and on the Smoky Hill (North) Route.

Although the Fort Morgan Cutoff lopped several miles and several hours off the stage route to Denver, it added to the dangers. The loneliness of the route made it more attractive to marauding Indians and highwaymen. There was also less water and game along this route, which made a big difference in those days.

THE HEROIC RIDE OF ELBRIDGE GERRY

Elbridge Gerry has never achieved his rightful place among Colorado pioneer heroes, although he has been called "Colorado's Paul Revere," and it is possible that he himself prevented the total destruction of Denver City and the northern Colorado settlements during the Indian Wars of 1864–65. He certainly was one of early Colorado's most colorful characters.

He is said to have been the grandson of a signer of the Declaration of Independence. He had the same name, and Colorado's Elbridge never disclaimed the honor. He came West in the 1830s as a trapper. He later became an agent for the trading post of Fort Laramie in Wyoming, and supplied some of the first participants in the gold rush of 1849. He was one of the founders of Colona near the mouth of the Cache La Poudre.

His real story began after he established a small trading post at the mouth of Crow Creek and the South Platte, at about the site of the later farm town of Kuner, which was about ten miles east of Greeley and seven miles east of FORT LATHAM, the prominent site in the area at the time.

Gerry was a "Squawman." He had as many as four Indian wives, not all at the same time. His most remembered wife was a Cheyenne.

On August 20, 1864, a relative of Gerry's wife (some say her brother) came into the Gerry Trading Post and warned the woman to take her children and run for cover. He said hundreds of Indians were gathering for a massive attack of all settlements along the Platte River Trail. They planned to destroy all communications to Denver and then attack and destroy Denver and all its inhabitants. The attack was planned in three days. On hearing this, Gerry jumped on the first of the four horses he would need for the frantic ride to Denver. He first warned all the settlers in and around Fort Latham, and then all the settlements and settlers between there and the capital city.

It is said that he dragged himself into the governor's home in the middle of the night, nearly two days after his ride began. He was exhausted. Some accounts say he was more dead than alive. The governor acted quickly. He mustered every gun and man available to set up a strong defense for Denver. He telegraphed all sites along the Platte River Trail that still had their lines up, and warned them of the impending attack. He immediately dispatched all troops he could spare to Fort Latham, to protect that key spot on the trail.

When the Indians discovered that Denver was prepared for the attack, as was Fort Latham and the sites between, they called off the all-out assault, although they destroyed most of the lines and the communications from Fort Latham eastward.

Elbridge Gerry became an immediate hero. But his deed almost did him in. In revenge for his act, the Redskins made Gerry's Trading Post and his possessions a special target. They continually ran off all stock Gerry could accumulate, and plagued his life and family with nuisance attacks and threats.

Gerry was penniless. But the settlers he'd saved seemed to have forgotten Elbridge Gerry sooner than the Indians did. He petitioned the government time and time again to make good his losses.

Finally, in 1872, the government compensated Gerry. The sum was $13,200, about half his total losses. With part of the funds Gerry built the "Gerry Block" in the nearby booming town of Evans. Completed in 1875, the Gerry Block included the Gerry House Hotel, "one of the finest hotels in the Territory."

Gerry died at his ranch a short time later, at the age of 57. A small headstone was placed over his grave on the site of his earlier trading post, on a little knoll about a mile and a half from the onetime town of Kuner (later a part of the Monford Feed Lots).

Elbridge Gerry and his little grave were all but forgotten until the 1930s, when some citizens of Greeley restored the grave site, and built a little iron fence around it. They have maintained the site ever since.

VALLEY STATION
(Morgan County)

Sterling's Overland Trail Park contains a marker dedicated to historic VALLEY STATION, which was located 3.8 miles northeast of the marker toward Julesberg, on the Platte River Trail.

The station was established in 1859 on the Leavenworth and Pikes Peak Express. The following year it

Valley Station marker at the spot of the historic stage station, just north of Sterling.

Stone remembrance of Valley Station at the colorful Overland Trail Museum in Sterling.

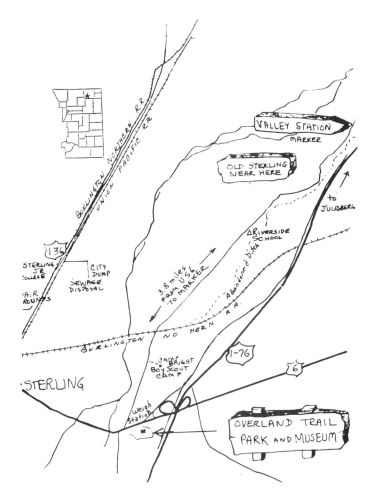

became a telegraph station for the Pacific Telegraph Company.

The sod stage station was built for protection against Indians and became a refuge for settlers and travelers, though it was not very effective against the massive onslaught during the Indian Wars. On January 28, 1865, an estimated 300 Indians attacked the post, wounding three defenders. The "Red Devils" burned 100 tons of government hay and ran off cattle, the number of which has been reported as all the way from 400 to 680 head, plus many mules and horses.

Eighteen soldiers took off after the band of Indians and after a 20-mile chase engaged in a valiant three-hour battle. The results as reported were at least twenty Indians killed, many wounded and the recapture of 300 to 400 cattle.

It was during this phase of the war that the Indians were successful in burning down virtually all of the telegraph poles along the Platte River Trail, cutting off communications almost all the way to Denver City.

Immediately, the army set out to re-establish the lines of communications. A Lieutenant Ware led a troop of soldiers with a "telegraph-pole train." Valley station was a major headquarters for the operation, but what remained of the stage station was not deemed suitable to hold off further Indian attacks. So the resourceful Ware built a fortification of bags of shelled corn. The unusual fort was inpenetrable and served the important operations well. Lieutenant Ware was commended for his part in the speedy work of restoring communications to Denver City.

Not only was the improvised fort safe during those difficult times, but it was also the site of certainly the only gourmet dinner along the Platte River Trail during the Indian Wars.

Unusual visitors to the "Corn Fort " were two Germans who made it through despite the continuous presence along the trail of Indians on the warpath. The two Germans traveled by night and hid themselves and their wagon by day. They didn't carry the usual prairie fare in their supplies. Hidden in the pit of their wagon were cans of oysters, kept cold by fresh snow each day. As Dr. Margaret Long reports in her classic "Smoky Hill Trail," Lieutenant Ware sat on his bastion after sunset and ate a can of freshly-thawed oysters "as delightful and fresh as if they were just out of Chesapeake Bay."

VALLEY STATION lingered several years, even after the railroad came through. It was a tiny farm center, not nearly as colorful as it had been as a stage station, the first settled site in the area. When the railroad came, the nearby town of Sterling took over.

"FORT WICKED" (Wisconsin Ranch, Godfrey's Ranch

(Logan County)

About three miles southwest of Merino, where U.S. 6 crosses to the south side of the Platte River is a marker. (see p. 65).

(see p. 65).

FORT WICKED
Originally Godfrey's Ranch.
Famous Overland Stage Station and one of
few forts withstanding the Indian uprising
of 1864 on the road to Colorado, named for the
bitter defense made by Holon Godfrey.

It was immediately after the Sand Creek Massacre that the Indians regrouped and intensified their attack on the Platte River Trail. They attacked and destroyed every station along the trail—every station but one. The one station was GODFREY'S RANCH, sometimes known as WISCONSIN RANCH. The "roundhouse" on Godfrey's Ranch had six-inch thick adobe walls with portholes for rifles. But some of the other stations along the trail were built as well, and they could not withstand the fierce Indian attacks.

Holon Godfrey, proprietor and hero of Fort Wicked. (*Courtesy Colorado Historical Society.*)

This drawing of Fort Wicked was one of a series of sketches by James Gookins which appeared in *Harper's Weekly*, October 13, 1866. (*Courtesy Colorado Historical Society.*)

On January 14, 1865, an estimated 300 Cheyennes in war paint attacked the Godfrey Ranch. Godfrey, three other men, and four women who valiantly melted down metal for molding bullets and reloading the guns, successfully held off the Indians during the day-long battle. Many redskins were killed and wounded. After nightfall, one of the defenders, a man named Perkins, escaped in the dark to get help from an encampment of soldiers near Fort Morgan. Only five soldiers were available to return with Perkins, but they succeeded in getting back into the ranchhouse unmolested. With fresh help, the entrapped party was able to repel (or tire) the Indians in the ensuing battle—and finally the Indians left.

After that the Indians named Godfrey "Old Wicked." Godfrey was said to have been so proud of the name that he hung a sign saying FORT WICKED over the door of his ranch.

The nearby AMERICAN RANCH was destroyed by the Indian attack and Godfrey's Ranch became the official stop in the Overland Stage run. Godfrey became

famous along the trail. His station was a popular stop. Inside his "fortress" was a long adobe cabin which contained a well-stocked store, a major supply station along the trail. Godfrey was noted for being genial and interesting.

It is not clear exactly when Godfrey came to this area, reportedly either 1861 or 1863. However, he remained after the Indian Wars to become a key figure. In the late 1860's and early 1870's, he "hand dug" a mile-long irrigation ditch to water his private garden. In the spring of 1872, he and six other men filed on the construction of a much larger irrigation ditch. First called the "Fort Wicked Ditch," it was said to have been the first ditch surveyed and dug along the South Platte in eastern Colorado and one of the first in the state.

The ditch was later called the South Platte Ditch (see "Farm Centers"), and is still in operation. In fact, on May 1, 1972, local residents celebrated the 100th anniversary of the ditch.

SOUTH PLATTE and then MERINO replaced FORT WICKED, but Holon Godfrey is still a local hero, and his exploits will be long remembered.

AMERICAN RANCH
(Kelly's, Morrison Ranch)
(Logan County)

AMERICAN RANCH did not fare as well during the Indian Wars as did Godfrey's Ranch or Fort Wicked, a mere three miles to the southwest along the Platte River Trail (see p. 65). American Ranch was destroyed twice.

In August of 1864, when the first scattered Indian attacks began, American Ranch was burned down. It was quickly rebuilt, mostly of sod construction rather than wood. Then on January 15, 1865, while Godfrey and his mixed crew were holding off a large band of Redskins, American Ranch was completely destroyed again, although there was a larger crew on hand than at Godfrey's. It is said seven men at American Ranch were killed and mutilated, and the two women, a Mrs. Morrison and her daughter, were kidnapped, never to be seen again.

There is some question as to the beginnings of American Ranch. Most probably it was jointly established. Local history says that "Uncle Jimmy" Chambers first settled here, but it is also said that Charlie Moore settled here in 1859, before the Overland established a stage route through the area. Moore named his place KELLY'S for some reason. The site is also sometimes called MORRISON RANCH, for the Morrison Family, early settlers.

Apparently both "Uncle Jimmy" and Charlie Moore survived the January 1865 Massacre, or they weren't present at the time, because both were heard from again. Moore and his brother James Moore, a famed Pony Express rider who was said to have made the second longest ride on record, moved to the Sterling area and established the WASHINGTON RANCH, three miles north of Valley Station. And Uncle Jimmy became a prominent figure in the Sterling area.

Although it is said that the American Ranch stage building was never rebuilt after its second destruction, and Fort Wicked became the official stage stop, Chambers was a longtime leader in the region. Chambers was said to have donated an acre of his land for the first school in the Sterling area. He also joined with Godfrey and others in the survey and construction of the region's first major irrigation ditch, the Fort Wicked Ditch, which later became the South Platte Ditch.

So although American Ranch had a short life, especially as a stage station, its inhabitants played a prominent part in the development of the region.

FORT MORGAN CUTOFF

BIJOU STATION
(Morgan County)

The site of BIJOU STATION was historic before it became an important stage station. Here, or very near here, on Bijou Creek, famed mountain man Sam Ashcraft had a trading post. It was built in 1861, primarily to trade with the Indians. It is said he became well known to Plains Indians, and he often knew their movements before any one else.

In July of 1862 a Mrs. Thomas Tuttle recorded in her diary that her party camped near the station which "... was to be torn down the next day."

It is not clear if the trading post was torn down or if a new building was constructed near the same site in 1864 when the Fort Morgan Cutoff was established and

Bijou Station became the first major station off the Platte River Trail, southwest of Fort Morgan. Although the Cutoff lopped several miles off the Platte River Trail into Denver, and saved precious time, the Cutoff became the most isolated and dangerous section of the stage run. It was the longest run between St. Louis and Denver without a change of horses, twenty miles from BEAVER CREEK STATION on the Platte River Trail.

About the same time Bijou Station was established, the Colorado Volunteers under Col. John Chivington camped near here prior to their infamous attack on Sand Creek, a precipitous event in the Indian Wars.

It remained a popular hangout for soldiers protecting the trail and those from Fort Morgan, a few miles to the northeast.

In 1865, famed Colorado mining man and politician N. P. Hill recorded arriving at Bijou Station with some friends, en route to Denver. He found the station so desolate and so overrun "with drunken rabble of soldiers" that he paid the stage driver another fifteen dollars to continue the trip into Denver.

BIJOU STATION remained a key point on the stage run into Denver until the railroad came through to the north. There was a later town along the railroad on Bijou Creek that was also called Bijou or Bijou Station, but it was a little north of the old Stage Station. Today it too is just a vague memory.

There was another stage stop called Bijou Station much further south on Bijou Creek on the Smoky Hill North Trail. It was a short distance south of present Byers. The trail joined the Fort Morgan Cutoff further west at Kiowa Station (near present Bennett) for the final leg into Denver.

LIVING SPRINGS STATION
(Adams County)

LIVING SPRINGS STATION was the other major stage station on the Fort Morgan Cutoff between present Fort Morgan on the Platte River Trail and Kiowa Station (just east of Bennett) on the Smoky Hill (north) Trail (see p. 106). Living Springs was located near the confluence of Wolf and Comanche Creeks about midway between Bijou Station and Kiowa Station. It was named for the springs found in a bed of the usually dry Comanche Creek. Living Springs was also a telegraph station for the Pacific Telegraph Company.

Living Springs was well built and also served as a "fortress" against Indian attack, as did most of the other stage stations in eastern Colorado. The author found no records of Indians ever attacking the station, although there were many in the neighborhood and many 'scares' during the Indian Wars.

After its usefulness dwindled as a stage station in the early 1870's, the isolated site lingered as a small farm and ranch center. "Grand Balls" were held at the old stage station. Settlers came from several miles distant.

Dr. Long reported in "The Smoky Hill Trail" that many of Colorado's greatest cattlemen grazed their herds nearby, including John Iliff and Billy Adams. The Coles and Earp Brothers were other interesting visitors to the station.

The May 20, 1893, issue of *The Denver Republican* told of "irregularities" in a special election at Living Springs, forcing another election. A total of 25 votes were cast in the election.

Dr. Long, who devoted much of her life to tracking down the early pioneer stage trails and locating the stations along the way, said the Living Springs station house where the dances were held burned down many years ago. She said some newspapers found in the walls of the ruins dated back to 1849, and lumber saved from the ruins was used to build a shed that stands today on the site of the historic stage station.

The last building from Living Springs, a one-room schoolhouse, has been relocated at COMANCHE CROSSING Historic Park in Strasburg (see Chapter XVIII).

Santa Fe, Overland and Other Trails

VIRGINIA DALE (Rocky Ridge)
(Larimer County)

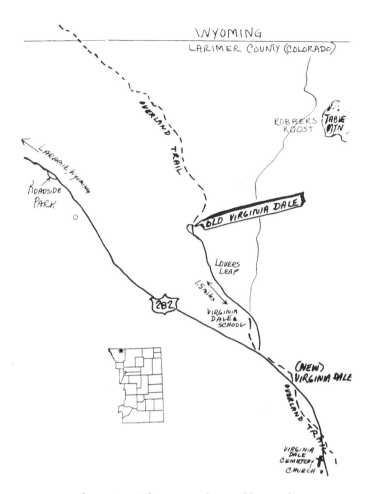

Perhaps Colorado's most notorious stage station (with the possible exception of Julesburg 1) was OLD VIRGINIA DALE. The station itself was little different from many others. It was its onetime agent, Joseph "Black Jack" Slade, who attracted attention.

Mark Twain, who passed this way, characterized Slade as the "cruelest looking man" he ever met. When he was sober, Slade was said to be almost pleasant and most competent. But when he was drunk, he was cruelly ruthless and lived up to Twain's appraisal of him. He demonstrated that in killing Jules Beni (see JULESBERG, Chapter XVIII). Slade not only operated Virginia Dale, he was division manager of the Overland Stage Route that included Beni's station in extreme northeastern Colorado.

The stage station was located 4.5 miles south of the Wyoming border, about a mile east of present Virginia Dale on U.S. 287. The original station, established in 1862, was 20 by 60 feet, built of hand-hewn logs, with a great rock fireplace and chimney.

Slade named the place for his wife, who, some say, was even meaner, and meaner-looking, than Slade. (Perhaps that is where he got his unhappy demeanor.) Slade helped the government build the station. The shingles were freighted from St. Joseph, Missouri, at $1.50 per pound. Large stables and barns and a corral

were near the station. The stages changed horses here, so fresh horses were always available.

There were several Indian "scares" at the station. At one time, a lookout was stationed atop a nearby hill to give warning of the approach of Redskins. Vice President Schuyler Colfax and other government officials were detained here several hours around 1870 due to marauding Indians in the neighborhood.

There were persistent rumors that Slade was the center of hanky panky going on at Virginia Dale. Whether Slade was getting his share or not, there were frequent stage robberies in the area, as the naming of a nearby hill "Robbers Roost" attests. Some say it was the growing rumors of Slade being a double agent for the stage line and a local robber band that caused his dismissal after little more than a year on the job. Others say that it was just his growing reputation for meanness. Whatever the reason, Slade was relieved of his post, and he wandered off to Montana, where he was hanged a couple of years later.

The stage station remained a key station until the railroad replaced the stage line in the 1870s. Bill Taylor and his wife relieved Slade and Virginia Dale. The Taylors operated the station and hotel, and were said to have successfully fought off an Indian attack by arrang-

Early drawing of "Black Jack" Slade. Mark Twain said he had the cruelest eyes of any man he had ever met. (*Courtesy Colorado Historical Society.*)

Virginia Dale Stage Station as it looked in 1883. The little knoll in the background, from which highwaymen could see stagecoaches approach, was called Robber's Roost. (*Courtesy U.S. Geological Survey.*)

ing stovepipes and wagon wheels to look like cannons. When the Taylors left, S. E. Leach became agent until the station closed.

When the railroad came, the stage buildings were sold and became part of a ranch. The old stage hotel had been the site of many local dances in the intervening years. Some of the old buildings were torn down, still showing some bullet holes, most from Indians but no doubt some from Slade's own gun. The old stage house, still in good shape, and the other remaining buildings are well integrated into the ranch at the site today.

The modern highway missed the old station by almost a mile. The roadside site by the same name doesn't have a history anything like the OLD VIRGINIA DALE.

FOSTER'S PLACE (with Augusta and Apishapa)
(Huerfano County)

Many stage stations were noted for their hospitality and good cooking, but few, if any, achieved the reputation of FOSTER'S PLACE, located on the Apishapa, about four miles east of Aguilar.

The stage station was established around 1862–63. It was just a drab little station until Colonel (some reports say Captain) James Allen Foster took over in 1868. Colonel Foster came from Virginia and was a southern gentleman of the highest order. He had fought with the Eighth Cavalry for the Confederate States of America. His wife Susan was a magnificent cook.

Foster began building a large, commodious hotel immediately. It was a two-story adobe and wood building with large rooms, four huge fireplaces and a veranda that extended entirely around the second floor.

It didn't take long for Mrs. Foster's reputation as a cook to spread throughout the region. Foster's Place soon became the most welcome stop along the line. But one needn't be a stage passenger to partake of the hospitality at Foster's Place. It became a clubhouse for trappers, traders, freighters, lumberjacks, traveling salesmen and any and all traveling down the road or living in the neighborhood. There was always a gathering around one or more of the fireplaces, and tales of adventure or just tall tales filled the air.

Foster farmed a small plot near the station and ran a few cattle, and the cuisine featured home-grown products.

There were many Indian "scares" in the vicinity, but no record of any raids on Foster's Place. Stagecoaches usually signalled their approach with rifle fire to let Foster know the hoofbeats were friendly.

The "good old days" ended at Foster's Place in 1876 when the Denver & Rio Grande Railroad built a narrow

gauge track through here (it became standard gauge in 1888). But Foster adapted. He established a railroad station along the tracks, about a half mile from his hotel. He called the new site AUGUSTA. A few years later, the railroad built another station about a half mile further east and called it APISHAPA. Apishapa (pronounced a-pish-a-pa) is an Indian word meaning "sticky" or "smelly" water, believed named for the overflowing river water that formed stagnant and odorous pools along the banks of the river.

During their long history Augusta and Apishapa have been confused, principally because of their proximity to each other. The post office and map makers often showed it as "Apishapa (Augusta P.O.)" and vice versa.

Foster and his wife built another hotel and eating place at Augusta. It was not as large as his original house and it never became the famous stopover the first one did. There was a large stockyard at Augusta, near the station, as well as a school and a couple of other businesses. Augusta also became a water stop on the railroad.

The old hotel was maintained as a home and guest house for a few years. Later it was turned into a sanitarium for tubercular patients. Even later it became headquarters for the Dupont Powder Company.

The first Mrs. Foster died in 1889, and Foster retired to Virginia, leaving his Colorado holdings to his adopted son. A short time later, however, Foster married another elegant Southern belle, and returned to Colorado to run his hotel. He died in 1895. His second wife died in 1908. Foster and his two wives were buried side by side in the little graveyard on a knoll about a half mile from his original home.

The entire area is now ranchland operated by Valentine Coppa, who was born in the ranchhouse next to his

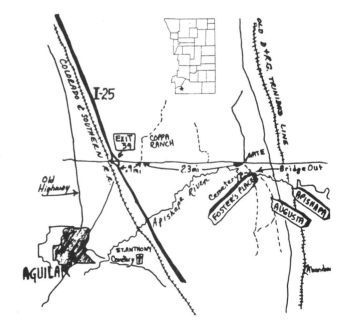

GHOSTS OF THE COLORADO PLAINS

Two views of Foster's Place Stage Station. High winds in early 1982 blew away part of the roof of the old station. At one time a veranda completely circled the second floor of the building. It was used as a lookout for Indians as well as for sitting in the open air.

The barn behind Foster's Place still stands. It may have to be torn down soon, however, because the waters of the Apishapa River are undercutting its foundations.

The old stockyards is all that is left of Augusta, a small railroad community that replaced Foster's Place stage station. The stockyards last shipped cattle in the mid-1930s.

present, modern home in 1916. He has seen many changes.

Coppa and his wife and three children have dearly loved Foster's Place Hotel and attempted to protect it as best they could. But they have stood by helplessly as the old building slowly deteriorated. Coppa said the last family to live in Foster's Place moved out around 1941, when heavy rains and some flooding made the building unsafe for occupation. Heavy rain during the summer of 1981 caved in part of one side of the building. Galelike winds in March of 1982 toppled much of the roof. Coppa said vandals and insensitive gun-toters have done more damage over the years than time and the weather. The old veranda was torn down many years ago.

The old Foster barn still stands proudly behind the house, but Coppa said it will probably be torn down soon because the river is undercutting its foundation and it could collapse into the Apishapa.

The Coppas encouraged and fully cooperated with efforts by regional historians to raise funds to preserve and restore Foster's Place and the barn, but too much money was needed and too little was available.

Coppa said the last cattle was shipped from the stockyards at Augusta in the mid-1930s. The railroad was abandoned in 1937. All that is left of the station is the large stockyard and the windmill that pumped water for the railroad. Nothing is left of Apishapa.

The little graveyard would be obscured by time and the weeds had not a 4-H group from nearby Gulnare,

led by teacher June Valentine (it is just coincidence that her last name is the same as Coppa's first name). A few years ago the club took on the historic little graveyard as its community service project. Club members cleared it of high weeds and built a little fence around it. Nonetheless, vandals have taken their toll. A 1968 photograph in a Pueblo newspaper shows a short marble marker for Foster. The heavy marker is gone. Its base remains, a short distance from a tall marble marker for both of Foster's wives. One side reads: Susan Foster 1833–1889. The other side reads: Margaret Elizabeth, 1838–1908. In front of this marker is a tiny white marker that says:

Corp.
James A. Foster
Col.
8 Va. Cav.
C.S.A.

No one seems to know what the "Corp." stands for.

Valentine and her young friends also built a panoramic marker on the top of the knoll. About a dozen markers are scattered around the little cemetery. The latest date on any marker is 1915.

One wonders where the Foster marker is today. It is gone, and soon his colorful and historic hotel will be just a memory—an important Colorado memory.

GREENHORN (Hicklin's)
(Pueblo County)

The mountains, the river and the later towns were named for the Comanche Chief Cuerno Verde (Green Horn) was was killed near here in 1779 by Spanish troops under Captain de Anza.

The start of modern activity began not too many years later. In 1846 and 1847, William Kronig and western wanderer Ruxton reported some French-Canadian families living and farming on Greenhorn Creek. In 1853, when Captain Gunnison passed by here on the way to his ambush death in Utah, his guide reported that a Mexican family was farming in the Greenhorn Valley.

Famed mountain man Alexander "Zin" Hicklin, who married the daughter of New Mexico's governor Charles Bent, wrangled himself a land grant, part of the Vigil and St. Vrain Grant, and established a trading post and ranch along the Greenhorn. He was a good friend of Kit Carson and many of the other notables of the time, who visited here often. Hicklin became a bit more notorious during the Civil War. A southern sympathizer, he began training other rebels in nearby Mace's Hole, preparing for the "takeover" by the South. The secret was discovered and troops from Fort Garland headed in that direction. Hicklin's "troops" became

The grave marker of Foster's wives, one side for Susan, the other for Margaret Elizabeth, stands in the little cemetery behind the famous old stage station. John Foster's marker sat beside it until it disappeared recently.

Alexander "Zin" Hicklin and (*below*) his house at Greenhorn.
(*Courtesy Pueblo Library District.*)

Greenhorn Mountain, named after the Indian Chief killed by De Anza, stands above the little stage stop of Green Horn. The picture
is dated 1889. (*Courtesy Denver Public Library, Western History Department.*)

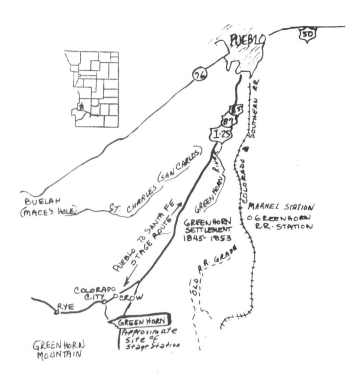

dred years later his grave was moved during the construction of Colorado City. Local people finally complied with his wishes and put some whiskey in his new grave. After a long dry spell, Hicklin can now entertain his friends.

BLOOM (Iron Springs)
(Otero County)

In 1862 Henry C. Withers established a stage station at IRON SPRINGS on the Santa Fe Trail, about 30 miles southwest of Bent's Fort, between it and Trinidad, on the Timpas River. It was a home station, which on the Southern Overland Mail Co. meant the horses were changed here and the passengers could eat and prepare for the trip ahead.

The Diary of Episcopalian Bishop Joseph C. Talbot tells of stopping here, arriving here at 4 A.M. after leaving Bent's Fort at 6 P.M. The Bishop called the station a "miserable, dirty place" where they stopped for a "greasy breakfast of antelope."

An early operator of the station in the late 1860's was named Brigham Young, no relation to the Mormon leader. In fact, he wasn't even a Mormon. He married one of "Uncle Rick" Wootton's daughters.

When the AT&SF Railroad replaced the stage in 1872 the site remained a station and cattle shipping point. It was about this time the name of the site was changed to BLOOM, for Frank Bloom, pioneer Trinidad banker and businessman and son-in-law of the most prominent rancher in this area, M. D. Thatcher.

The population has wavered up and down much of the time since. The 1915 Business Directory said the population was two whites and 40 Mexicans. The post office was discontinued in 1938, although the population was listed as 51 in 1940. Today it is still a flag station on the railroad and is still seen on some maps, but no population is listed.

aware of it and scattered. Hicklin convinced officials he had nothing to do with it by pretending to be a country bumpkin.

In the early 1860s a key stage station was established here on the north–south route between Santa Fe and Pueblo. In addition to its stage activity, a small farm and ranch community grew around the station. It remained a small center for several decades, up to modern times, although the Denver & Rio Grande built a short distance east of the site in 1876.

Hicklin, known for his hospitality and his humor, asked to be buried with whiskey in his grave so that he could entertain his friends who had gone·before him. When he died on February 13, 1874, his wishes were ignored for one reason or another. Nearly one hun-

CHAPTER III

BY THE SIDE OF THE ROAD

Every sign of civilization along the trail, no matter how minute, could be a major milepost in the long, lonely, slow-moving travel through the frontier West.

But some were more welcome, became more historic than others.

BIG TIMBERS

There were no buildings here to speak of, no specific center, or boundaries. But before Colorado became a territory, this was the starting point of our history, the commercial and social center, the nerve center of Colorado.

BIG TIMBERS was a grove of trees that stretched nearly 25 miles along the Arkansas, the Santa Fe Trail, west-

ward from about where present Lamar is today. It was a linear oasis, a lengthy trading post, a long brawling, laughing, lusty meeting-place of different cultures.

From the beginning of the Sante Fe Trail in the 1820s, this was a major camping place for the long caravans of freighters and emigrants. Here was respite from the heat and the dust of the trail, wood for the fire, water for man and animals.

Before and after that it was a camping ground for Indians: the Plains Indians, the Comanche, The Cheyenne, Arapahoes, Kiowa. They fought many battles for the rights to Big Timbers.

And this is where the earlier trappers and traders, the mountain men, met with the Indians, bartered beads and baubles for animal pelts—the Indians in full ceremonial dress, the mountain men boozing, brawling,

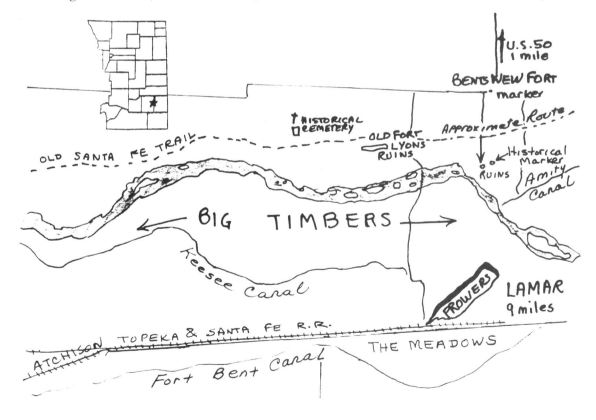

21

boisterous. There was always excitement and danger when the air reeked of "Taos Lightning," and there was plenty of that.

Near the western end of Big Timbers, William Bent did his first bartering in his "Old Trading Post," before he moved upstream to establish his famous trading post. In the end he returned to Big Timbers to build the New Bent's Fort, which he sold to the army and which became the original Fort Lyon.

Most of the famous western explorers and wanderers passed this way. First it was Pike and his party in 1806. In 1820, Maj. Long returned to civilization this way after crossing what he called the "great American Desert." The "Pathfinder," John C. Fremont, and his usual guide, Christopher "Kit" Carson, knew Big Timbers well.

Lt. Edward Beckwith, who took over the Gunnison Expedition after its leader was killed by Indians in Utah, passed through Big Timbers in 1853, and described it in great detail in his report of the expedition.

Alexander Barkley visited in 1846. So did Jacob Fowler and Rufus Sage, and most of the other western wanderers. And almost all of them reported the area thick with Indians. It was a Cheyenne campground in 1846.

In 1860, the U.S. Government used a building of Bent's New Fort, after Fort Lyon was moved to higher ground upstream, and made an Indian Agency for the surrounding Comanche reservation that had been established.

In 1863, the Government realized it had given the Comanche too much good land and tried to stick them in the farm village upstream, with almost devastating results (see Point of Rock, Chapter I).

Civilization took its toll on Big Timbers. Travelers and settlers tore down the big timbers for firewood, for homes, to make room for roads and other "modern improvements."

U.S. Highway 6 follows along much the same route as the Santa Fe Trail, and it is civilized along the way. Here and there are some trees, no groves. The last vestiges of Big Timbers is long gone.

NAMAQUA STATION (Mariano's Crossing, Fort Namaqua, Laramie Crossing)
(Larimer County)

There is a large stone and cement marker about 3 miles west of Loveland where Mariano (or Mariana) Modena established one of the earliest and most historic sites in early Colorado.

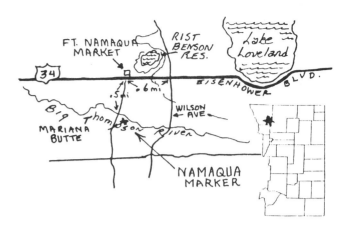

Modena was born in Taos, New Mexico, in 1812. He joined some beaver trappers while still in his teens and for the next few years did just about everything there was to do in the western wilderness. He was a trapper, trader, scout, guide, Indian fighter, rancher. After a most difficult trip as a guide with Captain Marcy, Modena decided to settle down.

Modena and his Indian wife laid claim to a large section of land here in 1858. Near a crossing of the St. Vrain River, they built a large, fortified stone building. He built a large stables and other buildings. Here would be a stage station, trading post, refuge for the early settlers during the Indian scares, as well as the site of the first school and first church services in this region.

It was the crossing of many trails, north–south and east–west. It was the north–south crossing of the Texas–Oregon or Denver–Laramie Trail. Offshoots of the Oregon Trail and the Platte River Trail passed by here, to the gold fields and points west.

There has been much discussion concerning the meaning of the name. Modena was said to be a self-educated man and a voracious reader. Although many believe that Namaqua means "near water," some say it is an African term while others say it is Indian. There are many other suggestions. One says it means "wayside inn," another says it is the name of a long-tailed African pigeon, and another says it is an Indian proper name. It really didn't matter, because virtually every oldtimer called the site Mariano's Crossing.

During the '59 gold rush to Colorado, a constant stream of traffic passed through here, many travelers dropping down from the Oregon Trail, at the Fort Laramie (Wyoming) turnoff. Others left the Platte River Trail and went directly westward into the golden mountains. Modena usually had a good supply of staple goods to sell, including whiskey. His wife and children helped with chores.

Modena built a bridge across the St. Vrain, and when

much of the early "learning" to his own children and then to neighbor children. The first little school opened in 1870–71. The first official teacher was Arah (or Sarah) Sprague, who was paid $200 for teaching from June through September of 1871. The first church services in the county were held in an adobe building here.

William McGaa, another pioneer leader in the region, joined Modena and others to build the first irrigation ditch.

After the railroad took over most of the duties served by this station, Namaqua remained a tiny farm center. Modena and his family farmed several acres.

Over the years most of the buildings at the historic crossing were torn down or moved, or were vandalized. Modena's home on the south side of the river is gone. The old fortified station was on the north side of the river and has become a part of another farm building. However, the portholes once used for rifles can still be seen.

The historic site might have been forgotten today if it weren't for the efforts of a local historian, the late Harold Dunning, who worked many years in gathering information and promoting the historic marker seen at the site today.

Modena died in 1878 at the age of 66. He and members of his family are buried nearby. The marker is a fine tribute to an unusual man.

Mariano Modena in customary garb. (*Courtesy Denver Public Library, Western History Department.*)

the river was too high to cross, he charged a small fee for use of his bridge.

In 1862, Namaqua was made a home station on the Denver–Laramie Stage. Modena's large corral always had fresh horses. It was here on June 30, 1862, that the first white child was born in the Big Thompson Valley. The first grave along the trail was that of H. L. Peterson. Others would follow, and a tiny graveyard was established. A person known only as "Mexican Joe" was killed by lightning in 1870, and joined the others.

Namaqua became the post office for the region during the 1860s. It is said that Modena himself dispensed

An impressive marker was built at the approximate site of the stage station operated by Mariano Modena. Longs Peak is in the background.

FREMONT'S ORCHARD
(Weld County)

This historic site was so named because Pathfinder John C. Fremont camped here on one of his expeditions, and because the thick grove of stunted misshapen cottonwoods along the river looked to Easterners like a fruit orchard back home. It was long known as a haven to Indians and weary mountain men. It was also a meeting-place for Indians and traders, a rendezvous, pow-wow site where Indians traded valuable furs for baubles and beads brought from the East by the mountain men.

In 1861 it was a logical site for a stage station, an oasis after 16 barren and difficult miles from the previous stop (see p. 110).

As with other stations along the Platte River Trail, Fremont's Orchard became the center for early settlers in the region. It was a supply center, social center, a place for settlers to congregate to learn the latest news from "the states" or just to watch the hopeful emigrants go by.

As was necessary for stage stations of the day, FREMONT'S ORCHARD had thick sturdy walls, "a fortress" for

John Charles Fremont, famed "Pathfinder of the West" who broke many trails through Colorado. Many places in the state were named for him, including Fremont's Orchard, where he camped before one of his mountain excursions. (*Courtesy Denver Public Library, Western History Department.*)

settlers during the Indian scares—and there were many.

One of the first battles of the Indian Wars of 1864–65 originated near here. Soldiers camped nearby in April of 1864 were told that a party of Cheyenne warriors had raided a nearby ranch and made off with four mules. Forty soldiers gave chase, routed the Indians, killed many and chased the others northward, after recapturing the mules.

One of the first post offices in the region was established at Fremont's Orchard on August 28, 1863. It was discontinued the following year on April 9, 1864.

That was about the time that the Fort Morgan Cutoff began routing most of the stages southwestward to Denver from a point east of Fremont's Orchard, bypassing the stage station. Although Fremont's Orchard continued to be a stopping place for wagons and travelers along the Platte River Trail, the stage station was abandoned.

In 1890 a new community was established on the north side of the river about four miles west of the site of the old stage station. It was named ORCHARD for the old site. Another little community began on the north side of the river, almost opposite the site of the one-time stage station. It was called GOODRICH for G. T. Goodrich, pioneer settler and a member of the first county board.

McBROOM'S CABIN
(Arapahoe County)

John McBroom was born in Kentucky on July 26, 1822. He came west as a wagon master or "bull whacker" with General Stephen W. Kearney in the latter's bloodless capture of New Mexico in the war with Mexico in 1846. The following year he became a hero in the recapture of Taos during the Indian Mexican insurrection.*

McBroom remained in New Mexico Territory to farm and work with the military. He drove herds of cattle over the Santa Fe Trail to New Mexico. He was a guide and scout for the Army, and a translator after learning the language of Indian tribes. He fought against the Apaches under Colonel Kit Carson, and stood beside Carson in 1857 when the Apaches signed a treaty ending the war.

That same year, McBroom once again became wagon master when Captain Randolph Marcy led an expedi-

---

*On the arrival of the troops, the well-armed and well-supplied insurrectionists took refuge in an old adobe church. They could have held out here indefinitely had not McBroom, at great personal risk, maneuvered a cannon into place to fire on the church at point-blank range and rout the rebels.

tion of troops and supplies to relieve beleaguered forces in Utah during the Mormon conflict. ·

On the return trip, the contingent was deterred by high spring runoff water on the South Platte River, near its confluence with Cherry Creek, at what would be the site of Denver City–Auraria a couple of years later. While soldiers were building a ferry to carry the troops across the swollen river, McBroom, grazing the stock, was able to explore up and down the river. A few miles south of the camping site, at the confluence of the Platte and Bear Creek (then called Montana Creek) he found "the youngest and fairest wonderland," according to his diary.

A few weeks after returning to New Mexico with the Army, he headed north once again, with only his horse, "faithful hound" and a rifle. Near the Platte-Bear Creek site he built a crude cabin, and planted his first crops. Before winter set in, however, he joined a wagon train headed for Santa Fe, where he spent the winter gathering materials and supplies for his return to Colorado the following spring (1859).

In the spring he built a sturdier cabin near the confluence of the Platte and Bear Creek, close to what would now be Dartmouth Avenue at the southern city limits of Denver. He filed on two claims and a short time later began construction of the first irrigation ditch, from Bear Creek to his crops.*

McBroom was ready for the gold-seekers that began arriving in greater and greater numbers during 1859 and 1860. Of course, he could not provide for all of them, but he had eager customers for all he could supply. He grew fresh corn and several other crops, including strawberries—the first in the region and a great treat for the newcomers. He also raised turkeys and planted the first orchards in the region.

John's brother, Isaac, arrived from Council Bluffs, Iowa, in June of 1860, and filed on land just west and adjacent to John's land. He is also said to have brought John the first honey bees in the region, and honey became another rare delicacy for the argonauts.

"Uncle John" McBroom's cabin and orchard became hospitality centers for the entire region. His old friend and former commanding officer, Kit Carson, stopped by many times, as did Father Dyer, the "Snowshoe Itinerant," Scout Jim Baker, "Uncle Rick" Wootton, Tom Tobin and all the other famed visitors to the region. John always had a hot meal for anyone passing through, and huge pots of hot coffee. His orchards attracted families from as far away as Denver City for weekend and holiday picnics. Fourth of July gatherings became

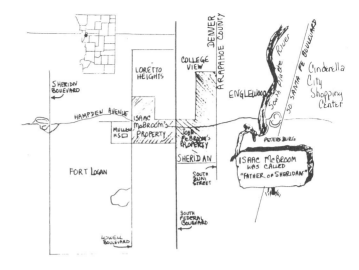

the tradition at Uncle John's. Father Dyer conducted a big camp meeting of Methodists on John McBroom's property.

One gathering was one of the most unusual in the short history of the region.

John McBroom had learned long ago how to deal with the Indians. In many cases he spoke their language and they respected him for his fairness and honesty. When the Indians became more and more antagonistic toward the settlers during the early 1860's, the settlers began organizing their resistance. With his background, it seemed natural enough that McBroom was elected captain of the "Bear Creek Rangers," a group of local volunteers organized to protect the infant settlements.

Captain McBroom scheduled a training session on his property just a few days after the Rangers were organized. Unbeknownst to the volunteers he also invited several Arapahoe "warriors" camping nearby. He sent couriers to tell the volunteers to leave their weapons at home.

Instead of a training session, all were treated to a grand feast of antelope and buffalo meat. Before it was over, the Indians agreed to stop their raids on the local gentry who in turn promised to provide the Indians with supplies and foodstuffs when available.

In 1866, McBroom married Emma Burnett. The couple had five children; two survived and also became prominent in the history of the area.

In 1870, McBroom built a large, modern home on a small hill overlooking his cabin. Within a year, the new house burned to the ground. John and Emma McBroom and their oldest son barely escaped with their lives. Within hours their neighbors gathered in force, and began construction of another home for the McBrooms.

In 1876, McBroom ran for a seat in Colorado's first State Legislature and won. But after only one term he

---

*McBroom's first homestead claim, filed November 1, 1859, was patented six years later and signed by President Johnson. The second claim was signed four years after that by President Grant. Patent on the ditch was not decreed until 35 years later but still retained the Number One priority for this section of Colorado.

The John McBroom cabin on Bear Creek; McBroom appears at right. On the back of the original photograph was written the following: "I was built in the year 1859 and occupied as a bachelors residence by John McBroom until 1866 when he got married and deserted me. During the time I was occupied I entertained the following noted mountaineers: L. B. Stewart, Tom Boggs, Tom Tobin, Calvin Jones, [and] Jim Baker; Col. A. G. Boone, great grandson of Dan Boone; Kit Carson, the noted trapper; and Colorow, the noted Indian Chief." McBroom's first cabin, built in 1858, is attached to the rear side of the newer one.

Below, John McBroom's cabin, in a photo from 1910, with John's brother Isaac seated next to his wife Emma. Standing at left is Mrs. McBroom Player, daughter of John, and at right, Mrs. Etta Neviheiser, who crossed the plains in the same wagon train as Isaac. (*Photos courtesy Littleton Historical Museum, Littleton, Colorado.*)

The McBroom Cabin being preserved and restored at the Arapahoe County Fair Grounds is actually Isaac McBroom's, moved from its site near South Federal Boulevard and Hampden. The John McBroom cabin, much like this one, burned down years ago. The window and door placement was about the only difference. (*Courtesy Littleton Historical Museum.*)

had had enough of politics, and returned to his farm, orchards and turkeys. Instead of politics he turned his attention to horse shows and county fairs.

He saw many changes over the years. He saw the railroads cross or pass his property. He saw the construction of Fort Logan nearby. He and his brother, Isaac, filed the first lot in Sheridan.

In 1885, John McBroom built a large brick home on his property. His son lived in the house for many years.

John McBroom died on January 15, 1891, after a short bout with pneumonia. His wife died a month later. The two of them are buried side by side on a hill in Littleton, overlooking the Platte River that they settled so many years before.

Due to the sturdy construction of the cabin he built in 1859, it remained in good condition until recent years. McBroom had used it as a guest residence for many years and kept it in good repair. A few years ago, it was saved from being torn down when George Turner moved it to Tiny Town, on Turkey Creek. But it burned down a short time later.

The building moved to the Arapahoe County Fairground and called "McBroom's Cabin" is actually the cabin built around 1860 by Isaac McBroom. It had been moved from its original location on about South Federal Boulevard beside Bear Creek. It is the oldest remaining construction (in the original shape) in Arapahoe County and probably in the entire Denver area. The Englewood JayCees stabilized the building. The Littleton Historical Museum hopes to eventually move the building to the Museum grounds, and restore it as a focal point of an 1860's historical farm.

GOLDEN GATE (Baled Hay City)
(Jefferson County)

It was a logical place, perhaps, for a small camp: at the entry-way and toll house to the road to the gold fields. It doesn't seem like a logical place for a "great city." That, apparently, is what GOLDEN GATE aspired to be—*the* "big city" of Colorado territory.

It was founded in the summer of 1859 at the mouth of Golden Gate Canyon, which allows Clear Creek to exit from the mountains. The camp, the town and the canyon were named for Thomas L. Golden, one of the key organizers of the Golden Gate Town Company, and later, when GOLDEN GATE died, a leader in Golden. Some oldtimers said the name came from the "golden opportunities" waiting down the road, at the gold fields.

The toll road to the fields was built through Golden Gate in 1860, and it was a busy road for several years, until the railroad came. One toll house was at Golden Gate.

Golden Gate's growth paralleled that of Golden, but was about one-third as fast. A *Rocky Mountain News* report in September of 1859 said there were ten houses in Golden Gate and thirty in Golden. In January of 1860, in the vote for county seat of Jefferson County, Golden Gate citizens, realizing they didn't have the votes to win but not wanting Golden to win, cast 79 votes for Arapahoe City and only four for Golden. Tom Golden, who

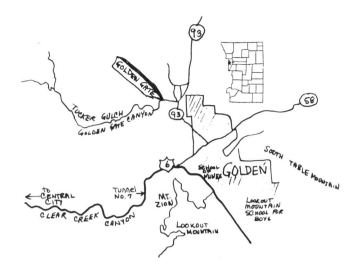

still lived in Golden Gate, received the bulk of the Golden Gate vote for County Recorder, but lost to Eli Carter of Golden. Tom Golden was a pioneer merchandiser, and said to be the first to advertise, in early 1860.

That same year the Golden Gate Town Company was granted 640 acres maximum for its plat by the Jefferson Territory Government. Some 40 blocks were platted. The townsite claim was challenged by one Alfred Tucker, who maintained that many of the lots being sold were on his farming claim. His challenge was somewhat successful in steering would-be buyers away from Tucker Gulch.

The superintendent of the St. Vrain, Golden City and Colorado Wagon Road, Dan McCleery, pushed the toll road through the rugged canyon, through Chimney Gulch (named for the tall chimney of the toll house), and built the first bridges across Clear Creek. To help bring the toll road into shape   Cleery was said to

have allowed toll-free passage of some 400 teams hauling heavy machinery through the canyon.

McCleery also built a "large" hotel and restaurant in Golden Gate. There were at least two other hotels built here in 1860. In April of 1860 the Gate City Hotel had a "grand opening" with all the "elite" attending.

Despite the auspicious beginning, Golden City and Denver City rapidly outgrew the little community with a big name and oddball location. Most Golden Gaters eventually moved to the other nearby cities, or on to the gold fields. There was some activity here until the railroad chugged through in 1870. All traces of Golden Gate are gone now, much of it washed away by the periodic floods that come splashing down the canyon.

An early nickname for Golden Gate was BALED HAY CITY for the bales of hay piled high to sell to travelers en route to Central City and beyond.

An even shorter-lived community—if one could call it that—was ROCKY MOUNTAIN CITY, located up the canyon beyond Golden Gate toward the Gregory Diggings (Central City).

Alfred Tucker (of Tucker Gulch, above) laid out the abortive community in June of 1859. Tom Golden had a hand in it also. They envisioned a large trading center. However, all reports say that it was never more than a "tent-grocery" and a couple of covered wagons. Those were gone, along with the grand visions, by 1860.

APEX *(Magic Mountain)*
(Jefferson County)

APEX was one of the busiest travel towns around in the early 1860s. The Apex and Gregory Wagon Road was

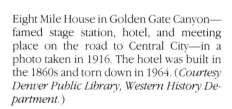

Eight Mile House in Golden Gate Canyon—famed stage station, hotel, and meeting place on the road to Central City—in a photo taken in 1916. The hotel was built in the 1860s and torn down in 1964. (*Courtesy Denver Public Library, Western History Department.*)

incorporated on October 11, 1861, by the Territorial Legislature, the first toll road to be incorporated. One of the leading incorporators was R.W. Steele, who was said to have spent his time between his "Governor's Mansion" (a cabin) at Mt. Vernon and here. Apex was located on the busy highway to the gold fields, the first major stop out of Denver, and at the crossing of the road to Bergen Park.

Both roads were busy, and Apex soon became cluttered with freighters and others to supply the needs of the travelers. And the grounds all around were stacked high with supplies and goods headed for the mountain towns.

Golden, a couple of miles down the road, soon took over most of the responsibilities from Apex. Reports said Apex was "nearly deserted" by 1867.

Still a choice location, the site of Apex apparently remained the site for substantial homes. Some reports claim that Steele built a large home here, and that George Pullman, while making his first fortune lending money at high interest in Central City, had some farming acreage nearby. An 1878 news item said that the "Metcalf Residence" burned to the ground November 1. An 1893 item in the *Denver Republican* said that fire destroyed the "old Binder Residence, the last remnant of a little town that was quite a thriving settlement in pioneer days."

The site, still a choice roadside location, continues to pile up history. During the 1950s, a young Boulder tycoon, Allen J. Lefferdink, began to build and promote a colorful make-believe village called MAGIC MOUNTAIN, billed as the "Disneyland of the Rockies." After several buildings were up, the scheme collapsed along with the rest of the "financial empire" of the young tycoon. (It was only the first of his empires to collapse; a second one fell in 1976 in Florida.)

The make-believe village remained. In many of the years since it was known as EAST TINCUP. Popular Denver radio personality Pete Smythe broadcast from the country store in a make-believe town named after one of Colorado's most colorful mining towns.*

Even later the original Magic Mountain buildings were restored and incorporated into one of the region's most colorful centers, HERITAGE SQUARE. Apex and its site may have finally found their true calling.

---

*Pete Smythe actually broadcast from a site about a half-mile away. This Apex should not be confused with the colorful mining camp above Central City.

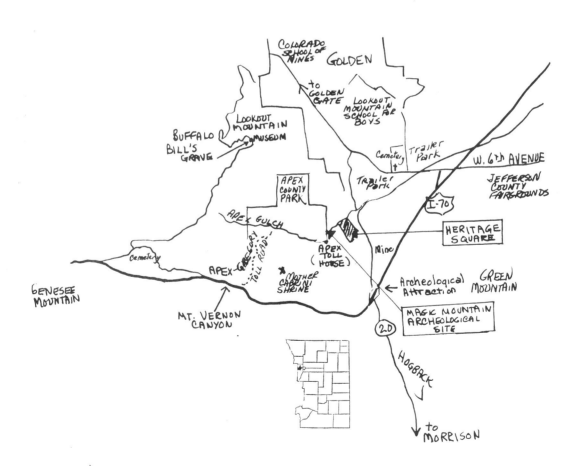

BRADFORD CITY (Bradford House, Twelve-Mile House)

(Jefferson County)

In 1859–60 Major Robert B. Bradford and associates built a toll road running southwest from Denver to the gold fields in South Park, Oro City (Leadville) and beyond. The full name of the road was Denver, Bradford, and Blue River Toll Road. At a point about twelve miles southwest of Denver and about four from Morrison, he built a sturdy two-story hotel, with even blocks of thick sandstone. The entrance was impressive, with six pillars. The large rooms inside had high ceilings, and there were two stairways to the second floor.

The BRADFORD HOUSE Hotel would be a major stopping place along the toll road, and it would be a toll station. Bradford also built some buildings around the hotel, the beginning of BRADFORD CITY. Reports as to the number of buildings vary considerably. Most passersby said there were no more than three buildings, a "Dutchman's domicile, Stone's Chateau" and the Bradford House. But a traveler in 1863 said there were thirty houses. All reports agree, however, on the fact that all the buildings were empty or almost empty by the mid-1860s.

Bradford had few takers at his hotel. It was too close to Denver City, going and coming. Many travelers complained that his toll was too high, $1.50. And the road was too steep out of Bradford City over BRADFORD HILL. A better road up Turkey Creek replaced the Bradford Road.

After only about two or three years (before 1867), Bradford gave up his dreams of empire. He still had several acres around his hotel. It is said that he farmed here until his death a few years later, in 1876.

The old stone hotel still stands now. It was lived in until about 1926. The door, roof and other parts are gone. The ruins were further damaged by a fire about 1967 and there are other vandal scars. It is located on the Ken-Caryl development. Originally, developers planned to bulldoze the old building, but now there is hope that the sturdy old building will remain, a landmark, a touch of history in the middle of the modern new environment.

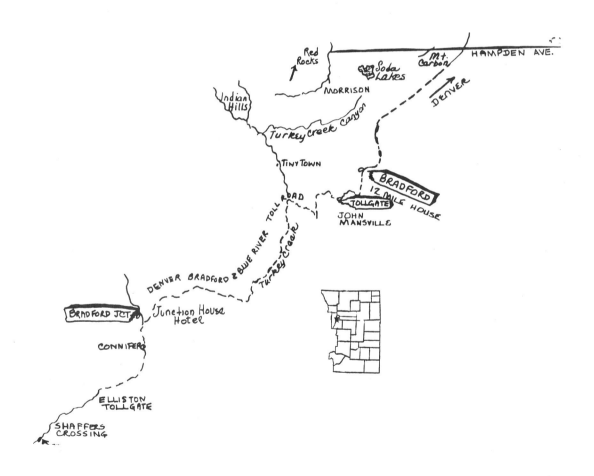

Some views of the ruins of Bradford House

The Perley Farm used the old buildings of Bradford House, shown at left in this old photo (no date is given). The sketch below, showing Bradford House as it used to look, is based on a 1972 interview with George Perly, who was born and raised on the property. (*Denver Public Library Western History Department*)

BRADFORD HOUSE
KEN-CARYL RANCH

BRADFORD JUNCTION
(Junction House, Hutchison, McNassar's Junction)
(Jefferson County)

This was the next toll station southwest of Bradford City, over the steep hill, just northeast of CONIFER and its predecessor. HUTCHISON was at a fairly important junction in the roads for the early 1860s: the Denver, Bradford and Blue River Road, and the wagon road to Bergen Park.

A large two-story hotel was built, called JUNCTION HOUSE Hotel. The toll here was $1.25, a quarter less than that at Bradford City. Being at the junction of two roads, this site was busier and longer lasting than Bradford City. In the mid-1860s, there was a general merchandise store, a saloon, a post office. Early reports from Hutchison boasted of the resident inventor, B. Aschenbach, who invented matches made of rye straw instead of wood which bend but do not break. Another resident was named James McNassar, and sometime in its early history the site was called McNASSAR JUNCTION.

Directories in the mid-1880s and later still listed HUTCHISON, and said the population was 50. The Junction House Hotel was still operating.

In fact, the site never did die. It became CONIFER, named either for the trees or for a George Conifer who operated a roadhouse here.

A rare picture of Bradford Junction, showing the Junction House Hotel. The site became known as Conifer in later years. *(Photo courtesy Francis Rizzari.)*

OLD RIVERBEND and NEW RIVERBEND

(Elbert County)

OLD RIVERBEND (the original RIVERBEND) was primarily a stage station during the 1860s. It was named for the big bend in the river.

During the frantic construction of the Kansas Pacific in 1870 what little there was of Old Riverbend moved about two miles southeast to NEW RIVERBEND on the railroad. For a short time while Riverbend was railhead for the railroad construction this was perhaps the wildest site in Colorado. Hundreds were here. It was the construction crews against many times as many people, men and women, out to take their money away from the crews by any means at hand.

At this tumultuous period there were said to be some twenty saloons in town, and only two or three were in permanent buildings; the rest were in wagons, tents, leantos, etc. It was during this time that the little graveyard was started on the hill above town. Many of the first markers are for those who died with their boots on.

A story is told about Riverbend (similar to stories about other wild towns through the West). It seems a young man was rendered unconscious during a brawl. Unmoving, he was considered dead. He was lugged up the hill, and was just about to be lowered in the hole made ready for him when he came to and declined the honor of a "decent burial."

When the construction crews moved on, Riverbend settled down to being a lusty railroad town. Its peak came in the early and mid-1880s. There were only two or three saloons, but enough to serve the smaller population. There was a post office, a grocery, general merchandise store, a school house, a depot, railroad section house and other railroad facilities. This was one of the busiest cattle shipping points along the Kansas Pacific.

It was the coming of another railroad that did Riverbend in. The Chicago, Kansas and Nebraska Railroad (to become the Chicago, Rock Island and Pacific in 1891) sliced through east-central Colorado in 1886. It crossed the Union Pacific line at a point a little southeast of Riverbend. This became LIMON.

Riverbend was too stubborn to give up easily, although much of its activity was transferred to the new town. Riverbend became a quiet little farm center, and some token chores were given it by the Union Pacific. It was listed as recently as 1915, and is still shown on some detailed maps.

Today, only one dilapidated building, plus some

Available information does not say whether this is Old or New Riverbend, but it is probably New Riverbend. (*Courtesy Denver Western Public Library, Western History Department.*)

Riverbend Cemetery, overlooking the place where the old town of Riverbend used to be.

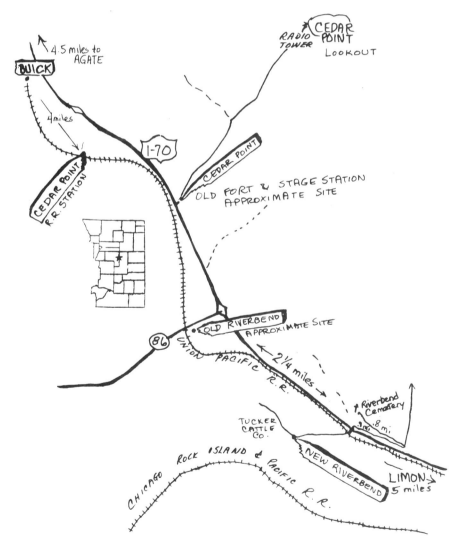

recent ranch construction, can be seen by the side of the road. The headstones can be found among weeds on the little hill above the site.

CEDAR POINT (with Riverbend)
(Elbert County)

During the early years of the Smoky Hill Trail there was a fort established near Riverbend to protect the isolated trail, from highwaymen as well as Indians. It was also a woodchoppers' camp, and it furnished much wood for the early construction of houses in Denver.

It was named CEDAR POINT for the promontory landmark a short distance east of the trail. The site was described in the 1860s as one stone house and stable, a subterranean fort and barracks of Company F., U.S. Army Regulars. There usually were several piles of cut timber to be hauled to Denver, by wagon until the Kansas Pacific railroad came through and made the job easier and faster.

There were countless stories of murder and marauding along the trail. Dr. Margaret Long in her classic book, "The Smoky Hill Trail," told of one story that had a happy ending—for one party. It seems a family from Paris exchanged stage tickets with another family in Atchison, Kansas, in their eagerness to reach Denver sooner. Near Cedar Point, their stage overtook an earlier stage. It was afire and its occupants murdered and scalped.

The Indians suddenly appeared again and gave chase. This stage would have met the same fate as the last one had not soldiers from Cedar Point arrived just in time, chased off the redskins and escorted the stage to safety.

There were other stories of close calls, of emigrants playing dead, hiding among the rattlesnakes, in dead buffalo skins and using other means to escape the wrath of the redskins. No doubt the tales would have different endings and would be more lurid had not the soldiers been nearby to protect the trail.

Cedar Point had a post office from about 1860 to 1865. The soldiers were on hand to protect the construction crews of the Kansas Pacific, but then they were no longer needed. There was some lumbering here until about 1870. George Crofutt still mentions CEDAR POINT in his Gripsack Guides of 1881 and 1885, noting that it is a "stock-raising" center.

Faint outlines of the outpost have been seen in recent years, but one has to know where to look. Stones from the buildings here were used in the construction of the Harper Ranch House, about a mile to the northwest. Most of the hastily made graves along the trail have long since disappeared. Here and there one can still see the ruts made long ago by the stages along the Smoky Hill Trail.

WOOTTON
(Las Animas County)

It would be difficult to find a more colorful character in the Old West than "Uncle Rick" or "Uncle Dick" Wootton, born Rickens Lacy Wootton in Virginia in 1816. He had been just about everything there was to be in the West before the '59ers came, and he knew the country.

He came west in the late 1830s, a trapper and scout. He served in the Mexican War, then started a buffalo ranch near the present site of Pueblo. He is credited with the first cross-breeding of cattle and buffalo, called cattelow or beefalo. Snickers over the wild experiment ended when he sold the results to the Central Park Zoo in New York City at a good profit.

Shortly after the rush to the gold fields in California, Wootton saw more riches in providing meat to the mining camps. He herded nearly 9000 sheep through and over the rockies to California, losing only a few en route, an amazing feat considering all the possible hazards along the way.

But perhaps his most heroic deed was making the first Christmas in Denver City festive for the hungry and thirsty settlers. Wootton defied Indians and all other hazards along the trail and rumbled into Denver City just before Christmas with wagonloads of "Taos Lightning" and provisions. He is credited with operating the first saloon and grocery store in Denver, and with the construction of the first two-story building in the city.

Having done just about everything else, and becoming bored with other things (see HUERFANO SETTLEMENTS, in "Colorado Kingdoms"), Wootton decided in 1866 to take on something new—road building. He acquired rights to build a toll road over Raton Pass. Wootton's 27-mile "modern highway" was not much better than the road used by travelers over the Santa Fe Trail for decades. He did level some of the more tilted sections and bridged some of the gaps along the way. Although he hired a team of men to maintain the road during the ensuing years, he did most of the original grading and construction himself. It took him almost a year.

He erected his toll gates and his home near the top of the pass, about two miles from the New Mexico border. His home was large and well-stocked with food and drink. It was said to be a stopping place for friends, travelers and "roadmen." But Wootton, they say, never had trouble near his toll station. He ran off troublemakers post haste. WOOTTON was also a stage station, where the charge was 75 cents for meals (see p. 77).

Although he was known for his hospitality, Wootton was all business when it came to his toll road. He had a heavy chain across it, and he didn't remove it until the toll was paid. It is said he had to collect some tolls at the point of a gun or "with a club," but generally his size and his reputation were enough. He stood 6 feet, 6 inches tall, more than 200 pounds of solid muscle.

"Uncle Dick" Wootton, seated, with his longtime friend, Jesus Silva. (*Courtesy Denver Public Library, Western History Department.*)

There was a classification for all travelers over the pass, and a different price for each: wagons $1.50; smaller vehicles, $1; horsemen and pack animals, 25 cents; cattle and sheep five cents a head. Indians passed free, because Wootton considered it their land. Mexicans claimed it was their land also, and complained that they were charged for passing, although they were given a discount. Lawmen, clergy, renegades on the run passed through free, as did funeral processions.

Wootton's greed cost him quite a bit of money when the first cattle drives made their way into Colorado. The first was made by Charles Goodnight and Oliver Loving shortly after the toll road was established. There were several hundred head of cattle in the herd. It is said that Wootton saw that it would have been an impossible job to turn the herd around, so he charged ten cents per head instead of the regular five cents. Goodnight was so furious, he vowed he would never come this way again. He never did, and there is no record of any other large drive going by Wootton. On the next drive, Goodnight found an easier way, Trinchera Pass, a short distance east of Raton. And it didn't cost a cent. The Goodnight–Loving Cattle Trail was a "one-shot deal," while thousands of cattle traveled Trinchera Pass (or Goodnight Trail) and other trails further east.

Although Wootton lost some from that one greedy experience, he continued to make a good living. It is said that he sometimes made up to $600 a month in tolls. It is also said that he threw the toll money in barrels, and when the barrels were full he loaded them on a wagon and took them down to a bank in Trinidad.

Although Wootton and his large family lived well, things were getting dull for the legendary figure. The final chapter of his toll road era was as classic as the character himself.

The Denver & Rio Grande Railroad was racing toward Raton Pass from the north. The Atchison, Topeka & Santa Fe was racing to the pass from the east. Both arrived at the northern foot of the pass at about the same time. This, however, is where the D&RG made a fatal mistake. Officials stopped at El Moro to plan their negotiations with Wootton for rights to the road. AT&SF officials didn't wait. In the dark of night they climbed the pass and negotiated with Wootton immediately; by daybreak they had acquired rights to the road. D&RG and the city of El Moro had lost. D&RG would come back, but El Moro never recovered and Trinidad became the "big city" of Las Animas County.

Wootton had money in the bank and he had won and lost fortunes before, so he didn't want payment from the railroad, which offered him $50,000. Wootton asked for a small monthly payment of $25 a month for food for his family, and lifetime passes on the railroad for his family and himself. Although the "deal" was sealed with only a handshake, the railroad stood by the terms. When "Uncle Dick" died in 1893, at age 77, the agreement went to his widow, his fourth wife, who had given him ten children although they married when she was 16 and he, 56.

When she died in 1916, the agreement was taken over by her children. The monthly allotment was increased to $50 in 1925 and to $75 in 1930. When the children died, the agreement ended. Wootton still has many descendants in southern Colorado and northern New Mexico. Wootton and his wife are buried at the Catholic cemetery in Trinidad.

The famous Wootton mansion all but burned to the ground in 1890. The ruins and a large acreage around it was acquired in 1906 by Col. James A. Ownbey, who was some character himself. He borrowed more than a million dollars from eastern millionaires, such as J.P. Morgan, to rebuild the Wootton mansion and develop the land around for ranching and coal mining. He used the wall ruins of the old Wootton house to rebuild an "exact replica" of the original building. The only difference was the interior, where it was furnished fit for the many millionaires Ownbey expected to visit here. (There is no record that any did.) The coal mines developed by the Wootton Land and Fuel Company never paid off, and Ownbey got involved in several

The Wootton Mansion on Raton Pass before and after it burned to the ground in the early 1890s. No date was given for the photo above, but it was probably taken in the 1880s. (*Courtesy Denver Public Library, Western History Department.*)

The second Wootton home on Raton Pass, built after the fire destroyed the first one, is shown at left. It was torn down in recent years despite efforts to save it. (*Courtesy Denver Public Library, Western History Department.*)

lawsuits and other problems, and died "penniless." Title to WOOTTON and the land eventually was acquired by the Colorado Fuel & Iron Company.

In 1910, an official of the Wootton Company, Albert Berg, began renting and caring for the Wootton House. When he died, his son, Donald Berg, took over the property. He rented the Wootton House and about 6600 acres from Colorado Fuel & Iron. He tried to buy the property but CF&I has no plans to sell it.

The crumbling Wootton house was torn down in recent years despite local efforts to preserve it.

SHARP'S (Sharp's Trading Post, Buzzard's Roost Ranch)
(Huerfano County)

Far off the beaten track to the eastern foot of the Sangre de Cristos about 25 miles west-northwest of Walsenburg, beyond Badito and about a mile beyond the combination school-Baptist church (now abandoned) in Malachite a delightful surprise awaits the traveler.

Around a corner of the dirt road one suddenly comes upon a crumbling adobe home structure, once a commodious, fashionable home, set between huge cottonwoods which were a nesting place for buzzards.

This was once the longtime home of Tom Sharp, another one of the Colorado's storybook pioneers that few people remember today. The Colorado cattle and horse "industry" has not forgotten him.

Less than a mile farther on down the road is another fairly large building. It has been restored (many times) and is still being lived in. This was once SHARP'S TRADING POST, the start of it all (see p. 175).

William Thomas Sharp was born in Missouri. While still young, he joined the Confederate Army, but was wounded early in the fighting and mustered out of the army. Shortly thereafter he went west in a wagon train, and made a living as a hunter providing meat for mining camps in California. His reputation as a marksman began to spread. Later, in Wyoming, he helped provide telegraph poles for the Union Pacific railroad. In 1867 he became a deputy sheriff in Cheyenne.

The following year he headed south into Colorado. In the Huerfano Valley he met Captain Charles Deus, another colorful character, who first settled in the region in the 1850s. He reinforced Sharp's conviction of the beauty and hunting and fishing potential here.

Sharp selected a site alongside the well-traveled road (at that time) over Sangre de Cristo Pass, near its junction with a road over Mosca Pass, also well traveled. He built a cabin and other buildings at the site that grew into MALACHITE (see Chapter XIV). Most importantly he built a trading post, which became the busiest enterprise in the region.

In 1870 Sharp returned to his home in Missouri, where he wed Katherine Durrett and purchased some horses to bring to Colorado. This was the beginning of one of the most successful and significant livestock enterprises in Colorado. Sharp was more interested in quality than quantity, and his stock, both horses and cattle, became so famous throughout the state that he had difficulty meeting the demand.

He brought some of the first whiteface and Hereford cattle into the state. His cross-breeding of cattle was almost as successful as his horse breeding. He traveled as far away as Europe to find the right breeds. But this was primarily for his racing stock. His fame also included the development of strong, fast hardy horses that performed well for every purpose called upon for horses in those days. He crossed strong Indian ponies from Idaho with fast mountain horses to combine the best qualities of each.

His brands, the Lazy S Bar and Reverse S Bar, were known far and wide as top quality brands. He was instrumental in promoting the Colorado State Fair and was an official of the fair for many years, as well as being an official of the state and regional livestock associations. His animals were exhibited far and wide, his awards and ribbons were countless.

Sharp's marksmanship and hunting prowess were legend. Through the years, he learned hunting and fishing techniques from the Indians, and they learned from him. During the early years, Indians, mostly Utes, would camp near his trading post. One of the reasons would be to hunt with Sharp. A favorite pastime of Sharp's was shooting coyotes at great distances. He would usually ask his Indian friend which coyote in a pack he should shoot. He seldom missed.

Sharp's regular guest was famed Chief Ouray. Regional historian Ralph Taylor, in his "Colorado, South of the Border," told of the procedure followed during an Ouray visit. The great chief would wait patiently outside the door of the house until the steaks were ready. After a great meal, Ouray would offer a coin to Sharp to pay for the meal. Sharp always refused. Often Ouray's wife, Chipeta, would accompany her husband to Sharp's place. Taylor said Chief Ouray learned the white man's table manners at Sharp's place.

Taylor said that Sharp also became the first Colorado dealer in army surplus. Sharp would buy large stocks from the army and sell or trade them to the Indians and other travelers. It became fairly common to see an Indian walking around wearing an army tunic or cap.

Sharp, like many ranchers of his day, hated sheep almost as much as coyotes. When herds of sheep were brought into the valley, Sharp acquired several mules that had the same ovine aversion. And the mules kept sheep away. Sharp lived on his ranch until his death on November 26, 1929, at the age of 91. Few pioneers had more impact on the state of Colorado than Tom Sharp.

Tom Sharp at age 83 on Tonapah, one of his fine horses. (*Colorado Historical Society*)

Sharp's Place on Buzzard's Roost Ranch, long-time home of Tom Sharp near Malachite, is shown at top, and below it, Sharp's old trading post near the Ranch. Built more than 100 years ago, it is still being used as a residence.

CHAPTER IV

FARM CENTERS: "BIG CITIES" OF THE PLAINS

The tiny farm centers were the "big cities" of the Plains—and the Plains were sprinkled liberally with them. There was one every few miles, within a day's horseback or wagon ride by the settlers.

Most of the week the little centers were quiet and workaday. But on weekends and holidays they came alive, the exciting commercial, social and recreational hub for a wide area.

A center would usually begin as a rural post office on someone's farm or ranch house. Then came a general merchandise store, and the post office would move to the store. A small rural school was built, often by the settlers themselves. The one-room edifice, often with a sod floor, would serve as a meeting place and church until the settlers would build a church, too. Many social activities—the potluck dinners, dances, spelling bees and political meetings—were held in the school building and/or the church.

Sporting activities were not neglected. The first rodeos began as informal competition on one of the farms or ranches near the center. Early horse racing and foot races were held here. Later, many farm centers had baseball teams, and the rivalries were as lusty as the land.

Growing farm centers usually acquired a livery (which later became a garage and service station) and other commercial enterprises.

Although few farm centers ever had more than 25 to 50 fulltime residents, hundreds could be drawn to the site on weekends and holidays.

Some farm centers died quickly from drought or from economic depressions such as in the 1890s and 1920s. World War I drained many of the younger settlers into the army or defense plants in the city. Virtually all of the centers died eventually as transportation improved and the range of the farm and ranch families expanded. Iceboxes and then freezers and refrigerators made it unnecessary to shop as frequently for food. More of the needed services would congregate in larger and larger centers. The few cities and towns remaining on the plains today are the surviving remnant of scores of tiny "big cities" of yesteryear.

OLD ARICKAREE CITY
(Washington County)

It would be difficult today to pinpoint the exact location of OLD ARICKAREE CITY. We are told that it was east of Thurman, in south-central Washington County, on the South Fork of the Arickaree River near Duck Springs, and southwest of the later Arickaree City. No matter, they also tell us that a flood in 1935 washed away the last trace of the old town.

The early cattle trails marked and made use of every source of water along the trail. Duck Springs was a watering place along the Texas–Montana and other cattle trails that brought some of the earliest livestock into northern Colorado and Wyoming and Montana. Before that it was a buffalo watering spot and a popular site of buffalo hunters.

Hall's History said the town was laid out by James Minnich (also shown as Ulwinick) on December 5, 1877. It was named for the river, which was named for an Indian tribe.

It was a "thriving community" for a few years, with a newspaper, church, school and several houses and businesses. There was some hope the railroad would pass this way, but it didn't come close. And OLD ARICKAREE CITY faded almost as fast as it started, being there all by itself. It was virtually a ghost by 1890, and completely "washed up" 45 years later.

There were later sites in the same region that were called Arickaree. Around 1918 there was an Arickaree Post Office east of Anton on Highway 36. The third site was north of this, about 11 miles due east of Anton and 4 miles north of the highway. This post office was closed in 1961, the last of the wandering Arickarees, although the creek continues to meander.

AROYA (Arroyo)
(Cheyenne County)

A lighthouse marks the site of AROYA. This may seem an unlikely landmark for a near-ghost farm town in eastern Colorado. But then not every "near-ghost" prairie town has a sculptor as a last resident. In recent years, Aroya had two residents, Marvin Sargent and Owen (or Ben) Moreland. Moreland took up sculpting a few years ago. He uses mostly scrap iron and other rusting relics found on the plains.

One of his "masterpieces" was a 35-foot tower, built of scrap iron in the shape of a lighthouse. He wasn't offered what he considered a fair price for it, so it remains—undoubtedly the only lighthouse on the Great Plains.

A purist might not consider a two-resident town a real ghost town. But counting a hermit or two as a live town wouldn't be fair to a good many deserving ghost towns. Sargent and Moreland wouldn't want to be unfair, and Aroya is deserving. (Sargent died in December 1979.)

Aroya is, or was, located west of Wild Horse on Big Sandy Creek and the Union Pacific Railroad. The name is a corruption of Arroyo, Spanish for "deep gulch." Maps and directories over the many years have used all sorts of corruptions of the name; once in a while it is even shown as ARROYO.

There was an Old Aroya, a short distance west of the present site. But it burned down and the town moved to the present site, where the land was lower and wells easier to dig.

There was a stage station on the Smoky Hill Trail, on or near the old site before 1872.

When the Kansas Pacific Railroad built through here in 1869–70, Aroya became a station on the line. It was a farm and ranch shipping point. George Crofutt's 1881 and 1885 guide spelled it Arroya, and said, "Cattle, sheep, horses, and 'cow boys' possess the whole country."

Major property holder here was the G.O.D. Ranch owned by T. C. Schilling of the Schilling Tea Co.

The site grew slowly. Although all the surrounding land was settled by hopeful people, the town itself had just a few buildings until after the turn of the century. The peak years seemed to be between 1910 and 1920, when there were about 20 families and close to 100 persons living in the community. There was a school and several businesses.

The school is boarded up today. There are about twelve other old buildings at the site, only one still occupied.

The town was hard-hit by the crash of 1929. Moreland said that his father, who owned much of the town, lost more than $100,000 himself. When the main highway, which had run through Aroya, was moved a short distance east, the town died quickly. Moreland, who was called "Aroya Red" in the region, inherited much of the ghost town. He still makes all manner of interesting things in his home in what is left of the old hotel. He will sell them to you at a good price, too. Otherwise, they pile up; he doesn't get too many visitors these days.

BADITO (Boyce's)
(Huerfano County)

BADITO was one of the most historic towns in southern Colorado and one of the earliest settlements in the state. Actually there is a wide divergence in dates given in its early history. Many sources claim that the settlement began in the early 1860s, while others claim it began about ten years earlier, around 1853. It is possible that the town was not heard from in its first years and only emerged in the 1860s when it became the most important town in the region.

Badito had many "firsts," but it was not the first county seat of Huerfano county as many sources claim. Huerfano was one of the original counties when Colorado Territory was created in 1861, and it covered all of southeastern Colorado, from the mountains to the Kansas border. AUTOBEES or AUTOBEES PLAZA was named the first county seat (see "Colorado Kingdoms"). Badito became a county seat a short time later, in 1863.

Among the firsts attributed to Badito: the first chain store magnate in Colorado; the first "Literary Society" in southern Colorado and possibly in the state; the first courthouse in southern Colorado; and among the first flour mills, orchestras and schools in the region.

There has also been some question as to Badito's lineage. Most sources claim it was a Spanish-American community, settled, as were many other southern Colorado communities, by emigrants from New Mexico. However, many of the early residents were Anglos.

The schoolhouse at Aroya.

The Moreland family operated the gas station (*right*) at this onetime crossroads, as well as the hotel and other businesses of Aroya. In the background is one of Ben Moreland's sculptures—surely the only lighthouse on the Great Plains.

Moreland's handiwork is seen everywhere around his home: unique iron fences, a furnace, lamps and chandeliers.

The building on the right was the first courthouse for Huerfano County, as well as post office, main store and trading post at Badito. The taller building behind it was a barn, and the tree-surrounded building across the street (*left*) was an inn, (*Photos courtesy Amon Carter Museum.*)

In fact, the most popular version of history says that F. W. Poshhoff was the first permanent settler. He is said to have opened a store on the site in the early 1850s. Others followed, and settled around the store. As Badito grew, Poshhoff prospered. He added to his goods and became a major supplier for a wide region. He did so well that he opened several other stores over the mountains in the San Luis Valley. He had a sutler store at Fort Garland, and other outlets in San Luis, Conejos, Costilla and Questa and a commisary for cattle camps at La Loma.

"The Literary Society of Huerfano County" was in full bloom by the early 1860s. Along with the local orchestra, it entertained during the lavish Christmas Eve celebrations and other holidays.

The population during the 1860s and early '70s rose as high as 500.

Most of the activity here involved sheep and wool, but there was also some cattle and farming. There were several other commercial enterprises in addition to the Poshhoff store, including the "commodious" Johnson's Hotel.

The population of the neighborhood jumped to an "uneasy" 3000 in 1865 when a large Indian campsite was established in the hills nearby. Badito residents experienced several tense days and sleepless nights before the Indians moved on. No harm done.

The Pueblo *Chieftain*, on January 4, 1872, told of the community's continuing prosperity. Reporting the Christmas Eve celebration, the newspaper said: "This place is the county seat of government for Heurfano County . . . the county of democratic majorities, good whisky and dark-eyed senoritas. At least, that's its reputation abroad." The writeup said the courthouse, "a first-rate building," would be finished in a few days and "Judge Hallett is ready."

It also said that there was a "big interest" in schools.

If one likes controversy, one might delve into the naming of Badito. One source went so far as to say Badito is Spanish for "little bandit" for a highwayman or highwaymen along the Taos and Sangre de Cristo Trail. A more down-to-earth version, however, is that Badito means "crossing" or "little ford," for the crossing of the Huerfano River here on the once-busy trail over the Sangre de Cristos.

The name BOYCE or BOYCE's also appears now and then in regard to Badito. The Diary of Bishop Talbott tells of visiting the site in 1863, and he called it Boyce's. He further commented that the "bedbugs were terrible" here.

Ruins of the Badito school (*above*) and front and side view of the old Badito inn. The inn was occupied until a few years ago and still appears to be solid.

Badito lost many of its residents to other nearby communities in the late 1870s. The county seat was transferred to the blossoming town of Walsenburg. Badito lingered on as a tiny center until well into this century. Today there are just a couple of adobe ruins left of the onetime community, but they are colorful ruins as befitting the onetime historic stature of Badito. There is the roofless, adobe church on the hill, that once stood proud over the community. The last home is a large adobe structure which had once been a hotel, surrounded by ancient but stately trees. Across from it are adobe farm buildings, indicating that a once-prosperous operation was well established here.

BEECHER ISLAND
(Beecher, Glory)
(Yuma County)

BEECHER ISLAND was similar to many another farm town on the Plains but distinguished itself by being located very near to, and naming itself after, the historic battlefields at Beecher Island. Here, in September 1869, a detachment of about 40 to 50 soldiers and Indian scouts led by Col. George Forsythe and Lt. Fred Beecher valiantly held off an estimated 1000 Cheyenne, Arapahoe and Ogallala Sioux Indians, led by famed Indian Chief Roman Nose. The battle lasted for eight days. When the Indians finally abandoned the battle, five soldiers, including Lt. Beecher, had been killed, and an estimated 75 Indians died, with many more wounded. It was one of the last battles the army had with the prairie tribes.

The scattered residents of this region petitioned for a post office in 1902. At the same time, four local residents contributed $40 each to build a sod schoolhouse, 12 by 24 feet. The school year was only four months long in the beginning. The first post office was in the dugout home of the Ekbergs. The third postmaster,

Garrette Van Wyke (1904–1906) shot and killed his sister-in-law and was sentenced to life in prison.

A new frame schoolhouse was built in 1912. A little later another schoolhouse was built about 3 miles northwest of the battle site. It was called EAST BEECHER, while the original school was called WEST BEECHER. Church services and other community meetings were held at the West Beecher school. In 1949, the school district was reorganized and the students were bussed to Wray, 16 miles to the north.

The early post office was discontinued after a few years, then reopened in the Miles store in 1925. At that time several names were submitted for the post office, including BEECHER ISLAND and GLORY. The post office chose the latter, but residents later petitioned and won the designation of Beecher Island. Most maps and other references later shortened it to Beecher. The post office was finally closed in 1958.

Although the center was losing patrons over the years, a new chapel was dedicated in 1950, and is still used from time to time.

The Beecher Island museum was opened in 1956 in a small abandoned building near the Oberg store. In the fall of 1966, after the museum was closed, the Beecher Island Memorial Association reopened a part of the museum collection in Wray.

There are still a few scattered homes and buildings in the area near the onetime battlefield, which is no longer an island.

The story of the Battle of Beecher Island is told at the base of this monument, and on markers surrounding the monument are the names of those killed here, including Lt. Beecher, for whom the town was named.

The Battle of Beecher Island, from a painting by Robert Lindeux (*Courtesy Colorado Historical Society.*)

Below, looking down on Beecher island from Squaw Hill, where wives and children of the Indians watched the battle in September 1869. The marker can be seen in the center, between the large community building at right and the church at left. (*Courtesy Colorado Historical Society.*)

CLARKVILLE

(Yuma County)

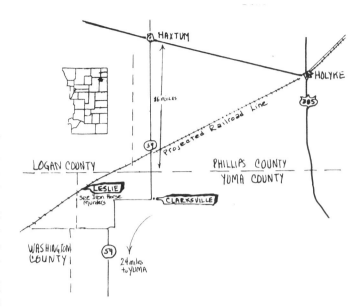

Clarkville, 17 miles northeast of Yuma, was a late bloomer and the most recent ghost town in the county. It is not completely dead, as the church and meeting hall are still used from time to time.

In the early 1930s Louis Nielsen leased five acres of land and built a home and a service station. After only a year, Nielsen sold out to Ted Clark. At the time Nielsen had $700 in credit on his books, but despite the depression he collected all but $4 of it.

The site officially became CLARKVILLE in 1937 when it received a post office and Clark became the first postmaster. It was a predominantly Swedish neighborhood, and was the largest, most active farm center for several miles. Most weekends were busy with social events.

The church formerly served the FORD neighborhood which was located about two miles west and two miles north of Clarkville. Clarkville citizens built a foundation for it near the center of town. Virtually the entire town turned out to move the church to the new location. The Ford community building was moved to Clarkville shortly thereafter.

Clarkville was very baseball minded. There were three community teams at one time, "The Fruit Jar Drinkers," the town team, a church team, and a boys' team.

The Clay Chamblins purchased the Clarkville site in 1947. He brought in an interest in turkey shoots. The Chamblins also installed blown-glass windows in the church.

In 1940 Clark purchased what was said to be the first school building in Haxtum and moved it to Clarkville. The two-room, false-fronted building was used as a grocery, variety store, cafe and, finally, a barn.

In 1961, when the Chamblins sold their home and store at auction, it marked the end of Clarkville as a community. Most of the buildings that hadn't been torn down before were eventually torn down or moved and used for other purposes. The Swedish Lutheran Church and community center still stand, but are used less and less.

Many of the farmers that used to live in or frequent Clarkville remain in the area. They get together often and swap memories, as they used to swap stories on the "liars bench" in Clarkville. They remember the Sunday school classes and throwing pennies not in a wishing well but in the "Little White Light House," to make a wish. The money was used for special parties. They remember the bells in the steeple of the church, ringing for the few weddings held here, and birthdays and other special occasions; the fireworks, baseball games, and potluck suppers on Independence Day. They remember the free cookies they got at the Chamblin store on one's birthday or for doing something special. They

Last buildings at the farm town of Clarkville: (*right to left*) Clarkville church, now boarded up; community center, still used infrequently; Church of the Nazarene, presently in regular use.

remember when the Nielsen service station was stripped one time by a man posing as a tire salesman. He was later caught with the goods.

Another time the Nielsen house was robbed of most of its food when the whole town was out watching a baseball game. Mrs. Nielsen told the menfolk not to chase after the culprit because he apparently needed what he stole more than the Nielsens did.

And there are a lot of other memories in between.

CORNISH

(Weld County)

CORNISH was best known for its Stone Age Fairs. In fact, the little farm center northeast of Greeley became known internationally for the annual event. Now that Cornish is a ghost town, the artifact display continues each year in Loveland.

The dry land farm area around Cornish was settled long before 1911 when the Union Pacific built a branch from Greeley to Briggsdale. The town was founded along the railroad by Henry Brady (or Breder) and named for the civil engineer on the railroad. Edwin Miller, a former state legislator and Denver printer and saddler who moved to Cornish to appease his ulcers, opened a store here. His wife's sister, Irene Shirk, became postmistress, a position she held for 33 years. All told she had 53 years of government service.

Although other farm produce was shipped from Cornish, it primarily was a cattle shipping point on the railroad. There was a stockyards here. There was also a race track, and Cornish became a popular racing and rodeo center.

It wasn't long after the town was founded that its citizens found that there were countless artifacts in the region from ancient Indian civilizations, some dating back 10,000 years and more. Most of the artifacts—

Only this old sign marks the site of the farm town of Cornish, where the colorful Stone Age Fairs were held many years ago.

arrowheads, stone axes, spear points, grinding and cutting implements, etc.—were found along nearby creek beds, and many of the ancient treasures were uncovered by windstorms. For years Cornish citizens gathered their treasures, proudly displaying newfound artifacts to their neighbors. In 1934 several townsfolk decided to make the collections available to any and all who wished to see them, and in July the first Stone Age Fair was held. There were some 25,000 exhibits, one of the largest collections of artifacts anywhere in the world. Governor Ed Johnson gave a speech. The next year it was even bigger. Archaeologists from around the country attended, and gave talks. The Fair had some 10,000 visitors from 41 states.

It grew each year for six years until it became too much for one fading little town to handle. The fair was transferred to Loveland, where it is an annual event. It is getting so large and sophisticated that few people recall that it all began in a little town, now a ghost town, along a ghost railroad branch.

In the first years of the fair Cornish had already begun to fade. The final touches have come the last few years. The Cornish school closed in 1948 and the remaining youngsters in Cornish were bused to nearby towns. The grocery store went in the early 1950s, and the church about the same time. The railroad line was

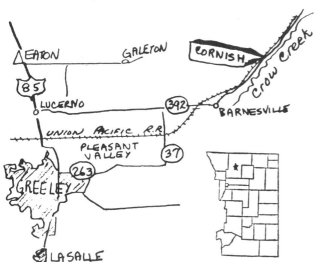

discontinued, the tracks torn up in 1966. The post office was closed in March of 1967.

CORNISH is more fortunate than most other Colorado ghost towns. It left something of which it can be proud: the annual Stone Age Fair.

EASTONVILLE (McConnellsville, Easton, Old Eastonville)
(El Paso County)

Of the many farm centers in eastern Colorado that are now ghosts, EASTONVILLE, in northern El Paso County about 12 miles south of Elbert, was probably the most prosperous. Its citizens called it the "potato capital of the world." Some years they couldn't find enough field workers to harvest the crops. Large advertisements were put in Colorado Springs newspapers offering top wages to any who would come to Eastonville and work.

There were many productive farms in this region when the Denver & New Orleans Railroad built through in 1881. (After other name changes, it became the Colorado & Southern Railroad.) A station was estab-

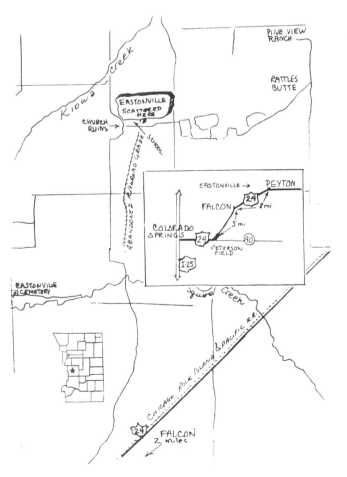

lished and originally called MCCONNELLSVILLE. A short time later, a post office was designated and called EASTON, for John Easton, a pioneer. The post office department found that name was too much like Eaton. another farm town in eastern Colorado, so residents made the name EASTONVILLE. And before the community became too well established, it moved a short distance to its final site, supposedly at the request of the railroad, so we also have an OLD EASTONVILLE in the picture.

The earlier post office in this area, dating as early as 1872, was at the sawmill operated by Jerome Weir on Squirrel Creek. His son, Austin, was the postmaster. The post office was moved to Eastonville in late September 1883, with John Brazelton as postmaster.

By the early 1890s, Eastonville had had three churches, Presbyterian, Methodist Episcopal and Baptist; three hotels; a newspaper, *The Eastonville World*, published by J. B. King; and all the other businesses found in other communities, only more of them. Also listed was a corporation known as the Colorado Implement Manufacturing Company, which made "potato shakers." The horse-drawn shakers harvested potatoes, separated them into two sizes and shook them into the proper sacks. It was considered the latest thing in farm equipment and was used for many years until more modern methods were devised. A two-story school building was completed in 1898.

The most prosperous years for Eastonville were from about 1900 to around 1910. The population was listed anywhere from 350 to 500 and more. That was just in the city and didn't count the many prosperous farms surrounding it. As many as nine or ten passenger trains and as many, or more, freight trains passed through the station daily. The depot never closed. During harvest, several freight cars were being loaded with potatoes and other produce on the side track.

Eastonville had all the social and service clubs the big cities did. The school building and the churches held frequent meetings. There was a race track, ball field, and other facilities for leisure-time activities.

In the many reports from the community on the social events, only one major scandal was reported. On October 28, 1898, a dance given by the Knights of Pythias was disrupted by an uninvited drunk who caused much trouble and antagonized several people before he was escorted forcefully from the building. He was found dead the following day, an obvious victim of murder. The suspects were cleared of any involvement, and the crime was never solved, officially.

Many reasons have been given or could be given for the gradual demise of such a prosperous community. It is still surrounded by prime agricultural land and there are still many prosperous farms and ranches close by. It just faded away for all the many reasons that most of the other farm centers in eastern Colorado did. Eastonville had potato blight, drought, and a big flood in 1935 that washed away many buildings.

The buildings and homes remaining at Eastonville are scattered over a wide area (*above*).

At right, a church building later used as a school, and below, an abandoned house.

A large portion of the homes and buildings are gone today. But there are also many relics of once large and handsome homes, and many barns and sheds. The little Episcopal church was converted into a barn. The Presbyterian church was burned down around 1970 by vandals or careless transients. The cemetery is off amid the large evergreen trees. It is visited often by old-timers and relatives of former settlers. In fact, each June some old-timers and their offspring meet to discuss old times. They used to meet in the church until it was burned down. Now those who gather picnic nearby.

There's still a lot to talk about. Eastonville was a large happy community and had a long life.

HAPPYVILLE and HEARTSTRONG (Headstrong)

(Yuma County)

Richard John Gilmore came to Colorado for his health, and homesteaded in east-central Yuma County. He built a large barn and dug a well. He lived in the barn until his home was built. In the years to follow many a dance was held in the loft of his barn.

In 1908–09 he was also instrumental in the development of a small crossroads center near his homestead, about 12 miles due south of Eckley (see p. 46). In early 1910 he volunteered to carry the mail for three months at no pay to demonstrate the need for a post office. When the post office was authorized, Gilmore and his neighbors submitted five names to the post office department, which decided on HAPPYVILLE. The post office was established on July 26, 1910.

One of the last houses at Heartstrong.

This school, which was in use until a few years ago, is a short distance east of the former site of Happyville.

A schoolhouse was built in 1911. There was also a well-stocked store, dairy, storage rooms for oil, seed and feed, and later a garage and machine shop. Another garage was built and, being larger than Gilmore's hayloft, became the site of community meetings and dances.

In 1915 Cleve Mason built a large store and purchased or built most other business enterprises in Happyville. They say he owned the town. He later sold his store to a group of farmers who turned it into a cooperative store, but Mason built an even larger store. Differences with other townspeople came to a head in 1920, and Mason decided to start another town of his own.

He platted a new townsite on ten acres of land two to three miles west of Happyville. He moved the store and three other buildings to the new site, and many of his friends followed suit. It took three days and 96 horses to move the large store the distance.

At this late date there is some dispute over the naming of the new community. One story goes that it was named HEARTSTRONG, but those staying behind in Happyville nicknamed it HEADSTRONG for its obstinate residents. Another story goes that Mason and friends actually asked that the community be named Headstrong, but the post office department named it Heartstrong instead.

The early 1920s saw the rapid growth of Heartstrong and the rapid demise of Happyville. A remaining Happyville store burned down in 1921 and was not rebuilt. The few other buildings remaining in Happyville were either torn down or put to other uses. The schoolhouse built by the settlers became a dairy barn. The old Gilmore house and barn are still standing, now owned by other farmers. Gilmore, who had come to Colorado for his health, died in Akron, Colorado, on March 22, 1950, at the age of 93.

Several buildings were moved to Heartstrong and

others were built. Mason set his big building he had moved from Happyville at the north end of Main Street. He used it for the same purposes as he had in Happyville: service station, general store, post office, and dance hall. He also built a creamery across the street. The Mason dance hall was sometimes called the "Opera House" as it also served as the site for local and traveling entertainment.

There were many of the usual businesses at Heartstrong, and some of the more unusual. Cleve Mason was also the agent for Denver's Fairmont Cemetery. He worked for the cemetery in Denver the last few years of his life, and died in Denver in 1969 at the age of 92. During 1927 and 1928 there was a demand for rabbit hides. Charles Lowe had a good business buying the hides from his neighbors at $1.35 a pound (it took about three furs to make a pound). When he got a truckload he took them to Yuma, where they were shipped to Denver.

Heartstrong had a close call in 1928 when a twister did heavy damage to one store. But no one was killed or injured and the store was repaired.

Heartstrong was much more than a commercial center. Its most remembered function was as a social center for a large region. There were regular dances held in the large hall over the "north store." When there were no traveling bands or musicians available, the Lowe family furnished the music. Heartstrong had a good baseball team for several years and competed with other nearby communities. There were also frequent horse races and local rodeo events. There was almost continuous horseshoe competition. Less physical were the spelling bees, literary readings, little theater dramas, and community sings.

Independence Day was always the big event. One Fourth of July a beef and a half were barbequed and 40 gallons of gravy served. There were many homemade and store-bought fireworks. One year a small girl was severely burned when a sparkler ignited her calico dress, but she survived.

The social functions changed over the years. By 1929 the racing and rodeos had ceased, but the baseball games continued. "Grandpa" VanMatre took over operations at the big store. Soon after, the dances became more infrequent, but other entertainment began. There was usually a town meeting on the third Wednesday of every month. The menfolk visited while the women prepared the potluck supper and visited, and the youngsters scampered around at the games—outside if it was nice weather. The after-dinner entertainment was usually provided by local talent, but if any could be imported, it was welcome. The "entertainment committee" was always looking for new talent. In addition to musical numbers there were plays put on by visiting local clubs, and by the schools; a group of Yuma businessmen put on a play called "Shot Gun Wedding."

In 1932 the Orton Brothers brought their circus to town, but the tent was no sooner up than it began to rain. The heavy rain continued for the better part of a week, and the circus had to move on, without performing in Heartstrong. It did leave behind quite a bit of elephant litter.

There was never a wedding or a funeral in Heartstrong. Heartstrong never had a school or a church of its own. Many church services were held in the meeting hall, particularly when an itinerant preacherman was passing through. Otherwise. local families traveled to the Betchel Church, about six miles distant. And Heartstrong youngsters attended the rural schools a few miles distant: SUNNY SLOPE, WHITE EAGLE, WILD CAT, HAPPYVILLE (for a very short time), and CENTER.

Heartstrong went the way of most of the other farm centers on the eastern plains. The farm depression which began before the 1929 crash was a staggering blow. The "Dust Bowl" drought of the 1930s did most of the rest. In 1940 "Grandpa" VanMatre suffered a stroke. While he was being rushed to the hospital in Kansas, his store burned to the ground. The store had held the community together. Now it was gone, and so was HEARTSTRONG after twenty years. Just three or four buildings remain today.

HYDE
(Washington County)

An 1886 newspaper story said of HYDE; "Few towns in Colorado have better prospects." Such a statement might have counted for more if it hadn't been printed in *Colorado Topics*, Hyde's own newspaper. Nonetheless, during the middle and late 1880s Hyde was about the fastest-growing town in the eastern Colorado plains. More so than Yuma, it was the destination of many newcomers to Colorado arriving on the Burlington line. And the *Colorado Topics* was the most read newspaper in eastern Colorado.

Gary Dogget filed on this section of land in 1885, and sold it to the Burlington Railroad for $200. The railroad turned it over to the Lincoln Land and Livestock Company, which platted the town and began selling lots in May of 1886 for $100 to $500. Few towns anywhere grew as rapidly, being settled by an "energetic, intelligent class of people," according to *Topics*.

Burlington completed a well in April of 1886, then built a large windmill and pumped the water into tanks of 70- to 100-barrel capacity. The town plat was built around a cistern 90 feet deep and 25 feet across. It was equipped with a double-action pump that required two men to pump. The settlers all hauled water from the cistern, the only source of water here.

One report claimed that there were 50 new homes in the community within weeks and that number was doubled by the end of 1886. This could have been a great exaggeration as compared to later reports; however, more than one directory claimed the town had a population of 500 within months of its founding. In additon to the newspaper, and the Lincoln Land and Livestock Company, Hyde soon had a bank, a hotel and other business listings.

The two-story school was built in 1888, and was also used for town meetings and social events. The Hyde Congregational Church was built about the same time.

Like most other eastern Colorado farm towns, drought and grasshoppers took their toll. The Hyde bank closed in 1895, after many of the town citizens had moved away. Before moving, most settlers attempted to sell their lots for a small part of what they paid for them. Others just abandoned their homes and land.

The town was virtually empty by 1910 when two men, Smith and Cluny, bought up much of the lots. Cluny built a store and attempted to promote the town once again with a little success. There were two grain elevators—the Shannon Grain elevator and the Wager Grain Elevator that was later bought by the Farmers Union M.&M. Cooperative. There was also a lumber yard and a bulk station for gas and oil. A new regional school was built south of town. The new hardware store and some other buildings eventually burned down.

Hyde's second life ended during the 1920s and '30s, during the Dust Bowl days and depression. There are some buildings left, and a grain elevator. Some one-time homes and businesses are now used for farm purposes. Only stone and marble markers remain in the little cemetery, since a fire in 1920 burned all the wooden ones.

PLATNER
(Harmon, Millet, Plainer)
(Washington County)

One source says PLAINER was the post office for MILLET, but that probably was PLATNER, since there is only one letter different. Then some sources say "Millet, see HARMON". We know the name of the town was Harmon in 1893 when two boys, Fred Platner, 16, and his brother David, 11, saw some smoke in the distance. They rode their ponies to the smoke and found a railroad bridge over Sand Creek afire. They rode hard the other way and flagged down the Burlington train "just in time," as most stories say.

From that day forward, all the Platners could ride the railroad free. However, a greater honor was changing the name of the town from Harmon to Platner.

The town was established along the Burlington during the 1880's. There were some railroad facilities here. It was a grain-shipping point on the railroad. There was a U. S. Department of Agriculture experimental station here that tested the various crops that could grow in the region. It may have been responsible for the extensive growth of bird seed, shipped from Harmon/Platner, and also the cultivation of millet grain.

There was a fairly stable population during the 1880s and most of the '90s. The town had several stores, a bank, and what was considered "a very fine school"—one of the few in the region with a bell.

The original Platner brothers, one a father of Fred and David, moved here in 1891 and began farming near town and operated a grist mill near the railroad.

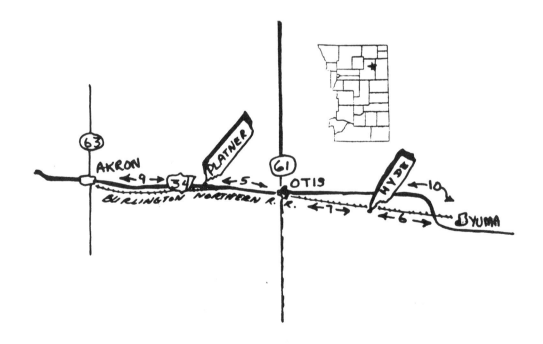

They almost endured the drought and depression of the 1890s, but finally had to close the mill around the turn of the century and move to Denver. The Platners were more fortunate than most of their neighbors who followed suit; they could use the railroad, free of cost.

Platner is still a name on the railroad, about 8 miles east of Akron. A few people still live and farm in the area, but there has only been a dozen or so since about 1915.

KEOTA

(Weld County)

One of the Indian meanings given KEOTA is "the fire has gone out." Another is "gone to visit." There's no question the fire has gone out of Keota.* Its pioneer residents have long since left Keota to "visit" greener pastures. The handful who remain don't like to see visitors at all—visitors have stripped the once-proud farm town clean. Outsiders only mean trouble.

The town was platted by the Lincoln Town Co. in 1888, shortly after the Colorado & Wyoming Railroad built a branch from Sterling to Cheyenne. Many of the first settlers were from Iowa, Indiana and other states to the east. The town was believed named for Keota, Indiana, hometown of some of the early settlers, although there were Keotas in Oklahoma, Missouri and other states. Its Indian meaning is also subject to debate.

The town didn't make much progress until about twenty years later when another wave of homesteaders came. That was about the time (in 1908) when the Chicago, Burlington & Quincy took over the line and promoted settlement. Wheat was the major shipment.

In the next few years Keota boomed. It had everything a modern, thriving farm town could want: bank, school, church, five stores, and even a fire station with two hose carts. The quaint Keota Methodist Church with its unusual corner bell tower was built in 1918. There was also a doctor, a lawyer, a railroad agent, and a resident minister. No saloon was allowed.

Another of Keota's joys was its weekly newspaper, *The Keota News*, published by Clyde Stanley, beginning in 1911. Stanley began publishing in Lafayette, Colorado in 1908. His first publication was *Quest: A Journal*

---

*A "new fire" threatens to greatly heat up activity in and around the ghost town of Keota. As the book goes to press, a joint venture by Union Energy Mining and Power Resources Corporation of Denver is in the final stages of launching a massive uranium mining program under 2000 acres of Keota ranchland. The companies also plan to build a plant to produce a projected 500,000 pounds of yellowcake a year. The mining of the so-called "Pawnee Deposit" has met some opposition based mostly on environmental concerns, including the possible contamination of underground water resources.

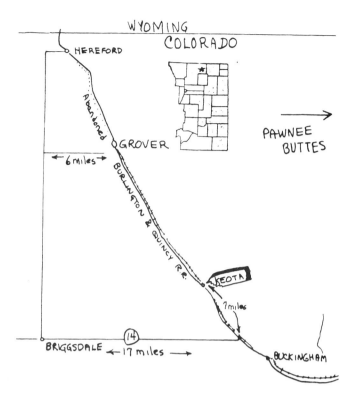

of Aspiration, containing poetry and words of inspiration, ideals, etc. He published more than 33 *Quests* in the next four years. But shortly after arriving in Keota he became so busy putting out the newspaper and doing print jobs for a wide area, that he neglected *Quest* for a while—for 46 years, in fact. He didn't get around to publishing another Quest until 1958, many years after he stopped publishing *The Keota News*.

Even during its halcyon days, just before World War I, Keota never had a population of more than 150, but it seemed much larger—on weekends and holidays especially. The town served some 1000 to 1500 homesteading neighbors, and on special days it was bursting at the seams. The town was incorporated and had a full set of officials.

Then things began happening to Keota.

Before World War I, Keota had daily passenger service on the railroad. Then service became weekly, then not at all. Soon it had only whistle-stop freight service.

The water tower, once a beacon of the town's pride, a complete water system with fireplugs and all, soon became a questionable monument to the town's major problem: water. The water from wells became undependable. During driest years water was shipped in by railroads and trucks. When water in the tower was low there was concern about it being contaminated. The town well was contaminated by a dead man one time, believed murdered.

The bank failed in 1923. Two years later, Stanley published the last issue of *The Keota News*. Stanley

Keota is shown in an early photograph. (*Denver Public Library Western History Department.*)

Little evidence of past activity at Keota can be seen today. At right is a building that once was among the many lining Main Street. Church in the background is shown close up below.

stayed on, however, and did job printing for a wide area. He and a half dozen others were the last residents of the community. The last minister left town in the 1920's. A couple of years later, the two-story Cottage Inn Hotel closed.

The high school, built in 1915, closed in 1951 after graduating two seniors.

All the while, there was the heat and cold, snow and dust, to make the remaining residents more uncomfortable.

About the last hope Keota had was that it was a "crossroads" town, the crossing of two unpaved dusty roads. Then a few years ago the highway department paved Colorado Route 14 and ran it south of Keota, giving travelers more reason to bypass the town.

However, for the most part, the few remaining citizens of Keota are glad to be left alone. Weekend visitors, many thinking the town is abandoned, pick up anything that suits their fancy. Someone took the "town bell" that had tolled for the church meetings, weddings, funerals, and other major events, whether local or international, for 42 years since 1918.

The town was still incorporated into the 1970s, the smallest incorporated town in the state. There were only a half dozen residents and each was a town official. They also owned much of the town; only a few ruins remain, including the church and the cement front of the hotel. Roanoke Avenue, once the main street of Keota, is weed-covered and strewn with tumbleweeds and dust.

Around 1912 there was some talk of making a new county to be called Pawnee, out of eastern Weld County. However, the batttle between Keota and Grover over the county seat became so bitter that the idea was forgotten.

The county would have been named after the ageless sentinels that dominate this region—the Pawnee Buttes. The Buttes, called "Rattlesnake Buttes" in James Michener's "Centennial," played a prominent part in that novel. The Pawnee Buttes have seen many things come and go. Keota was more temporary than most.

KOENIG
(Weld County)

KOENIG was one of the more memorable little farm towns that lived and died at the whim of the railroad. Located five miles north northwest of Johnstown near the Larimer County line, Koenig is a complete ghost today except for the old hotel which is now a family home.

This region was deeded to the Denver Pacific Railroad by an act of Congress when Colorado was still a territory. In the late 1880s Rudolph Koenig emigrated to Colorado from Switzerland and bought some land

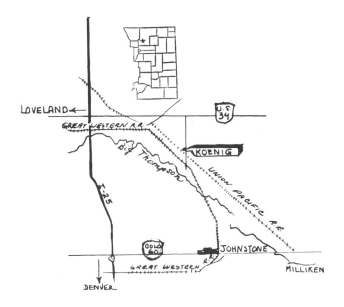

here from the railroad. Koenig, who later became mayor of Golden, began ranching and farming on the land, while he and his wife lived in Loveland.

In 1911 the Union Pacific ran tracks through the Koenig Ranch and erected a rather large station here. Rudolph's widow Emma, and her sons, Fred and Godfrey, still worked the land. Encouraged by the neighbors, the Koenigs platted an ideal community composed of twelve square blocks, with numbered streets and avenues named for trees. The plat included stockyards, coal sheds, potato docks and an area for a sugar beet dump near the railroad.

That same year, the Koenigs built a rather large hotel. It was full by year's end, the first guests being cattlemen, railroad men and traveling salesmen. The station was also busy. The station master lived in the station house and was available 24 hours a day.

Water was a problem from the beginning. Mrs. Koenig fancied herself a "water witch." Her pronged stick method did locate some good wells, but she also struck many a "dry hole." Much of the water had to be hauled in by rail from Loveland. For the hotel the water was stored in a large cistern, which also caught rainwater. When water was scarce much of the used water was captured and recycled for use in washing, irrigation, feeding livestock, etc.

Myron Hamilton, who operated a store at Hamilton's Corners, now called Johnson's Corners, moved to Koenig and opened the first store here. One of the Koenig enterprises here was a cheese factory, called the "Swiss Cot," located about a mile east of town near the Mountain View School, which Koenig youngsters attended.

The station and hotel were the economic and social centers of the community. Many salesmen and buyers and other commercial people passed through

The once-colorful railroad town of Koenig was known for the stately trees lining the road in front of the Koenig House hotel.

the station. Much livestock and farm produce was shipped out. And many Koenigites, with nothing else to do, came to watch the buzz of activity around the station and watch the trains come and go.

A dance marked the grand opening of the Hotel in 1911. Some 80 or more people attended, and it lasted all night. It set the tone of future events, and many other dances followed.

Despite the difficulty in maintaining an adequate water supply, two of the most disturbing experiences came in the form of too much water—in the form of snow. As in virtually all of Colorado, the big blizzard of 1913 completely crippled the community. The snow lasted for nearly a week and buried wagons, fences and everything else. It took days to dig out, and things never got back to normal until the snow melted in the spring.

Another snowstorm in 1919 stranded a trainload of passengers in the town for several days. The 40 to 50 people jammed accommodations and went through almost all the provisions the little town had in stock.

Perhaps the most unique feature of the little town was its colorful landscaping and trees. Mrs. Koenig herself was responsible for many of the stately silver maples and cottonwoods shading the ghost town today. The station master was what might be called a "flower freak" today. He tended the land around the station with loving care, producing a veritable rampage of color from the flowers he planted. He also set the tone for other citizens near the station. Many yards there were well tended and displayed many flowers and shrubs.

KOENIG had all the needed features of a permanent town, and it was a welcome, upstanding member in Colorado's family of towns. But, alas, appearance is not all. Koenig's life was short. In a consolidation of

schools, the Mountain View School closed its doors in 1918. Koenig felt the impact of the depression beginning almost ten years before the crash of 1929. Old-timers claim it was the unavailability of "credit buyin'," and bank loans had much to do with Koenig's demise. It was a vicious circle. By not extending credit, business could not move their wares. One by one they had to close and move to greener markets.

And water remained a problem. Some years it was more of a problem, almost attaining crisis proportions.

Emma Koenig and her sons attempted to keep things going, but without much luck. Emma moved into the hotel in 1924, and then to Greeley in 1944. She died there in 1960 at the age of 98. Her long life recalls one of the many stories told about her. It seems a fortune teller told her she would live to be 75—so although she lost several teeth just before she turned 75, she didn't buy dentures until she turned 76.

Only a half-dozen buildings remain at Koenig today. The hotel has been converted into a private home. The old general store is now used to store farm machinery and other things. There is another building that has been converted into an "antique" shop.

A local citizen tore down the once-colorful depot in 1938 and used the material to build a barn and other outbuildings.

The foundation of the depot is almost obscured by the weeds that replaced the flowers that once bloomed here.

The Amen family bought the townsite and much of the surrounding land from the Koenigs in 1946. They have a deep interest in the history of the site and have maintained their stewardship well.

KUNER
(Weld County)

An early brochure of the Kuner Improvement Company stated that KUNER "should be the center of a farming community of from 10,000 to 20,000 people who should produce over $5 million in crops annually. This amount of produce and money handled there will make Kuner one of the richest and best towns in the State of Colorado."

It wasn't that, but it was the only town in the whole state of Colorado named for a pickle.

Settlement began in the 1880s, but it wasn't until 1908 that the town was platted around and named for the receiving station of the Kuner Pickle Company. It was an elaborate plat, with two "great" boulevards, Conner and Cottingham, bisecting the center of town at Miller Park. Most of the businesses were on these streets—the post office, blacksmith, creamery, Aunt Susie's Cafe, the service station and the hardware store that boasted of handling more hardware and dry goods

Max Kuner, "The Pickle Man."
(*Denver Public Library Western History Department.*)

The old Kuner school (*below*) today stands in the lower right corner of the huge Monfort Feed Lots shown at bottom. (*Bureau of Reclamation, U.S. Department of the Interior.*)

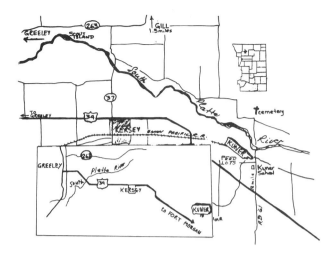

than "any other establishment between Kansas City and Denver."

But perhaps the economic pulse of the town was the street near the northern edge that ran parallel to the tracks and was called "Beet Shovelers Road." It led to the sugar beet dump, alongside the Union Pacific tracks. Here was the pickle house and the little frame depot. Loads of sugar beets and cucumbers (made into pickles) were shipped from here, and some barley, grain and other farm products.

The predominantly Dutch settlers* attempted to make this a potato center, which was part of their undoing. It was before farmers were encouraged to rotate their crops, especially such soil-demanding crops as potatoes and sugar beets. The soil was drained of its nutrients, and the problem was compounded by the drought and other plagues.

The town's pride and joy was the Kuner Christian Reform Church, organized on May 1, 1909. The church was dedicated six weeks later. Total cost of construction was $1400, although there was much volunteer work by church members. It was the first public building in Kuner and the site of many community meetings and social gatherings. The school was built the following year.

Despite the high hopes of the community it never progressed much beyond the first two or three years. The population never exceeded 100, if that. The town was virtually a ghost by 1920, and the little church was torn down during the 1920s. The belfry was turned into a tool shed.

The site, about 13 miles west of Greeley, became part of the new Monfort Feed lots, which feeds about 100,000 cattle.

---

*Many early Colorado settlers from Deutschland (Germany) were sometimes called Dutch by mistake. However, the first families to settle in Kuner were members of the Dutch Christian Reformed Church and were called "Hollanders" as well as Dutch.

There was a fairly large town near here called BROOK- FIELD (see Map 31), but all evidence of it was gone (except four lonesome graves on a hill) when new settlers came around the turn of the century. The little town they started was located on Two Butte Creek, about 18 miles northwest of Springfield. There is no source for the name today, but it apparently was a family name.

The community of MAXEY had a post office by 1910. There was a country store and a few homes, some built of stone. There was need for a cemetery early, so they located one just at the edge of town on a small promontory. The graveyard was apparently never platted officially. It is said there was no charge or special arrangements made for burial. Family and/or friends made all the arrangements, dug the hole, and bought or made the headstone.

In that difficult region and those hard times the cemetery acquired a growing number of residents. Maxeyites thought it was time the town had a church, not only to prepare them for the journey ahead but to make the transition period easier for those left behind.

A town meeting was held in 1917, and it was decided that the only way such a poor community could have a church of its own was through money-raising activities. And for the next several months most of their activities were directed toward raising money for the church through dances, box lunches, bazaars, etc. One of the best money-raisers was selling homemade ice cream. By 1918 enough nickels and dimes had come into the town piggy bank that work began on construction. The fund-raising continued as the townsfolk pitched in to build the church. Since construction was on a "pay-as-you-go" basis, the church was not completed until 1921.

But how proud they all were of their little stone church. For such a remote little place, the interior was magnificent, all hand-carved with tender loving care, especially the pews and the rostrum.

The church was located adjacent to the graveyard. Of course, such a poor community could not afford a full time pastor, but is was frequently blessed by a visit by a man of God from Springfield, Las Animas, or other nearby "cities." The whole town turned out whenever one came to town, no matter what time or day of the week. A regular Sunday school had been organized even before the church was completed, but having a church made it seem more meaningful.

An indication of how much of a force religion was in the lives of Maxey residents is the record that on one day no less than 30 persons were baptized in a water hole in nearby Two Butte Creek.

Years passed and times changed. The surrounding

This old school building and the stone church are about all that's left of the isolated farm town of Maxey. (*Photo courtesy Sarah McKinley.*)

Walls of the Maxey general store and post office, made of native rock, are crumbling rapidly. (*Photo courtesy Betty Cook.*)

"Old Number Nine" windmill at Maxey. These 18-foot wooden towers marked an unofficial post office: the homesteader nearest a well received mail for all in the area, and the well number became part of the address.

ranches had to consolidate. Some got bigger to survive the drought and the times; others were sold or abandoned, and the owners moved away. And it didn't pay people to "do business" in the little crossroads town when they could travel in good cars or trucks over good roads to "the big city" to do their business.

There is no one left in the little town of MAXEY today. There are a couple of old buildings, and the little stone church and graveyard. Silent today, but not completely forgotten. The large J-Lazy M Ranch covers much of the surrounding area. Its owner, James "Jim" McEndree has taken it upon himself to protect and preserve the little church, as much from grazing cattle as vandals. He built a fence around the church, and he and his men keep an eye on it.

Long ago Millie Ely built a fence around the graveyard, which now contains about 50 headstones. Other Maxey citizens planted iris around the fence in profusion. Today, each May, youngsters in the Big Rock 4-H Club, many of them grandchildren of Maxey residents, weed and clear out the little graveyard. When they are finished, you can still see the colorful iris planted so long ago.

NEPESTA (Santa Fe)
(Pueblo County)

There is little left of the onetime busy community of NEPESTA, located 27 miles east of Pueblo, south of the river that gave the town its name. The Indians and the Spanish called the Arkansas River Rio Nepeste (Big River) or Nepeste, and that was the name known to mountain men and travelers along the Santa Fe Trail (see Map 28).

In the early 1870s, Nepesta was a busy stage station. In 1876, the A.T.& S.F. built a station and section house here, and the town was on its way. For awhile the railroad called it SANTA FE STATION. The same year the post office opened under the name NEPESTA. The railroad shortened the time for mail delivery from points east from thirty days to ten.

The original store was a two-story building near the river. It sold everything from party dresses to nails to groceries. The store was the social hub of the community. Old-timers would while away their time here swapping stories. Many a major political controversy was won and lost around the pot-bellied stove in the store, or in front of the store when the weather was warm. On shopping days, usually Saturday, settlers would come from miles around in every sort of conveyance to join the old-timers in discussion or trading the latest news.

Later the store was moved to higher ground to protect it from the frequent flooding along the river.

Settlers built an irrigation ditch during those early years, using hand tools and horse-drawn scrapers. The ditch, whose headgate was a short distance upriver from the town, was originally called the Enterprise Ditch, later changed to the Oxford–Farmers Ditch Company.

Shortly after the railroad established a station here, a large stockyards was built with cattle shoots. Cattle and many other farm products were shipped from here. One product shipped from here was tons of buffalo bones picked up off the prairie. The bones, shipped east to make fertilizer, brought $8 a ton.

The first school was built on the north side of the river on Kramer Creek and was called the KRAMER SCHOOL. Later, the school was built in town and called WEST NEPESTA and finally a large modern brick schoolhouse was built. The school burned in 1948, and the students were transported to Fowler.

Since there was no bridge in those early years, the river was usually forded on foot or horseback. Almost every spring travel was hampered by high water. Flooding was a frequent problem, and eventually most of the community moved away from the river to high ground.

The community had a Union Church and later the Nepesta Methodist-Episcopal Church. The church was transferred to Fowler, seven miles away, in 1914.

During the early years, there were many Indian scares and battles in the region. But there is no record of any attacks on the town. One early settler, Kip True, who died in 1949 at the age of 104, often told of watching a Ute scalp dance from a treetop nearby. The Utes had just returned from battle below Fort Lyon with several scalps taken from Plains Indians. Another oldtimer was "Jackie" Moore, said to be the first settler in the region and a onetime pony express rider. He died in 1927 at the age of 92.

Across the highway from what's left of the community is a small graveyard where many a pioneer was buried—several in the diphtheria epidemic of 1879. Six children of one pioneer couple died during that period.

Much of the onetime community has been washed away by floods. Other buildings have been torn down or converted to other uses. However, descendants of pioneer settlers still live in the region. Whenever they get together they recall stories of the community with the unusual name.

RINN
(Weld County)

RINN is another once-prosperous farm community that evokes only fond memories—so much so that for the past twenty years former residents and their descendants get together, eat tons of food at the annual smorgasbord and talk about the happy past. In recent years as many as 800 gathered from miles around.

Early Nepesta sat close to the river, shown in the old photo above, and was flooded a few times before most of the buildings were moved to higher ground. (*Pueblo Library District.*)

The old Nepesta school (*right*) was moved, and is now used as a barn.

The church at Rinn is the place where former residents of the old farm town gather each September for smorgasbord and memory exchange.

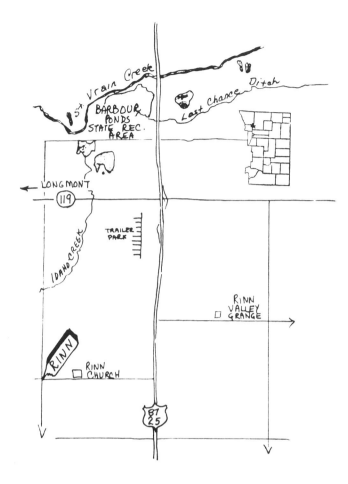

There were three schools in the near area, two frame and one made of stone. All were active by 1890. There was also a blacksmith.

Samuel Rinn ran the store for two decades before he sold it to go into farming full time. During good years, he and his partner Fred Jillson, were among the leading wheat growers in northern Colorado.

However, the primary crop in the vicinity was sugar beets. The Great Western Sugar Company purchased all the area could produce.

Although the soil was rich during good years, irrigation was important during dry years and for sugar beets. The first water rights went back to the 1860s, and it continued as a sensitive area during the history of the region. During dry years, the availability and use of the precious water would often turn neighbor against neighbor.

But there were always other things to drink, even during prohibition. Everyone knew about "Jimmy Smith's Barn." In fact, knowledge of it went further than the neighborhood. Strangers were directed there. Going price was one dollar per pint.

Dances were held on the big wooden floor above the horse stalls, usually on Tuesday and Saturday nights. One year someone stole the cash register from the barn with all the cash raised that night.

Samuel Rinn was a longtime member of the local school board. In 1928 he ran for the state legislature on the Republican ticket. However, the wheat crop was so good that year that he had little time to campaign and lost by a narrow margin in the primary.

He died on March 1, 1930, and his wife took over the business.

Due primarily to the growth of irrigated sugar beet farming, most farms have smaller acreages than they did at the turn of the century. Hardly anyone lives in Rinn anymore. They live in Longmont or other nearby "cities."

Two of the schools have been converted into private homes. The third, the stone schoolhouse, has seen other uses since it was last used as a school, and is now falling into disrepair.

The blacksmith shop still stands at the crossroads. Now it's surrounded by cars, trucks and farm machinery waiting for repairs.

But the church still stands proud. It is still the hub of the neighborhood, a larger neighborhood than that of years gone past—at least one day a year. People come from throughout northern Colorado and some from even farther to attend the smorgasbord reunion. One wonders if it's the food or the nostalgia that brings a growing number back each year. The extent of the feast is almost beyond comprehension: long tables crowded with barbequed meat and other delicacies, all manner of beans, potato salads, probably 100 different kinds of salad and deserts.

The first reunion was held in 1949. The church was in

They meet on the last Thursday in September at the church, which, along with the Rinn family, constituted a dominant force in this community located ten miles southeast of Longmont, in Weld County near the Boulder County line.

This lush farmland was settled in the 1860s and '70s. Among the early settlers were the Rinn Brothers, Jake and Samuel, who came to Colorado from Pennsylvania. Jake Rinn started a store and post office out of his home. Samuel Rinn purchased the property in the 1890s and managed the post office for about seven years until Rinn was established on a rural postal route. He continued to run the general store for several years.

Many others settled during those years. Whenever needed, one or more of the Rinns was always available to lend a helping hand. The Rinn women delivered many a baby and nursed many sick persons back to health. The Rinn menfolk helped neighbors build or repair farm facilities.

Samuel Rinn gave land for the construction of a church. It was dedicated in 1906. A parsonage was built in 1911. The original church burned to the ground in 1924, but was rebuilt immediately. The church and the parsonage were moved to their present location in 1936 to make room for the highway.

GHOSTS OF THE COLORADO PLAINS

a sad state of disrepair. The neighbors got together to clean it up, paint it and repair where needed. The clean-up gathering occurs every year just before the reunion. The smorgasbord has grown into one of the greatest money-raisers anywhere. The funds are used to keep the church in repair.

There was a special celebration in 1956 to celebrate the golden anniversary of the church.

Even today, the name of Rinn is ever present. The Rinn family Bible is encased in iron in the church's steeple.

SOUTH PLATTE
(Logan County)

During the 1870s, SOUTH PLATTE was the most important point along the South Platte Valley from Greeley to Julesburg near the Nebraska border.

It was settled in 1872, although there was some farming and ranching here along the Platte as early as the 1860's. There were also some important stage stations in the area: AMERICAN RANCH, GODFREY'S RANCH ("FORT WICKED") (see Chapter II). However, South Platte is considered the first community in Logan County. It was mentioned as one of the three populated communities in the "entire Platte Valley" in 1873, although the population of Sterling, South Platte and Green City "was not more than 250."

That year, 1873, a school was started at South Platte, thus becoming the only community for 200 miles east of Greeley to have a school.

The schoolhouse was built on land donated by "Uncle Jimmy" Chambers, who settled the American Ranch stage station and was an early leader in this region. He and others were instrumental in the construction of the local irrigation ditch in April and May of 1872. It has been called the Fort Wicked Ditch Company and the Holon Godfrey Ditch Company, both for the stage sta-

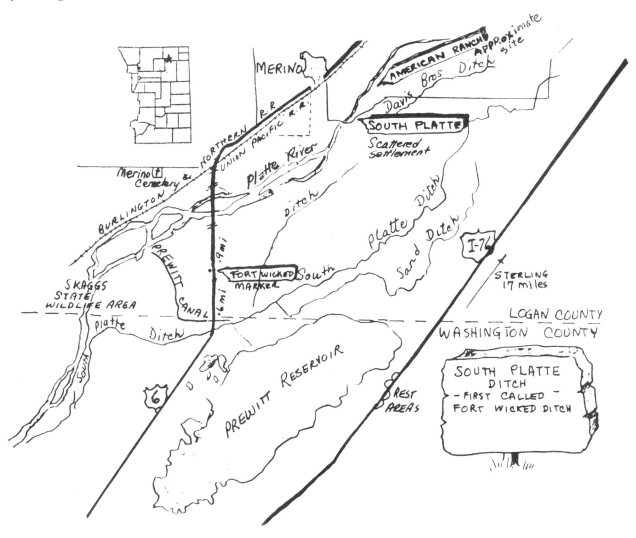

The once-busy depot at Thatcher (*above*) was closed down in the 1960s. (*Denver Public Library Western History Department.*)

Thatcher rodeo grounds (*above*) haven't seen much action in recent years, but this once was the liveliest place for miles around.

The center of activity in this farm and ranch area was the Thatcher school, which still stands today (*left*).

tion operator nearby (see "Stage Stations"), but the irrigation ditch is known historically as the SOUTH PLATTE DITCH. And although Godfrey is credited with building his own irrigation ditch a short time earlier, the South Platte Ditch is usually said to be the first ditch in the South Platte Valley east of Denver, and one of the earliest in the state.

South Platte didn't last long, as Sterling and other communities got more attention, including BUFFALO (now MERINO) just across the river from South Platte.

Crofutt said of South Platte in 1881 and 1885 that "grazing lands, cattle and sheep occupy the country with a few cowboys." The post office for South Platte was discontinued in January of 1883.

THATCHER
(Las Animas County)

People come from all over each year to remember THATCHER. Now they are meeting in Fowler, 80 miles away, because there is not much to remember in Thatcher and no place to get together.

Thatcher was a colorful cowtown a few decades ago. It was named for the Thatcher family, who had cattle, horse and banking interests here and in and around Pueblo. Family members founded the First National Bank in Pueblo. Their colorful three-story mansion in

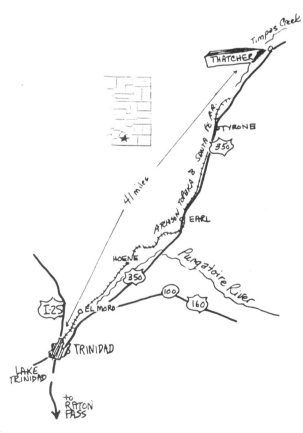

Pueblo, covered with rose-colored stone and called Rosemount, is now the Pueblo Metropolitan Museum.

The family also had a fancy ranch just a short distance out of town, and their cattle and beautiful horses ran free over hundreds of their privately owned acres as well as on free-grazing land.

This was in the 1860s, and for many years after that.

The town was founded shortly after the A.T. & S.F. Railroad came through here, en route to Trinidad and New Mexico, in 1872. A large, colorful station was constructed, and for several decades it was open around the clock. A large general store sold everything from fertilizer to petticoats. There was a fine high school; that is where the Thatcher reunions first took place in 1958.

Like other rural communities, Thatcher was a busy and colorful place on the weekends. Families would come to town in all manner of conveyances to buy supplies and participate in the activities. The prestigious cowpolks from the Thatcher ranch would come to town to spend their money. Youngsters, hopeful waddies of the future, would follow them around.

Thatcher's fate was little different than hundreds of other farm and ranch communities on the plains. But at one time Thatcher planned on being world famous. Thatcher's "Edsel" was a helium plant. During the early years of this century, when dirigibles looked like the way to fly in the future, the helium plant was installed, with an expanding capacity to fill orders from around the globe. If they had produced airplane gas it would have been another story.

The Thatcher interests slowly withdrew as more homesteaders came, broke the sod and put up fences on the free range. The family still has cattle and financial interests in Colorado, but the cowpolks aren't seen in Thatcher anymore. Hardly anybody is.

The depot closed down in the mid-1960s. Ira Smoot, who had been station agent and telegrapher for 45 years, no longer came to work. The old smoke-eating locomotives no longer bring excitement to Thatcher. Now an Amtrak streamliner streaks through the town, seldom bothering to even toot its whistle.

The post office closed a few years ago. The general store burned to the ground, and no thought was given to rebuilding it. The high school, the town's pride and joy, is in ruins. Any school kids in the Thatcher area are bused to Hoehne, about 30 miles away.

TOONERVILLE (Red Rock)
(Bent County)

Rural families living in this neighborhood thought they were something special although they weren't much different from other rural families throughout eastern Colorado.

Only rubble remains of the Toonerville church which used to be the social center of that farm community.

The truck outside the former general store at Toonerville hasn't made a delivery in years.

Their rural center was originally known as RED ROCK. And the families that gathered there each weekend thought they had something special going. Red Rock had a church, a school/meeting hall, a country store and a couple of other commercial businesses. It even had its own station on the AT&ST railroad, about 22 miles south southeast of Las Animas.

What they thought was special was the fun and games they had on the weekends. There was always something planned: baseball games, dances, rodeos, potluck suppers—and all the other things the other rural centers enjoyed.

But Red Rock had more fun. Virtually everybody in the surrounding area came together at Red Rock on the weekends. Everybody knew everybody. Finally, they figured that such a close-knit group ought to have its own set of officers. So they elected a full slate of officers, from the mayor on down. They conducted mock town meetings and trials, etc.

Of course, with such a fun group, a nondescript name like Red Rock just wouldn't do. So for a couple of weekends they thought up some possible names. Then they voted; TOONERVILLE won. That was the name of a popular comic strip of the time, "The Toonerville Trolley." Everybody thought that was a grand name. They adapted it to just about everything there was. They became "Toonerville Folks," the train became their own "Toonerville Trolley," and the ladies became "Toonerville Toots."

But even a fun town like Toonerville couldn't giggle its way through the "Dust Bowl" and the depression. The school/meeting hall is still in good shape today,

and it is used from time to time. Otherwise, one finds only the foundation of the church, the ruins of the country store and a couple of other buildings. They even changed the name of the nearby railroad marker. It's called RUXTON now.

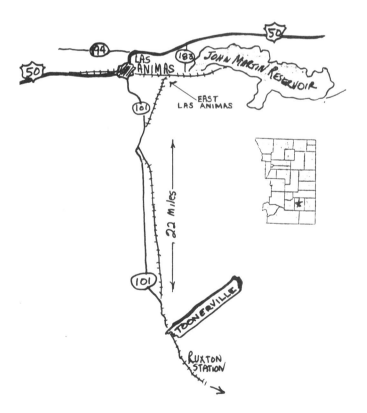

GHOSTS OF THE COLORADO PLAINS

CHAPTER V

COLORADO KINGDOMS

Colorado's best-known cattle kingdom is the John Iliff ranch, which covered all of northeastern Colorado during the 1870's and '80's. It was fictionalized in the James Michener epic, *Centennial*.

But there were other Colorado kingdoms.

Most of the others were in southern Colorado. Some were encouraged by the large Mexican land grants that were generally made to encourage settlement in a virgin territory. The seemingly endless amounts of free or near-free land was mouth-watering to those with visions of empire. With their use of cheap Mexican labor to go with the land, some could be better described as feudal empires or fiefdoms. Autobees was an example.

Several years before Colorado became a territory there was extensive commercial and agricultural activity in southern Colorado. After its founding in 1822, the Santa Fe Trail and the branches thereof were busy highways to New Mexico. One of the first, and certainly the most prominent pioneer to set up shop along the Trail was William Bent, who established his famous trading post in 1833, after experimenting with other sites along the Arkansas prior to that.

The trappers and mountain men of the day traded their furs for provisions at Bent's Fort. The great agricultural and commercial leaders of early Colorado and New Mexico worked for Bent in one capacity or another, many freighting for him.

Bent's Fort was the most famous trading post in southern Colorado, but there were others. More notorious was Fort Pueblo (El Pueblo, etc.), which was established around 1842 and met its bloody end on Christmas Day 1854, when its occupants were slaughtered by Indians. The fort had been established primarily by George Simpson. Fortunately for him and other prominent settlers of that time they were away from the fort when the massacre occurred.

There were also agricultural settlements that supplied livestock and farm products for the trading posts and the early travelers. The most prominent of these were the Hardscrabble settlements, further up the Arkansas River near present Canon City, and smaller, shorter-lived farm efforts along the Greenhorn and St.

Charles rivers south or east of present Pueblo. Most noted of all were Autobees and the Huerfano Settlements.

There are several good books on the Santa Fe Trail and on Bent's Fort. Leading expert on most of the other early settlements, especially Hardscrabble and the Huerfano Settlements, is Janet Lecompte. She has written several articles on pre-territorial activity in southern Colorado, and has brought much of it together in her most interesting and well-documented book, *Pueblo–Hardscrabble–Greenhorn: The Upper Arkansas, 1832–1856*. It is highly recommended for anyone interested in delving further into the history of this fascinating region before territorial settlement and the Colorado gold rush began.

AUTOBEES (Autobees Plaza, Huerfano Abajo)
(Pueblo County)

Charles Autobees came west when he was only 11 or 12 years old. Orphaned when very young and running wild on the streets of St. Louis, he joined a party of trappers heading up the Missouri river in the early 1820s. In the next few years he learned all the rules of survival in the western wilderness, and he himself became known and respected throughout the west by mountain men and Indians alike.

In the 1830s he found himself in New Mexico, where he became an agent for Simeon Turley, who operated Turley's Mill, a large distillery north of Taos. Autobees became one of the west's first legitimate liquor distributors.

He also took the first of his wives.*

---

*For most of his adult life Autobees had two wives. One, Serafina, spent much of the time in New Mexico with the Autobees children. His constant companion in Colorado for more than 20 years was an Arapahoe squaw named Sycamore. He had other "wives," mostly Indian, from time to time.

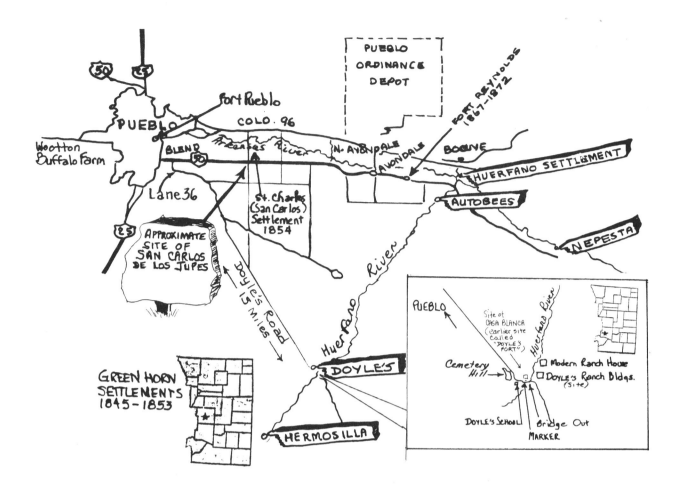

Turley's Mill was destroyed and Turley was killed during the Mexican uprising of 1847. Autobees no longer had a product to sell.

During the rebellion he fought under Ceran St. Vrain. During this time and the years that followed, St. Vrain saw in Autobees the toughness, courage and intelligence that was needed to lead the settlement of huge Vigil and St. Vrain Land Grant in the Arkansas Valley, in what is now Colorado. Primary purpose of the land grants was to encourage settlement in virgin territory. St. Vrain was anxious to "prove up" on the grant when it came under review by the United States Government.

Autobees was finally convinced. In February of 1853 he set out with about 60 pack animals loaded with provisions and equipment, much of it provided by St. Vrain, and 25 men. Some of the men, such as William Kroenig and Marcelino Baca, would later be residents of the Huerfano Settlements (but now had other errands): most of the rest were "peons," primarily Mexican and French.

There was heavy snow en route and the traveling was slow, but the party reached the confluence of the Arkansas and Huerfano Rivers by late February.

(Kroenig and Baca continued on to Big Timbers for trading.)

Autobees, who had his choice of the land, selected lowlands along the Huerfano and south of the confluence. The bottom lands along the river were heavily wooded, and the soil was deep and rich.

At the early signs of spring, the first crops were planted. The primary crop was corn, but others such as potatoes, beets, etc. were planted to sustain the little colony.

The following year, 1854, Autobees was joined by his illustrious neighbors, "Uncle Rick" Wootton, Joseph Doyle, William Kroenig, Marcelino Baca and others, who built their placitas near the confluence (see HUERFANO SETTLEMENTS, below). The new settlement was built with permanancy in mind, but Indian raids that same year would chase all but Autobees and his wife and workers back to New Mexico and end the short life of the settlements.

In October of 1854 Autobees, with his wife Sycamore and some of his workers, was surrounded by Utes west of the settlement. The Indians ordered Autobees to turn over his wife and other Arapahoes in his party. Autobees refused. The battle lasted more than two

GHOSTS OF THE COLORADO PLAINS

This marker tells the story of Autobees, the man and the site.

hours. Autobees was wounded and some of his stock was stolen. But the Indians finally left—without Sycamore, who had fought valiantly beside her husband.

In 1855 Autobees built his permanent residence on the west side of the Huerfano, about 2 miles south of the confluence. Here he had his workers construct several buildings, primarily of adobe and wood, around a large square. This commodious oasis became known far and wide as AUTOBEES PLAZA, HUERFANA ABAJO, or just AUTOBEES. *Abajo* is Spanish for "low" and could mean the lowlands along the river or the "lower" Huerfano below its mouth.

In addition to living quarters for the family and workers, there were guest quarters, a livery and large corral, a large dining room and kitchen, work and storage rooms, and a "trading" room where Autobees negotiated with the Indians and other traveling salesmen of the day.

The guest rooms were temporary homes for many of the more famous men of that time—Kit Carson, John C. Fremont, St. Vrain and many others, including Autobees' famed brother, Tom (Autobees) Tobin,* best known for his tracking down of the "Bloody Espinozas" who cut a bloody trail through Colorado Territory in the 1860's. To prove that he killed them, he brought back their heads and rolled them across the floor of Fort Garland.

During the years of 1855–57, Autobees continued to farm on a sufficient scale to feed his settlement and

---

* The relationship between Autobees and Tobin has been the bane of western writers. They have called them "brothers-in-law" and "half brothers," etc. Janet Lecompte said they were brothers.

provide for what travelers there were. He made frequent trips to New Mexico, to visit Fort Union and his "other family," Bent's Fort and elsewhere.

In 1858 and 1859, when reports of gold finds in Colorado were rampant and the "great migration" began, Joseph Doyle, Wootton, William Kroenig, Thomas Fields and others returned to make their fortunes—not from locating gold mines but by feeding and supplying the miners and mining camps. Within months the "new Huerfano settlement" around AUTOBEES became the most productive agricultural region in the Territory.

While his neighbors made their fortunes supplying the needs of the "new cities" and the gold camps, Autobees continued to farm and hunt on a moderate scale. Visions of great wealth did not seem to pursue him through his farming activity. However, he did serve the gold rush in other ways.

Autobees first received Territory then military authorization to operate the ferry across the Arkansas, anywhere within 2½ miles of the mouth of the Huerfano. His original ferryboat was so small that a wagon had to be dismantled to be carried across the stream. Nonetheless, business was brisk, as more and more gold hungry immigrants poured into Colorado.

A later ferryboat built by the military, was one of the largest in existence, and could carry a fully loaded six-mule team. Autobees had a crew operating the ferry

Charles Autobees. (*Courtesy Colorado Historical Society.*)

night and day. The cost for a non-military wagon drawn by two animals to cross on the ferry, was one dollar. A four-animal team cost $1.25. Every horse or mule with rider paid 25 cents. One person on foot was 20 cents. Livestock was 10 cents each.

Nearby Fort Reynolds relied on Autobees in many ways. His "saloon" was popular with the soldiers (though not with the officers). In addition to operating the ferry for the military, he also was frequently employed as a guide and scout, generally in forays against marauding Indians.

When Colorado Territory was created, Huerfano became one of the original 17 counties, and AUTOBEES became the original county seat. Charles Autobees and Joseph Doyle became two of the three county commissioners. Originally, Huerfano County comprised virtually all of southeastern Colorado Territory.

When a bridge was built across the Arkansas around 1866, most of Autobees' ferry traffic was lost, but the commandant of Fort Reynolds employed Autobees to operate the ferry for the military exclusively. (It was said that one provision was that Autobees close down his saloon. There is no record that he did.)

During the Indian War of 1868, Autobees and his son, Mariano, served as guides and scouts for a contingent of soldiers sent from Fort Lyon, plus about 100 Mexicans, Indians and half-breeds, to put down the Plains Indians in southern Colorado. The Indians led them a merry chase and the small army became stranded without provisions. They were rescued by Mariano Autobees, who got through with wagonloads of food and supplies.

From 1870 to 1872 Autobees was employed virtually fulltime by the military as a guide and a scout. Much of his activity involved chasing down horse thieves and other lawbreakers.

Over the years, Autobees relied more and more on his sons to farm his land. Shortly after Colorado became a Territory, the U.S. Government reviewed all earlier land grants. It was estimated that some 3 or 4 million acres was involved in the original Vigil and St. Vrain Land Grant. On review, the Congress whacked this down to about 100,000 acres. Autobees' land was trimmed to about 686 acres.

Shortly after the Indian troubles subsided on the Colorado Plains the Army abandoned its posts along the Arkansas. Autobees had little to do. In the mid-1870s what land was not farmed by his sons was leased or sold to Thomas Fields, and Autobees lived in near-poverty the last few years of his life.

In 1879, the Colorado General Assembly voted a pension to Charles Autobees. It was not enough even to provide for his simple needs. In 1882, the U.S. Congress received a bill to grant Autobees a pension as an Indian fighter. Before the measure came up for a vote, Autobees died on June 17, 1882, at the age of 70. He was buried in a simple grave at the St. Vrain Cemetery, not far from his plaza, the ruins of which have since been washed away by floods.

There is a marker to this man who matched the Colorado mountains. It is a short distance north of U.S. Highway 50 on the west banks of the Huerfano, where he pioneered settlement so many years ago.

The land around the Upper Huerano remains some of the most fertile and productive in Colorado. Southern Colorado historian Ralph Taylor estimates that Autobees may have had as many as 700 descendants, many who still live and farm in this region. Descendants gave land for the construction of the old St. Joseph Church and for the cemetery nearby, and were largely responsible for the development of the community of Avanodale.

In fact, much of the development of southern Colorado is a monument to Charles Autobees.

HUERFANO SETTLEMENT and DOYLE'S (Doyle's Mill, Doyle's Ranch, Casa Blanca, Hermosilla)
(Pueblo County)

Within months of the establishment of AUTOBEES, some very important people moved into the neighborhood. Actually, "Uncle Dick" Wootton, Joseph Doyle and William Kroenig had helped Autobees build his headquarters in 1853, and returned a few months later to build

William Kroenig, photographed in the middle or late 1890s. (*Denver Public Library Western History Department.*)

their *placitas* nearby, along the bottom lands near the confluence of the Huerfano and Arkansas Rivers.

Wootton used some of his profits from the 1852 venture when he trailed thousands of sheep to the goldfields of California, and Doyle and Kroenig utilized the profits from their trading activities to build substantial homes here.

It was the largest and the most significant settlement in southeastern Colorado up to that time. And although the original HUERFANO SETTLEMENT lasted but a few months, it was the key to the future development of southern Colorado, and its residents were bulwarks in the early settlement of the entire state.

Unlike Autobees, who built in the form of a large plaza, his new neighbors constructed random placitas along the river bottom. In addition to five or six large homes, there were a number of smaller cabins and dugouts for the "peons", who were primarily Mexican and French. At one end of the settlement were several tepee-like structures (called "sweat-houses") for Indian residents. The main placitas were sturdy and commodious, with rooms for families of the principal residents and their guests. They were built to be their permanent homes.

Wootton constructed what was called a "substantial fortress," surrounded by a sharp-pointed log stockade with thick, bullet-proof bastions at opposite corners. His placita contained several rooms, additional living quarters for guests and servants, a livery, work and storage rooms, a huge shed for wagons and heavy equipment, and a corral. One unusual aspect of the shed was the roof. It was covered with soil and was farmed by the women.

Wootton was primarily the stock raiser in the settlement, raising cattle, horses and mules. He found a ready market at Army installations in New Mexico.

Doyle and Kroenig were expert farmers.

After accompanying Autobees to the Huerfano in 1853 and helping him get established, Kroenig continued on to do some trading at Big Timbers (see "By The Side of the Road") and then began farming near the mouth of the Greenhorn, about midway between the Huerfano and the present site of Pueblo.

Originally from Germany, Kroenig was in his twenties when he settled near the mouth of the Huerfano and began farming in partnership with Autobees. He furnished the seeds and expertise while Autobees furnished the peons.

He took his share of the harvest to Fort Laramie (in present Wyoming) on the Oregon Trail. A steady stream of immigrants passed through the fort en route to the California gold fields or the Northwest. They were desperate for food, and to lighten their load or to help finance the remainder of the trip, many left their livestock behind or bartered them (usually to the Indians) for very little in return.

So, in addition to buffalo robes, Kroenig acquired

When he died in 1864 at the age of 46, Joseph Doyle was considered the richest man in the Territory, and one of the most powerful. (*Denver Public Library Western History Department.*)

about 100 head of cattle for one dollar a head or less, and some 200 sheep. He trailed these back to New Mexico, where he sold them at a good profit. With these funds he was able to build his placita at the Huerfano Settlement.

Joseph Brainbridge Doyle was born in Shenandoah, Virginia. His father was a captain in the militia during the War of 1812, and the family moved to St. Louis during the 1830's. In 1839 Joseph Doyle signed on with William Bent and headed west for Bent's Fort. He was a hard worker, imaginative and honest. In the coming years he became known and respected throughout the west and attained a high level of success in all he attempted.

He worked for Bent for several years, primarily as a freighter, until he left Bent's employ in 1844. He was a partner of Alexander Barclay, George Simpson and others in the Hardscrabble trading post operations up the Arkansas River, near present Canon City. He and Barclay built and operated Fort Barclay, a trading post near Watrous, New Mexico. In New Mexico, he married Marie de la Cruz Suaso from a prominent New Mexico family.

He too assisted Autobees in 1853 in establishing the first settlement along the Huerfano. The following year, he began farming further up the Arkansas, near the mouth of the St. Charles (San Carlos) River, just east of the present site of Pueblo. He also had a good harvest, but concern over the frequent flooding at his location influenced him to move to the Huerfano Settlement in the fall of 1854.

He built the largest placita of all, 75 by 60 feet, which included guest rooms for George Simpson and his family.

Residents worked with Autobees to put in a crude irrigation system. Captain John W. Gunnison passed through the settlement in 1854 on the ill-fated expedition which ended with his death at the hands of Indians in Utah.

This settlement had Indian troubles of its own. In 1854 and '55 frequent Indian forays drove the settlers to distraction. In January of 1855, a wagon train had just passed through heading west when it was set upon by Indians. All the immigrants were killed and their wagons burned.

Still hungry for blood, the Indian band continued on toward the Huerfano. All the settlers fled to Wootton's fortress. Doyle was away at the time, but his wife Cruz and their two children joined the others. As the Indians approached they were met with some fire from the bastions above, but not enough to deter them. Just as the approached the main gate of the Wootton stockade, the remainder of the settlers that had been waiting behind the gates rushed out, completely surprised the attackers and sent them fleeing in disarray.

But the raids and threats of raids continued. By mid-1855, all but a handful of the settlers had returned to New Mexico. Autobees remained through it all. Wootton stayed through early May, as his wife Dolores was in the last stages of a difficult pregnancy. She died in childbirth, and the disconsolate Wootton left the settlement also.

It spelled the end of the original Huerfano Settlement.

Autobees and William Bent continued their operations, despite the ever-present threat of Indians.

Wootton, Kroenig and Doyle continued their activity, most of it centering around New Mexico. Alexander Barclay died in 1855 and Doyle sold Fort Barclay shortly thereafter. He also operated a commercial freight line between St. Louis and Santa Fe.

They returned to the Huerfano in 1858 and 1859 with the first reports of gold found in Colorado and the beginning of the "great migration." Wootton, Kroenig and Doyle became three of the earliest success stories of the gold rush. They didn't waste their time searching for the precious metal; they made their fortunes supplying the argonauts with their needs.

Wootton became a major supplier of food and liquid nourishment in Denver City, where he opened one of the first stores and saloons in the infant city.

Kroenig returned to the land above Autobees, near the confluence and not far from the old Huerfano Settlements, and began farming on a large scale. Soon this area became the most productive agricultural region in the territory, largely due to his efforts. Kroenig expanded his food and mercantile business with out-

lets in Denver City, Colorado City (early Colorado Springs), early Pueblo and the first gold camps.

Most successful of all was Joseph Doyle. With the profits from his freighting business, he headed a pack train loaded down with food and other goods to Denver City, where he sold his supplies under the name of J.B. Doyle & Company. Almost from the beginning his became the largest mercantile business in the Territory, with outlets in Denver, Colorado City, Pueblo, the Canon City area, and the early gold camps. He did a half-million dollars' business a year. He was called the richest man in the Territory and Colorado's first millionaire.

In 1859 he purchased a large tract of land along the Huerfano, south of Autobees' land, and established headquarters at a point about 15 miles below the confluence. He brought in lumber from the east and built a large, two-story home, somewhat in the grand style of the mansions of his native Virginia. He furnished the house lavishly and staffed it with many servants.

In 1861, he built a large flour mill nearby, one of the first in the territory, and increased his acreage to 600 acres. In addition to his cropland, he ran hundreds of head of livestock in the surrounding fields.

Doyle's headquarters and its buildings gave reasons for the many names given the site. DOYLE'S RANCH or just DOYLE'S were often used. He painted his house white and called it CASA BLANCA. The site was also called DOYLE'S MILL for the flour mill. Doyle also built the first school in the region, where his children and the children of his workers attended. The first teacher at Doyle's School was said to be O. J. Goldrick, who left here after a short stint to become Denver City's first schoolteacher. Successor of Goldrick was Ernest Porter. Church services were also held in the school.

Local people still call the site DOYLE'S FORT for a building across from the school. A post office opened here on February 25, 1862. One name used was HERMOSILLA or HERMOSILLO, Spanish for "a beautiful place," for the landscaping and natural beauty of the place.

When Colorado Territory was divided into the original 17 counties and AUTOBEES became county seat of Huerfano County, Doyle became one of the three county commissioners. In 1864, Doyle was elected to the Territory Council (which became the Territory Senate), representing all of southeastern Colorado Territory.

Joseph Doyle did not live to serve his term. He died suddenly in Denver on March 4, 1864, of a heart attack. He was just 46 years old. At the time of his death, he was considered the richest man in the state and one of the most politically powerful.

Territorial Governor John Evans led a large delegation of luminaries to the funeral.

The obituary in *The Rocky Mountain News* called Doyle "One of the best-known and most highly re-

The structure above is said to be an early residence of Joseph Doyle at his ranch. At left is Casa Blanca, Doyle's longtime home. (*Pueblo Library District.*)

Headstones of Joseph Doyle and his wife Cruz stand above the ruins of the schoolhouse. "Uncle Dick" Wootton claimed that foul play caused Mrs. Doyle's death in an attempt to take over the vast holdings of her husband.

Remains of the Doyle schoolhouse.

Students at the Doyle school with their teacher, no date given. (*Pueblo Library District.*)

spected among the pioneers of the Rocky Mountains, where he spent almost a lifetime first as a trapper, then a trader, and, since the settlement of the country, as a most active businessman in furthering all of its great enterprises."

An obituary also said that ". . . he had at all times a piece of good land, seed and teams for any man who was broke and wished by labor to repair his lost fortune . . . no honest, industrious man can say that he ever went to the deceased for aid and did not receive it."

Janet Lecompt quoted a Pueblo correspondent as saying ". . . the countenance of every citizen of southern Colorado wears a cloudy and gloomy look . . . and well it might, for the whole economy of the Arkansas Valley was more or less involved in his many enterprises and dependent upon his steady generosity and good sense."

Joseph Doyle was buried on a small hill on his land, overlooking the Huerfano River that he loved, and just above the Doyle School. His wife, born Marie de la Cruz Suaso, died a year later and was buried beside him.

Wootton had lived with the Doyles frequently. After Joseph Doyle's death he had indicated his intention of marrying Cruz Doyle, and when she died he hinted at

the possibility of foul play because of her wealth. He was at his ranch near Pueblo at the time of Cruz' death, and shortly after that left for his new life atop Raton Pass (see Wootton, "By the Side of the Road").

George Simpson and his family had lived with the Doyles since 1861. They moved on to Trinidad after the death of Cruz Doyle.

There was a frenetic battle over the Doyle fortune and land by family members and hangers-on. Consequently the family fortune was squandered and the family disintegrated.

The site of Doyle's kingdom was listed in post office and business directories for several years, under the various names, DOYLES, DOYLE'S MILL, HERMASILLA being the most frequent. Population was listed at 50 as late as 1876.

There are three or four scattered ranches here today. A large attractive ranchhouse sits on a hill overlooking the east banks of the Huerfano close to where CASA BLANCA once stood. (Casa Blanca burned down in 1942.)

The bridge over the Huerfano was washed out in recent years but the river can usually be negotiated by an ordinary automobile much of the year. Several mailboxes stand together at the west bank of the river. A

GHOSTS OF THE COLORADO PLAINS

short distance up the road to the west is a large marker to Doyle, which was dedicated in 1978.

The ruins of Doyle's School is a little further up the road. The letters spelling out "Doyle" can barely be seen from the road. Above the school is the hill where Joseph Doyle, his wife Cruz, family members and others are buried. Off to one side are two tiny markers that say simply "unknown" on them. One wonders who the unknown people were and how they came to be buried on the hill with this great man and his family.

Standing on the hill, looking at the markers, the roofless school below and the beautiful Huerfano river, heavily lined with trees and greenery, one can wonder about the river and the onetime world of Joseph Bainbridge Doyle.

The well-graded gravel road runs from the hill, northwestward in a straight line from Doyle's world, 15 miles to Pueblo and the real world of today.

BARELA (El Porviner) and RIVERA (San Francisco Plaza, Glenham, Barela Junction)
(Las Animas County)

The castle headquarters of the extensive political and financial empire of Casimiro Barela, known as the "Perpetual Senator," was southeast of Trinidad in Las Animas County, near the New Mexico line. Near Trinidad, Barela built two lavish homes for his two gracious ladies. From here he ran his multi-million dollar, multi-faceted empire in Colorado, New Mexico, Mexico and South America. He lived here while State Senator for forty years, longer than any man in the nation.

It all began in New Mexico where Casimiro was born on March 4, 1847, in Embudo, an ancient Mexican-

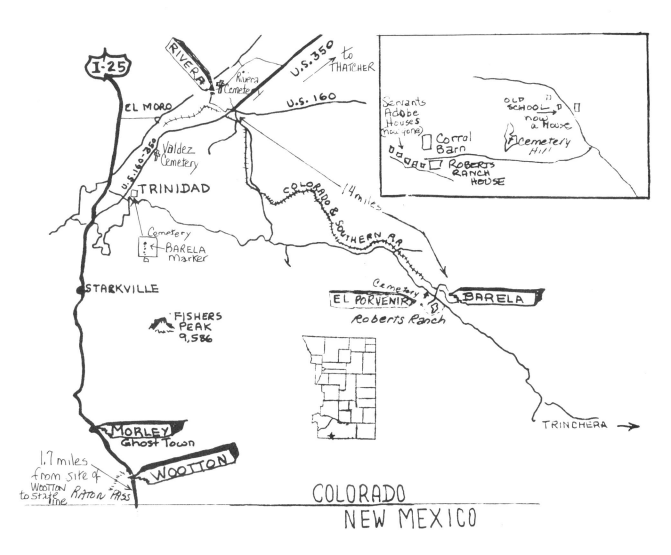

Casimiro Barela, "the perpetual Senator," and his first wife, Josefita. (*Denver Public Library Western History Department.*)

Indian town about midway between Taos and Santa Fe. While he was still a youth the family moved to Mora, New Mexico, where he, his father and his brothers operated a mercantile business. Although education was difficult to come by in those times and places, Casimiro was given the best education available, and he was hungry for knowledge.

Casimiro first visited Colorado while a teenager on a grain-buying trip with his father. he liked the land around Trinidad and convinced his family to take up farming here. Casimiro Barela moved to Colorado in Jaunary, 1867. On March 4, 1867, his 20th birthday, Casimiro married his childhood sweetheart from New Mexico, Josefita Ortiz.

The couple lived on land southeast of Trinidad, Josefita bore Casimiro four girls (though the first child died); the first three letters of the oldest girl's name Leonor was used as his cattle brand (LEO). It became a well-known brand, not only in Colorado.

Besides attention to the rapid growth of his farflung business enterprises and his dedication to his family, more was demanded as his neighbors saw in him the leadership they needed to represent them in the raw frontier.

He was already justice of the peace and county assessor in 1871 when he was first elected to the Territorial Assembly in Denver. In 1874–75, when Colorado was approaching statehood, he was one of 49 selected to write the state constitution. His role was important in protecting the rights of minorities, and it was his insistence that caused the state constitution to be printed in Spanish as well as English. Colorado became a state in 1876, and Barela was elected State Senator to the first Colorado legislature. He would be re-elected to the post for the next 40 years.

Barela worked diligently as a senator. While the legislature was in session, he usually lived in a large house near the Capitol, with his family and many servants. His house in Denver was a center for many social gatherings, especially when foreign dignitaries were in Colorado.

His soirees at home in southern Colorado were more like royal affairs, largely due to their setting. When Casimiro married Josefita he said she would be a queen. He began building her "castle" shortly after their marriage—the most lavish such palace to flower in the sage and sandhills plains of eastern Colorado.

He called the home EL PORVINIR ("The Future"). It was like a fairyland castle amid endless gardens and long rows of trees, and with a lake nearby, large enough for boating. There were miles of irrigation ditches to water the gardens and trees.

From the tower of the "castle" could be seen the wide beauty of the land and the growing town of BARELA.

The grave marker of Casimiro Barela (*left*) is in a Trinidad cemetery. The graves of Josefita and other members of the family (*above*) are on a knoll near El Porvenir.

The residents were primarily the families of workers for Barela. The town had a hotel, school, several stores and good homes.

Barela also built a small but colorful chapel near El Porvenir. It boasted a fine bell, and Catholic ceremonies of every kind were held here. Barela's first child was buried near El Porvenir. In 1878 his father José died and was buried near his granddaughter; by 1883 his beloved wife Josefita was gone too, and the little cemetery had its third occupant.

For many years Barela was considered the richest cattleman in southern Colorado. But that was far from his only interest. His burgeoning empire included the most famous racing and breeding horses in the region. Many of the stories and legends surrounding Barela concerned the famous races held here or elsewhere by his horses. Barela operated a giant sheep ranch near Taos. He had a 500-acre ranch in Old Mexico and a coffee plantation in Brazil. He also had some cattle interests in Kansas City. He was a director of the Trinidad & San Luis Railroad and of the Trinidad National Bank. He ran two bilingual printing businesses, in Trinidad and in Denver. He had other business interests in Denver, southern Colorado and in New Mexico, including the family's mercantile business in Mora.

He also had time and donated much money to charity and other programs to help Spanish-Americans. He was instrumental in the building of a modern hospital in Trinidad.

In 1884, Barela married another New Mexico lady, Damiana Rivera. She was as gracious as Barela's first wife, and more outgoing. The family continued to do much entertaining wherever they went. Damiana Barela became a good friend and confidant to individuals and families over a wide area. Her door was always open to those needing advice or help. She and Casimiro adopted a son shortly after they were married. During the next few years they adopted eight more youngsters, orphans or children of impoverished families. Barela started another brand—DB—his wife's initials.

Barela built his second wife her own little "castle" about six miles northeast of Trinidad. It was more ranch-style than castle-like, built in the Spanish "quinta" style: meandering, multi-level, with many windows, verandas and fireplaces. Extensive lawns, flower gardens and trees surrounded the house, which Barela named RIVERA. Lilac bushes, purple iris and roses dominated the gardens. There were cement walks through and around the gardens, which were lit with many colorful lamps.

The Denver, Texas & Fort Worth Railroad (1888–90), Union Pacific, Denver & Gulf (1890–98) and the Colorado & Southern (today) ran lines near Rivera. Barela

Below, a photo of Porvenir in 1931 when Earl Roberts purchased the property. He later moved the cupola and made other changes to modernize. Earl's son Tom and family live in the house today (*left*). (*Photos courtesy Tom Roberts.*)

convinced the railroad to make a stop there. The walk to the station from Rivera was lined with flowers and trees and well lit. The Senator built an attractive shelter at the stop, with a sign saying RIVERA.

The railroad also stopped at BARELA. It is said that the town was on or very near the site of an early Mexican plaza, one of several in Colorado called SAN FRANCISCO. Before it was renamed Barela, it was also called GLENHAM; later it was also known at times as BARELA PLAZA, BARELA JUNCTION, BARELA STATION.

During Barela's more than 40 years of public life he was a forceful, influential figure in state government, a hard worker and honest. He had a strong, melodious voice. He was a spokesman of many liberal causes, for minorities and for agriculture. He was instrumental in establishing many agricultural experimental stations throughout the state. In addition to being State Senator, he was Consul for Mexico and other Latin American countries, and a leading host of dignitaries of all races. He once threw a lavish dinner for U.S. Grant in Trinidad.

The later Barela home, Rivera. (*Aultman Studios, Trinidad.*)

Once during a political speech in Hoehne, another community near Trinidad, he was wounded by a would-be assassin. The audience caught the gunman and wanted to string him up immediately, but Barela himself persuaded the mob to turn him over to the local authorities for a proper trial.

The longtime Democratic leader changed parties in 1900, believing he could better represent "his people" as a Republican. That year he won a close election from Dr. Beshoar, a liberal doctor to the coal miners who would become famous during the coal-field wars. The election was so close that Dr. Beshoar protested possible "irregularities." It is said that Barela helped pay the the recount himself, and won.

Barela was finally defeated in 1916. Nearly 70, he retired to Rivera with his wife Damiana. His three daughters were married and lived elsewhere, as did his adopted children, but they visited frequently.

Casimiro Barela, the "Perpetual Senator," died on December 18, 1920. Instead of being buried at EL POR-VENIR, he was buried in Trinidad.

His final tribute came when he was elected one of the sixteen original outstanding Colorado pioneers to be included among the stained glass portraits in the rotunda in the Colorado Capitol building. He will be remembered as long as there is a Colorado.

HIGBEE (Nine Mile Bottom): JJ Ranch; Prairie Land and Cattle Co.

(Otero County)

The onetime town of HIGBEE in southeast Otero County was once the headquarters for two of the largest cattle kingdoms in the nation, and, for a few short years one of them was said to have been the largest in the world: the JJ RANCH and the PRAIRIE LAND AND CATTLE COMPANY.

Following the Civil War three brothers—Jim, Peyton (Pate) and Steve Jones—put together a large herd of longhorns in Texas. Jim Jones then headed north into the virgin country of Colorado to look for an ideal location. He found it in what is called the Smith Canyon area in what is now extreme southeastern Prowers County and southwestern Bent County in southeastern Colorado.

In June of 1869 the Jones brothers set out for the promised land, trailing 1100 head of longhorn cattle and many good breeding horses. They entered Colorado over the Goodnight Trail, opened a short time before by Charles Goodnight. Their families followed in covered wagons. Thus was established the JJ CATTLE RANCH, named for Jim Jones.

The brothers were ambitious, industrious and innovative. They immediately began acquiring new land and bringing in more cattle and horses. They improved their herds by crossbreeding longhorns with shorthorns. Within a few years they were herding cattle over

an estimated 2,250,000 acres (3500 square miles), all of southeastern Colorado from the Purgatoire River to the Kansas line and from the Arkansas River to New Mexico. Estimates of their herds ran all the way from 30,000 up to 50,000. There were more than 50 different brands. There were almost as many brands for the hundreds of horses.

Such a large operation was not without its problems. The scattered herds were easy prey to rustlers. One report said that a large neighboring ranch was started by simply altering one of the JJ brands. There were also extreme weather conditions to contend with. Drought and winter blizzards took their toll. The Jones brothers had continual battles with sheepmen to save the precious grassland for their cattle.

Travel distances cost valuable time and money. The situation was greatly alleviated with the construction of the Pueblo & Arkansas Valley Railroad (later the AT&SF) in 1875. In 1878, the JJ Ranch loaded some 2000 cattle for shipment to St. Louis, filling 98 rail cars.

Naturally, record-keeping was the biggest headache. Most of the records that were kept were later destroyed.

In 1881 and '82 the Jones brothers disposed of their empire to the Prairie Land and Cattle Company. The 3500 square miles of land, 55,000 head of cattle and some 300 horses sold for $625,000. The brothers believed later that they sold far too cheaply.

The Prairie Company was backed primarily by Scottish and English money and promoted by Underwood Clark & Company of St. Louis. It is said they were capitalized at $3.5 million.

Shortly after acquiring the JJ Ranch the Prairie Company purchased the Cross L. Ranch in Northern New Mexico and Oklahoma, nearly as large as the JJ Ranch, as well as other spreads that extended them into New Mexico, Oklahoma and Texas. Grazing at times more than 150,000 cattle, it was the largest cattle empire in the world.

The longtime manager of the Prairie empire was Murdo McKenzie, known widely as "King of the Cattlemen." He set the tone for the distinguished operations. He never rode a horse, but covered the area in a buckboard or in a plush private railroad car. He dressed as a king cowboy, impeccably. He never wore a gun. He was paid some $20,000 a year, an astronomical amount for that day and age.

The many foreign investors who visited also rode in private Pullman railroad cars and were entertained lavishly. They introduced Old-World traditions that seemed out of place in the dusty prairieland of the southern plains.

McKenzie and his distinguished visitors also learned the harsh lessons of such an empire. They learned of drought, and other extreme weather conditions, of great distances, erratic transportation and fluctuating markets.

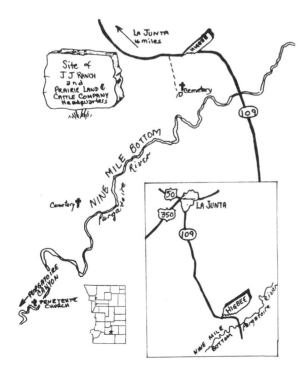

The house above was the home of Charles Carson (son of Kit Carson) at Higbee, headquarters of the JJ Ranch and the Prairie Land and Cattle Company—two of the largest ranch empires in Colorado history. (*Denver Public Library Western History Department*.)

At right, the J. B. Dean family at their home in Smith Canyon, 1889. Dean was an employee of the JJ Ranch. (*Colorado Historical Society*.)

Nonetheless, it was probably the longest lasting of the old cattle empires, and it paid dividends to its investors virtually every year. During its years between 1882 and 1916, when it went out of business, it marketed more beef in Kansas City than any other cattle company.

The Prairie Company began disposing of its land and holdings in 1912, and had its last great roundup in 1916. The land and cattle herds were sold piecemeal to buyers throughout Colorado, New Mexico, Texas, Kansas and Nebraska. The huge ranch that was purchased for $625,000 in 1881–82 was valued up to an estimated $30 million and more in its prime. Much of the land sold for around $2.50 an acre and the cattle went for an average of $19 a head.

Details of its operations are impossible to come by. Whatever records were kept were deliberately destroyed after the company was liquidated. Its long and colorful story would have made fascinating reading, but it can only be speculative fiction today.

A few years before the Prairie Company was dissolved, McKenzie went to Brazil to manage the Brazil Land, Cattle and Packing Company, which became one of the largest such operations in the world, if not the largest.

Much of the Prairie cattle was shipped from Hasty and other shipping stations along the railroad, but for all the years that the JJ Ranch and the Prairie Land and Cattle Company were in business, most of the activity centered in the improbable little community of HIGBEE, an isolated site in southeastern Otero County, about sixteen miles southeast of La Junta.

The tiny community was named for Uriah Higbee, who settled in southern Colorado in the early 1860s. Toward the end of the decade he built a fort-like home in the bottom lands along the Purgatorie River. He and other early settlers dug the first irrigation ditch in this area, one of the first in southern Colorado—making the bottom lands even more lush, during dry periods as well as during the good years. The bottom lands containing water gates were long known as NINE MILE BOTTOM, indicating the extent of the rich farm area.

Other settlers built homes around Higbee's fort, where all gathered during periods of Indian scares, and the settlement of Higbee emerged. By 1880 there was a general store here and a post office. Later a two-story hotel was built, a dance hall and meeting place, a livery and other businesses. But Higbee never achieved city status. It was never more than a functional center for the ranch families in the neighborhood, which were sparsely scattered to suit the dry land needs around the river bottom lands.

However, even the bottom lands were hit hard by the drought and depression of the 1920s and '30s. Higbee, as significant as it was, was just another victim of the Dust Bowl that decimated southeastern Colorado.

It was significant enough to be remembered, however.

A lone marker was first erected where the town used to be by Otero County 4-H club members in 1959. But on December 19, 1965, some 35 families made up of former settlers and descendants of settlers (many for-mer employees of the Prairie Company) who came from a wide region of southern Colorado and northern New Mexico, met in a snow-covered field to re-dedicate a plaque commemorating the historic site as HIGBEE VALLEY ROADSIDE PARK. No one lives in Higbee today, but even after the ruins of the last buildings are gone Higbee will have a plaque to show where it used to be.

Also remaining is the little Higbee cemetery where many of the pioneers are buried, including Charley Carson, a son of Kit Carson.

CHAPTER VI

TRAIL TOWNS

Among the wildest towns in the early West were the towns born along the historic trails, many leading from Texas for stocking or replenishing northern herds. The trails also led herds to market, or to the railroads which went to more distant markets.

Perhaps the most famous trail towns that survived the many shootouts and rowdy visits of the hungry, thirsty, dusty, sex-starved waddies are Dodge City and Abilene.

Most of the others didn't survive. They were among the least-known "cities" in the Old West, mostly because they were short-lived and died with the trails themselves.

Most of the herds developed in Colorado and the states north of it came from Texas, trailing up through southern Colorado. The earliest cattle in Colorado were brought from Texas, driven through northern New Mexico over Raton Pass, an extension or variation of the Chisholm Trail called the Goodnight–Loving Trail for its leaders, Charles Goodnight and Oliver Loving.

Goodnight did not like the exorbitant prices charged by "Uncle Rick" Wootton, who had the tollgate atop Raton Pass, and vowed he would never come that way again. He didn't. The next time he trailed over an easier—and absolutely free—pass a short distance east of Raton Pass, called Trainchera Pass.

These herds fed the Iliff herds in northern Colorado, and some north of that, as well as Goodnight's own herds in southern Colorado.

The rowdiest trail towns exploded upon the scene in far southeastern Colorado during the 1880s. They accomodated the National Cattle Trail, which existed for about two years in the mid-1880's, which in turn fed the Texas–Montana Cattle Trail and the other variations thereof.

It is doubtful that even Dodge City and Abilene—which have provided scads of material for movies and televison versions of the Old West—were as loud and/ or noteworthy as, say, Boston and Trail City during their brief existence.

ALBANY
(Prowers County)

ALBANY was about midway between Boston and Lamar, just north of the Baca County line in Prowers County. The town was begun in 1886, at the height of the frenetic activity along the National Cattle Trail east of the town.

The site was on a known water source, near the George Lanning Farm. The little town grew around the well, which was 200 feet deep and dug by hand. Not nearly as wild as Boston to the south and Trail City to the north, Albany nonetheless had it moments. During its short service at the end of the trail-dusting days there were some saloons that provided gambling and girling opportunities. There was also a newspaper here for a short time, *The Albany Advance*, published by Dr. Silsby.

Most sources believe that the town was named by settlers from New York, who named the prairie town after its capital city. At any rate, the name is in keeping with the presumptious names of the other cowtowns.

Perhaps because of its saner character, Albany outlived the cattle trail days. It served as a small ranch center during the 1890s and early 1900s. It had a post office as late as 1907.

ATLANTA
(Baca County)

ATLANTA had a reputation of being more orderly than its cowtown neighbors. Perhaps its more savory reputation was due to the fact that it was off the "beaten trail" of the major cattle drives and was also a ranch center and roadside town along more conventional lines.

Atlanta was in northwestern Baca County on Freezeout Creek, along the wagon road between Granada and Fort Union, New Mexico. Troops, freighters and some cattle drovers had used the trail over the years. Some

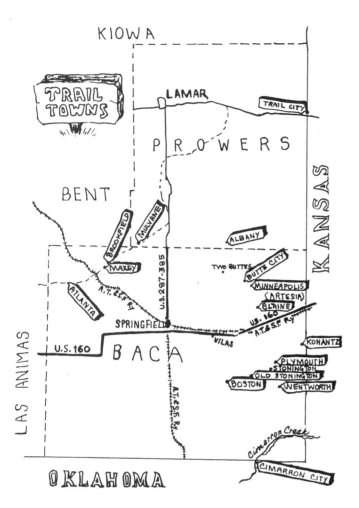

from time to time and there was some farming and ranching in the neighborhood, MAXEY (see "Farm Towns") to the north became the commercial and social center for the neighborhood. And other roads replaced this road.

BLAINE-ARTESIA

(Baca County)

Few townsites in Colorado had the identity problem this one did. It began as BLAINE, which soon died. Then came ARTESIA, which also died. Finally, it came back to BLAINE. Little wonder many mapmakers and directory compilers played it safe with such designations as Blaine (Artesia) or Artesia (Blaine). Actually the two were a short distance apart . . . but that's getting ahead of the story.

To add to the confusion, when Blaine first appeared on the maps, it looked for all the world as though it was on the exact same spot as Minneapolis (see below).

Blaine was born of Minneapolis. After the latter townsite was abandoned for failure to pay off the bonds, most of the businesses moved a short distance across the section line and began the town of Blaine, named for an early settler. The bonds were floated again and Blaine lived awhile on promises. Then it too faded, like Minneapolis.

About 1909 artesian wells were located at a site about a mile south of the Blaine site. The town of Artesia was developed along with the wells. It also lasted a few years. In 1914–15 it had a newspaper, *The Artesia Call*.

The well water was used for irrigation, but it wasn't as plentiful as at first thought, particularly during dry years. The water table fell and the wells failed, and the little town faded.

When it came back again a short time later, it was as Blaine. This remained a farm center up to modern times. It is still shown on some maps, and is listed as a rural center in recent directories.

BOSTON

(Baca County)

BOSTON and TRAIL CITY in Colorado were perhaps the wildest frontier cowtowns in the West during their short life spans. And that includes Dodge City and Abilene. But Boston and Trail City both died almost as quickly as they boomed, after a short violent life.

It is curious that so little is known or heard about Boston, Colorado. It is never mentioned in the history books. Perhaps proper historians choose to overlook it for its short, unsavory place in the overall picture of frontier Colorado. But during its short span Boston was

considered it another rarely used branch of the Santa Fe Trail.

Freezeout Creek was said to have been named for a small group of soldiers traveling along the Granada–Fort Union road when a blizzard hit them in a canyon along the creek. They sought shelter under an overhang in the canyon but froze to death. Their frozen bodies were found later and they were given a proper burial.

Atlanta was said to have been named by a group from Georgia who filed on the townsite in May of 1887. At that time it was in Las Animas County.

The small town that grew up there was strung out along the road for a distance of about a half mile, as most of the businesses catered to the traveler. There were several saloons, a couple of eating places, groceries and other businesses. It also had a weekly newspaper during 1887–88, *The Atlanta Democrat*. There was a post office until 1899. The top population was about 100, not counting the people passing through.

Virtually the entire lifespan of the town was between 1886 and 1890. Although the road continued to be used

The class of 1922 poses in front of the Blaine School

In 1912 the post office was moved from Blaine to Artesia. The photo shows the move, with Postmaster U. J. Warren at far left. Below, opening day in Artesia.

indeed a force to be reckoned with. It was the fastest-growing town in southeastern Colorado—in all of eastern Colorado, in fact. It came verly close to becoming the first county seat of Baca County. It was known throughout cattle country and the western underworld.

Perhaps now we can begin giving it the recognition it deserves.

Boston was born in 1886, named by settlers from New England. It was located 12 to 13 miles south southeast of present Vilas, and less than 20 miles north of the Oklahoma Panhandle. It was a needed center at the time, to serve the growing ranch area and the cattle trails from Texas.

By 1888, it had a population from 300 to 500. There were several saloons, three livery stables, a bank, and two weekly newspapers: *The Boston Banner*, edited by G. W. Daniel, and *The Western World*, S. M. Koukle (or Konkle) editor. There was another newspaper, *The Baca County Journal*, which apparently came later and didn't last long.

Vilas, to the north, was growing about the same time, but not as rapidly. *The Colorado Graphic* (of Hyde) commented at the time that eastern Colorado newspapers were becoming as numerous as "grasshoppers in Kansas." It noted *The Western World* of Boston and the *Vilas Democrat* as the "well-known booming kind . . . although we have never heard of Boston and Vilas, yet according to these sheets they are the greatest towns in the state."

That Boston was flamboyant from the first is evident by the story of Lamar's first anniversary on May 24, 1887. The celebration was "the most spectacular event in the early history of the Arkansas Valley," and the "most spectacular feature of the parade" was the floats, band and citizens of Boston. The Lamar paper said Boston had 1000 citizens at the time.

Some headstones in a corner of an isolated field is all that's left of Boston, the onetime wild trail town.

Boston's growth and Boston citizens had lured the bank, drug store and other businesses away from Vilas. Thus it was understandable that Vilas citizens refused to join with Boston's attempt to be designated county seat of the new Baca county. Boston couldn't woo any allies in the cause, and Springfield won out. Some say this was the beginning of the end of Boston. But with all the other things that happened, it is doubtful that one loss spelled the end.

Another disappointment Boston suffered concerned railroads. It lived its life in anticipation of the railroad. One after another, rumors of new railroads surfaced, that planned routes would hook up Boston with the rest of the world. The rumors were kept alive by town promoters and land speculators who sold land along the projected routes. The "paper" railroads, included such lines as "The Boston, Trinidad & Western," and "The Dodge City, Montezuma & Trinidad" railways.

Boston was the gathering place of the worst and the wildest from throughout the Panhandle region. The rustlers and roadmen came here to spend their ill-gotten gain. The "regulators" (bounty hunters) came to sort out the rustlers and get rid of them. Lawmen found Boston happy hunting for the "most wanted."

The Coe gang passed through often. Boston was general headquarters for the Jennings Gang. A well-known rustling outfit known as the "Gang of Thirteen" also headquartered here. Its leader was a man named White, who had been range boss for a nearby outfit until he got into bad company and discovered money was easier to come by on the other side of the law.

The "free-lance" and hired regulators who got a price for rustlers, dead or alive—usually dead—did little more to upgrade a town than the men they sought. They were more apt to shoot up the town than those running from the law.

Nor did the attempts to bring law and order to the chaos do much good. Cornelius Smith was hired as town marshall. He was a known cattle thief and outlaw but was considered "the toughest of the tough," the kind of man needed to deal with his kind. There resulted charges that Smith "played favorites," sheltering his friends and running off the competition.

Another time, a citizens "vigilantes" committee was formed when things seemed particularly bad. This only seemed to further fortify the warring factions, and almost caused open war. Maybe it did. The "Law and Order Committee" was formed after the city marshall shot down Newton Bradley, local cowboy. This caused additional rivalry among surrounding outfits. The vigilantes only seemed to add fuel to the fire.

There are generally two stories about the "final straw" and the end of Boston. They both involve a man named Bill Thompson in two opposing roles. Perhaps there were two Bill Thompsons, or maybe it was the same Bill Thompson from different viewpoints.

The story that is told more often is that Bill Thompson was deputy sheriff, a brave lawman who had formerly served in Dodge City. He had a warrant for the arrest of White, the leader of the "Gang of Thirteen." When he attempted to arrest White on the Main Street of Boston, Thompson was shot down. As a result the "bad guys" laid siege to the town and shot up just about everything in sight, scaring away the "normal citizens" that hadn't been frightened away before.

The other story has Bill Thompson playing the role of a regulator (perhaps a self-appointed "deputy"), in a small band of regulators that hung around together, boozed together, and frequently shot up the town together. They really shot up the town when some horses belonging to one of their members were stolen. The spree ended in the middle of town on Main Street, with a gunfight (one version says with members of the Jennings gang). In the fight, a merchant was said to have shot and killed a regulator. After the shooting the regulators laid siege to the town, blocked all roads, broke most of the windows on Main Street, and attempted to set fire to the town. (It is said the merchant who did the shooting escaped by being smuggled out of town in a box.)

To further confuse the issue of Bill Thompson, the following item was a front page story in the *Denver Republican*, dated May 14, 1893:

LAMAR—Sheriff Dobson of Barber County, Kansas, came in from the south with two men heavily ironed. They were Bill and Gid Thompson of Boston, Baca County, who he had arrested for murder, said to have been committed in Barber County, Kansas, in 1886.

It appears a Missourian named McQuinn suddenly disappeared, and as he had upwards of $4000 on his persons, foul play was at once claimed. The Thompsons were suspected, but no direct evidence could be found against them. The officers, however, had not given up the case, and recently arrested a party in Barber County, who has made a full confession, and the arrest of the parties from Baca County followed.

The Thompsons came to Baca County in 1887, are well-to-do, and were highly respected citizens of that part of the county. Sheriff Dobson left on No. 4 last evening for Medicine Lodge, Kansas, with his prisoners.

At any rate, a Bill Thompson, or a couple of Bill Thompsons, played an important part in Boston's history, if only in its demise. The good people of Boston found it safer to stay off the streets of their town. The wiser ones left early; life became completely impossible after the rough element took over the town. The last good citizens left by or during 1892. They moved to Vilas, Springfield and other points. And when there was nothing left to prey upon, the underworld characters went elsewhere also.

There is no trace whatsoever of the townsite today. It is in a field and has been plowed over time and time again.

The only memorial to Boston is found in Vilas. C. F. Wheeler, who had built a mercantile store and a saloon side by side in Boston during its early days, "escaped" in 1887 and moved his two false-fronted stores to Vilas, where he continued his businesses for many years. The store has served many purposes since. It was the Sunrise Saloon, then an all-purpose store. After 1932 it was a cafe, drug store and even a school lunchroom. Then it was empty for many years and began to deteriorate.

However, during the Centennial year of 1976 the citizens of Vilas restored the building and turned it into a regional museum. It retains its false front and the flavor of the old West. If it could talk, the store from Boston could tell much interesting history about early Baca county.

BROOKFIELD
(Baca County)

BROOKFIELD was another town in northwestern Baca County on the old Granada to Fort Union, New Mexico, wagon road—about midway between MULVANE (in the extreme southwestern corner of Prowers County) and ATLANTA, and very near the later farm town of MAXEY (see "Farm Towns").

The wagon road was here long before, but the town of Brookfield was started in late 1886 or early 1887. It was said to have been started by the Brookfield Town Company of Kansas, and the official plat was not filed until August 24, 1888.

It was a larger town than Atlanta, platted on forty acres. One report said the town had three banks and five saloons. It also had a weekly newspaper, *The Maverick*—Grant Turner, editor and publisher—which survived until June 1889. There was a weekly stage through town from Mulvane to CARRIZO SPRINGS in southwestern Baca County (see "They'll Mine Anywhere").

Brookfield participated in the "county seat war." In the proposal to form four separate counties instead of the one that was eventually formed, Brookfield was promoting the county of Keokuk, and itself as county seat.

Despite its relatively large size, Brookfield died rapidly; it was dead by the early 1890s. There was no trace of it when Maxey sprung up a decade or so later, except for four unmarked graves on a small hill beside where Brookfield was. The four stone mounds (or cairns) protected the bodies beneath them from predatory animals. Although unmarked, local legend says one grave is that of a sheepherder, another is that of Amanda King, an aunt to Bent King, a pioneer. The third is said to be that of a boy named Boggs, and the fourth is unknown.

BUTTE CITY

(Baca County)

BUTTE CITY had probably the briefest life of all the many short-lived trail towns in southeastern Colorado. It was named for two buttes which had served as a landmark for cattle drovers since the first herds went through here in the 1870s. The town was apparently close to the present town of TWO BUTTES, which grew up long after Butte City died.

Butte City was on an old wagon road from Texas to Granada and other points. Other projected roads and railroad lines never happened. The Crill and Bowdel Stage line was initiated at Butte City, running to Granada. When Boston quickly surpassed Butte City in growth, the line ran between Boston and Granada.

Butte City was started, like many of its neighbors, in 1886 and 1887. But its neighbors continued to grow, at least for three or four years. MINNEAPOLIS, 2 to 3 miles away, was rapidly becoming the exciting town Butte City wanted to be. Within about a year of its hopeful start, most of the residents of Butte City had moved to Minneapolis, and whatever little there had been of Butte City was gone.

MINNEAPOLIS (Corinth)

(Baca County)

MINNEAPOLIS was the most prominent city in southeastern Colorado for about two years. It was even larger and had more saloons than Boston, but it was not as wild a town.

Minneapolis was located about 9 miles almost due north of the present Walsh. There was some settlement here in 1886 but the town plat was officially filed on February 11, 1887. It was the largest and most comprehensive plat ever filed in that region, with some eighty blocks laid out.

Its growth was phenomenal. Within the first year an almost constant stream of wagons carrying building supplies rumbled into town from Granada, and still didn't keep up with the demand. A tiny town named CORINTH had started a short distance to the east a few months before and had been granted the first post office in Baca County. It was soon lost in the dust of the feverish activity at Minneapolis, and the post office was transferred to the new city. It was believed named for settlers from Minnesota, and in keeping with the other "big city" names in the area.

It was said that there were some 500 people here within the first year, and there were about thirty businesses. It had a daily stage to Granada and Boston, a sorghum factory, a broom factory, the Grand Central Hotel, another hotel, the Universalist church, a rather large school, a print shop, and more saloons along its main street than any other town in the region. It also had two newspapers, *The Minneapolis Chico* (1887–90), a weekly published by L. A. Wikoff; and *The Minneapolis Republican* another weekly published during 1888–89.

Demonstrating their faith in its future, Minneapolis citizens took time out from hectic activity and elected a full slate of city officers, including a mayor, Dr. J. F. Rickenbach, and a town council. And the city government did what all city governments are wont to do. They drew up a budget for city improvements, and sold bonds to finance them.

Minneapolis was also prominent in the so-called "County Seat War." Being the largest and fastest-growing community, except possibly for Springfield, it seemed a logical choice for county seat—particularly in the original plan to make four new counties. This plan was fostered by Minneapolis, Boston, Atlanta and Carrizo Springs, with each of them planning to become a seat of county government, rather than Springfield becoming the seat of one large county. There was plenty of back room and barroom politics involved, and lobbying at the local and state level. It would take a good investigative reporter to unravel it all, after all these years.

Surprisingly, Springfield went along with the four-county scheme. There were a couple of reasons local historians give for Springfield's move: first, Springfield leaders knew the four-county plan wouldn't work, and there would only be one county; and second, they didn't want to antagonize the other communities hoping for their support for Springfield if only one new county was formed.

It came as a surprise to all involved (except possibly Springfield) when Senator Casimiro Barela, "the perpetual senator" from Trinidad, introduced a bill in the state legislator calling for one county. It passed on April 16, 1889. The new county was named BACA for a prominent Trinidad Family.

The wheeling and dealing continued into November, when citizens of the new county voted for Springfield, Minneapolis or Stonington for the permanent seat for the new county. There were many charges and counter-charges before and after the election. There were charges that Minneapolis votes were improperly filed and improperly counted. The immediate outcome of the vote made Springfield the county seat, but the longtime result was continued resentment among the many people involved, and a rivalry within the county more bitter than found in other counties.

The first result of that bitterness came shortly after the vote, when the building purchased as the first county courthouse was burned mysteriously while en route from Boston to Springfield. A similar fate befell the next two courthouses.

Some blame the downfall of Minneapolis on the loss

The Crill and Boudle Stage, which ran from Granada on the Arkansas River and railroad to Baca County trail towns, is pictured above in 1886. Below is a Baca County wagon train operated by the Crill and Boudle line.

Business card (*top*) advertises services provided by Gabriel Crill and John Bowdle. Below it, one share of stock in the Butte City Land & Town Company, dated 1886.

Students at the Minneapolis school (*right*) with their teacher, Mamie Herbert, in the late 1880s. Jim Crill is second from left.

(*Photos courtesy Jack Crill.*)

of this vote. It may have had something to do with it, but of much greater impact was the rapid decline of good water sources and crop failure. The town was unable to pay off the bonds issued for its development. By 1890 the population was down to 100, and the site was virtually abandoned by 1892.

The new town of BLAINE picked up some of the pieces but the first town of Blaine didn't last much longer than Minneapolis. The Minneapolis Cemetery was used years later by ARTESIA, but it was still called the Minneapolis Cemetery, the only reminder today of a fabulous, flash-in-the-pan "city."

OLD STONINGTON

(Baca County)

Actually there were two Old Stoningtons. The first was no more than a post office at a ranch. During the town boom during the late 1880s, the post office was moved about three miles to a new community called Stonington, believed to be a local family name.

Stonington experienced the phenomenal growth of the other boom towns. It was a trading center for a large area to the Kansas border, as well as for those who did not choose to risk a visit to Boston, about five miles to the southwest. The town had a hotel and many business listings, including two newspapers, *The Stonington Journal* (1888–89) and *The Stonington Sentinel* (1889–90).

Stonington was a finalist, with Springfield and Minneapolis, in the 1889 vote for a permanent county seat. It was charged that Minneapolis conspired with Springfield against Stonington to give Springfield the victory in that election.

Stonington faded slowly during the 1890s. It had a population of only 100 by 1900, and only half that in 1905. It was nearly gone by 1909, when changes in the Homestead Act encouraged more migration, even to this dry farm region. The new settlers established a center about six miles east of Old Stonington and took over the post office. For awhile the new community was called NEW STONINGTON, and then just STONINGTON. The latter is still a point on the map, although it lost many of its residents during the depression and Dust Bowl days of the 1920s and '30s.

TRAIL CITY

(Prowers County)

If TRAIL CITY and BOSTON in extreme southeastern Colorado had lived longer and/or had better press agents, they would have been as infamous as Dodge City or Abilene as wild and lawless Western cowtowns. In fact,

Trail City and Boston could well have set the standard for wildness and lawlessness—for other cowtowns to shoot at, so to speak.

Trail City lived only two or three years. It is just as well. It packed enough life and excitement into those few months to last most other towns and cities a lifetime.

And wouldn't you know it, this Colorado nightmare was caused by Texas.

By early 1880s Texas cattlemen were hurting badly. Their northern markets were drying up as better strains of cattle than longhorns were found for those areas. And cattle drives were finding more resistance and difficulty getting to those markets anyway. Sodbusters were putting up more and more fences, plowing up fields and using the available water along the trail. And they were touchy—even testy—about Texas cattle tearing down the fences, trampling the crops and using and/or contaminating the scarce water sources.

A telling blow came in 1883 when Kansas passed a quarantine law that forbid Texas cattle drives from entering that state.

Cattlemen in Texas were already calling for a "National Cattle Trail," a ten-mile-wide protected highway going north from Texas to the northern markets. The plan called for the trail to pass along the eastern border of Colorado to Ogallala, Nebraska, with branches heading northwestward into north-central Colorado, and into Wyoming and Montana.

Texas leaders exerted much pressure on Congress. There were many tales—Texas-style—of undue pressure, bribery, etc. The measure was defeated in Congress, but the cattlemen finally established a three-mile-wide trail along the eastern Colorado border.

Prominent Texas cattleman Martin Culver, who had been a leader in getting the trail, wasted little time in capitalizing on the new "cattle freeway." He saw the need for a "city" at a key location along the trail. The obvious location would be where the trail crosses the Santa Fe Trail and Santa Fe Railroad along the Arkansas River, a major watering spot before the hot, dusty and usually dry road northward. The site was just into Colorado from quarantined Kansas.

Culver and some associates began laying out a town in 1884, on a 15-acre plot. Within a short time some 100 lots were sold for $100 to $200 each, most of them along one long north–south street that abutted the Kansas border.

The character of the community was caused by a set of circumstances. It was the first pay stop for cattle drovers who had just completed a long hard drive and faced another, and a major watering stop, where cattle (and cattle drovers) could wash off the dust of the trail and be prepared for the long road ahead. It was also the place where officials from Colorado and Kansas checked the brands of the cattle for strays and possible rustled cattle.

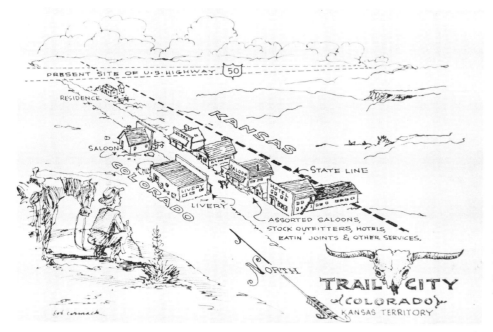

The drawing of what Trail City may have looked like in 1886 was made by Bob Cormack, Denver artist, for an article that appeared in a publication of the Denver Posse of Westerners. (*Denver Public Library Western History Department.*)

Thus, elements from far and wide—including many interests from Dodge City—came to compete for the waddies hard-earned wages, generally about $30 a month. Most of the rapidly hoisted buildings along the long main street were saloons, gambling dens and brothels; the majority of the 30 to 40 buildings along the street were of this nature. And most of those were on the eastern (sunny) side of the street. The front doors opened to the hitching posts on the Colorado side. The back doors opened on or near the Kansas border. There were many restrictions in Kansas, including no booze, but one could do just about as he pleased in Colorado. A man being pursued by the local gendarmes could go through one door and out another to escape the jurisdiction of the law-enforcing pursuers.

And the stories are endless about the "unbelievable scenes—reaching the utmost depths of degradation and debauchery," as described by the *Lamar Register*. Lamar, a new and growing community at the western end of the county was safer than closer neighbors, although Trail City was not too far for Lamarites to travel to for fun and depravity. Closer neighbors suffered more. The Trail City dissipation spilled over onto them, and they suffered raids by Trail City citizens seeking mischief and/or booty.

Staid and quiet Coolidge, Kansas, just two miles away, suffered the most. Sodden waddies during the early weeks of Trail City found many ways to shake up Coolidge, such as racing down the main street shooting wildly at signs and lights at all hours of the night and day. A favorite sport in Trail City was horse-racing in the main street, and for a time, to and through Coolidge as well. These weren't your normal horse-races. The racing cowboys often had naked whores sitting behind them, holding on for dear life and shouting and screaming as if there were no tomorrow.

It didn't take the conservative city fathers of Coolidge long to build up a distaste for this sort of thing. Within a few weeks they took turns standing guard at the edge of the city to greet any unwelcome visitors with rifle fire.

Even so, Murph Ward continued to run a hack line between Trail City and Coolidge. It cost fifty cents one way. The oft-told story is that when business was slow Ward would try to stimulate things by giving a painted lady or two a free ride.

Of the countless stories told about Trail City, the most notorious concerned the gunning down of I. P. "Print" Olive. Olive himself was a most controversial character. He was a powerful force, with ranching interests in Kansas, Nebraska and northwestern Colorado, near Wray. Many claim he was ruthless, stepping on anyone who got in his way. It is said that he shot down suspected rustlers in Texas.

Joe Sparrow had been a trail driver for Olive and had borrowed money from him. Some say Sparrow never intended to pay it back. On August 15, 1886, Olive told Sparrow he needed the money by the next day since he was leaving town.

The next day Olive found Sparrow at the Haynes Saloon. Olive was in shirtsleeves and was obviously not armed. As Olive walked into the saloon and walked toward the bar, Sparrow suddenly drew his gun and shot him in the chest. He shot him again, and when Olive slumped to the floor, Sparrow stood over him and shot him again in the head.

The bartender wrestled the gun from Sparrow, who

Author Harry Chrisman took this photograph of the last ruins of Trail City in 1957. He described the site as fifteen acres of broken glass, old wagon tires, bits of houses, rusty nails, etc. Today this ruin has collapsed and joined the rest of the debris. (*Denver Public Library Western History Department.*)

ran into the street. He was soon captured, however. After three trials he was finally found innocent and released.

Harry Chrisman tells the whole story including the aftermath in his book *The Ladder of Rivers*.

There was some evidence of permanancy in Trail City. Most obvious was Culver's Canfield Hotel, a two-story stone structure that dominated Main Street. And there were a few "normal" businesses, such as general merchandise and grocery stores—a man has to eat, too—and livery, etc. The Santa Fe Railroad built a large stockyards, and actually shipped cattle from here.

But the "National Cattle Trail" only gave Texas cattlemen a brief reprieve. The northern markets had just about all the Texas longhorns they wanted or needed. It was estimated that nearly a quarter of a million longhorns traveled to or through Trail City in 1885 and 1886. But in 1887 about 100,000 head were stalled at Trail City or turned back farther north for lack of a market—equal to the number sold at Trail City or at the northern markets. It was obvious that the usefulness of the cattle highway was already past.

The fulltime population of Trail City was never more than 200, although during peak times the transient population was more than double that. The population dropped to 100 in 1887 and half of that the following year.

As rapidly as Trail City died, so did the National Cattle Trail. Within a short time much of the region was homesteaded. Fences and broken sod lined the trail that was created to overcome such obstacles.

A branch of the National Trail passed northwestward and crossed the Smoky Hill Trail east of Hugo. At this point the State Historical Society erected a stone monument and plaque in 1939. The original bronze plaque which was later stolen, read: "This monument stands on the Smoky Hill Trail on the Republican–Big Sandy Divide, the route of the Butterfield Stage 1866–1870. Fifty yards east the Texas–Montana Cattle Trail (National Cattle Trail) crossed the Smoky Hill Trail."

They say deep ruts chiseled by the great herds were once prominent in the eastern plains. Some small sections were still visible in recent years. They will all be gone unless they are fenced off and preserved.

GHOSTS OF THE COLORADO PLAINS

J. B. Silvis traveled in his own railroad car (above) on the Union Pacific Railroad, selling "historic" and scenic photos of the early West, as well as doing routine photographic work for local citizens. One photo he sold was called "The Olive Gang"—but the "gang members" shown included adversaries of I. P. Olive as well as his brothers and friends. The photograph of Olive had been taken about 1866 in Georgetown, Texas. (*Photo from* Ladder of Rivers *by Harry E. Chrisman, reprinted 1982 by Swallow/Ohio University Press.*)

Absolutely nothing remains to mark Trail City, the "Sodom and Gamorra of the plains." Some of the old buildings were torn down or moved to be put to other uses. Time, vandals and flood waters have done the rest. From time to time, explorers claim to have found some broken glass, empty bullet shells, and other artifacts at the site. The site has been trampled by many herds and been plowed up many times in the years since all the sinning, shooting and selling cattle days. In more recent years, the land was purchased by the widow of onetime movie star Andy Devine.

Isn't it ironic that the west's "wickedest city," "the hell hole of the Arkansas," became something Devine.

CHAPTER VII

COLONY TOWNS

As the New World was nirvana to all matter of humanity from throughout the world during the 1600s and 1700s, the wide-open West was the promise of paradise to the dreamers and doers a century or two later. It was the promise of fresh air and elbow room to those suppressed by the lifestyles in eastern cities and oppressive conditions around the world.

The wide-open, wonderful vistas of the west meant many things to many different people, but to most it meant the chance of a new life, the foundation of their dreams.

As with everything worth dreaming about, unprincipled persons took advantage of the dreamers to line their own pocketbooks (GREEN CITY is an example; see "Con Towns"). But by and large the colony leaders were well-intentioned, hard-working pioneers, as were the settlers they led to the promised land.

AGRICOLA

(Weld County)

AGRICOLA was the first farm colony along the Platte River Trail, and a promising one.

A report in the February 1, 1860, *The Mountaineer* said the new farm community was in "the midst of one of the richest agricultural districts in the region," and the "projectors are enterprising gentlemen who will spare nothing to make this an important point."

The report further stated that a military and stage road was planned eastward along the Platte to the stage station in Old Julesburg. The Western State Company was to make a station at Agricola. A sawmill would be up by spring so logs could be floated down the Cache La Poudre to the site.

Actually, many old trails converged at this site, including the old Cherokee Trail along the Poudre. Some logs were floated down the Poudre, and the sawmill here was kept busy.

It would seem as if Agricola—Latin for "farmer"—had everything going for it. However, a site a short distance to the southwest, at a major crossing of the Platte, quickly outdistanced Agricola. LATHAM not only had the only good crossing of the Platte for many miles, it soon had the stage station, and had better connections north and south, and west into the gold fields. As Latham grew, Agricola waned . . . and soon disappeared.

FRIEND (Frontier Legion)

(Yuma County)

FRIEND was a Quaker colony about five miles southwest of Idalia, seven to eight miles by road, in southeast Yuma County near the Kansas line.

Reed Decker, James Dudgeon, Sylvester Andrews and Frank Elliot came to the site in 1886 from Friend, Nebraska. They began a center where the four homesteads met and named it for their home in Nebraska, which was named for the Quaker faith. Several sources claim that the site was originally named FRONTIER LEGION, but none of the sources say why, and there is little evidence that there was a site worthy of a name before 1886.

Within a few months several other families arrived from Nebraska, and the farm center grew rapidly. A couple of newspaper reports even called it a "boom town."

By the time Friend was incorporated in July of 1887 there were about twenty buildings in the community, including a bank, two hotels, a restaurant, drug store, two livery stables, two general stores, a newspaper-printing office and even a saloon. Mail came twice a week from Haigler, Nebraska. Water was supplied by a town well and was hauled in buckets and barrels.

The settlers worked together to build a school which was also used as a place of worship and a meeting hall. The community had a literary society, and the meetings were always crowded.

The population here was never very large, but the town served a large number over a wide area. Weekends, holidays and other social events saw a great many people in the little center. One report estimated that there were 200 in the area.

As with many other high-thinking towns, Friend had hoped for railroad connections. In the early 1890s there was a rumor that the Rock Island would come this way. It didn't. This disappointment, on top of drought and other economic problems had a decimating affect on the community. The last of the settlers in the little town had moved elsewhere by the late 1890s. Most of the buildings were torn down or moved to be used as farm buildings. No trace remains of the onetime community.

MUSTANG (Larimer)

(Huerfano County)

It was called a "picturesque Swedish village," this site settled by Swedish immigrants around 1894. Located in northern Huerfano County, just south of the Pueblo County line, it was on both the Colorado & Southern and the Denver and Rio Grande railroads.

Like most other colonies settled by families from abroad, this one retained most of its Old World customs, and even attempted to follow its native architecture in the buildings here.

The site was originally named LARIMER, but when it applied for and received a post office in 1908, the easily confused post office department was concerned about the similarity to the county in northern Colorado. It is said that the railroad suggested the name MUSTANG for nearby Wild Horse (mustang) Arroyo.

Over the years, the community lost much of its Swedish flavor, due largely to the influence of the railroad. But it was a rather stable, long-lasting town.

It still had a population of 35 in March of 1940, when an item appeared in the Colorado Springs *Gazette-Telegraph* which said ". . . two mail pouches have been thrown from speeding trains (at Mustang) for 32 years.

But today there were no mail sacks tagged Mustang. C. Eklund has been retired because of his age and the post office discontinued."

Mustang is still shown on some maps, and many descendents of the original settlers live in the region.

PELLA and NORTH PELLA

(Boulder County)

George Webster and Charles True settled here in 1859, began an orchard and broke ground for planting. Within a year, other families from Pella, Iowa, joined them, bringing farm animals and seeds to be planted. They named the community after their former home town.

The community was located in lush farmland along the St. Vrain, about five miles west of present LONGMONT. For several years PELLA and OLD BURLINGTON were the only towns in the region.

The community took on an air of permanence in 1861 when a grist mill was built, one of the first in Colorado. It soon had a nursery, a school, several other businesses, and one of the most popular race tracks for miles around.

Pella became one of the busiest trading centers north of Denver for nearly twenty years. The community prospered, although it lost some buildings and much topsoil in the flood of 1864, and the crops were decimated by grasshoppers in 1867.

There were also a couple of destructive fires. Otherwise, life was good at Pella. Like most other farm communities, it was a very sociable town, with all matter of social events planned throughout the year.

A new influx of emigrants joined with some families from Pella to form another community about 2½ miles north around 1870. It was named, surprisingly enough, NORTH PELLA. There apparently was not any rivalry between the two close neighbors, and their history was intermingled for the next few years as long as the communities lasted.

In 1879 a Dunkard preacher named Jacob Flory selected a site between the two Pellas for a Dunkard colony. The Dunkards were a form of German-American Baptists, militant only in their quest for peace and an end of war. Flory and his followers built a church and a sanitarium. He called the sanitarium HYGIENE, which was also the name given to the new community. Flory also published a newspaper, *The Home Miner*. The new settlement received a post office in 1883.

For two decades the Denver, Utah & Pacific Railroad had snubbed Pella, bypassing the community on its line from Longmont to Lyons. In 1885, it built a new depot to welcome people to Hygiene. It was about the last straw for Pella, both Pellas. More and more of their activities centered in Hygiene.

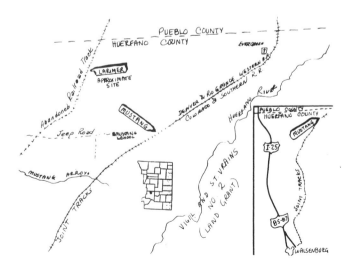

GHOSTS OF THE COLORADO PLAINS

The McCaslin cabin, built in 1860, was called Fort Pella because it was a gathering place for settlers during Indian scares. Above, the family is shown in front of the enlarged cabin about 1902, just before the new McCaslin house was built. Six-year-old Ted McCaslin is sitting in front of the group.

After the move into the "big house" the cabin slowly fell into ruin, as shown at right, just before it was dismantled, log by log—each log numbered for eventual reconstruction as an historic attraction.

Below, the McCaslin barn (which is still in use today) is shown thirty or forty years ago, when it was a landmark known as "The Crossings" for its location at the upper crossing of the St. Vrain.

An old cottonwood (*below*) near the McCaslin farm is said to be the largest cottonwood in North America.

(*Photos courtesy Pat Jones.*)

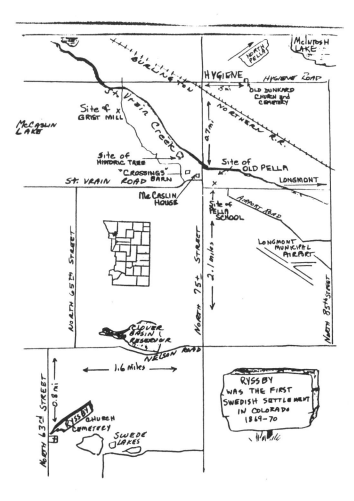

RYSSBY WAS THE FIRST SWEDISH SETTLEMENT IN COLORADO 1869-70

The old McCaslin cabin has fallen into disuse in recent years and efforts to preserve it through the Boulder County Park and Open Space program have faltered.

Less than a half-mile west of the cabin is what local residents claim to be the largest Plains cottonwood tree in North America. Residents say that the tree was there when the first settlers entered the valley; otherwise, no one is sure of its age. The Forest Service is afraid to make a tree-ring cut to establish its age, fearful that it would also establish disease in its limbs. The famed tree, although on private property, has also seen abuse in recent years. The giant, gnarled old tree has attracted many curiosity seekers and picnickers, who have carved their initials and have otherwise left their imprint on the tree.

RYSSBY
(Boulder County)

Sven Johnson was an agent for the White Star steamship line. In the late 1860s he convinced many of his neighbors in his native village of Ryssby in Smaland, Sweden, of the opportunities to be found in America. Johnson led a group of about a dozen families to settle in Colorado in 1869, at a site about six miles west of Burlington (Old Burlington, now Longmont).

Children and women helped clear the fields of boulders and brush. Crude irrigation ditches were dug in 1871 (and improved upon subsequently). That year the settlers gathered at Johnson's home to celebrate their first Julotta, traditional Swedish "Early Yule" ceremonies.

The village, which they named Ryssby for their native village in Sweden—also located at the foot of majestic, snow-covered peaks—was founded officially in 1872.

The settlers had very little money, but they were good workers. Whole families cultivated the land during spring and summer; many of the menfolk worked during winters in the mines around Central City and Blackhawk. The first few years of farming were disastrous, plagued with drought, locusts, hail and floods. But in 1875 and '76 the crops were good, and settlers were able to send some money back to bring more families to the new country. A log school house was built, and church services, town meetings and celebrations were held in the building.

The good harvests also gave the settlers enough confidence in the future to ask the Augustana Synod of the Lutheran Church of America for affiliation and the assignment of a pastor. The Reverend Frederick Lagerman arrived in the fall of 1877. During the first two months of 1878 the congregation was organized, a constitution adopted, officers elected and new members admitted.

It wasn't a sudden death to the Pellas, however. Many of the last remnants of the communities disappeared only in recent years. The stones from the ruins of the old Pella school were used to rebuild the steeple of the nearby RYSSBY Church (see below).

About the only material remains of Pella are a few time-worn, unreadable markers in a tiny fenced area. Here was buried the small child of Jim and Mary Ellen Weisner. This site became the Pella or Weisner Cemetery, and many other pioneer residents were buried beside the Weisner child. For many years people believed—some still do—that "Rocky Mountain Jim" Nugent, one of the region's most colorful characters, was buried here. Others claim he sleeps in an unmarked grave in various other nearby cemeteries.

The McCaslin family still lives in the region. The fourth and fifth generation lived in a home near the old Pella community. Matthew McCaslin, after prospecting for gold, settled here in 1860 in one of the original cabins in Pella. The family since has been most prominent in the Boulder–Longmont area. Matthew was a Boulder County Commissioner, as was his grandson, Ted McCaslin.

The Ryssby Church before (*right*) and after the tower was rebuilt with stones from the old Pella School.

Midsummer Day picnic at Ryssby. (*Colorado Historical Society.*)

The pastor's salary was $300 a year, and he was given 40 acres for the prastgard (pastor's garden). He could work ten days for a share in the irrigation water (Table Mountain Ditch). A parsonage was built at a cost of $425. But differences arose between the congregation and Reverend Lagerman. He resigned in February, 1881.

Despite their loss of a pastor, the settlers continued with plans to build a church. Hugo Anderson donated three acres of land, and August Olander contributed sandstone on his land. The cornerstone was laid on Reformation Sunday, October 31, 1881. The little stone church was designed to match the one in their native Swedish town. All volunteered to help build the church. Charles Olson was the stonemason. On June 24, 1882, Midsummer Day on the Nordic Calendar, the settlers celebrated completion of construction with dedication ceremonies.

The land just east of the church was set aside for the community cemetery. The loved ones of settlers that had previously been buried in other nearby plots were reburied near the church.

In 1883, after more than two years without a pastor, the congregation welcomed Reverend L. J. Sandeen. The little colony prospered, and by the late 1880's the congregation had grown to about 50 families. The language and customs of the old country were retained; but the children were learning English in school, and more and more English was heard.

As the settlers prospered, farming activity began to spread to fertile lands in all directions, particularly to the east and north. In the years around the turn of the century, more and more families joined the larger Elim Swedish Evangelical Church in Longmont. The Ryssby congregation grew smaller and smaller. The last minutes of the Protocols Book of Ryssby were recorded on January 3, 1905, and the little church was deserted. In 1914, the Ryssby congregation joined Elim to become the First Lutheran Church, in Longmont.

For several years the little church building in Ryssby was allowed to deteriorate. The bell tower, once the pride and joy of the community, was toppled by lightning and not rebuilt.

It wasn't until 1924 that Elim Pastor Luther Stromquist was successful in generating interest in the little church and its proud legacy by instituting Midsummer services at the church. It became an annual affair, and each year more Ryssby settlers and their children and grandchildren would return for the full day of worship, reunion and eating the famous Swedish smorgasbord.

Reverend Stromquist and others led efforts that resulted in the Ryssby Church becoming a Colorado Historical Site on June 25, 1933. A bronze plaque telling the story of Ryssby was embedded in a large boulder in front of the church. The records of the Ryssby congregation since its inception were presented to the State Historical Society.

In 1938, the first Christmas celebration was held there, reuniting the old congregation at the annual Julotta celebration. This and the Midsummer festivals have grown each year. In 1977 more than 1700 persons from near and far attended the weekend Christmas ceremonies, including some visitors from Sweden.

It was with particular pride that the ceremonies were held in the little church building that looked almost as good as new. The tower that toppled long ago had been rebuilt with stone from the old church at Pella. The church had been restored and painted inside and out, still retaining the original appearance. The friends of the old church had collected more than $25,000 in a few years to restore the church that cost less than $1000 to build.

Although the little church is now equipped with electricity, the services used 200 candles and seven kerosene chandeliers, as it did long years ago. And although modern heaters have been installed in the baseboards, the old pot-bellied stove still stands near the altar.

The 1977 ceremonies were special, marking the hundredth birthday of the Ryssby congregation, known as the "cradle of Lutheranism in Colorado." Although the little church and its adjoining cemetery are all that remain of the first Swedish colony in Colorado, they are proud reminders and getting more attention each year.

CHAPTER VIII

THE TOWNS BEFORE

Today's maps are neat and uncluttered, at least compared to what they would look like if all the towns that ever were and all the names the towns had before were listed on the maps. There wouldn't be room for roads.

Even the towns that survived aren't necessarily what they seem. Some are many incarnations removed from their origins. Others were just a hairsbreadth away from being called something else. Denver, Colorado Springs and Pueblo might well have had different names. There were well over 100 names involved in the development of Denver, including some 120 suburbs and independent communities that were absorbed. Some had aspirations of absorbing the absorber, and giving it another name.

There were countless reasons for a town to change its name, as some changed their locations: to be near a railroad, to consolidate local settlers or purposes, etc.

Bear in mind, the following represent just a cross-section of "the towns before." There are others throughout the book that could have been included in this chapter, and there were others in the state that aren't included in this book at all.

ARAPAHOE CITY

But for the grace of God and a few pioneer votes, the capitol of Colorado could well have been ARAPAHOE CITY today. It was located between Denver and Golden a little to the north, around West 44th Avenue, near the south shores of present Standley Lake.

Although it never became the capitol of the state, and only lasted about three years, it was pretty historic.

Some placer gold was found here in 1858. It was enough to begin a settlement. On November 29, 1858, the Arapahoe Town Company, named for the Indian tribe, was organized. G. B. Allen laid out a proper townsite. During the winter months the development at the site was rapid. Reports of its growth range from 20 to 50 cabins and 100 to 300 souls those first few months.

Although no one became rich from the nearby placer gold, a couple of Arapahoe citizens helped precipitate Colorado's gold stampede for sure. During the winter months George Jackson sneaked off into the mountains to look for gold. Under ice and snow at a site near present Idaho Springs, now marked with a historic plaque, he found his gold. He took careful note of the site and returned as soon as the thaw began in the spring. But he was not able to shake his suspicious followers. Within a few weeks Clear Creek and its tributaries near Jackson's Diggings was elbow-to-elbow with gold-hungry men.

John Gregory, another Arapahoe citizen, took off in a slightly different direction in the spring of 1859. He was rewarded with a fine discovery on what is now called Gregory Gulch, running between today's Blackhawk and Central City. Soon that small area, called then "The Richest Square Mile on Earth," was mobbed with argonauts, and hopefuls from all over the world couldn't get to the new promised land fast enough. Colorado was on its way.

Arapahoe sent seven delegates to the territorial constitutional convention in Denver City in August of 1859, but it didn't have the delegate strength to win the day.

Arapahoe lost another election in January of 1860 when it vied with Golden for county seat of Jefferson County. Although Arapahoe predated Golden, its growth was not as rapid, and Golden won the vote 401 to 288.

It is remarkable that Arapahoe could muster that many votes at that time (though it got 79 votes from Golden Gate, which didn't want Golden to win) because by June the community was virtually deserted. Although there were sluice boxes all over the landscape for a while, Arapahoe had little commercial activity except off the back of a wagon or in a tent. It had no school, church or cemetery. Even the first good road from the Denver area via Arapahoe to the gold fields, begun in early 1860, came too late.

Nothing's left of Arapahoe today but a marker on West 44th Avenue on the first bridge crossing Clear Creek. It says:

In this immediate area once stood Arapahoe City, a pioneer placer mining camp, the earliest town in Jefferson County, named for the Arapahoe Indians. Town Company organized Nov. 29, 1858.

From here went George A. Jackson and John H. Gregory to make their historic gold discoveries near Idaho Springs and Central City. Arapahoe's population was 80 in 1860. Extensive gold dredging operations of 1904 covered part of the site.

Before the Air Force Academy

(El Paso County)

The once-thriving community of HUSTED would be located at about the main (north) entrance of the Air Force Academy today. It was primarily a lumber town with a huge sawmill operated by Calvin R. Husted. It was also a major railroad shipping point for farm produce and cattle.

Husted constructed his sawmill in the late 1860s. Soon the community around the mill had some 200 people. There were many business listings, including a liquor store. There was also a church and a school, and a weekly newspaper, the *Husted Banner*. The little depot had a prominent sign that said: "Husted, Elevation 6596 feet, Denver 62 miles, Ogden, 716 miles."

There was much tragedy in the neighborhood. In addition to the many Indian raids and battles (see below) and a lynching, there were two train wrecks. In 1888 a Rock Island and a Rio Grande train collided head-on about one mile west of Husted. The engines were demolished and fire blazed through much of the wreckage. Miraculously only two persons were killed, but many were injured. Another accident on August 15, 1909, killed seven and injured nearly 60 persons.

Husted operated his mill for many years. Calvin Husted was one of the earliest county commissioners in El Paso County. He was known to be a generous man; during his prosperous years he was said to have given many a handout and grubstake. He died in the poorhouse in Colorado Springs.

The town lingered on for many years after the sawmill was abandoned. It remained a shipping point for the nearby farms and ranches, and it was a roadside stop along the highway. The shacks and buildings disappeared one by one over the years. One of the oldest was the Branding Iron Cafe; it became a saloon, then a store and post office, and finally a church. The service station and store closed in 1956. The last signs of Husted were completely destroyed with the construction of the Academy and the U.S. 85–87 freeway.

PRING SIDING was near the north end of what is now the Air Force Academy, about 3½ miles due north of Husted, on the railroad. It was settled around 1880 by J. W. Pring, who eventually accumulated 1000 acres.

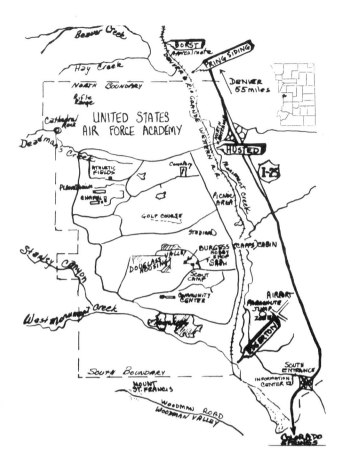

For many years it was a farm shipping center and railroad site. It had a water tank and section house, the ruins of which were still visible when the Academy was built.

Perhaps the most historic site within the Academy today was the site of the old TEACHOUT RANCH. It was settled by Harlow "Leafy" Teachout in the 1860s. The most prominent ranch building was the "fortress," much used by neighboring residents during the Indian Wars of 1864–68. The walls were said to have been more than twelve feet thick in places, with several portholes for rifles. There were many Indian raids in the region, particularly in 1864, 1866 and 1868. In 1866, 20 to 30 settlers were killed within a 20-mile radius of the Teachout Ranch. Some 100 horses from the ranch were stolen by the Indians. During those years as many if not more neighboring Indians were killed who were innocent of any wrongdoing. Those were superfrenetic times and both sides overreacted; damages were exaggerated as well as the restitution.

A picture of the fortress was taken as late as 1878. An almost obscured foundation of the old Teachout ice house was reported seen in the late 1960s, near the onetime ranch headquarters, close to the southern entrance of the Academy, about four miles south of the site of Husted.

The Burgess Cabin, oldest building on the Air Force Academy land, is often known as the Capps Cabin because of the adjacent grave markers of the Capps family, who actually lived in a different cabin nearby.

EDGERTON was located near the southern entrance to the Academy, not far from the Teachout Ranch. In fact, Teachout was the longtime postmaster of Edgerton.

Edgerton was settled in the 1860s, and was originally called MONUMENT or MONUMENT STATION, for nearby Monument Park. This used to be the jumping-off place for visitors to the park. In 1874 the Post Office was named Monument and the D&RG station here was called HENRY. A short time later, both became EDGERTON.

An 1865 business directory said hides and pelts were shipped from here, in addition to the Monument Park activity, and ranching. But the most significant activity here for several decades was lumbering.

According to the 1900 business directory, ice and some coal was shipped from here, in addition to lumber and cattle. There were ten business listings and a population of 250.

Unfortunately, Edgerton is best remembered for one of the most brutal, unsolved murders in Colorado history.

In 1886, neighbors found an elderly woman, Mrs. Kearney, in the barn of her ranch with her head split open by an ax. The horribly mutilated body of her six-year-old grandson was found in a nearby grain bin. (The boy's widowed mother was in the East attempting to get on the stage.) The table in the house was set for three, but no one knew who the third party was to be. Friends and relatives put together a $500 reward for the murderer, although many were questioned in the case, the murderer was never found.

No trace of Edgerton can be found today.

There was another obscure camp that was located for a short time in or near the north end of the Academy, four miles northwest of Husted on Stanley Creek. *The Denver Republican*, on December 19, 1893, reported: "Another discovery of gold made at STANLEY CAMP."

Another source said there was the "Stanley Camp Mine" here, as well as placer mining. A search for the site could give the cadets something to do during their free hours.

About the only reminder of the past found on the Air Force Academy today is the Burgess Ranch Cabin. The ranch building was constructed in 1869–70 by William A. Burgess, making it one of the oldest remaining buildings in the Pike's Peak region.

It was spared during the construction of the Academy, moved from its original location and restored. The restoration is faithful to the original, save for the sturdy stone foundation. Outstanding features of the cabin are the hand-hewn exterior logs and the large stone fireplace.

The cabin is on the National Register of Historic Places. A tiny cemetery nearby was also moved from its original site, and contains the graves of some of the pioneer neighbors of the Burgesses.

By contrast, the old cabin was located in the Douglass Valley housing area, about 200 yards from a modern home, built by an architectural engineer, with solar heating.

East of Denver
(Adaurs and Arapahoe Counties)

Traveling east out of Denver are several quiet little towns that were significant stations on the old Kansas Pacific. But most of them were there—on the old Smoky Hill Trail—before the railroad came.

About 15 miles due east of Denver was one of the more important stage stations in early Colorado. It was called BOX ELDER, and it was not only the first major

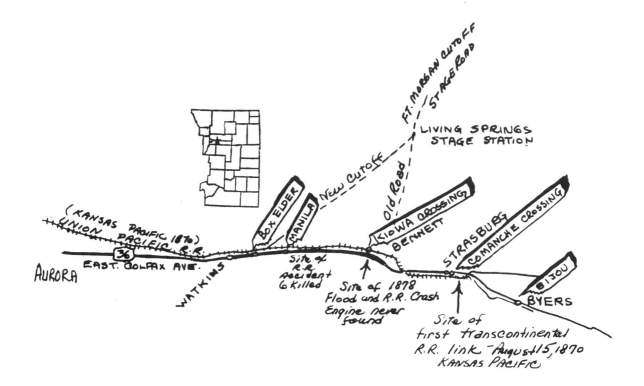

stage stop out of Denver on the Smoky Hill Trail (North), but it was also on the Fort Morgan Cutoff from the Platte River Trail.

When the railroad came the station, established about a mile west, was renamed WATKINS for a local rancher, E. L. Watkins.

Five miles further down the line was MANILA, now a ghost. Manila is historic in that there were two early train wrecks near here. One, just east of Manila, involved a head-on collision between two trains, one loaded with iron. Six men were killed and eight were injured. The track was cleared and the trains ran again. But the following day another train smashed into railroad cars used as bunkhouses for railroad workers, killing another six men and injuring about a dozen. The engineer was almost lynched. It was determined that the locomotive brakes had failed.

Another five miles down the tracks is BENNETT, known back in the 1860s as KIOWA CROSSING or KIOWA, for the nearby creek. It was the site of a stage station and a popular overnight stop, the home of the Mack family. It was also the scene of one of Colorado's worst and weirdest train accidents.

On the night of May 21, 1878, a flash flood washed out the railroad crossing on Kiowa Creek, just a short distance from the Mack home. A freight train out of Denver was traveling almost full speed when it reached the creek. The engine, tender and 18 freight cars plunged into the churning waters. Only six flat cars and the caboose remained on the tracks.

The body of the engineer, John Bacon of Denver, was found six days later seven miles downstream. The fireman, Seldon, and another man were found about a mile and a half downstream. The conductor and brakeman were safe in the caboose. A tramp who was sleeping in one of the boxcars was pulled from the stream alive, although he claimed the boxcar had rolled over "more than a thousand times."

More miraculous, perhaps, is the fact that the engine of the train has never been found, although persons have sought for it all the decades since.

The town was renamed for the widows of the engineer and fireman, two sisters whose maiden name was Bennett. Another source says Bennett was named for the Honorable H.P. Bennett, pastmaster of Denver. Going a step further, another source said the postmaster was the father of the Bennett sisters.

Next station down the line is STRASBURG, originally known as COMANCHE CROSSING (see "Very Special Places"). It was the most historic railroad point on the line.

Around 1912 there was a promotional campaign to establish a "full service" farm community, named COMANCHE, about a mile north of Strasburg. The promotion, although it was more than that, was primarily the work of the Thaden family. They had an elaborate community laid out and offered good lots to any and all who would settle there. There was a real estate agent and building contractor standing by. A regular stage run was inaugurated between the site and Strasburg. A combination drug–tobacco–candy store was built, a grocery store and a post office.

World War I didn't help the promotion, but it was pushed again right after the war. By 1920 the Thadens gave up. Apparently not enough people cared to live even a mile away from the railroad and "civilization."

Another five miles east from Strasburg is BYERS, another early stage station that was named BIJOU before it was renamed for William N. Byers, Editor of the *Rocky Mountain News*. Bijou is French for jewel, and the site was named for the nearby creek.

OLD BURLINGTON
(Boulder County)

OLD BURLINGTON* was one of the earliest and largest communities in northern Colorado. It began in the early 1860s, originally as a stage station, but it soon became a thriving farm crossroads town, coming into full maturity with the coming of the railroad believed to be its namesake.

By 1862 Burlington had a post office, and the Allen Hotel and the stage station were the centers of activity here. By the 1870's there were two hotels and several businesses, and a population of some 300.

But Old Burlington's trademark, known throughout the state, was its race track. Many of the best horses in early Colorado came here to test their speed.

It is said that the bad blood between Will Dubois and Ed Kinney began at the race track. Kinney was one of the top horsemen around. Dubois was the son of good pioneer stock, but he fell into bad company. He developed a reputation as a braggart and somewhat of a gunslinger and all-around "bad guy." His "bad company" numbered quite a few. Many lived in Left Hand Canyon, where Dubois often stayed. The large following of both men compounded the feud.

Some say the feud came about when Dubois attempted to bribe one of Kinney's riders to throw a race. There were other things. It is believed the final straw came when Dubois was arrested and accused of one of the many stage robberies that took place in the region. Dubois was acquitted for lack of evidence, but he held the notion that he'd been framed and that Kinney had something to do with it.

A few days after the trial, Dubois met Kinney and another man along the trail leading into Burlington. Dubois demanded compensation for the time and money lost while on trial and in jail. There were words, and . . . it was bound to happen somewhere, sooner or later. Kinney was no match for Dubois.

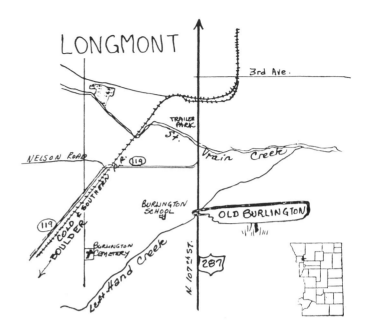

When Kinney's body was brought into town, a posse was formed immediately, and it set out for Left Hand Canyon.

Dubois escaped capture the first time around with a daring dash for freedom aboard his trusty steed, as they say. He stayed overnight with friends, who urged him to skip the country. But Dubois, either foolishly or foolhardily, didn't do things that way. In fact, he thought he could ambush the posse. Well-armed, he dug into a protected site in Left Hand Canyon and waited. Eventually, a posse of a dozen men or so approached. Dubois put up a long and good fight, but couldn't overcome the numbers. He was shot dead.

The Chicago–Colorado Colony was formed around 1870 and land was purchased about a mile north of Burlington. An elaborate townsite was platted, and colonists began to arrive. Many Burlington citizens, particularly the commercial establishments, joined the new community. Allen's Hotel, long the center of Old Burlington, was moved to the new city—called Longmont—and became the Silver Moon Hotel, a mainstay for many years. Independence Hall, with the Burlington Community Center on the second floor, was moved to Longmont in 1872. But Old Burlington didn't die overnight. It still had a population of 300 in 1874.

It died slowly. There are still some reminders of Old Burlington adjacent the south end of Longmont. The cemetery there was originally the Burlington Cemetery; in a corner of it sleep pioneer Burlington residents, some dating back to the 1860s. The Burlington School, built in 1867 to replace the original school, still stands and has been restored.

---

*There was another OLD BURLINGTON, located about two miles east of present Burlington, a live town in eastern Kit Carson County near the Kansas line. This Old Burlington was platted in 1887 by the Lowell Townsite Company and named for Burlington, Kansas, from whence the Colorado settler came.

CHEROKEE CITY, LATHAM, FORT LATHAM

(Weld County)

In late 1860 a small community and stage station was established at the only crossing of the Platte for many miles. The settlers formed the Cherokee Town Company and named the new community CHEROKEE CITY, for the Cherokee Trail which passed nearby.

One of the founders, a Dr. Bell, planned to build a road along the Platte all the way to Julesburg. By December of 1860 there were several houses here, a stage station and a sawmill, built and operated by John Quincy Rollins, prominent businessman and road-builder in early Colorado. A fortified stables was built to protect man and beast against Indians. Cherokee City was granted a post office in November of 1862.

However, it was a futile gesture. Rollins abondoned his sawmill and moved on to other things. More settlers realized that Cherokee City was located too close to the river bottom.

In 1863 the settlers selected a site about a quarter-mile away, farther from the river bottom. They named the new site LATHAM, after the California Senator, Milton S. Latham, a strong advocate of the Overland Route. Since it became the stage station, it was also called LATHAM STATION. And since it also had a sturdy fortress, often used by settlers during the Indian Wars, a very common name for the site was FORT LATHAM.

An early newspaper had called Cherokee City "the metropolis along the Platte"; Latham became it in fact. It was a key junction point for stages and wagons traveling along the Platte River Trail, to points north to Cheyenne

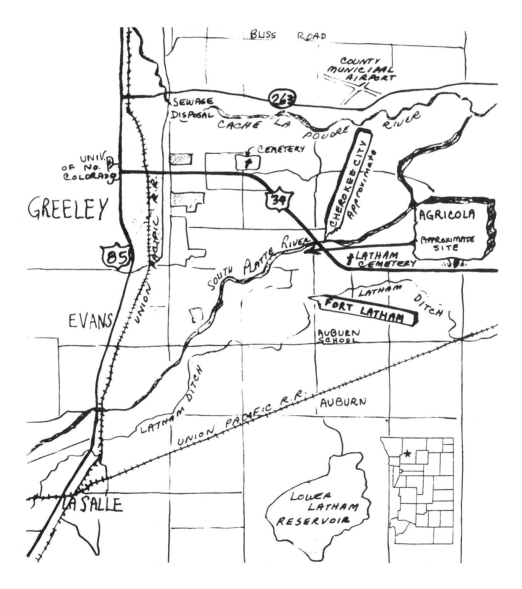

and beyond, and west into the goldfields. It continued to be a busy junction point even after the Fort Morgan Cutoff, established between Fort Morgan and Denver in late 1864, took away much of the Platte River traffic.

During the "Indian War of 1864," Fort Latham became a training ground for the "100-Day Volunteers." A flood on May 20 of the same year threatened the community. The high water held up stage traffic and the mail for several days.

In October, 1868, Latham was made county seat of Weld County. But the designation came near the end. In the late 1860s the Denver-Pacific Railroad bypassed Latham and in 1869 established a station about two miles northwest, called EVANS. In January of 1870, Evans was made County Seat of Weld County. Citizens of Latham had already started moving to the new community.

About all that is left of the once-important community of Latham is a tiny graveyard and a marker. The nearby cemetery, probably used by Latham and Cherokee City has a headstone that says:

> Only known buried here
> Magdalena Simon 1809–1861   and two infant sons
> Several others unknown

The marker erected in 1927 on a corner of a house on the site reads:

> Site of Latham Station at junction of Denver and California Overland Stage routes 1859–1870. Refuge from warring Indians. Camp of Colorado 100-day volunteers 1864. U. S. Post Office, store and school 1864–1870. County seat of Weld County, Colorado Territory 1865–1876. [error]

OLD CHEYENNE WELLS (Indian Wells)

(Cheyenne County)

The original CHEYENNE WELLS was located about five miles north of the present community, and was also called INDIAN WELLS. It was an early stage station located near a cave which showed signs of early Indian habitation.* There were Indian graves nearby, and wells long known to Indians, the reason for the station's name.

When the stage station was established along the old Smoky Hill Trail in the 1860s, the cave was used as a stables. The station was operated by Johnny White, a colorful figure along the desolate route. More welcome

to travelers than White was the saloon he operated across the road from the cave.

In addition to the saloon the cave–stables and the station–residence, beside the cave, White built a small fortress–lookout on the bluff overlooking the site. A trench (moat) was dug around the small fort. There were many Indian "scares" in the region, and the little fortress was frequently used as a haven for settlers and travelers, but there is no record of any battles here.

However, early Colorado historian Baskin** tells of the death near here of Joe Lane, who was lured away by Utes and murdered.

When the Kansas Pacific Railroad rushed through in 1870, not far south of the stage station, it made the latter extraneous. Anything worth moving from OLD CHEYENNE WELLS was relocated in new CHEYENNE WELLS.

The only evidence remaining of the old town is the ancient cave (although, for some reason the Civilian Conservation Corps. [CCC] blew up most of the caves in the area in the 1930s). Even the ancient springs, so welcome to early travelers, have dried up.

CITADEL and NEW MEMPHIS

(Douglas County)

A group calling itself "The Independence Colony" filed on some land about 30 miles south of Denver on Plum Creek. This was in 1872. The settlers named the site

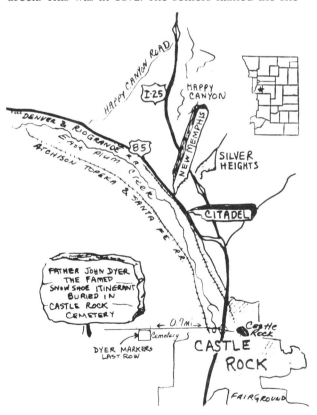

---

*The remaining caves and overhangs can be seen in the sides of the low mesas two to three miles east of U.S. 385, from a point about five miles north of Cheyenne Wells. There is a dirt road here that will take you to a closer view.

**O. L. Baskin, *History of the Arkansas Valley*

after the impressive table mountain that looked to some like a massive castle or citadel.

The new site, according to plan, received a boost in 1873 when the Santa Fe Railroad laid its track through here and CITADEL became a station on the line.

However, the boost was short-lived. In 1874 some industrious settlers from the east platted an ambitious community just north of Citadel. They named the site after the big city in their native state, hoping or expecting NEW MEMPHIS to be the Western equivalent of the Tennessee city. The industriousness of the new settlers seemed geared in that direction. The frequent hopeful reports from the new community received much attention.

It grew rapidly, quickly absorbing the settlement of Citadel. For a short time in the late 1870s New Memphis was the largest and most important town between Denver and Colorado City.

But then another new community, two miles to the south, began to flourish. It was named for the same mountain which gave Citadel its name, but the new settlers called it CASTLE ROCK.

For a short time Castle Rock and New Memphis competed for dominance and for designation as the county seat. But fate and the railroad soon began to frown on New Memphis and smile on Castle Rock. Soon New Memphis settlers gave up and moved to the new center.

The former Citadel and New Memphis are on farmland today.

JUNCTION (Junction House, Fort Junction, Old Fort Morgan) SANBORN, CAMP WARDWELL (Camp or Fort Tyler, Fort Wardwell), ASHCROFT'S RANCH

(Morgan County)

This area had many names before it finally came together as Fort Morgan.

In 1864 the famed Fort Morgan Cutoff was estab-

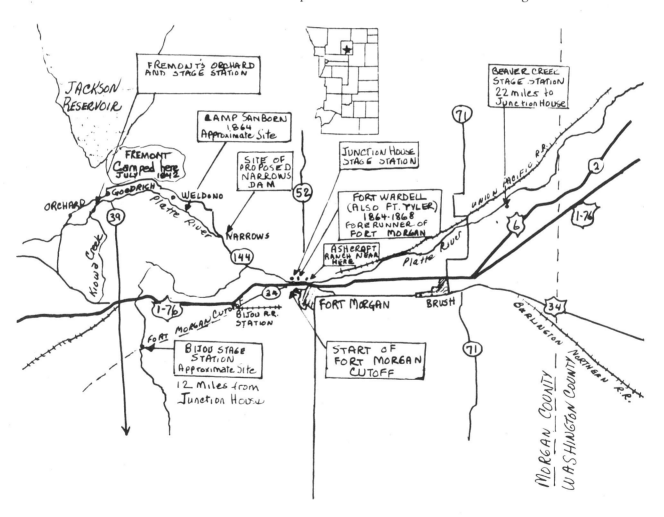

A rotting chair frame bars the door of a sod house in the Narrows area, a reminder of early days around Fort Morgan. (*U.S. Bureau of Reclamation.*)

lished. It left the Platte River Trail and cut across country southwestward, saving a full 20 miles into Denver. A stage station was established at the junction point, a short distance east of the present site of Fort Morgan. The station was variously called Junction, Junction House, Fort Junction, Junction Station and Old Fort Morgan.

When Indian troubles broke out all along the stage line in 1864, volunteers came out in force. Hastily trained civilians and a smattering of regulars patrolled along the line, some riding along the stages and wagon trains into the territory. Several hastily built camps were established along the route.

Camp Sanborn was established in 1864 about six miles east of Fremont's Orchard (see, "By the Side of the Road"). This camp lasted less than a year, and when it was abandoned the ragtag troops were sent to Fremont's Orchard and then to another nearby camp.

To better protect the Fort Morgan Cutoff and the isolated ranches in the region, another fort was built overlooking the Junction House in 1864-65. It was originally called Camp or Fort Tyler, for the Tyler Rangers, volunteers from Central City. It was renamed Camp or Fort Wardwell, and eventually Fort Morgan in 1866, honoring Colonel Christopher A. Morgan, a local volunteer in the Civil War who was killed in 1866.

Although abandoned in 1867-68, it had grown to a sizeable outpost at the time. The fort consisted of a collection of buildings, mostly sod. It was situated on a plateau about 60 feet above the river. There were comfortable quarters for the officers, servants' quarters, lookout towers and a flag tower, magazines, guard houses, mess rooms and bunk houses.

Two hundred wagons could be accomodated within the enclosure. And at various times, from one to six companies of soldiers were stationed here. The entire fort covered an area of about one city block. The outer walls, made of sod, reinforced with logs, were surrounded by a ditch-like moat. There were numerous slots for rifles in the walls and cannons protected the fort from the northeast and southwest corners. There was a tall flagpole in the center. A marker at the approximate location of the fort can be seen in Fort Morgan today.

The fort was never attacked although the troops protected activity all along the Platte River Trail and Fort Morgan Cutoff.

The fort was abandoned May 18, 1868, with proper pomp and rituals. The buildings and moveable objects were sold at auction. Most of the troops departed for Fort Laramie.

About the same time railroads were racing toward Denver, making the stage lines along parallel routes useless. Later the Colorado Central Railroad selected the best site near the old fort and stage station, and built its station, and named the station for the old fort.

There was another historic site near early Junction House and Camp Wardwell. It was the ranch and small trading post called Ashcroft's Ranch. It was established in 1861 and was said to have been located about a half mile northeast of the fort. There is a small cemetery on a knoll due east of the site of the fort, overlooking the ranch site. No information is available on the graves.

Samuel P. Ashcroft (sometimes spelled Ashcraft) was married to a Sioux woman, whose information apparently kept her husband and others in the neighborhood informed on the activities of the Cheyennes and Arapahoe War parties.

OLD KIT CARSON
(Cheyenne County)

Old Kit Carson, located about three miles west of the present site, was far lustier than the present community. In fact, during 1869–70, when it was railhead for the construction of the Kansas Pacific, it was about the wildest town in Colorado.

During those first years it was estimated that there were between 1500 and 2000 persons here, and only a small portion of them belonged to the railroad construction crews. There were the "lively ladies" and the gamblers and con men, all eager to get their hands on the hard-earned money of the construction crews. There were the "Taos Lightning dispensers," and other camp followers.

The ragamuffin community consisted of tents, dugouts and a few permanent buildings. Much business, especially saloon business, was carried out from the back of a wagon.

While it was the railhead, Old Kit Carson was the distribution center for much of eastern and southeastern Colorado, and northeastern New Mexico. In such a wild, disorganized environment there was much illicit traffic and stolen goods. One historian said that the only employment in Kit Carson, other than gambling, prostitution and the like, was "robbing the trains." Whole freight cars were robbed of their contents. An undercover Denver railroad detective, posing as a tramp, led to the arrest of many thieves and the recovery of stolen goods, but it was just a token gesture in the flood of illegal activity.

When the railhead moved further west many of the buildings, particularly the railroad buildings, were loaded on flatcars and taken to the new site. So, too, went most of the tents, lean-tos, gamblers, "gals," and camp followers—"following the action."

But Old Kit Carson, unlike many wild and woolly railroad construction towns, did not die. It collected itself after the tumultuous, temporary element moved on, and became a better, more stable community, far safer and saner that it had been, a fairly respectable "railroad city." There was a station here, stockyards for cattle to be shipped, and other railroad facilities. In 1871 it won a post office designation. The following year, the community gained in status when the Grand Duke Alexis of Russia headquartered here for a few days while hunting buffalo on the Plains.

A better site was found for the station in 1882 about three miles east of the site of OLD KIT CARSON. Much of that town was loaded on flatcars and taken to NEW KIT CARSON, where an even more permanent town was established. Of course, both Old and New Kit Carson and the county to their north were named for the famous scout.

THE MEADOWS and PROWERS
(Bent County)

PROWERS, now a rural post office, was for many years one of the more prominent towns in southeastern Colo-

rado. The site was first called the Meadows, after the lush bottom-land fields in the area.

When the Pueblo & Arkansas Valley Railroad (later the AT&SF) chugged through in the mid-1870s, it set up a station which was called, simply, THE MEADOWS. However, the site began to grow immediately. It soon needed a post office and acquired other necessities of a farm center. A more dignified name was needed.

One of the most prominent names in the region was that of John Prowers. He came to Colorado from Missouri at the age of 18, got work at the right place, Bent's Fort, and did many jobs for William Bent, including freighting in supplies and items for trading. Within a very short time, Prowers became a force in the region. He became one of the largest landowners in the Arkansas Valley, partially through the friendship and influence of Bent.

Working for Thomas Boggs (see BOGGSVILLE, "Very Special Places"), he introduced many successful innovations in farming and ranching in this area. While the reputation of this area as "the Cradle of the Cattle Industry" in Colorado might be debatable, Prowers and

John Prowers, one of southern Colorado's first businessmen. When he died in 1884, at the age of 46, he was one of the state's richest men and largest landholders. (*Denver Public Library Western History Department.*)

Prowers' wife Amache was the daughter of Cheyenne Chief One Eye, who was killed at the Sand Creek massacre. The Prowers lived first at Old Caddoa and later had a large home at Boggsville. (*Denver Public Library Western History Department.*)

Boggs did begin big-time ranching in this region, with Bent.

Prowers was also a good friend of Kit Carson. In fact, Kit and his wife, Amache, were originally buried in a section behind Prowers' House in Boggsville called "The Gardens." Later they were reburied in Taos.

Prowers died in 1884 after crowding a lot of life and much pioneering into his 46 years.

Although the name of the station and the Post Office has been called PROWERS, the surrounding area and often the community center continue to be called THE MEADOWS.

LA PLAZA DE LOS LEONES, TOURIST CITY and WALSENBURG

(Huerfano County)

Miguel Antonio Leon, with his family and another family, the Atencios, settled in the shadows of the Spanish Peaks in 1859. They built several cottages around a Spanish-style plaza. The place came to be known as LA PLAZA DE LOS LEONES for Don Leon, who became the Alcalde or mayor.

Local historian and legend-collector Louis D. Sporleder once described life at the plaza:

Life was idyllic in the first two decades of the plaza's existence. When the rising sun gilded the tips of the big trees on the round knob south of the creek, the people began to stir. Smoke rose from the chimneys, girls carried water and the men chopped wood. The livestock in the corrals in back of each house became noisy; lambs bleated and calves bawled. A half hour later, after milking, the different herds and flocks were driven beyond the fields and gardens to graze.

Amiable children, in the early days of the Plaza's life: Boys doffed their hats to all elders; girls remained silent until spoken to. With but few exceptions the children were well-behaved and suitably trained. The girls assisted in household duties and the boys herded the stock.

Thus it was at the Plaza until the mid-1870's when the "iron horse" changed the idyllic life. People with names nothing like Leon and Atencio took up residence here. They took up different occupations. And, of course, the railroad and its black smoke brought a more frenetic style.

When the railroad and a different kind of settler came to the site in the 1870s, to the "new town" adjacent to the 50 Mexican huts here, the town was incorporated as WALSENS, then WALSENBURG, for Fred Walsens, a

new leader in the community. Some of the earliest coal in the region was found nearby.

In 1887 town expansion and a new image was attempted, primarily by the railroad. Part of the new image was promotion of the SPANISH PEAK HOT SPRINGS, about a mile and a half away. An effort was made to rename the town TOURIST CITY. Some sources claim that the name actually was changed by the post office department for a short while. Whether that is true or not, it became WALSENBURG for good.

OLD GRANADA (Zuck, Barton, Byron, Adana)

(Prowers County)

OLD GRANADA was the start of it—the beginning of the riotous reputation that would be southeastern Colorado's, one upheld nobly by BOSTON and TRAIL CITY in the years to follow. It is doubtful that anyplace in the west had three such notorious neighbors.

Colorado can be proud.

Actually, it was a peaceful site in 1872. T. B. Nolan operated a little general store and commissary alongside what had long been known as the Santa Fe Trail. Business was brisk, as there were more travelers every year. But it was peaceful.

Then came the railroad in 1873.

The railroad made this site, at the mouth of Granada Creek, its railhead for construction. Overnight Granada became another typical construction town, only larger and wilder than the others, because the railroad went broke after it reached this spot and it was nearly two years before they raised enough money to continue the construction.

Meanwhile, the railroad workers and the hundreds of unsavory types that follow the construction crews whooped it up. Anywhere from 1000 to 1500 people were here: the railroad workers, the gamblers, the girls, and a smattering of legitimate businessmen. There were several general stores and at least a dozen saloons, some in tents or in the back of wagons. Since this was a railroad terminus, it also became the supply center for a wide area of southeastern Colorado. Freighters were plentiful and they were also fair game for the con men and women, the gamblers and the girls.

The biggest con game was played by town promoters. Chick, Brown & Company bought up most of the land around the railhead, and they promoted a permanent and promising townsite. Lots sold fast. The trouble was, buyers were given receipts for their money, but not the deeds to the land. They got the run-around that helped keep the community in an uproar. Finally, when the railroad moved on, most of the people followed it, leaving the land (and the money) to the company.

Among all the gunsmoke, gambling and girlie stuff, there were some who actually wanted this to be a proper and permanent town. A sizable hotel was built, large warehouses for the railroad and the freighters. There was even a school, big enough to accomodate not only the local students but kids from Coolidge, Kansas, who were transported back and forth each day by the railroad.

For nearly a month during the winter of 1874 there was no activity on the railroad. A severe blizzard closed the line between Dodge City and Granada, which was virtually cut off from the rest of the world. Food and other supplies became scarce. When the first train made it through the drifts after 24 days, it was cause for a grand celebration—as if Granada needed a cause to celebrate.

Perhaps the wildest (and most sincere) celebration of all took place in the spring of 1875 when construction began again. By September the tracks reached Las Animas (East or Old Las Animas), and the construction crews moved to the new railhead.

Almost as quickly as Granada exploded upon the scene it was defused. Only the debris of two years of hard living remained for the most part. Granada had its first quiet night in two years. There were still a few ranchers around and a few "die-hards" that continued to promote Granada as a permanent town along the railroad. But the railroad selected a site three miles farther down the line. One might think the railroad wanted to get away from the reputation of the original city—but the name GRANADA was retained. The old site, as long as its memory lasted, became OLD GRANADA.

Some early residents claimed Granada means "end of the road." The old and new Granada were named for the creek. Some believe that its name came from the city in Spain, famous in song. The name can also mean "pomegranates" in Spanish, but no pomegranates were raised here—only hell. And the natives don't pronounce the name as it's spelled. They shorten the first couple of "a's," making it sound like "gre-ne-da."

The site had other names after Granada. A small ranch center here was originally called ZUCK in the 1890s, it was later changed to BARTON. The railroad at one time called it BYRON and the ADANA. It has been a longtime headquarters for the XY RANCH. There is also some irrigated farming, and sugar beets and alfalfa are shipped.

OLD GRANADA and its reputation aren't totally forgotten. New Granada holds an annual celebration and barbeque called "Shoot 'em Up Days," to commemorate the excitement that once was here.

OLD STERLING
(Logan County)

OLD STERLING was located about three miles northeast of the present site of STERLING. A member of the railroad engineering party surveying through here in 1870, David Leavitt, returned shortly thereafter and began a ranch. He and some other early pioneers built an irrigation ditch, which Leavitt named the Sterling Ditch after his hometown in Illinois.

In 1873–74, a party of southerners, primarily from Tennessee and Mississippi, settled at the site. It was a hard-working group, and Old Sterling became a growing, rather prosperous community. Like the other farm centers on the Plains it was a most sociable community, with large gatherings for activities on the weekends and holidays. It is said to have been the site of the first sod schoolhouse in Logan County.

When the Colorado Central Railroad (forerunner of the Union Pacific) entered Colorado and began building along the Platte in this direction, Old Sterling residents got together and offered the railroad 80 acres for a station. The railroad selected a site nearby and the pioneer residents moved to the new STERLING.

WINONA (Douty's Mill, Old St. Louis) and BIG THOMPSON
(Larimer County)

In 1864 Andrew Douty built the first flour mill in northern Colorado on South Boulder Creek. But he soon realized his mill was too far from the farms, so in 1867 Douty constructed a large mill alongside the Big Thompson for $10,000. The mill was run by water power. Douty imported huge buhrs, or grinding stones, from Italy, to grind the flour and feed. (The buhrs are now in the Loveland Museum.)

Douty built himself a nice home. Others came and did likewise. Soon there were other businesses, a drug store, blacksmith, the largest mercantile store in the region and a commodious hotel. There was also a school, eventually a church, and the post office was named WINONA, for the daughter of Judge Washburn.

But the most popular name for the site was OLD ST. LOUIS, for a ruse Douty used in order to sell his flour. Douty produced good flour and could sell it at a price competitive with or even lower than that of the major producer of flour sold throughout the West. The problem was that the other flour, produced in St. Louis and marketed in a widely known, colorful bag, was soundly established. So Douty used a bag that looked almost exactly like the St. Louis bag. It worked.

WINONA, or OLD ST. LOUIS, prospered. The regular dances held at the hotel were well attended. Another hotel was built near the mill, and other businesses were established.

Railroads, however, care little for the established in their route-planning process. In 1877 the Colorado Central, heading for Cheyenne, selected a site about a mile away for a station and named it LOVELAND, for H.A.W. Loveland, president of the railroad.

Most of Winona or Old St. Louis picked up and moved to the new city. What didn't move was eventually absorbed anyway.

About a mile away was another fairly prosperous community, BIG THOMPSON, which met the same fate. Named for the river, Big Thompson was here even before WINONA. (When Big Thompson received a post office in 1864 it was located in the home of Judge Washburn, whose name was used for WINONA.) It was the site of a large dairy operation and farm center.

This center had a population of about 150 when Loveland was established. They and their homes and businesses soon became a part of the new town.

CALIFORNIA RANCH (Frank's Town)

(Douglas County)

This was the predecessor of FRANKTOWN. Frank Gardner made claim on the land just south of the present town, and almost immediately it became a key stage stop on the old Smoky Hill Trail. Gardner constructed a sizable hotel with rooms and a dining hall on the ground floor. The large dance hall on the second floor became the social center for the region, often with entertainers from Denver featured on the weekends. Large stables were also built, and barns. Later a saloon and jail were built at the site. There was also a sawmill here operated by Thomas Bayaud.

Bishop Joseph Talbott, en route to New Mexico in 1863, described this as the first stop "for the driver" south of Denver, and "an excellent place."

In 1864 the Third Calvary mentioned stopping here while on the way to escort the surviving members of the Reynolds gang to Fort Lyon. The gang, in an early Colorado classical farce, had been prevented from robbing the Colorado treasury to help finance the Rebel cause during the Civil War. In the final chapter of their tale, they were shot, a short distance south of California Ranch while being escorted to Fort Lyon. According to the soldiers, they'd attempted to escape.

As the community grew (to the north) it became known as FRANK'S TOWN, finally just FRANKTOWN. It became the first county seat of Douglas County. Frank Gardner was named first county treasurer in 1861 and elected to the post the following year.

OLD ELBERT (Clermont)

(Elbert County)

The first man to make claim to land in this region was a Duke Benard or Bernard. In 1860 he sold his spread to Adam Rinnert, who made many improvements over the years. He profited from the growing number of travelers over this north–south trail, connecting just to the north with the Smoky Hill Trail. He built a hotel with five bedrooms, a big kitchen, a dining room and a parlor. There was also a large corral. The site was named for the county, which was named for Samuel Elbert, territorial governor (1873–74).

ELBERT became a changeover station on the stage route between Denver and Pueblo. In 1875 it received a post office, with Charles Hutchins as the first postmaster. Louisa Carver became postmistress in 1880. Later she went elsewhere, only to return shortly after, wanting to be postmistress again. Unable to wrest the job away from the current jobholder, Louisa set up her own post office at the site and called it CLERMONT. Exactly how she did this is now lost to history.

Anyhow, in 1882 the Denver & New Orleans Railroad (later the Colorado & Southern) built through about seven miles to the northeast. The following year the CLERMONT–OLD ELBERT post office was moved to the railroad. Many of the buildings at the old site were dismantled and moved to the new or used for farm and ranch buildings at nearby locations. Floods have since obliterated all that was left.

HENDERSON'S ISLAND (Denver's Poor Farm, The Pest House)

(Adams County)

HENDERSON'S ISLAND is now the Adams County Fairgrounds and Regional Park, a busy, colorful place. But it had a long and colorful history before it became what it is today.

Colonel Jack Henderson (there is some question as to how he received his commission) was said to be the first resident of what is now Adams County. He came here in 1858 and settled on an island in a wide area of the Platte River. He introduced cattle and horses to the region, and noticed how fat they became on the lush green grasses of the river bottomlands.

However, he failed to make proper claim to the land. One story claims that he traded the entire 360-acre tract for two barrels of whiskey. At any rate, when Henderson left at the start of the Civil War others filed on the land, which was originally a part of Arapahoe County.

In the years before Arapahoe County was broken up and this area became Adams County, 1902, the land saw many owners and many uses. The influx of settlers

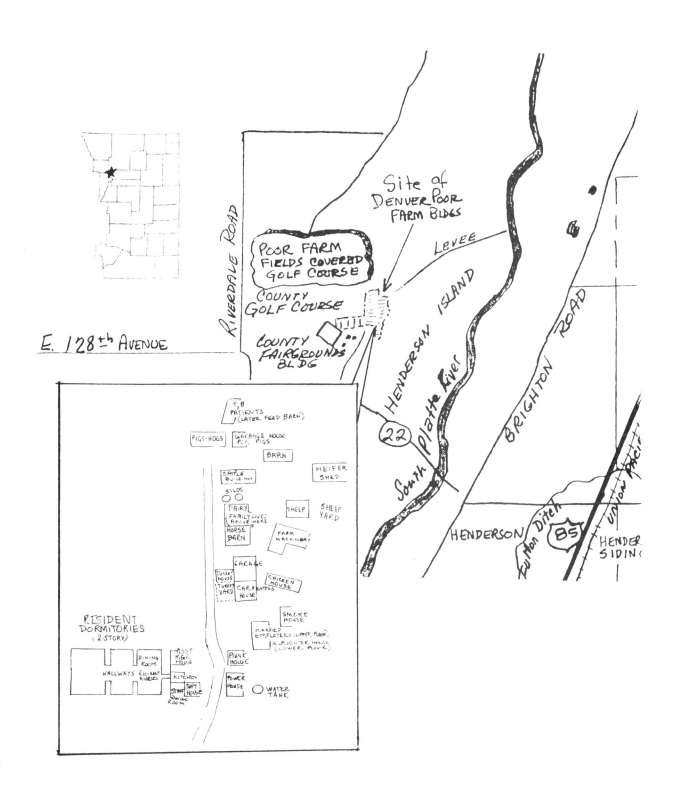

John Foos, farmhand at the Denver Poor Farm, stands in front of the huge horse barn. Beyond the barn is the dairy. (*Photo from around 1940; courtesy Albert Foos*)

caused the permanent creation of HENDERSON on the banks of the River.

In 1908 it was deeded to Denver, and it became the DENVER POOR FARM, better known in those days as "The Pest House." It was little more than an isolated "skid row" and "drying out" center* until 1931, when Denver officials put Harold "Duke" Lascelles in charge of the entire operations. The changes were immediate and amazing. He turned it into an efficient irrigated dairy farm. The Holsteins raised here won many awards, the herd was considered one of the best in the state.

However, due to overcrowding, local harrassment, and other reasons, Denver closed down the facility in the 1950s.

In 1960 Adams County purchased the property for $176,500, razed the old buildings and began development of a golf course, fairgrounds and a regional park. County fairground facilities were moved from Brighton. Over the years new buildings were added.

Today, Henderson's Island contains one of the most complete and modern county fairgrounds in the nation. Many of the facilities have been added since 1968.

It is a far cry from the questionable beginning more than 100 years ago, and certainly worth more than two barrels of whiskey.

*Most early so-called "Pest Houses" also maintained isolated wards for indigent persons with communicable or incurable diseases.

ST. VRAINS (St. Vrain)
(Weld County)

ST. VRAINS was one of the most important sites in Colorado during the early 1860s. It was built around the ruins of the famed trading post, FORT ST. VRAINS, near the confluence of the St. Vrains and the Platte rivers.

In 1859 and early '60s it served as a stage station for stages going north and south between Denver and Wyoming and east–west along the Platte River Trail. It was a key jumping off place for the argonauts heading for the gold fields to the west.

The Golden Mountaineer on February 8, 1860, reported that "the proprietors" of St. Vrains "claim the advantages of being more centrally located in regard to different mines in the mountains than any other [town] and that it is a proper point for all immigrants to cross coming to or going from this country." The item said, "Persons coming to Blue, South Park or Gregory's Diggings [Central City] . . . will save 25 miles by crossing here and going to Golden City." The glowing story also said that "contiguous to the town is a large body of excellent land which can be cultivated without irrigation."

At a governing convention held at St. Vrains the first governing rules for northern Colorado were drawn up. Shortly afterward, at the constitutional convention for Jefferson Territory in Denver, St. Vrains County was named one of the twelve counties in Jefferson Territory, with ST. VRAINS as its seat.

Of course, Jefferson Territory never came to be, and the creation of Colorado Territory shortly thereafter ended all talk about it.

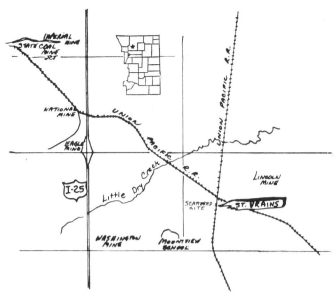

County buildings were built in 1861 of logs. The first county proceeding and the first court proceeding were carried out in these log buildings.

More important to the growth of the city was the fact that is was a major highway into the mountains. St. Vrains was terminus of the St. Vrain, Golden City and Colorado Wagon Road. Almost as much as Golden City, St. Vrains was a "jumping off" site for the gold-seekers. It was also where the disgusted and disappointed rejoined the roads back to "civilization."

The *Mountaineer* reported in February of 1860 that a "large and commodious" hotel was completed and a "wholesale store" was being built. But in the diary of one of the emigrants says that in June of that year he reached a "city" which contained only three frame houses "at crossing to Golden City and on site of St. Vrains Fort . . . we were obliged to drive about five miles further to camp for dinner."

Some early reports, in giving distances, reported that St. Vrains was only 55 miles from "Shian Pass," no doubt Cheyenne Pass.

The St. Vrain Ditch Company was formed in 1863 and construction began on one of the earliest ditches in this region, to expand the productivity of this fertile area.

Partially rebuilt Fort St. Vrains and the other fortified buildings at the county seat made St. Vrains a stronghold against the Indian takeover during the "Indian Wars" of 1864–65.

In October of 1868 the county seat was moved to Latham, a few miles to the northeast. The move was undoubtedly too soon. Latham didn't last long as county seat and it was soon located elsewhere. St. Vrains kept on rolling along. Today it remains the center of lush farm county with some coal nearby, although a city as such is difficult to find. It was easier a few years ago when it was a station on the railroad. The entire area is busy today and there are buildings and facilities of all sorts. No doubt some were once part of the community of St. Vrains, but it is virtually impossible to define the limits of the once historic settlement.

CHAPTER IX

CON TOWNS

Town promotion was a big thing in the Old West. And it didn't always involve the railroads, mining and other "normal" ventures. There were many capricious motives for town promotion. To make a quick buck was an important one.

GREEN CITY (Greensboro, Old Corona)

(Weld County)

There were many town promoters in early Colorado. Then there was Colonel David S. Green.

Green, originally from New York and a latecomer to Denver City, bought up hundreds of acres of government land along Platte River bottom 25 to 30 miles downstream from the current site of Greeley. He got it for $1.25 an acre.

On this land he laid out an elaborate metropolis of some 5600 lots on nearly 250 blocks, including an abundance of sites for schools, churches, businesses,

and just about everything else a "big city" would need.

Then he began advertising his concoction in newspapers throughout the eastern U.S., particularly in the South and Midwest. Aye, there's the rub! His advertisements were something to behold. They showed many commodious, well-built homes, most of them two stories high. The ads showed churches and schools and thriving businesses. Most of all they showed plush grasses, and towering shade trees along a wide and beautiful river. One ad showed a large steamboat docking at a pier at what was presumed to be the thriving metropolis of Green City.

The ads offered lots for "as little as" $150 to $200 each, two-story homes already in place, and irrigation promised—although the land was so fertile, additional water was just an extra benefit.

The ads were sufficient to stir the dreams of many a work-weary family. The Southwestern Colony was founded in Memphis, Tennessee, with D. S. Green as its president. About 100 families, primarily from Tennessee, Kentucky, Ohio, Indiana, and Illinois, sold their homes and most of their belongings and headed West. Another 100 families followed during the summer,

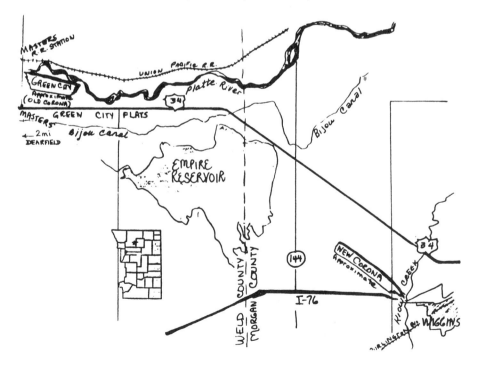

before the original settlers were able to get back and tell them the truth.

What they found in Colorado was a far cry from what was pictured in the ads. There were only 15 to 20 homes built, as cheaply as they could be and only one room each. Yes, there were a few two-story houses, with one room on each floor. The lush farmland promised turned out to be gravelly alkaline soil, too dry and thin to cultivate anything. There was a hasty attempt to build irrigation ditches, but the water soaked into the gravel before it could be used.

Some families had brought heavy stump removers across the prairie to clear the forests on their land. No need. There wasn't a tree within miles. In fact, the first logs to build the first homes in Green City were floated down the river from Greeley.

It is said that they even tried to bring supplies to the new settlement by riverboat. A boat—a much smaller one than the one depicted in the advertisements—headed downstream from Denver loaded with needed supplies. Interest ran so high in the project that most of the citizens of Green City headed down the banks of the river on horseback or on foot to meet it. A few miles before reaching Green City the boat hit a sandbank and tipped over, spilling all of its goods and the three-man crew.

By 1872 the greatly disappointed settlers had had enough. They voted to oust Green as president of the colony. It is said that Green had made a quick $60,000 on the exchange of land. He had no talent for farming anyhow.

The settlers reorganized, and renamed their community CORONA. They worked hard and tried to make the best of a bad situation. But they couldn't overcome the handicaps of the location. They suffered another blow when the promised railroad passed it by. A handful stuck it out through the 1870s and early '80s. The post office was discontinued in 1878.

A homesteader with a sample of his melons raised without irrigation in Lincoln County, Colorado

Two Grandsons of W. S. Pershing feasting on melons raised without irrigation

These are typical of the post cards, posters and other promotional material that saturated eastern and midwestern states boosting dry land farming in eastern Colorado. (*Photos courtesy Mrs. Jack Owen, Karval*)

In September of 1888, NEW CORONA was platted about eight miles southeast of the old site, on the Burlington Railroad.

The original town of GREEN CITY, or GREENSBORO, had been long forgotten. The bad dream was over.

BULGER CITY

(Larimer)

BULGER CITY was a one-man promotion. Col. James C. Bulger wanted to build an illustrious city. He wanted it to be named after him, and he wanted to be just about every official in it.

In the first years of this century he found what he considered an ideal location, about 5 miles north of Wellington, 15 north northeast of Fort Collins, in Larimer County. He laid out an elaborate townsite, organized and made himself president of the Bulger Land and Livestock Company, and got himself designated postmaster, deputy sheriff and district agent for "all kinds of insurance."

Although he was impulsive, erratic and egotistical, he apparently was also persuasive. He lured some commercial types here and a couple of dozen families or so. According to Don and Jean Griswold's *Colorado's Century of Cities*, the hopeful individuals included Edward Combs, assistant postmaster; B. Duran, hotel keeper; Henry Garrett, blacksmith; A. Wilson, general merchant; William Hall, livery and feed store owner; E. D. Wilson, well digger; and Walston and Gloser, farm equipment.

But according to the Griswolds the town didn't grow very fast, probably because of Bulger's reputation as a hard-drinking, quick-tempered man. Bulger himself got discouraged when fire destroyed his property. He moved on to bigger and better things, such as organizing a regiment of Spanish-American veterans, to be battle-ready in case the Mexicans gave the United States any trouble. A short time later his hard drinking and quick temper got him into an argument where he shot and killed a man. He was sentenced to the Colorado State Penitentiary, where in 1916 he was committed to the insane ward.

The other residents of BULGER CITY had long since moved on to other things too.

SCHRAMM

(Yuma County)

SCHRAMM was a short ego trip east of Yuma.

Dr. (not medical) Raimon Von Herron (Horum) Schramm, a rich, highly educated German of noble descent, moved to Yuma from New York by way of Texas. He had originally planned to start a new life in Hyde, Colorado. But when the railroad stopped at Yuma, he decided to cast his lot at this sleepy little site. And he had a lot to cast. This was 1887.

It is estimated that he quickly invested some $50,000 in land and construction in and around Yuma. Within a short time he had built three two-story buildings on the main street as well as other lesser buildings. They were constructed of brick, from Schramm's own brickyard at the edge of town. The first building was completed in 1888, and there was a grand opening to signal new life in the small community. In the years to come Schramm's buildings housed much of the commercal activity of Yuma, including a bank. He built a hotel and a building called the Stock Exchange, which was really a department store.

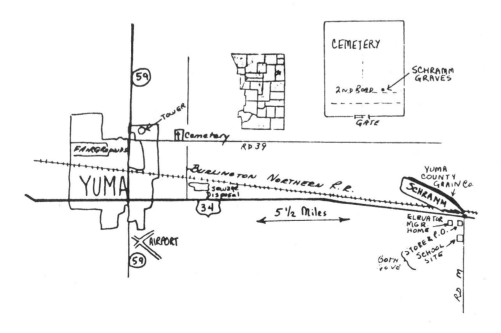

A family crest said to stem from German nobility decorates the Schramm headstone in the Yuma cemetery.

The grain elevator at left, built in 1918, and the remains of the manager's house across the highway (*see below*) are the only buildings still standing from the old town of Schramm.

At the site of Schramm today are modern grain elevators (*below*), with the former manager's house. The general store and post office building was on the corner to the right of the house, and the Schramm school was located along this road, toward the foreground of the photograph.

Schramm definitely perked up the little community. All he wanted in return was a little appreciation. He considered himself the town father, and he wanted to make it official. He wanted to be burgermeister, or mayor.

Yuma-ites didn't mind all what Schramm did for the town, but they didn't want a "foreigner" as their mayor. Schramm let it be known that if he wasn't so elected he would move all of his buildings elsewhere and begin another "city" that would put Yuma out of business. Yuma-ites wouldn't be threatened.

So, Herr Schramm purchased a tract of land along the railroad track about six miles east of Yuma. He got the Burlington Railroad to put a siding there. Then Schramm began to move a couple of his smaller Yuma buildings on flatcars to the new site, and made preparations to dismantle the larger buildings for removal also. He called the new site SCHRAMM, and began construction of a modern ranch nearby.

Yuma town leaders called an emergency meeting. Darned if they didn't elect Schramm Burgermeister of Yuma.

The town of Schramm didn't collapse, however. It lingered for many years. In fact, it is still shown on some outdated maps. It was a farm and ranch center and shipping point. Herr Schramm wasn't an absentee owner of his town. Being mayor of Yuma wasn't all that time-consuming. He spent much time at his ranch at SCHRAMM when he wanted to get away from the rigors of public office.

Many people left the area during the mid-1890s, due to prolonged drought and grasshoppers, and the panic of 1893. However, Schramm remained to look after his interests, and the interests of his neighbors. He was the benefactor of many people and saw them through the difficult period when they might otherwise have joined the migration.

Many residents in the region are descendants of those who stayed, thanks to the beneficence of Burgermeister Schramm. The brick buildings on main street in Yuma, still in use, are further monuments to the man. Some of the buildings in the little town he created along the tracks were used for other purposes in later years, and others were torn down. The site is now ranch land, although it is said some foundations of his buildings can still be seen.

The town of Schramm also had a school, a few stores and a post office, which was discontinued in 1927. Two grain elevators are all that stand today.

The last few years of Schramm's life were not happy ones. He was sick much of the time. Much of his fortune faded and his "dreams of empire" faded with it. He died in 1907, and his wife Mary in 1916. They are buried side by side in the Yuma cemetery. His noble background is shown on the crest that adorns his marker . . . and in the brick buildings still standing on the main street of Yuma.

SHERIDAN LAKE
(Kiowa County)

SHERIDAN LAKE is still a living town in eastern Kiowa County, near Kansas. It's a pleasant place for its some 765 residents, and the colorful lake attracts others during duck and fishing seasons.

But this town is one of the better examples in eastern Colorado of how far town promoters went in the old days. It was built on a lie—and a buffalo wallow.

Sheridan Lake like, TOWNER (see "Tragedy Towns"), a short distance away, is an exception to the naming of towns along the "ABC Railroad." A place very near this site was named Arden, as the first town inside Colorado along the railroad (which became the Missouri–Pacific) to be named alphabetically by Jessie Mallory Thayer, daughter of the president of the railroad's town company.

Even before the railroad entered Colorado, town promoters bought up a lot of marshland along the anticipated route. They incorporated the Sheridan Town Company, created an elaborate town plat and began selling lots—"at reasonable prices."

However, since the railroad did not own the property, officials intended to bypass the Sheridan site and lay out their own town, Arden, about three miles farther on.

The Sheridan Lake town promoters did not give up easily. They hired Homer Norris, colorful editor of *The Granada Exponent*, to sing the many benefits of the Sheridan Lake site. Through his imaginative prose, the buffalo wallow became a "beautiful lake," named for one of the great heroes of the day, General Phil Sheridan—because this was, the promoters said, General Sheridan's most favorite camping spot in all of eastern Colorado.

General Sheridan did lead troops through eastern Colorado and was said to have made one of his many camps in the state near this site. This site may have been a handy camping site, but one doubts that the great military man would classify a buffalo swamp in the far isolated plains of nowhereland as his favorite campsite, if he even remembered being there in the first place.

Some say Editor Norris never saw the site of Sheridan Lake, but he turned the trick. His stories lured some property buyers and eventually convinced the railroad that this would be a more appropriate site for a station than Arden.

The railroad moved its station, and Sheridan Lake became the first county seat of Kiowa County while Arden became only a railroad siding.

Of course, the town promoters dredged out the marshland and turned it into a couple of very presentable lakes. Some residents are even proud of the false premises upon which their community was founded.

CHAPTER X

IRON HORSE MURDERS

As the railroad was the mother of many towns and cities, so was it the cause of death to countless hopeful communities. The Iron Horse not only put the stage out of business and caused the downfall of many a stage station; it also indirectly or deliberately led to the early death of many other settlements.

The number of sites spurned by the railroads, or located badly by town promoters in anticipation of the railroad, seems endless. Countless communities were already in place when the railroad came, but the railroad saw no reason to go out of its way to honor an established settlement. Indeed, many a community which desired to latch onto the railroad had to pick itself up bodily and move to trackside to compete with new settlements.

Also, the route of a projected line was not always certain until it was actually built. And even then it sometimes was changed, with the discovery of a better water source, a better river crossing, flatter ground for

a station, etc. In some cases the railroad purposely went around a new site or straight through it without stopping, because the town promoters picked a bad location, planned too close to a better town, or just drove too hard a bargain with the railroad.

The following are just a few of the many towns born with the railroad in mind but done in because the railroad, for one reason or another, didn't cooperate with its dreams of growth.

BLACKWELL (West Farm)
(Prowers County)

A.R. Black had a ranch along the Pueblo & Arkansas Valley Railroad (which became the AT&SF in 1900). It was natural to have a station here. The frame 14 by 16 depot was located on what was known as WEST FARM, but

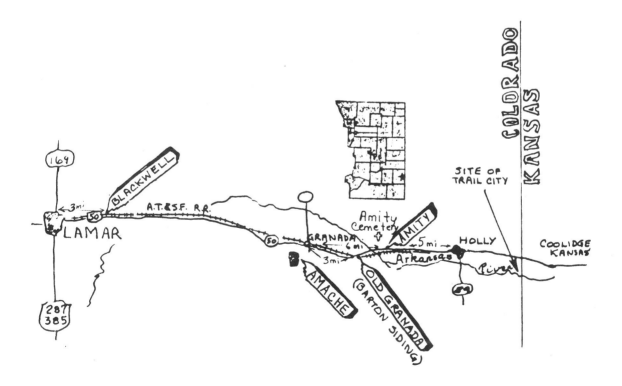

the tiny community at the site was named Blackwell. About the only things in the "tiny community" was what the railroad put there: the depot, a section house, stockyards, water tank, fences and a couple of storage buildings. But it was enough, apparently, to give Black visions of empire.

When a "more complete town" at a better station site was started about three miles west along the track, the railroad made plans to move its Blackwell facilities to the new location.

Black still had high hopes for his site, and threatened to enjoin the railroad from moving out.

So on May 22, Black received a telegram calling him to Pueblo, presumably on urgent business. Within hours after Black had left, railroad workers from up and down the line converged on the site known as Blackwell. It took them about 20 hours to completely dismantle the facilities there, load them on flatcars and take them to the new site. When Black returned from Pueblo he was completely stunned to see that the potentially "great city" of Blackwell was nothing but prairieland. He threatened all matter of action, but there was nothing he could do about it; the railroad took only what was its own.

The date—May 24, 1886—marked the final, sudden end of Blackwell and the "official" beginning of the important railroad city of Lamar, named after the then U.S. Secretary of Interior.

During the Centennial–Bicentennial celebration in 1976, local citizens re-enacted the May 24, 1886, incident. Some want it to become an annual event.

Kit Carson County Capers
Involving: Beloit, Bowser-Malowe, Carlisle, Crystal Springs and Oranola (Columbia)

As an example of just how extensive town promotion could be in anticipation of a railroad line, we can take just one Colorado county and the anticipation of just one railroad: Kit Carson County and the Chicago, Rock Island & Pacific Railroad originally named the Chicago, Kansas & Nebraska; the capers began when it entered Colorado from Kansas in 1886.

BELOIT
(Kit Carson County)

Of the many towns promoted in anticipation of the coming of the Iron Horse, Beloit was probably among the biggest, with the biggest promotion and the biggest error in anticipating the route of the projected railroad.

In the mid-1880s, when the Chicago, Kansas & Nebraska Railroad (which became the Chicago, Rock Is-

land & Pacific in 1891) planned an extension of their line into Colorado, entering Kit Carson County, town promoters wasted no time in planning for the "biggest" metropolis in eastern Colorado along the railroad. The Beloit Town Site and Land Company was organized. Posters and newspaper ads were circulated along the line in Kansas and Nebraska and elsewhere, boasting the benefits of the brand new town.

The promoters not only anticipated the new railroad but expected the site would be a junction interchange for tracks going to Pueblo and Colorado Springs.

Wells were dug and windmills and pumps installed. Sod and frame houses and buildings were constructed around a large city square with a hotel, saloon, general merchandise store, blacksmith.

The promotion did attract about 100 settlers. They discovered almost immediately that the railroad would miss the site by a full eight miles. Despite the disappointment, most of them hung on and attempted to make the most of a bad situation.

It was the drought and depression of 1893–94 that did them in. Beloit, "the metropolis of the prairies," was a ghost by 1895.

The site was located eight miles west and seven miles south of Burlington.

BOWSER-MALOWE (Flagler)
(Kit Carson County)

Before the Chicago, Kansas and Nebraska Railroad (which became the Chicago, Rock Island and Pacific in 1891) built through Kit Carson County, a tiny center near western county line had the unusual name of Bowser. It was named for the longtime pet dog of the storekeeper and postmistress, Mrs. Robinson. Other homesteaders convinced Mrs. Robinson to dignify the site by calling it Bowserville.

When the railroad came, it originally used Bowser or Bowserville as a stop. But the railroad soon found a good supply of underground water and springs a short distance west, and established a depot there. This was originally named Malowe, for M. A. Lowe, an attorney for the railroad. Malowe became a key cattle-shipping point.

The growing community was eventually renamed Flagler for Henry M. Flagler, a wealthy railroad man.

CARLISLE
(Kit Carson County)

Another townsite snubbed by the Chicago, Kansas & Nebraska Railroad (Rock Island) was Carlisle. It was even more of a snub than that given Beloit.

Carlisle was already established as a community, a

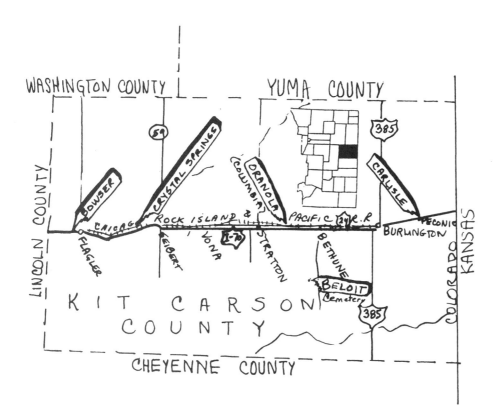

relatively thriving and growing town. It was the distribution center for goods brought into Colorado by the Kansas Pacific to the south and the Burlington to the north.

When word came in the mid-1880s that the new railroad was heading their way, Carlisle citizens planned a handsome new and larger town to greet it. A town plat containing 43 blocks was drawn up. A complete town was promised.

But the railroad missed the site by less than a mile. PECONIC or PECONIC SIDING, located between Burlington and the Kansas border, was made the station. Carlisle citizens moved everything to the new site.

CRYSTAL SPRINGS

(Kit Carson County)

Many promoters were disappointed by the projected route of the Rock Island (Chicago, Kansas & Nebraska) Railroad. There were many near-misses. One was CRYSTAL SPRINGS.

Stephen S. Strode selected a site about three miles west of present Seibert at a crossing of the South Fork of the Republican River.

He platted an elaborate town, 20 blocks, most of them 300 by 400 feet. The main street was 100 feet wide, the others 80 feet wide. He did everything to make the site enticing to the railroad. The streets running north

and south were named Chicago, Rock Island, Colorado and Railway. Streets running east and west were named Spring, Front, Second, Third, Fourth and Fifth.

Arch Cunningham joined Strode and got out the first issue of the *Crystal Springs Register* in July 4, 1888.

But little else happened in Crystal Springs after the railroad found a better crossing of the river about a half mile south. No lots were sold in 1889, and the townsite was abandoned by 1890.

ORANOLA *(Columbia)*

(Kit Carson County)

Another elaborate town promotion in Kit Carson County in an effort to woo the railroad was COLUMBIA.

Columbia was platted in May of 1888 by the Columbia Townsite Company on land homesteaded by David E. Scott. Several blocks were platted, 300 feet square. One block in the center of the plat was set aside as the "town square." Business lots 25 by 140 feet all faced the square. Streets were 100 or 110 feet wide.

A lumber and coal yard was built, as was a bank—just about everything prospective residents would need.

The first setback came from the post office department. It claimed that Columbia was too common a name in the West, and wasn't acceptable. So the name was changed to ORANOLA.

The second and more significant setback came when

the railroad favored a new townsite 3½ miles west, named STRATTON.

In 1880 the ORANOLA townsite and what little there was upon it was sold at sheriff's auction for taxes.

EAST LAS ANIMAS (Old Las Animas)

(Bent County)

In anticipation of the approach of the railroad LAS ANIMAS was founded opposite Fort Lyons on the Arkansas. The first county commissioners of Bent County met here March 12, 1870. In 1873, C. W. Bowman brought a printing press to town, and on May 23 he published the first issue of *The Las Animas Leader*.

A short time later, however, the Pueblo & Arkansas Valley Railroad (later the AT&SF) built through here and completely snubbed Las Animas, selecting a site about four miles on down the line. Since there was already a Las Animas, the new community was originally named WEST LAS ANIMAS. But in 1875 the county seat was moved to the new town, the "West" was dropped from the post office name, and OLD LAS ANIMAS became EAST LAS ANIMAS. Bowman moved his press to the new town and most of the other commercial enterprises soon followed.

But East Las Animas didn't die completely for several years. It was still listed, just listed, in an 1898 Directory.

JOYCOY

Unlike most other "Iron Horse Murders," JOYCOY was not a boo-boo by town promoters. The railroad itself pulled this boner.

In 1926 the AT&SF Railroad laid out a town in Baca County, an "ideal community" near the center of things. Lots were offered at attractive prices and additional inducements were offered to businesses, not the least of which was a railroad spur from Springfield.

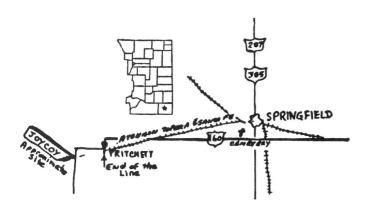

Ruins of Charles Campbell store (six miles north and west of Pritchett, 18 miles due west of Springfield), which was somewhat north of the onetime town of Joycoy. The Model T Ford was used as school bus as well as delivery truck.

They named the site JOYCOY, a delightful name that no one today seems to know the source of.

The railroad set out to carry out its promises, laying track southwestward from Springfield. When it was three or four miles short and Joycoy lots still were not selling, the railroad decided it would stop laying track and set up a town at the end of the track already built, naming it PRITCHETT in honor of a railroad official.

LESLIE

LESLIE was further along than most other towns established in anticipation of a planned railroad line. In fact, it was already considered a coming "city of the plains" before the big disappointment came.

It sprung up on the Washington–Yuma County Line, about two miles south of Logan County, along the projected Burlington spur between Holyoke and Akron.

The railroad even dug a well to make sure the site was feasible for railroad purposes.

The town site was surveyed by A. B. Smith on June 4, 1888, platted October 29, 1888, and filed on two weeks later.

It became a bustling community from the start. Several homes were built and more were being built, as were several business establishments. A weekly newspaper, appropriately called *The Cactus*, began publication. A school and a church went up, and became centers not only for the new settlers but for a large farm neighborhood.

But after several months of promises, rumors and

growing fears the official word came that the spur was not to be built after all.

Several still-hopeful residents joined together in the attempt to make their community permanent despite the lack of a railroad. But many more were realistic about it and moved away. The newspaper ceased publication in 1892, and the post office was closed shortly thereafter.

It remained a tiny farm center for a few more years. It is a complete ghost town today, located on farmland; some former residents erected a marker at the site a few years ago.

TROY*

(Las Animas County)

It is not clear today whether TROY was established in anticipation of the railroad or was already in place and attempted to woo the railroad to pass through the site.

In either case, the 1888 Business Directory said Troy was "new and growing" on the "proposed Denver, Texas & Fort Worth Railway." Already the town had 300 residents and some 20 business listings, including the Troy Hotel and a weekly newspaper, *The Troy Settler*, published by the Weeden brothers.

The promise of a railroad must have been strong since the 1890 Directory said Troy was "on" the DT&FW railroad. This may have been a branch line that was never built. Otherwise, the DT&FW or any other railroad never came close to Troy. There was good reason. Troy was located in eastern Las Animas County, with the closest point also in the middle of nowhere.

Even without a railroad, Troy lingered on for decades. It added a school and had a post office for many years. In 1910 it still boasted a population of 125. It didn't have a railroad but it had a regular stage from Folson, New Mexico.

It remains a rural site on the map today, with no post office (mail to Kim), no population, and no railroad. The last Troy Post Office closed in 1942.

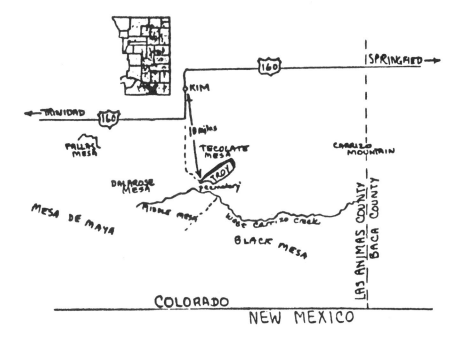

CHAPTER XI

DROWNED TOWNS

There is an elite fraternity of Colorado towns that have completely disappeared from the scene because of the unquenchable thirst of Coloradans and the land upon which they live. In the semi-arid state, water is more precious than gold. Snowpack from Colorado's high mountains provides much of the staff of life for a dozen states around. Fortunately, Colorado was able to hold a portion of it back for its own use.

Most or many of those natural bowls to trap the water were once sites for towns of every purpose.

Ghost-towners are familiar with some of the mountain mining towns buried by reservoirs—much as MONTGOMERY, at the foot of Mt. Lincoln in South Park, now covered with the waters behind Montgomery Dam, part of the Colorado Springs water system; and DORA (Gove), buried by the DeWeese Reservoir, north of Westcliffe in Custer County.

There are other Drowned Towns throughout the state, many lost to us only in recent years.

OLD CADDOA (*Caddo*)
(Bent County)

This historic Colorado town is buried under the waters of a reservoir—when it has water. It is named for its first and more temporary residents, the Caddoa Indian tribe. The small tribe was displaced during the Civil War, an unusual case. They found themselves in Texas, but sympathetic to the Union cause and vulnerable to Southern harrassment.

They sought asylum in the north. The northern officials selected this site along the Arkansas River, not far from FORT WISE (Fort Lyon). The government built three stone buildings to be used as tribe headquarters. They also promised the tribe protection and any other assistance within reason.

It is not certain whether the entire tribe or only several members came to spend the winter of 1863–64

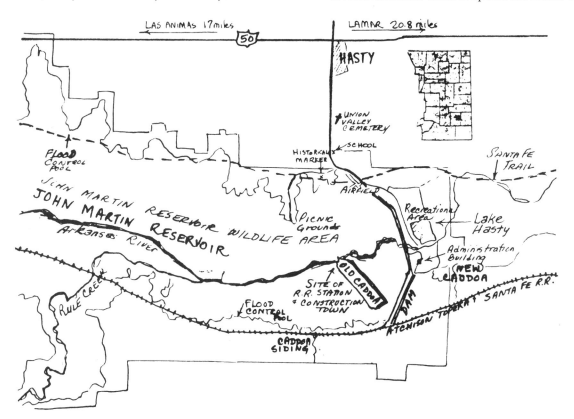

130

Its street overgrown with sage, the site of the town of Caddoa stands below John Martin Dam. The large fish on the front of the remaining building indicates that the owner might have dreamed of selling bait and tack to hordes of fishermen. However, John Martin dam seldom holds water, having been built strictly for flood control. (*Photo courtesy Bureau of Reclamation, U.S. Dept. of Interior.*)

here, but during that one season they decided to reject the site. The tribe found another location further south in New Mexico along the banks of the Canadian River.

The name CADDOA has remained to this day, named for the tribe that spent so little time here. It is said that the word has meaning in other Indian languages. It means sacred "Sun Dance" in Kiowa and Comanche. The name has often been misspelled and/or mispronounced over the years as CADDO.

Before the Indian settlement John Prowers had already, since about 1861, begun running cattle in this region. He has been called the "father of the cattle industry in Colorado" (see BOGGSVILLE, "Very Special Places"). Prowers was probably the first to run Herefords in Colorado, to crossbreed cattle and improve the stock. He furnished beef for the army at Fort Wise and elsewhere. It was considered the best beef one could find.

When the Caddoa Indians went south and left Colorado, Prowers took over that land and used the buildings built for the Indians as his headquarters.

Prowers had married Amache, an Indian princess who was daughter of Chief One Eye. He could speak several Indian languages and was often in demand as an interpretor. He was one of the very few friends the Indians had. It was about this time that "friendly" Indians were granted rights to live "in peace" on a hunk of land in east-central Colorado at Sand Creek. Prowers' father-in-law, Chief One Eye, went there with hundreds of other Indians, primarily Arapahoe and Cheyenne.

Apparently John Prowers' relations with the Indians were known far and wide. It is said the Prowers was put under guard when Colonel John Chivington brought his troops here for a surprise raid on the Indians at Sand Creek. The massacre is well known today. Colonel Chivington and his Colorado Volunteers slaughtered from 200 to more than 600 Indians—men, women, and children. One of those killed was Chief One Eye, Prowers' father-in-law.

Following the Sand Creek Massacre, Prowers became most vocal in protesting the deed. He went to Washington to testify on behalf of the Indians. The matter was investigated, but Colonel Chivington was never tried by a court martial.

What did happen was that the surviving Indians or relatives of those killed at Sand Creek were given in reparation 160 acres of land, primarily along the Arkansas. However, the Indians were nomads, not prepared to settle on the land. They sold their land and moved on. Many or most of the Indians sold their land to John Prowers.

With all the things said about the young Prowers, this easy and cheap purchase of land may be questioned. One answer could be that Prowers was there, already a large landowner and running cattle here. If he didn't buy the land someone else would. Before long Prowers was the largest landowner in southern Colorado, possibly in all of Colorado. (This was before John Iliff's rise to power in the northeast.) Prowers also ran more cattle than anyone, some say up to 50,000 head.

OLD CADDOA next attracted attention in 1873 when it became a railhead for the construction of the railroad, the forerunner of the Santa Fe. It was the usual wild construction town one always found at the railhead during construction. The excitement lasted for about two years before the railhead moved on to West Las Animas (the new Las Animas).

Old Caddoa all but disappeared again, remaining just a small station on the railroad, a shipping point.

The site burst forth again in 1887 when three brothers, Fred, Carl and George Trostle organized the Caddoa Land and Town Company (reorganized shortly thereafter as the Caddoa Land and Investment Company). They surveyed and platted an elaborate townsite around the tiny Caddoa station.

Despite the elaborate plans, however, very little of "the new Caddoa" was built. The brothers did not sell many lots. After a few months the company went broke. Only a few new buildings were added to the station facilities.

The final invasion was around 1939–40, when the U.S. Corps of Engineers moved in construction crews to build a high earthen dam, originally to be called Caddoa Dam and Reservoir but eventually named the John Martin Dam and Reservoir.

When this final major boom of the site came, Caddoa had a stockyards, two saloons, a few other buildings, and a tiny cemetery that hadn't had any new "residents" for several years. The little town, which was located just below where the dam would be, was hardly ready for the nearly 1000 workers who arrived. Makeshift frame buildings were built overnight. Dozens of trailers moved in and tents went up. Old Caddoa hadn't seen such industry since the railroad construction days. But with all the temporary buildings, it was obvious there was no tomorrow.

The only thing worth moving was the tiny cemetery. There were only seven bodies buried there, and they were buried so long ago—the last person in the 1890s. The few remains were carefully reburied in the southeast corner of the Hasty cemetery, about four miles to the north.

The dam was scheduled to be completed in mid-1942. Its water would cover the site of OLD CADDOA. In 1941, plans began for a "new city" just above the dam.

The NEW CADDOA had an elaborate plat also. It would be a great new resort town, where people could come and enjoy the beautiful large lake on the prairie. It never became the "grand resort" as planned. Several people still live in Caddoa. Sometimes they and others enjoy fishing and other recreational activities in the reservoir. However, frequently the water is too low or almost gone, due to drought and the need for its water elsewhere. Some years the water is so low that hundreds of thousands of fish have died.

OLD CADDOA had many lives, none of them very long-lasting or profitable. Maybe the Indians knew what they were doing so many moons ago when they left the place, only their name remaining.

SWALLOWS and TAYLORSVILLE
(Pueblo County)

These two towns were inseparable, but they never really got together in their lifetimes. Now they are together, finally, in death.

The two sites were directly across the Arkansas River from each other, about fifteen miles west of Pueblo. In the early 1970s when the Bureau of Reclamation built a dam across the Arkansas the few remaining buildings in SWALLOWS and TAYLORSVILLE were bulldozed to the ground. The dam began taking water about January 1, 1974. The huge conservation pool backed up and buried these longtime neighbors. The river long kept them apart; now it has brought them together.

Actually, most of the story is about SWALLOWS. There were scattered farm and ranch operations, as well as other activities, throughout the valley, but Swallows was *the* community. Probably the main reason Taylorsville had a separate name in the first place was that the first post office here, in 1878, was in the ranch house of Daniel Taylor. That's where the post office was much of the time over the years.

The two towns traded. At times both Swallows and Taylorsville had post offices. Taylorsville had the first school in 1877, a few years before Swallows did. When they both had schools, local youngsters would attend

This old stone and log building—an example of "add-on" architecture—survived the clearing of the Swallows area because it sits above the valley flooded by the Pueblo Reservoir.

The Bureau of Reclamation photographed these abandoned buildings in the area cleared for the Pueblo dam and reservoir. Above, the former Swallow schoolhouse, and at left, the remains of sheds and a building in the Sawmill area. Below, what's left of a masonry house and a 20-unit farrowing unit on the former Honor Farm.

different grade levels in the two schools. At other times the youngsters would attend one school certain months of the years and the other one other months.

The Santa Fe Railroad built on the north side of the river, the Taylorsville side, so it had a Santa Fe depot. There was a D&RG depot on the Swallows side of the river. Various bridges have crossed the Arkansas between the two communities over the years. There was a rickety foot bridge used in recent years until it was washed out.

Local residents and even writers and historians have tended to ignore Taylorsville, and call the whole site Swallows. Even Bureau of Reclamation officials who gave the author a day-long tour of the site in 1972 didn't mention Taylorsville. The tour included all the remaining buildings and ruins (now disappeared). A couple that were identifiable were a depot platform, a large cistern nearby, and the roofless ruins of a school. They called them the Swallows depot and school, although it wasn't until I became more familiar with the subject that I realized they were both on the Taylorsville side of the River.

Swallows was believed named for the birds seen nesting in bluffs surrounding the valley. A less believable source for the name was first published by George Crofutt in his 1881 Gripsack Guide and has been repeated many times since. The story goes that two stagers sought the affection of the same Indian lovely. When one won out the other made a vile statement regarding her character. They fought, and according to Crofutt,

" . . . one of them swallowed it. Guess which one? Continued in our next. . . . " That Crofutt was some tease.

In addition to the swallows overhead, the bluffs tell us that the Indians were no strangers to the area. Some crude pictographs and petroglyths and artifacts of varying vintage have been found here.

The first white men settled in the valley in the middle and late 1860s. Among them were the Richie brothers, who settled at the mouth of Rush Creek, the first site of Swallows. Another early settler was A. D. Hamlin, who brought a small herd of cattle with him from Texas and settled near the mouth of Turkey Creek. He set aside a part of his land for a family burial plot. As he prospered he enlarged the plot into a community cemetery, the Turkey Creek graveyard.

Most everyone prospered in the lush bottom land. Prosperity seemed limitless in the early 1870s when the railroads came, rushing westward to tap the endless wealth of the Colorado mountains. They greatly enriched the towns along the way.

Life was good in the green valley. Railroad activity enlivened the good life. The day-to-day news of the two railroads in the "Royal Gorge War" up the line was especially exciting. Many deep emotions surfaced in March of 1906 when the tragic head-on crash at blind Adobe Curve up the track killed more than 35. It happened because the young telegraph operator at Swallows fell asleep at the switch.

There was prospecting around Swallows over the years. They also looked for some coal, but nothing of a paying nature was ever reported. However, there was quite a bit of rock quarrying done nearby. There were small quarry firms. The largest, most active one was the Turkey Creek Stone Company that incorporated around the turn of the century, and shipped quite a bit of stone during the early 1900s.

Many blamed the demise of Swallows on the flood in 1921. It no doubt hastened the end. But close-knit farm communities were on their way out throughout Colorado and elsewhere. With better transportation and technology, it was just about as fast and as cheap, if not cheaper, to fill one's needs in Pueblo than at the little store on Main Street. And it was a whole lot more exciting.

However, Swallows–Taylorsville was still a plush, well–adjusted farm valley in June of 1921. It had had high water before that caused some problems, but nothing in the past prepared them for June 5, 1921. People who measure disasters would call it a "hundred year flood"—a flood of such intensity that it only happens on the average of once every hundred years. The torrent crest roared down the Arkansas, down, over and through the plush, green valley, washing away everything that wasn't anchored down and many things that were. What would be known to future generations as "the Great Pueblo Flood" left Swallows reeling.

Fortunately, the right people weren't asleep at the switch this time. Sufficient warning prevented loss of life.

They returned to what had been their homes. They salvaged what they could. Many rebuilt. Some cleared the land and continued to farm, but moved to Pueblo and commuted. Very few sold out.

But Swallows' days as a self-contained community were over. The post office was closed in 1947 and the school about the same time.

There were still many farm and other buildings in the valley in the late 1960s and the early '70s when the plans for the Pueblo dam were started and implemented. The Bureau of Reclamation moved slowly in acquiring the property and relocating the property owners. Many of the latter disliked leaving the green valley, and rightfully so, but there were no major problems. The buildings were leveled or moved one by one as the residents moved. When the waters came the only thing left of Swallows was its cemetery, which had been established on a hill above the community. The Turkey Creek Cemetery, begun so many years ago, would have been covered by water, so its graves were carefully relocated in the Swallows Cemetery, which still had plenty of room.

The Pueblo Dam and Reservoir is the largest facility

Pueblo Dam, which created a lake and a recreational area among the largest in the state of Colorado, has won many awards for its design. (*Bureau of Reclamation*)

in the giant Frying Pan–Arkansas Project. In fact, its 60 miles of shoreline makes it one of the largest man-made bodies of water in Colorado. The conservation pool will hold 357,000 acre-feet of water, although it is generally a shallow pool. The deepest spot is 90 feet, but most of it is no deeper than 25 feet.

The railroad tracks and major highways have been relocated above the water line. Many of the roads used in the construction of the dam have been preserved as access roads to the lake and dam.

The water comes from Turquoise and Twin Lakes on the Upper Arkansas. The multi-purpose dam provides Pueblo with water and flood control. And it provides Colorado with another major recreational facility and wildlife habitat. The recreational potential of the reservoir is endless. Countless events have been held here in the first years of its opening, including the International Speedboat Races in 1976.

The land around the dam and reservoir is blooming with new development, stark contrast to the longtime sleepy atmosphere of SWALLOWS and TAYLORSVILLE.

Before the Chatfield Dam
(Douglas County)

One of the first settlements in the Denver Metropolitan region was on or very near land now covered by the Chatfield Dam site. A journal of an early gold-seeking party tells of camping during the winter of 1858–59 at the confluence of Plum Creek and the South Platte. They named the camp PIKE'S PEAK CITY, but although the journal said that 38 cabins were built for the 82 persons in the prospecting party, they apparently did not intend to stay very long. As soon as the weather broke the following spring, the party headed for the mountains and abandoned their little camp.

A short time later a stage station on the run between Denver and Colorado City was established near the same site. It had two early names. One was ROUND CORRAL for the large peculiar-shaped corral at the station. The more permanent name was PLUM CREEK STATION or just PLUM CREEK.

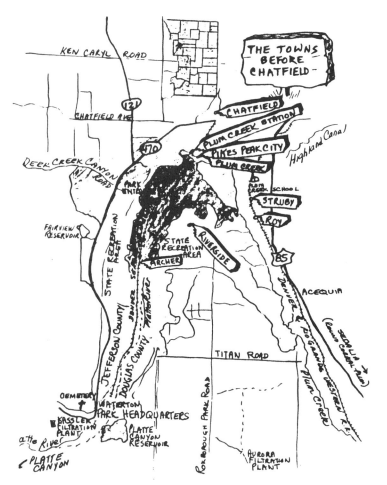

THE TOWNS BEFORE CHATFIELD

KEN CARYL ROAD

CHATFIELD AVE

(121)

(470)

DEER CREEK CANYON ROAD

FAIRVIEW RESERVOIR

CHATFIELD

PLUM CREEK STATION

PIKES PEAK CITY

PLUM CREEK

Highland Canal

SCHOOL

STRUBY

ROY

(85)

ACEQUIA

SEDALIA (Santa Fe →)

Denver & Rio Grande Western R.R.

PARK ENTER

STATE RECREATION AREA

STATE RECREATION AREA

ARCHER

RIVERSIDE

JEFFERSON COUNTY

DOUGLAS COUNTY

DENVER SOUTH PARK P. PACIFIC

TITAN ROAD

ROXBOROUGH PARK ROAD

Plum Creek

CEMETERY

WATERTON PARK HEADQUARTERS

KASSLER FILTRATION PLANT

at the River

PLATTE CANYON

PLATTE CANYON RESERVOIR

AURORA FILTRATION PLANT

The site was the scene of a major massacre during the Indian Wars of 1864–65. A letter from a traveler, dated November 27, 1864, told of coming upon the station to find survivors burying victims of an Indian attack. A party of about 80 Indians had attacked the station and a greater number of whites. The surprise attack had its effect. Seventeen defenders were killed, and only two persons escaped unscathed. There had been Indian attacks before, one in October of the same year, and there were others nearby later.

When the Denver & Rio Grande Railroad built southward from Denver in the early 1870s, a railroad station replaced the stage station. It retained the name PLUM CREEK (or PLUM CREEK STATION or just PLUM).

Glowing reports in the mid-1870s claimed that the rich agricultural and ranch land in the region "renders this station one of the best shipping points anywhere on the line."

Plum Creek was named after the wild plums found along the creek. It was shortly after the railroad station was established and a new town flourished that the site was renamed by a prominent settler for his hometown in Missouri, SEDALIA.

Another small station along the railroad was located about two and a half miles south southeast of Sedalia along both the Denver & Rio Grande and the Santa Fe; it was originally named ORSA and later named KING.

The name for the dam was prompted by another small farm shipping station which was named for Isaac W. Chatfield, a contractor for the railroad. CHATFIELD STATION was established in 1885 along the Denver, South Park & Pacific, which passed a short distance

Sugar beet dump was moved to Chatfield Station on the Colorado & Southern Railroad in 1939, after a third rail was added to the narrow gauge line from Denver to accommodate the sugar beet business. (*Littleton Historical Museum, Littleton CO*)

northwest of the later dam site. It was also surrounded by lush farmlands, and the station shipped a great deal of farm produce, most of it to Denver.

A dam on the river had been recommended as early as 1912. It was finally approved by Congress in 1950, but it wasn't until the disastrous flood of June 16, 1965, which did nearly a half-billion dollars property damage in the Denver Metropolitan area, that the project was finally funded and begun. The dam was closed in August of 1973 by then Vice President Spiro Agnew. This is one of the first dams in the nation where recreation and nature study areas and facilities were planned into the project, with the planning assistance of local citizens.

SOPRIS (Carpiosas, Sopris Plaza) and PIEDMONT, ST. THOMAS, JERRYVILLE

(Las Animas County)

A lot of chronology and facts and figures go into recounting the history of a town, particularly a ghost town—in an effort to preserve something real of something that is no more.

Cold facts and figures don't seem to fit SOPRIS. Sopris is an emotional thing. It's inexplicable. The author has only spent a few days there—before and after its final death. He has visited and studied hundreds, thousands, of ghost towns. They were all different. But Sopris came through strong. It had a personality different from any other. In its final days it had a vitality, even while being raped and humiliated. It had fallen on hard, deathly times. But it was still proud and colorful.

There was the emotion of seeing a good town, a once-proud town, a once youthful, once hopeful town die. One remembers the basketball hoop (with some strings attached) on the garage behind a broken house, and the worn "basketball court" amid the weeds below. There was the tricycle, well worn and rusted. And there were the homes, brightly painted inside and out, some even in psychedelic colors.

Sopris citizens had, not long before, not only displayed a happy, carefree face to the outside world but lived that way day to day. The paint wasn't faded or weather-worn, even though it was known for years that the end was coming. They kept it bright in Sopris, to the end.

Facts and figures are essential to history, although they don't feed the hopeful man, or satisfy his needs or emotions. But with Sopris, as with any ordinary town, facts and figures are the easiest thing to write about.

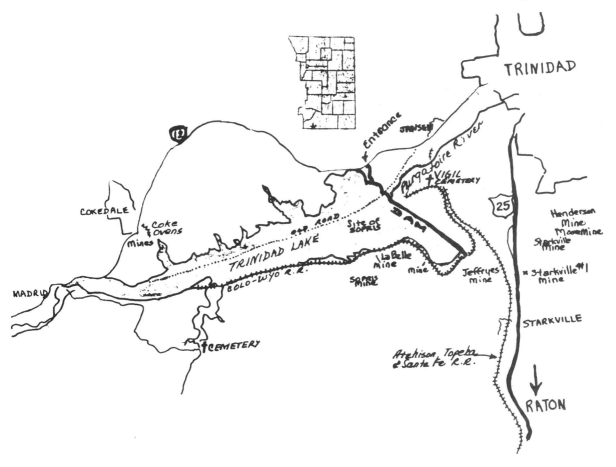

A kindergarten class at the Sopris coal camp. (*Pueblo Library District*)

Many Mexican (or New Mexican, Spanish American, or Hispanic, take your choice) families lived in the vicinity from around 1860 (maybe before) until the 1880s. Their little community, or plaza, was called CAR-PIOSAS.

In 1887 General Elbridge B. Sopris, onetime Indian fighter and leader of the Colorado Volunteers, promoted a coal town here on land that he had acquired over the years. Some sources say his community was originally called SOPRIS PLAZA, in deference to the original inhabitants. But it was soon called just SOPRIS.

Many of the first employees in the mines were Mexicans, but as the mining increased Italians were imported and soon dominated the scene. The Sopris Mine was the largest producer here and soon became the primary producer in Las Animas County. During its best years Sopris shipped an average of 1500 tons of good coal per day. Construction of 400 coke ovens, beginning in 1888, further boosted the economy.

At its peak nearly 2000 souls lived in Sopris. It was usually the second largest city in Las Animas County, second only to Trinidad. The coal production and the population would be shown as considerably higher if one included the nearby mines and the satellite camps such as JANSEN, opposite Sopris on the highway, and PIEDMONT, ST. THOMAS and JERRYVILLE.

Those, in greatly compacted form, are the facts and figures regarding Sopris.

Facts and figures don't mention the bells that tolled from the old Catholic Church every Sunday morning, reminding the citizens of their Sabbath duty, or at other times to signal a death or celebrate a special occasion. Nor does it mention the countless confirmations and spotless suits and dresses; the many festive high school dances and graduations; the rabid support of the athletic teams. Point out that 90 percent of the Sopris youngsters graduated from high school, and that a most disproportionate number—for a coal town—of those youngsters went on to college. Mention somewhere that the Sopris high school had one of the first adult education programs in the state. Immigrant parents wanted to fit in, to be good citizens, and set a good example for their youngsters.

In addition to the intense interests in sports and education, and the countless social events, Sopris was noted for its home-made wine. It became almost competitive. Home recipes were treasured, guarded or traded. But the socials and the wine-making and drinking never got in the way of progress.

Tragedy helped bring the community together. A mine explosion in 1922 took 17 lives. In 1925 things looked quite bleak for awhile when the CF&I closed

In the last days of Sopris, people carted away everything that looked usable before the bulldozers came. In the background above, Fishers Peak overlooks the scene; at right, a rusted and abandoned tricycle is left to share the fate of the empty buildings.

operations. However, some mining continued on a smaller scale, on a lease by Jack Deldosso.

When breadwinners found work elsewhere, the families moved away. Some found work in the Allen Mine, for a long time the only operating mine in Las Animas County. Some found work in Trinidad, and commuted from Sopris. But jobs became much more difficult to come by throughout the area as more and more mines closed, and what had shortly before been one of the more prosperous areas in the state became the most depressed.

The population of Sopris fell off dramatically during the 1930s—Even more so after 1940, when Deldosso ceased operations.

Sopris became little more than a "waiting" or a "bedroom" community. Virtually all the employable men worked elsewhere or were forced to go on relief. But, despite everything, they were still proud. They didn't want to leave Sopris if they didn't have to. They held out hope and were as happy as they could be.

Then the word came that the Trinidad Reservoir had been approved and the entire site was to be flooded. With everything else, their homes were going to be torn down. It was the final blow, but surprisingly, there was not the great uproar that might have been expected from such a once-proud community. Maybe those who remained were just too weak to protest. Or maybe this was the "out" that they needed, an excuse many needed to make them leave. There was little resistence by the some 400 third- and fourth-generation Italian families that had to leave.

The colorful Reverend John O'Flynn of Trinidad was most helpful in keeping the predominantly Catholic community together during the final years. However, for some reason the Catholic powers-that-be dispatched one Father James Koenigsfeld to the site in 1968. He arrived upon the unhappy scene in blue jeans, cowboy hat and boots, looking like anything but a priest.

With the help of the remaining families he wrote all the former residents of Sopris he could find and urged them to return one last time and give Sopris a fitting burial.

They came from as far away as California and Indiana, some 600 them, and Sopris got a decent burial.

Then the visitors went back to their new homes. Those who moved nearby watched the systematic final destruction of their community. There was little dignity in it. Before, during and after the ruthless bulldozers went to work the scavengers moved in. Weekends were field days. Trucks and station wagons from Trinidad and other nearby points headed for Sopris, and whole families stripped the community of everything they could, the door and window frames, the wiring, the plumbing, and everything else that may or may not be of value. Gaping holes were left in what used to be walls and rooms. Roofs were gone. All that remained were the ruined wall—brightly painted inside and out—the rusted basketball hoops, and crippled tricycles.

And when the bulldozers were finished all that was left—besides a lot of facts and figures and countless memories—was the cemetery, a fitting memorial to a dead town. It had been moved to higher ground, very systematically, so that the new site was arranged just like the old one.

For a short while some believed the whole project was a big mistake, that although the old town of Sopris had been bulldozed to the ground and a huge dam was built—it would never hold water.

One would think that every problem had been anticipated, with the Bureau of Reclamation, the U.S. Corps of Engineers, and local officials having planned, negotiated carefully for years, then planned and negotiated some more. But they forgot one thing: downstream water rights. There were some 200 water rights, some a hundred years old, that had to be satisfied before there would be any water to fill Trinidad Lake.

One Trinidad city councilman called the dam "the biggest blunder the government ever made."

Today, looking at the beautiful lake, one would find it difficult to believe the uproar heard on the land before the water began to flow.

There were many suits filed by downstream users. They were all settled. And the water began to back up behind the dam in 1977. To the amazement of many people, water continued to back up and a large lake was formed. It has been filled to about 70–80 percent of its intended capacity since. In early 1982 the lake contained 50,300 acre-feet of water, while the bottom of the flood capacity pool is 65,000 acre-feet. In fact, a contract was to be let in 1982 to add an additional spillway at the south end of the dam to better accomodate a hundred-year flood.

Recreational development by the Colorado Division of Parks was completed in late 1980, and the facilities were opened to visitors in May of 1981. Vehicle count to the lake from May through December was 450,000, with an unofficial people count of well over a million persons. There were 1,800 surface acres of recreational opportunity at the lake in 1981. Future plans call for the building of a marina.

The generations of those who dug dusty coal deep in the bowels of the earth, who lived and died on the surface above the deep mines, would never have believed that one day the marker above their memories would be a beautiful lake.

CHAPTER XII

TRAGEDY TOWNS

Life was difficult on the frontier. And for some towns, life was more difficult than for others. Tragedy then was the same as tragedy today . . . only it was more frequent.

Disaster in *EDEN*

(Pueblo County)

Despite the name, EDEN was no paradise. In fact, for a few days in its history, it was the closest thing to hell on earth. It was not a town. It was only one of those tiny sites the railroads used to maintain every few miles along the line for one reason or another. Much of its life, Eden was little more than a tiny railroad station and siding and a name along the tracks. It was located about eight miles north of Pueblo.

The name is ironic considering the fact that Eden, or just north of Eden, was the scene of the worst railroad disaster in U.S. history up to that time, and still the third worst in history. The August 7, 1904, disaster took place in usually dry Porter Draw, just north of Eden and just before it connects up with Fountain Creek. The French mountain men called the creek *la fontaine qui bouille* (the fountain, or spring, that boils) because of the thermal springs of Manitou at the foot of Pike's Peak that flows into the creek near its source. There have been many other disasters along the short stream, many in the neighborhood of Eden, which is located a short distance north of where the creek empties into the Arkansas River in Pueblo. One historian called the Fountain one of the "deadliest" streams in America—an unusual reputation for a stream that is so tranquil 98 percent of the time.

It wasn't tranquil the evening of August 7, 1904. Heavy rains west of Eden had sent Porter Draw and Fountain Creek into a rampage.

A combination Missouri Pacific and Denver & Rio Grande excursion Train Number 11 left Denver at 5 P.M. en route to Pueblo. Behind the locomotive was the baggage car, smoker, chair car and two sleepers, and a diner tailed the train. There were about 150 passengers. Walter Hinman was engineer, Dave Mayfield was fireman, and James H. Smith was conductor.

The train was due at Eden at 7:59 and in Pueblo a few minutes after 8 p.m., then on to Kansas City and St. Louis. However, the engineer was warned to slow down as he passed Colorado Springs because of the heavy rains.

The bridge over Porter Draw was 96 feet long and 20 feet high, built on piles. The Draw was running bank full as the train approached, but the bridge appeared safe. No one knew at the time that a wooden highway bridge upstream had been washed out and put extra pressure on the pilings under the railroad bridge.

Frank Jones was on duty at the Eden station. He reported later that he saw the headlight of the train as it approached the other side of the bridge. When the light didn't reappear on his side of the bridge he knew something was terribly wrong. He took a lantern and headed up the track.

It is believed that the momentum of the engine carried it across the bridge. However, the bridge gave way just as the engine hit the far side, and the baggage car, smoker and chair car plunged into the dark waters, pulling the locomotive back into the water. Miraculously, the front part of the train twisted loose from the last three cars, two Pullman cars and a diner, which remained on the track.

The fact that the engine crossed the bridge and then was pulled back into the churning waters was verified by the fireman, Dave Mayfield. Mayfield said he heard the bridging creak and crack and then the train wobbled perilously. Mayfield jumped clear, climbing ashore downstream a few minutes later. He said he heard the screaming of the victims mixed in with the creaking and hissing of the engine and the cars as they washed downstream.

There were three others who escaped from the first part of the train, and there were at least 26 safe in the last three cars.

Hysterical headlines immediately after the disaster put the casualties as high as 200. However, a close study following the accident put the best estimate at 97 victims lost, with a few more unaccounted for. The body of engineer Hinman was one of the first found. Many bodies were found days later, some miles downstream. It was claimed that one body was found near Holly near the Kansas border. Some skeletons found years later were possibly victims.

It is interesting that some accounts years later confuse this train disaster with the 1878 disaster on Kiowa Creek, northeast of this site, (see East of Denver, "The Towns Before") in which the engine was enveloped in

These photographs taken at the scene of the Eden train wreck are part of the Dow Helmers collection, Pueblo Library District.

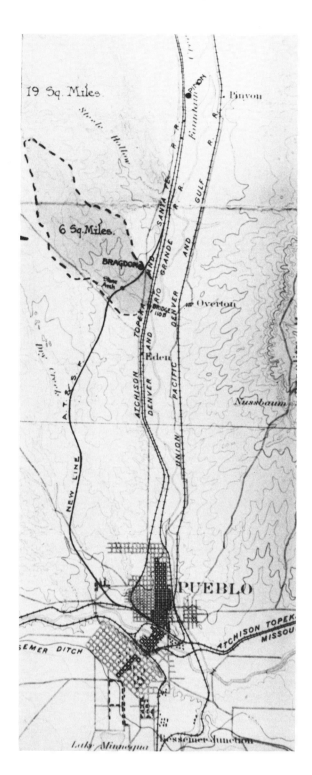

A steel spar set in concrete replaced the span that washed away to cause the Eden train wreck. (*Pueblo Library District*)

U.S. Geological Survey Topographical map showing the 6 square mile basin of Hogan's Gulch (shaded area at top) which drained into Fountain Creek under the Denver & Rio Grande Railroad bridge. Hogan's Gulch is better known today as Porter's Draw. To see how the area has changed since the tragedy, see p. 179. (Map first reproduced in Dow Helmer's *Tragedy at Eden*, 1971.)

quicksand and was never found. This engine was found a short distance downstream, half buried in sand and water. The other cars, smashed and broken, were also far downstream.

As soon as he saw what had happened, Frank Jones of the Eden station telegraphed up and down the track, blocking further use and calling for rescue workers. Within a half hour a rescue train had left Pueblo. The search for survivors soon became a search for bodies. The bodies were placed in baggage cars and taken to funeral parlors in Pueblo, where friends and relatives identified them. It was said that the disaster touched just about every family in Pueblo.

Many of the victims were found during the next few days. Search parties were hampered for three days, as the Fountain was still on a rampage. But the aftermath was almost as sickening as the original disaster. The days after the disaster the roads to Eden were clogged with sightseers and souvenir hunters. Some of the latter were better classified as ghouls. Most of the ladies' handbags and purses found along the shore had been relieved of money and valuables. Most of the watches left on wrists of the victims had stopped at about 8:15 to 8:30.

The investigation that followed cleared the railroad of any responsibility in the disaster, since it was caused by an "act of nature" and no one had known that the highway bridge upstream had been washed into the pilings of the railroad bridge. However, the railroad did come under much criticism for the speed in which they rebuilt the bridge and put it back into use— particularly for the fact that they rebuilt the bridge along the same lines as the old, on three piers instead of a single span bridge that would not wash away under similar circumstances. The railroad was also blamed for not maintaining a better system of inspections.

The railroad was credited with hiring 300 men to search for the bodies. Pueblo Mayor B. B. Brown offered $100 for each body found.

Heavy rains caused a similar accident near here on August 30, 1912, near Pinon, another tiny station a short distance north of Eden. A Chicago, Rock Island and Pacific railroad train using the D&RG tracks was also warned to proceed slowly due to heavy rains. Near Pinon an embankment gave way and the locomotive, tender, combination baggage and smoking car and another coach toppled into the flood waters. A day coach and a Pullman remained on the tracks. The exact count of victims was impossible since the conductor had just begun taking tickets when the accident happened. The official toll was finally set as six victims.

A devastating flood on June 3, 1921, did heavy damage throughout the Arkansas River Basin. Nearly 100 lives were lost, but most of them were in Pueblo.

There was another flood in 1964 that did heavy damage, but no more than two lives were lost.

LANSING (Kingsley, Kingston)

(Yuma County)

For a small prairie town, LANSING had more than its share of tragedy. One of its tragedies affected all of Colorado and the west. Among the first settlers were Russians from South Dakota, who brought with them the Russian thistle. It is said to have spread from here throughout Colorado and the plains—and it is still spreading.

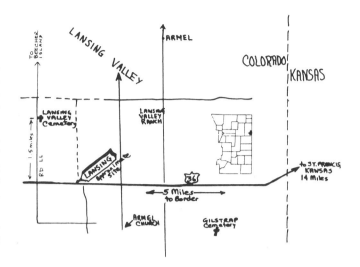

The site, first settled in the 1880s, was located in the southeast corner of Yuma County, 5 miles from the Kansas border and about 25 miles south southeast of Wray. It apparently was named KINGSLEY first, then KINGSTON, but the Post Office Department asked that the name be changed because of the other Kingstons in the West. So the final, ill-fated name was LANSING.

The settlement was on some of the best land in the county, and the community prospered for a while. During the 1880s and much of the 1890s, the population was around 200, with far more on the weekends and holidays when families from miles around would come to town to shop and join in the festivities.

A lonely graveyard off an isolated road is all that remains of the tragedy town of Lansing.

The town had all the conveniences and commercial establishments. There was a bank, a weekly newspaper (*The Lariat*), the "commodious" Ballard Hotel; the Beck Brothers and the Benson Brothers ran a merchandise store, as did A. F. Greatsinger. There were also two hardware stores, a lumber yard, a meat market, law office, and two saloons. A short time later a second hotel, the Ball Hotel, opened. Many participated in building a sod schoolhouse, where church services were also held. A little cemetery dates from the 1880s.

The one big excitement prior to the final tragedy was the robbery of the post office and the murder of a man named Beam.

Memorial Day, 1896, is a day the residents of Lansing could never forget. That was the day the tornado completely destroyed the town. One fortunate thing was that all the residents could see it coming and had time to run for their potato cellars and other underground rooms. By some miracle no one was killed. But every building in the community was turned into rubble— except the old sod schoolhouse.

Drought, grasshoppers and Russian thistle had already begun to reduce the population. Where there were about 200 residents in 1890, there were less than 40 by 1896.

Very little rebuilding was done. It was the sudden end of a dry land farm town. The post office was moved to Armel. All that is left of the once-prosperous little town is the little cemetery, covered by Russian thistle and other weeds.

TOWNER (Memphis): The Pleasant Valley Tragedy

(Kiowa County)

TOWNER is the first Colorado town on the so-called "ABC Railroad," and being the first town it was also the first town to become an exception to the naming process that gave the line its nickname.

Towner is about a mile and a half into Colorado from Kansas on what became the Missouri–Pacific line. The president of the railroad-affiliated Pueblo and State Line Town Company, S. H. Mallory, allowed his daughter, Jessie Mallory Thayer, to name the towns that grew up along the railroad line. She named them alphabetically, so the towns heading westward from the border were Arden, Brandon, Chivington, Diston, Eads, Fergus, etc.

However, the first three towns—Towner, Stuart (Stewart) and Sheridan Lake—were exceptions. Towner was originally named MEMPHIS by early settlers from Tennessee, but was soon renamed for a railroad official. It is still populated and remains a small shipping point on the railroad.

The small farm community gained national attention in late March of 1931, when tragedy struck during one of the sudden and vicious snow storms that frequently hit the plains.

Young Bryan Untiedt was rescued from a stranded school bus in a plane piloted by Denver barnstormer Captain Eddie Brooks, and taken to the hospital in Lamar. At right, Bryan is shown leaving for Washington D.C., where he was honored by President Hoover for his bravery. (*Rocky Mountain News photos*)

As happens so often in springtime on the plains, the day began almost pleasantly, with a warm chinook wind and no hint of the weather to come. Then suddenly the wind shifted.

The storm swept down shortly after some 20 students had begun their classes at the Pleasant Valley School, a small country school near Towner.

By mid-morning the hurricane-force winds began drifting snow window-high alongside the little school and was pushing snow under the cracks of the door. It was decided to close the school and bus the youngsters back to their rural homes.

Two miles from the school, Carl Miller, the bus driver, could not see the road in front of the bus due to the swirl of the snow, and the bus became stuck in the drifts. Miller, an experienced driver, tried desperately to get the bus moving again, but the vehicle only became more deeply cemented in the snow.

He kept the motor of the bus going, however, to provide some warmth. When the motor stopped, a makeshift stove was made out of a milk can, and Miller and the students began systematically burning their books, rulers, bus seats, etc. Miller also made the youngsters play games, wrestle and sing, to keep them active. Throughout the seemingly endless night, Miller was able to keep the children occupied, but, during the night, some of them began falling asleep and could not be awakened easily. Two children were dead at daybreak.

Miller decided that he would have to brave the still-raging storm to find help. Tragically, he headed in the opposite direction from the closest farm, which was only about a half mile away. He wandered two miles before he collapsed and died.

Back on the bus, 13-year-old Bryan Untiedt took charge and kept the youngsters active. He also stripped himself of most of his own clothing to warm the others. As some children fell off to sleep, he would slap them—some quite hard by his own account—to keep them awake and make them mad enough to stay awake.

It was nearly 36 hours later when one of the many search parties combing the region found the little bus. This search party included Bryan Untiedt's father.

On Sunday, March 28, Captain Eddie Brooks, colorful and courageous barnstormer from Denver, landed his plane on a hastily cleared landing strip a short distance from the bus. Five of the children had already frozen to death; most of the others were near death, but were flown to the hospital in Lamar. One of the dead was Bryan's 7-year-old brother, but a sister, 10, and another brother, 8, survived.

Among those rescued was young Bryan Untiedt, in his underwear. The Untiedt house would have been the first stop for the bus, but it never reached the house.

Bryan Untiedt became a national hero. He was invited to Washington by President Herbert Hoover, and spent the night at the White House. He was the honored guest of Los Angeles and honored by Colorado's governor. He also made a lecture tour.

He served in the Seebees in the South Pacific during World War II, and ran his own construction firm in the Denver area following the war. He died at his home in Aurora, Colorado, on December 29, 1977, at the age of 59. He was survived by his wife, Barbara, a son, three daughters, and two brothers and two sisters—one brother and sister he helped keep alive during the "Towner Tragedy."

PUNKIN CENTER (Pumpkin Center)*

(Lincoln County)

Although shown on most maps from the 1920s through the 1940s, and still seen on some maps, PUNKIN CENTER was never more than a crossroads center. Despite its tininess, it had more trouble and tragedy than real live communities.

It is located amid endless farmland in central Lincoln County, where Colorado Highway 94, straight as an arrow east–west, cuts across Colorado 71, straight as an arrow north–south.

In the early 1920s a bachelor named Howard Stevens purchased two acres of land on the northeast corner of the intersection. Here he built a combination service station/grocery store with living quarters. For some reason he painted all the buildings, including the outhouse, a light orange color. It is said farm children in

---

* Most recent maps show the name as Punkin, although earlier maps have spelled it Pumpkin.

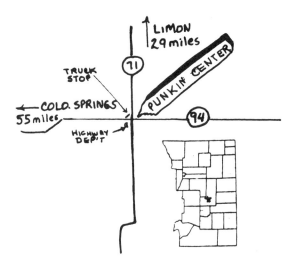

the area began calling the squat orange buildings Pun-kin Center.

Some local people give another reason for the name. They claim a local farmer, attempting to promote pumpkins as the major crop here as melons were promoted to the south, planted an extensive pumpkin crop, and the area became a center for pumpkins. In any case, the squat buildings were painted pumpkin color.

Stevens got his first taste of trouble in 1929 when he took in two young cowpolks, down on their luck. In repayment, the two waddies pulled out a gun and attempted to rob their host. Stevens wasn't an easy mark. In wrestling the gun away from them, he was shot in the shoulder. But he got the gun. One of the young robbers ran for it. Stevens, bleeding shoulder and all, marched the other man three miles to the closest neighbor's house to call the sheriff. The other young man was also caught. Both were sent to the State Reformatory.

Despite the loneliness of the site, Stevens wasn't beaten and robbed again until 1937. After that, he had a gun available at all times. It did him little good.

On August 29, 1941, Stevens, age 65, was shot and killed during another robbery. His brother found his body the next morning.

Ralph Haddock bought the center from the Stevens estate. He was AWOL from the army but soon returned to finish his time. While he was gone, his wife ran the store. She apparently didn't have any trouble.

In 1954 the Haddocks sold the store to Veryl Story. Story had owned the center just twelve hours when, returning from a trip to Colorado Springs, he saw smoke rising from the prairie in the distance. Yep, it was Punkin Center, burned to the ground.

Punkin Center survived, however. During the 1950s the Colorado Highway Department established a

Only the State Highway Department buildings at left retain the pumpkin color that gave this crossroads its name. The popular cafe at the site is behind the sign.

maintenance facility on the site. Since about 1970, the facility has been operated by Vernon Riemenschnieder, who lives in a trailer home with his wife and two children. Two older sons are in the Army.

A few years ago they were joined by Roger and Wanda Fisher and their five children, who left the hurley-burley of California to live the quiet life on the Colorado plains. The Fishers operate the cafe and gas station here. The Fishers' cafe, with Shirley Riemenschnieder filling in as part-time cook, has become a popular truck stop because of its food. In fact, on Sunday, some families drive all the way from Karval (16 miles away) to eat Sunday dinner here. The Punkin Center children are bussed to Karval for school.

And the violent history of Punkin Center continues, although in the most recent episode the tiny community served as a haven—a life-saving oasis. In March of 1981, a sudden and violent blizzard paralyzed eastern Colorado. Nineteen stranded motorists were fed and bedded down at the Punkin Center cafe until they were able to safely continue their journey.

Punkin Center has served as a welcome haven in other blizzards and during the dust storms of the 1930s and 1940s. So the community with the unusual name has some worthwhile memories, too.

PURCELL (Hungerford, Hungerford Station)
(Weld County)

Many Colorado communities were strangled by the drought of Dust Bowl days in the 1930s. Purcell, located about 5 miles east and 15 miles north of Greeley, virtually died of thirst. What made its death more heart-rending is that with it died its grandiose scheme to provide it and its neighbors with all the precious water they would ever need.

Purcell was born in 1910 when the Union Pacific Railroad reached out from Greeley with a spur to tap the lush grains and plump cattle in this region.

The site was originally named Hungerford, for J. J. Hungerford. However, a rather large townsite was surveyed and platted by the Purcell Land and Investment Company, run by Lawrence Purcell, a Greeley real estate man. When application for a post office was made, it was made in the name of Purcell.

The railroad built a turnaround track here. There were also two large grain elevators, a stockyards, and several businesses. It was also one of the first rural communities in northern Colorado to have its own telephone system.

When the first dry cycle came shortly after World War I, Purcell citizens led the fight for an elaborate

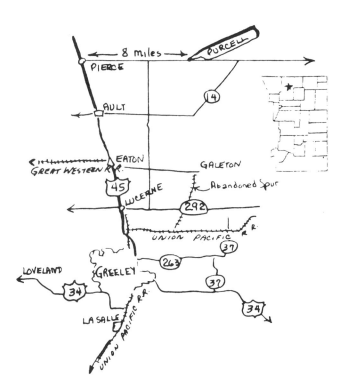

irrigation plan to divert water from Laramie, Wyoming, into the Cache la Poudre, to put about one million acres of northern Colorado under irrigation. The idea was put forth in more detail in James Michener's novel *Centennial*.

Wyoming desperately fought the idea, and it never came about.

If it had happened, or even if there had been some promise of relief, Purcell might still be with us today. As it was, it was buried in the dust of the Dust Bowl, according to newspapers of the time.

The railroad spur was abandoned. The government relief program of the New Deal bought up much of the land and set it aside for future grazing, relocating many of the Purcell families to other areas, many on the Western Slope.

Dust storms rolled over eastern Colorado during the 1930s. This photograph was taken in 1935 in Baca County, heart of the Dust Bowl. (*Denver Public Library, Western History Department*)

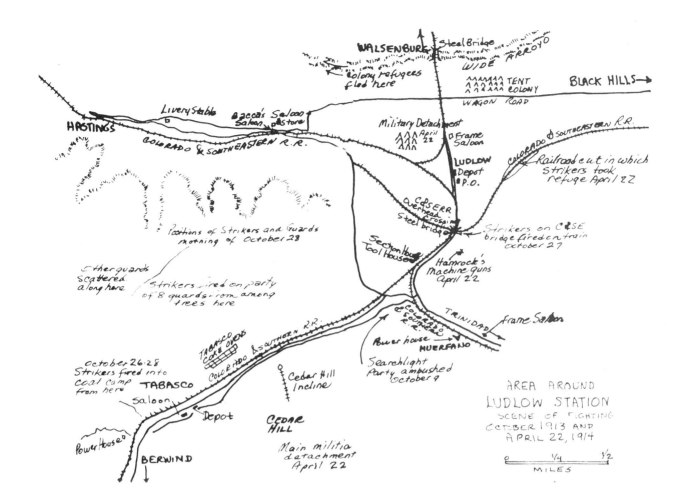

WALSENBURG Steel Bridge
WIDE ARROYO
colony refugees fled here
TENT COLONY
BLACK HILLS →
WAGON ROAD
HASTINGS
Livery Stable
Bacca's Saloon Saloon & Store
COLORADO & SOUTHEASTERN R.R.
Military Detachment April 22
Frame Saloon
COLORADO & SOUTHEASTERN R.R.
LUDLOW Depot P.O.
Railroad cut in which Strikers took refuge April 22
C.& S.E.R.R. Overhead Steel bridge
Strikers on C&SE bridge fired on train October 27
Positions of Strikers and Guards morning of October 28
Other guards scattered along here
Strikers fired on party of 8 guards from among trees here
Section House Tool House
Hamrock's Machine guns April 22
TRINIDAD
Frame Saloon
COLORADO & SOUTHERN R.R.
TABASCO COKE OVENS
COLORADO & SOUTHERN R.R.
COLORADO SOUTHERN R.R.
Power house
MUERFANO
Searchlight Party ambushed October 9
October 26-28 Strikers fired into Coal camp from here
TABASCO
Saloon
Depot
Cedar Hill Incline
CEDAR HILL
Power House
BERWIND
Main militia detachment April 22
AREA AROUND LUDLOW STATION
SCENE OF FIGHTING OCTOBER 1913 AND APRIL 22, 1914
0   ¼   ½
MILES

LUDLOW: The Ludlow Massacre
(Las Animas County)

The incredible story of the Colorado Coalfield War of 1913–14, remembered today for a single event, the "Ludlow Massacre," is told in great and gory detail in two or three fine books. Perhaps the classic account is *Up From the Depths*, by Barron Beshoar, the story of labor leader John Lawson. Another dramatic account, "The Great Coalfield War," is an early thesis by Senator George McGovern, published later with Leonard F. Guttridge. More recently the Colorado University Press has brought out a heretofore unpublished novel by Upton Sinclair, *The Coal War*. It has a long introduction by John Graham of the C.U. English Department which is as hard-hitting as anything written about those times.

All accounts demonstrate convincingly that the rich coal fields of Colorado were the lucrative playgrounds of the lords of eastern finance, led by the most ruthless baron of them all, John D. Rockefeller, Jr.

It is difficult to picture today the conditions which existed in the deep mines early in this century. Most of the miners were recent immigrants, primarily from Middle and Eastern European countries. Most had known only poverty in their lives. At least one third of them were illiterate, and few knew any English at all. Except for the "American Dream," the different ethnic groups had little in common and remained segregated. The mine owners encouraged and maintained this segregation, to hinder organization among the miners. Company spies were everywhere to weed out any "troublemakers." Union members attempted to counteract this by working their way into positions of company spy to get rid of anti-union miners.

Safety in the mine was of little concern to the owners 2000 miles away. It was an "unnecessary expense." In 1913 nearly 500 men were injured and 110 were killed in coal mines in Colorado. In 1910 more than 300 men were killed in nearby mines. (A scant three miles away from Ludlow, Colorado's worst mine disaster took place in 1917, claiming 121 lives [see HASTINGS].) A study at the time showed that Colorado mine accidents averaged four times more victims per capita than in other mining states.

Hours and wages were little different in 1913 than they had been during the strike of 1903. Although an eight-hour day had been approved years before, most company mines were still working ten to twelve hours per day. Pay was as little as 29 cents an hour with a maximum of $2.50 to $3.50 a day. At this time most wages were based on how much coal the miner produced during his shift ("sixteen tons, da, da . . . da"). The problem was that the weighmen were company personnel, and they subtracted everything they could.

The monetary exchange was company scrip that could only be spent within the camp. The rent for company-built houses was paid to the company in its scrip. Groceries and supplies were purchased at the company store, with company scrip. Studies showed that prices at company stores were higher than those in stores in town. Even the company saloon—if there was one—took only scrip, if the miner had enough left for a "monthly binge." In most cases the scrip ran out early in the month, too often on payday, so the miners' families lived on credit the rest of the month (". . . another day older and deeper in debt . . . I owe my soul to the company store. . . ."). There were usually many other payments each month that ate away at the small paycheck, such as health care (far from the best), and even education. Extra or emergency money needs were handled through the "friendly neighborhood (company) loan office," whose interest rates were exorbitant.

It was only through men like John Lawson—and others close to his towering dedication such as "Mother Jones," a fire-eater despite her 80 years—that a sufficient number of workers joined together in an attempt to fight the squalid conditions forced upon them by the all-powerful overlords back east.

There had been feeble attempts to stand up to their oppressors before, but the strike of 1903 was the first significant rumble by the discontented. Outward appearances might lead one to believe that the 1903 strike was somewhat successful. On paper, wages were stabilized, an eight-hour day was approved, the union received some recognition. But conditions changed very little. Or they changed briefly and then drifted back to what they were before—or worse. Indeed, the 1903 strike made the mine owners determined to "break" the union, utilizing any and all means available.

A strike of the proportions of the coal field strike of 1913–14 does not develop overnight. It was more than a strike. Some called it a "civil war"—the nation's second civil war, within Colorado.

It took much to bring so many different ethnic groups together to protest conditions that may have been little better than the conditions from which they left in the Old Country. One might say the 1913 strike began the day the 1903 strike ended. Labor unrest reached explosive proportions during 1911 and 1912. Ironically, the union's (unrecognized) demands in 1913 were little different from those made in 1903: an eight-hour day, a 10 percent wage increase, their own weighmen at the scales, the right to live in other than company houses and to shop in other than company stores, recognition of the union as bargaining agent for the miners, and pay for "dead work"—timbering, cleaning, picking slate, etc.

There was a meeting of mine union officials in Trinidad on September 15, 1913. The governor and other officials sent messages and/or representatives in an attempt to talk the miners out of a walkout, but the strike began officially on September 23. Some 12,000 miners and their families moved out or were evicted from their company homes in scores of mining camps throughout the Walsenburg and Trinidad area. Tent colonies were set up in a half-dozen sites in the region.

Perhaps the largest of the tent colonies was established just outside the town of Ludlow, where about 900 miners, with their wives and children lived in about 180 tents.

Shortly after the strike began the Governor called out the state militia. Base camps were set up near Walsenburg and Trinidad. In addition troops patrolled the entire area, and smaller camps of soldiers were stationed at "hot spots" or trouble spots when needed. Troops remained around the tent city of Ludlow.

The situation throughout the region grew more tense week by week. Each time a distant rifle shot was heard, each time a dead dog or other animal was found along the way, and particularly when a dead man was found along the road, striker or non-striker, the air became more tense. Random shots were heard in the distance night and day. Less frequent were the blasts of dynamite. To protect the women and children from getting caught in the crossfire, many of the strikers dug caves under the tents.

Although the situation worsened almost daily, many of the militia had to return to their homes, or found good excuses to do so. Their places were filled by hired guards—"gunmen" or "goons" professional strikebreakers hired by the mine companies.

The days passed into 1914. More and more the miners would spend each day in arroyos or behind railroad embankments near the tent cities, digging in in preparation for open battle and hoping to draw attention and fire away from the tent cities. As March turned into April, both sides helped increase the tension. With regularity striker marksmen would shoot out the huge searchlights that swept the tent cities throughout the night. Then the militia or guards would rake the night air with rifle or machine gun fire, sometimes shooting into the tents themselves.

Rumors were enemies to both sides. By mid-April, both sides expected an attack momentarily.

On the morning of April 20, 1914, the brittle silence was suddenly shattered by three dynamite blasts, apparently set on signal, near the area where the militia was bivouacking. The militia responded immediately with rifle and machine-gun fire.

The strikers had already taken their positions behind a railroad embankment and the arroyos. They returned the fire, hoping to draw the shooting away from the

"Mother" Jones and miners' strike leader John Lawson (*left*) with Horace Hawkins, another Colorado union official.

A group portrait was taken of strikers at the tent colony at Ludlow in 1914, where whole families camped, including babies in prams.

Both the Colorado State Militia and National Guard troops were sent to Ludlow to subdue the strikers. Two members of the militia, a ragtag bunch, are shown at left; above right, a Guards gunner on "Water Tank Hill" above the tent colony at Ludlow.

The Red Cross was on the scene of the devastation of the tent colony (below) within hours after the Ludlow Massacre.

Photos from Denver Public Library, Western History Department.

tents, where most of the women and children huddled in the pits below the tents.

The shooting continued into the afternoon. But, as the fire from the strikers became less and less frequent, it was obvious that they were running out of ammunition. They began to evacuate the tent city. With the aid of a locomotive and several autos to provide cover, many of the women and children were able to escape to a nearby arroyo.

Before many were allowed to escape, however, the militia and guards attacked the tent city, opening fire on the tents and pillaging them. Some accounts claim some of the womenfolk were attacked.

The most damage was done when they set fire to the tents.

When the smoke and noise had cleared, the charred bodies of two women and nine young children were found in one pit—known forevermore as "The Black Hole of Ludlow."

The number of casualties has varied widely over the years. Many hysterical accounts immediately after the massacre greatly exaggerated the number of victims. More careless accounts since claim all the casualties were women and children. Careful documents put the number at two women, eleven children, seven (or six) strikers and one militia. Some number an "innocent observer" among the seven strikers.

It is also interesting that most accounts of the "Great Coalfield War" indicate that the Ludlow victims were the total number of victims of that war. But it was just the beginning of what some have called "The Ten-Day War." Although apparently no one has been brave enough to count, or even closely estimate the total number of casualties throughout the state, it was certainly several times 21. In fact, more than 21 could have died at nearby Forbes and around Louisville and its Hecla Subdivision in the Boulder area in the days before and after the Ludlow Massacre.

Ludlow, however, was the one single event that sent shock waves throughout the nation and changed the complexion of the strike.

The "incident" cemented the resolve of the strikers. Long processions followed the caskets of the dead in Trinidad a few days later. There were more and more fiery speeches by Mother Jones and others, who said the strikers owed it to the dead to continue their fight.

A few days later, an army of strikers gathered and marched on Forbes, burning it to the ground and killing several guards and non-striking miners.

More than 400 indictments were made against the strikers, including murder charges against John Lawson. He was found guilty of the charge, but the Colorado Supreme Court later set aside the verdict.

Governor Elias Ammons was able to convince President Woodrow Wilson that anarchy ruled the state and Federal troops were needed to bring peace to the beleagered battlefields of Colorado.

Colorado's most colorful active participant in the Ludlow aftermath was Denver society matron Molly Brown, who became known as "The Unsinkable" after

The marker erected at Ludlow to commemorate the Ludlow Massacre is said to stand over the site of the "Black Hole," shown below, where two women and nine young children died during the attack.

The "Coalfield War" extended throughout the state, a Ten-Day War that involved Federal troops before it was over. *Above*, troops of the Eleventh U.S. Cavalry en route to the southern Colorado coal fields, May 2–6, 1914.

surviving the sinking of the Titanic. She cut short one of her trips to return to Colorado to lead the campaign for food and clothing for the strikers and their families.

Denver reporter Gene Fowler, who would later become the toast of New York and Hollywood, had been sent home early in the strike for his sardonic attacks on "General" Chase, head of the state militia.

The last structure at Ludlow is the facade of a former Main Street store.

But muckraker Upton Sinclair pulled out all stops in his enflaming attacks on the Wall Street "murderers". He even organized a physical attack on Rockefeller's mansion, but it fizzled.

Perhaps the most heralded but least useful result of the Massacre was the visit to Colorado, finally, of John D. Rockefeller himself. After all the fanfare, and tons of words and ritual, which appeared in newspapers as the "second coming," Rockefeller went home. Little changed, except that some of the dingy southern Colorado coal camps got bandstands and dance pavilions, and unionization of the mines was set back even further by what was called the "Rockefeller Plan," little more than a "company union."

Of course, some good things came out of the blood-letting. It did focus attention on the conditions in the mines, which helped establish new laws and legislation over the years. It gained sympathy for the United Mine Workers union. The "Rockefeller Plan" hindered progress in unionization, but Ludlow demonstrated dramatically that workers everywhere have a need and a reason for organization.

It also led to the creation, in 1915, of the Colorado Industrial Commission, formed to mediate differences between labor and management and neutralizing somewhat the anti-union Rockefeller Plan. The "company union" was outlawed by the Wagner Act of 1938. Ludlow was also said to be responsible for the state's first Workman's Compensation Act.

Each year, on or about April 20, union officials and union men gather to recount the progress made in unionism since Ludlow. They meet at an impressive monument that stands over the approximate site of the "Black Hole of Ludlow."*

Ludlow is no more than foundations and rubble today, except for the monument which will stand fore-ever, for union miners everywhere.

---

*In 1984 ceremonies nearly 100 union officials and sympathizers witnessed the burial at the monument of the ashes of Mike Lavoda, a key figure in the "Coal Field Wars." He came to America in 1910 from Yugoslavia and soon became a union organizer for the United Mine Workers. He was so tireless and effective during the strike that mine guards had orders to shoot him on sight. He died in New Orleans on March 31, 1984, at the age of 96.

HASTINGS: Colorado's Underground Inferno
(Las Animas County)

On April 15, 1981, fifteen miners died deep within the bowels of the Dutch Creek Mine near Redstone, Colorado. It was the worst coal mine disaster in several years in the state. But it was only the most recent of scores of similar tragedies that have marked the mining history of Colorado.

In the past 100 years 935* coal miners have lost their lives in 106 underground fires and explosions.

Colorado's worst coal mine disaster occurred in 1917 in the town of HASTINGS. Many other Colorado disasters were almost as bad. Each one, no matter how few lives are lost, is a tragedy.

The best account of the Hastings disaster was written by veteran Colorado ghost-towner and historian Francis B. Rizzari. His paper, "Colorado's Underground Inferno" was originally printed in the April 1968 *Denver Westerner Monthly Roundup*, and was reprinted in the 1968 *Westerners Yearbook*, Volume XXIV. Mr. Rizzari has granted the author permission to print the following condensation of his account.

* * *

On the morning of April 27, 1917, about 8:45 A.M., an explosion of methane gas (CH_4), known as Fire Damp, occurred in the Hastings Number 2 coal mine, owned

---

* Colorado Bureau of Mines statistics, 1884 to April 15 1981.

and operated by the Victor-American Fuel Company, at Hastings, Las Animas County, Colorado. One hundred and twenty-one men were in the mine at the time. There were no survivors.

Hastings first appears in the small town and post office section of the Colorado State Business Directory for 1890. It is listed merely as Hastings, Las Animas County, population 20. There are no stage connections nor distances noted from other towns in the vicinity. The same listing is carried in the directories for 1891 and 1892, but in the 1893 edition, it has been moved to the main section and now has a population of 50. Seven businesses are listed: the Hastings Hotel, operated by Mrs. C. T. Burton; P. J. Bocco and Company, grocers; Claudius Hart, meat; Nicolli Brothers, grocery and saloon; James Roberts, postmaster; and the Victor Coal Company, general merchandise and coal mining. It is also listed as being on the Union Pacific, Denver and Gulf Railroad. Actually, it was on a branch from the main line that was a mile away. The connection was called Ludlow.

In the directory for 1894, the population has jumped to 1500. It now lists a mayor, city clerk, Catholic Church, an assistant postmaster, and two justices of the peace in

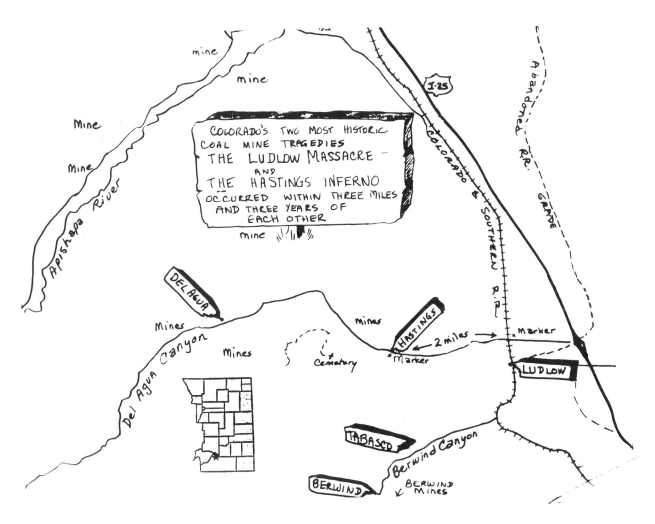

addition to the previously mentioned establishments. The Victor Coal Company is now listed as the Victor Coal and Coke Company. In 1895 a physician and a railroad agent were added to the list. From here on the population varies, dropping to 1000 in 1898 and to 600 in 1900. However the *Denver Times* for November 20, 1900, states that the Victor Fuel Company (note the name change) has 3600 men employed in its mines at Hastings, Downing, Grey Creek, Chandler, and Maitland. Another story in the *Times* for December 31, 1899, stated the town had a population of 1000 and that there were 100 coke ovens.

In the Directories for 1901 and 1902 the population is given as 2000 and there are ten businesses listed. From 1903 to 1909 the population is shown as 200 but I am sure this is an error where one zero was dropped and then carried over year after year by the editors and not corrected until 1909. However, also remember that 1903 was the year of the strike, so perhaps 200 is correct.

In the 1905 directory there are 16 businesses listed including an opera house, carpenter, barber, and music teacher. In 1909 the population is back to 2000 and there are 13 entries including a stage line, school principal, and the Mountain Telegraph Company. In the 1910 and 1911 editions, a blacksmith has seen fit to pay for the privilege of being listed. In 1912 the population dropped to 693 and the Victor-American Fuel Company is listed for the first time.

Statistics remained much the same until the year 1917 when the Continental Oil Company and the Trinidad Electric Transportation Railway appear. As nearly as can be determined, the latter company was a power company, although there was a Trinidad Electric Transmission Railway and Gas Company that operated the street and interurban railway from Trinidad to Starkville.

Since 1904, the town had been served by the Colorado and South Eastern Railway, a wholly-owned subsidiary of the coal company. The branch line built by the Union Pacific, Denver and Gulf Railroad in 1983 had been taken over by the Colorado and Southern upon that company's organization in 1898. Then in 1904, the company bought the track from the C&S, organized the Colorado and South Eastern and eventually extended its tracks up the canyon west of Hastings to Delagua. The railroad was scrapped in 1952.

The year 1917 was a fateful one for Hastings. Coal, being organic in nature, sometimes generates a deadly gas in the mines known as Fire Damp. It is highly explosive when it comes in contact with a open flame. The Hastings Mine had an unusually high content of this gas. In 1911 the State Bureau of Mines had recommended the installation of radiators and the injection of steam into the air intakes of all mines in Las Animas County south of Aguilar, in order to lessen the chance of an explosion due to coal dust. The Hastings mine developed an adobe duster, similar to those in use today, whereby adobe dust was sprayed on the coal facings. This machine, however, was not working on the morning of April 27.

Operations at the Hastings mine were not carried on through a vertical shaft as in most mines, but through an adit that followed the dip of the vein itself. The vein had an average dip of about five degrees. Tributary drifts took off the main adit so the coal could be worked on a multitude of facings at the same time. These drifts were called entries and were numbered one north, two north or one south, two south and so on.

The original entry of the mine had been made on the upper vein known as the Berwind "A." However, there had been a couple of explosions in previous years, causing a few deaths and setting the vein on fire. It had been sealed off about 2000 feet from the portal and left to burn out. From this point on the "A" vein, a sloping entry had been made to the vein 40 feet below known as the Berwind "B." The main face of the "B" vein was in over 8000 feet. Haulage was done by hand and mules. Labor in the entries was mostly done by hand while that on the main face of the vein was done by an electric mining machine. This machine was down for repair and, as was the case of the duster, was not operating the morning of April 27.

In order to minimize the danger of gas explosions in the mine, the miners were equipped with Victor electric lamps. The Wolf safety lamp, which had a flame encased in wire mesh, was carried by the superintendent, the mine foreman, the fire-boss, the company mine inspecor, shaftman, and some entrymen working in the entries known to be generating a high percentage of gas. The presence of gas could be determined by the dimming of the flame.

At 6 A.M. on April 27, the fire-boss inspected the mine to its utmost depths and, as he had done many times before, reported it safe for work. He checked the fan that circulated the fresh air through the "B" seam at the rate of 50,000 cubic feet per minute and O.K.'d it. At 7 A.M. the day shift consisting of 35 Greeks, 33 Austrians, 13 Italians, 14 Mexicans, 7 Negroes, 3 Poles, 1 Serbian, 2 Welsh and 13 Americans, entered the mine. David Reese, traveling inspector, was one of the group.

About 9:00 A.M. a trip of empty cars was descending the slope into the mine. Suddenly the cars stopped and the trip rider got off the cars to investigate the trouble. He had gone but a short way when he smelled smoke and saw a huge cloud of the billowing stuff approaching him. This meant only one thing—FIRE! He turned and ran back up the slope, his lungs straining and his aching legs seemingly held down by lead weights as he tried to outrace the deadly cloud. Bursting from the mouth of the mine, he gave the alarm. In a few minutes the smoke from which he had fled in panic began to emerge from the portal. Down in the powerhouse the engineer began to blow the disaster signal on the steam whistle, calling all off-shift miners to the mine headquarters to prepare for the work of rescue.

Hastings, a typical southern Colorado coal mining town before the mine disaster on April 27, 1917.

Tipple and surface buildings at Hastings on the day after the fire and explosion which killed 121 men, Colorado's worst coal mine disaster.

Photos courtesy Denver Public Library, Western History Department.

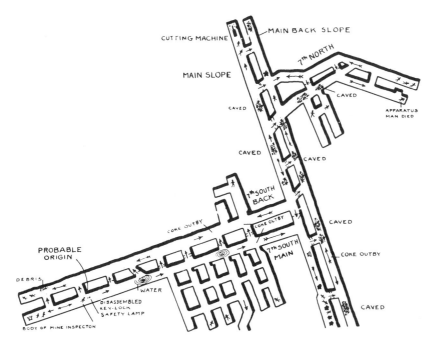

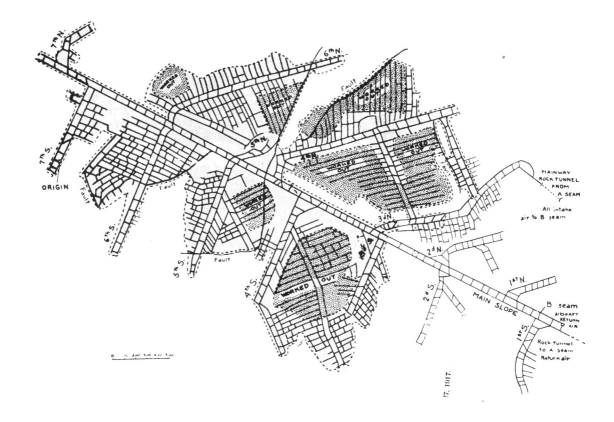

These diagrams show (*below*) the layout of the Hastings mine in Trinidad, with the area of the probable origin of the explosion indicated at left; and an enlargement of that section, showing more detail. (*U.S. Bureau of Mines*)

Telephone calls were placed to the towns around asking for help of their helmet crews.

No concussion or shock had been felt at the surface and at first there was some optimism that the smoke was caused by a fire and that some of the miners were safe. However, the smoke was so thick that it was some time before rescuers could attempt to enter the mine.

Henry P. King, Deputy State Inspector of Coal Mines, District No. 1, arrived at the mine at 2:30 P.M. and entered the workings twenty minues later. There seemed to be no damage as far as the third and fourth entries and hope was still held for some survivors. This hope was short-lived, however, as beyond this point they began to come upon bodies of the miners. These were burned, thus indicating an explosion of some kind had taken place. Below the fourth north entry they began to encounter damage and rock fall, thus slowing the recovery work. The great fan had not been damaged, but even so, it could not seem to clear the smoke from the mine and progress was slow.

James Dalrymple, State Mine Inspector, arrived on the scene early on the morning of the 28th, and after accompanying one of the rescue crews as far as possible, stated it was doubtful if any were still alive. By 5 o'clock that afternoon, 30 hours after the explosion, thirteen bodies had been recovered, and by 8 o'clock, two more. Dalrymple also stated that he thought there had been an explosion but could not be certain until the entire mine had been inspected.

All during this time the scene at the mine portal was one of total despair. Wives, sweethearts, and relatives of the trapped men huddled around waiting for some word. Some wept silently, others were almost hysteri-cal and had to be restrained forcibly from entering the workings. A few stood there numbly, saying nothing, remembering other days like this when there had been survivors, but realizing that today was the one day they had lived in fear of most of their lives.

Rumors ran through the crowd that the Austrians had blown up the mine in order to slow America's war effort. War had been declared on Austria and Germany only twenty-one days before. This theory was so strong that Governor Julius Ganter felt it necesary to make a public announcement that there was no evidence of foul play connected with the disaster.

As more and more bodies were recovered it was noticed that many had their hair burned off and the skin and flesh were blackened as if scorched, thus confirming a flash explosion. Looking back, at this time, we can visualize an explosion similar to one which occurs when a lighted match is thrown into a spreading flow of gasoline. The result is not a loud explosion but a "Whoo—oosh." The Hastings explosion must have been similar, only a thousand times greater. Coal dust may have been a contributing factor, as the duster was not working that morning.

As the work of clearing up the mine and recovering the bodies proceeded, it was noticed that the damage encountered to the seventh south entry had been caused by a force exerting pressure upward toward the mine entrance, while below that entry, the damage seemed to indicate that the force has been downward. This led to the conclusion that the origin of the explosion had occurred near that spot.

By the 8th of May, rescuers had reached the face of the main slope. Here they found the electric cutting

A lonely marker rising above the weeds at Hastings tells of Colorado's worst mine disaster.

The opening of the Berwind "B" shaft was sealed after the Hastings mine disaster. (*Denver Public Library, Western History Department*)

machine with its wires still disconnected, thus eliminating it as the cause. On the morning of May 10, the graveyard shift found the body of David Reese, Company Mine Inspector. The Wolf safety lamp that he had been carrying was found beside his body with the oil vessel disconnected. From this point investigators observed that the force of the explosion had travelled both inwardly and outwardly in the mine and that his lamp was not damaged nor blown away from his body, thus indicating that little or no violence had taken place at that spot. This led Inspector King to state that from his evidence, the explosion had been caused at this point by a naked light coming in contact with gas.

The entrymen working in the seventh south back entry also had Wolf safety lamps. They were one hundred and twenty-five feet beyond the point where Reese's body has been found. Most of the gas given off in this part of the mine came from the face of the entry. If the gas had been explosive where Reese was, it was more so where the men were, thus making it impossible for the Wolf safety lamp to burn. Therefore, it seemed evident that those men either did not know, or did not care what extinguished the lamp.

One hundred and twenty-one men died, and at the time the official report was written, only one hundred and one bodies had been recovered. The search went on well into the following year and before the final count of 121 was given out another man died from indirect causes of the tragedy. On May 6, 1917, Walter Kerr, 27 years old, married, father of three children, and a member of the Berwind Colorado Fuel and Iron Company's Helmet Crew, was carrying a body out of the mine. He suddenly left his crew and was later found dead in a cross-cut at the face of the seventh north entry. It was found that he had a defective heart and the overexertion had caused it to fail.

Production at the mine for 1917 dropped to 74,221 tons. In 1918 it fell to 11,944. This year, however, the state produced its greatest amount of coal, 12,658,053 tons. No production is recorded for Hastings for 1919 and 1920, but in 1921, it was 20,747 tons. None is recorded for 1922, and 1923 a mere 7049 tons are shown. The mine was then abandoned and the portal sealed.

The town of Hastings carried on somehow after that, but was only a ghost of its former self. By 1933 the directories list a population of 307. The publishers evidently did little research for the succeeding years as that figure is carried every year to 1939.

Just when the great tipples, trestles, and other structures were torn down, I do not know. They probably fell into decay gradually and the final cleanup was done in 1952 when the railroad was torn up. Today only the cement foundations with huge anchor bolts in them, a row of deserted and half-ruined coke ovens, and a polished granite monument to the memory of the dead miners mark the spot where 121 men died in Colorado's Underground Inferno.

CHAPTER XIII

MINING THE PLAINS (or "They'll Mine Anywhere")

Colorado's great mineral wealth—the Mother Lode—came from what was considered an almost continuous vein that cut through the heart of the state. But to the eager argonauts all of Colorado promised endless wealth in gold and silver. They turned over every rock and dug prospect holes in some of the strangest places. Oddly enough, they found what they firmly believed was their "fortune" in some of the most out-of-the-way places.

RUSSELLVILLE

(Douglas County)

Many historians mark this site as the true beginning of it all. William Green Russell and his party from Georgia, traveling northward from Pueblo over the Jimmy Camp Trail, panned some color on a Gulch, a tributary of Cherry Creek, in Central Colorado. The gulch which came to be known as Russellville Gulch, was located about five miles south of present Franktown.

The discovery was made during the summer of 1858. The gold was not in paying quantities, but it was enough to encourage the Russell party to continue. A short time later they found more color on Little Dry Creek at the southern city limits of present Denver. Here they established Placer Camp and spent the winter, before heading into the mountains the following spring—with hundreds of others—and making the first rich discoveries in Colorado.

But RUSSELLVILLE, the camp established on Russell Gulch, was not forgotten. The news of Russell's discovery brought many other hopefuls to the scene. A couple of accounts say "hundreds" flocked here, and there was placering all up and down the gulch. Nonetheless, there is no record of any fortunes made. It would have been a ghost after the first year if it had relied on placer gold. However, being the first settlement of any kind in the region, it became a stage station on the Smoky Hill Trail. There was also one of the first sawmills in Colorado nearby.

Along with the stage station there was an immense barn, a stockade, corral and an eating place. There is some argument about there being a saloon as well. It received a post office designation on May 22, 1862.

It was just about this time, however, that another ranch-house center was growing about five miles to the north. On September 8, 1862, less than four months after the first post office was designated it was moved to the new site, Frank's Town or FRANKTOWN.

There was evidence of some activity at Russellville until about 1867. Then it was all Franktown. Ruins of the stage station buildings were noted for a few more years. Then nothing. A modern subdivision of fine homes called *Russellville* has gone up in this area in recent years.

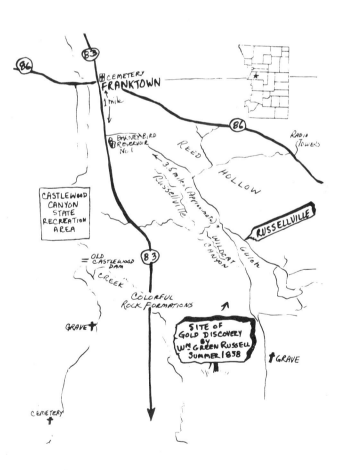

161

The Denver Gold Camps

After finding traces of gold in Russell Gulch, most of the William Green Russell party were encouraged enough to press on in their search for riches.

The Russell party searched the streams and rivers as they continued their way northward in the summer of 1858. By late summer party members found some more color in Little Dry Creek, near its confluence with the South Platte River. This is just south of the present city limits of Denver in Englewood.

The site was said to have been the first camp where gold was found in paying quantities and was largely responsible for the start of the gold rush to Colorado the following year.

Russell and his group of about a dozen Georgians established a camp here, built about a dozen cabins, and settled down to pan for gold and wait out the winter. The camp was called PLACER CAMP for the type of mining they did.

Although they found some color here, rumors of far greater riches lured them into the mountains with hundreds of others the following spring.

A monument to the camp was erected in 1927 on the north bank of the Platte River on the east side of U.S. 85, just south of the Denver city limits, in Arapahoe County.

Russell gave his name to another site, the rich mining area of Russell Gulch in the Central City region. Early in the Civil War Russell left the state to join the Confederate cause, returning to Colorado briefly in 1876.

The discovery of placer gold on Little Dry Creek was

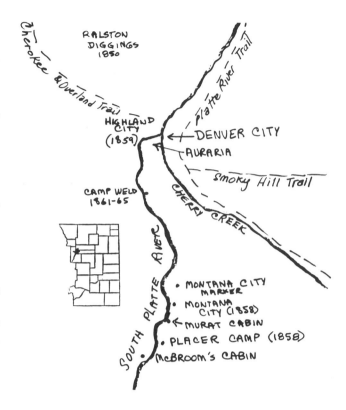

largely responsible for the founding of a far more historic town a short distance north of Placer Camp and the first Yankee settlement in the Denver area, MONTANA CITY.

A party of prospectors from Lawrence, Kansas, established a camp near what is now the south end of Overland Park, about a mile north of the site of Placer Camp. The group, headed by John Easter, believed that the discovery of gold nearby would lead to permanent settlement of the territory, and a center or capital would be needed to anchor the impending activity.

The party, which consisted of forty men, two women and fourteen wagons of supplies and equipment, organized a town company on September 7, 1858. They platted a fairly elaborate townsite about a quarter of a mile square on the east banks of the Platte River. Josiah Hinman was elected president of the town company, and William Boyer, secretary. In the first weeks of the new community, twenty cabins and homes were built.

The following year the community's most colorful residents settled here, the "Count and Countess" Henri Murat, from Hanover, Germany. The Count was a noted story-teller and plied the ideal trades to practice his calling: he was a barber and a bartender. The good Count gave a shave to the Territory's first distinguished visitor. Horace Greeley—New York publisher, presidential candidate-to-be, and the man who told all those young men to "Go West" in the first place—came west himself in 1859 to see if those rumors of gold were really true.

In a small park along the Platte River is this log house called the Murat Cabin, and said to be the first home of "Count and Countess" Murat, at this approximate location. In fact, the cabin is a replica of the original, constructed from the logs of several old cabins in the area—maybe even some from the Murat dwelling.

Denver, 1859. In foreground is Denver City; to left, across Cherry Creek, is Araria; in back, beyond the Platte River, is the site of the short-lived community of Highland City. (*Photo courtesy Denver Planning Office*)

On his visit to the region, Greeley wrote, "I had the honor to be shaved by a nephew (so he assured me) of Murat, Bonaparte's King of Naples—the honor and the shave together costing but a paltry dollar."

Greeley was doubtless the last historic figure to visit Montana City because the community didn't last much longer. The nearby mountains, for which the town was named, beckoned most of the early settlers. The few who remained at the foot of the mountains seemed to be gathering at twin "cities" about four miles down the Platte at the mouth of Cherry Creek. The fast-growing communities, facing each other across Cherry Creek, were Auraria and Denver City.

Within two years Montana City was a ghost town. A plaque commemorating its existence which was put up in 1929 was stolen a short time later. Another stone marker was established near the clubhouse at Overland Park. A short distance south of the marker, on the east banks of the Platte, a "faithful replica" of the Murat cabin was built from the ruins of early log cabins.

There was another little-known, short-lived camp called MEXICAN DIGGINGS about three miles up the Platte from Placer Camp. The residents were Mexican nationals who at that time and for several years to come, would not dare invade white camps. There were countless isolated camps or suburbs of mining camps that had such names as Mexican Flats or Chihuahua through the West.

This camp settled in the fall of 1858, had about the same lifespan as Placer Camp: by the following spring the residents followed the trail into the gleaming mountains.

The discovery of gold on RALSTON CREEK was even earlier than at Russellville and Placer Camp. A marker in Inspiration Point Park just off 49th and Sheridan Boulevard in extreme northwest Denver reads:

One mile north of this point gold was discovered on June 22, 1850, by a party of California-bound Cherokees. The discovery was made by Louis Ralston, whose name was given the creek (a branch of Clear Creek). Reports of the find brought the prospecting parties of 1858, whose discoveries caused the Pikes Peak gold rush of 1859, which resulted in the permanent settlement of Colorado.

When the Pikes Peak Gold Rush did eventually develop, RALSTON DIGGINGS became one of the first sites for placer mining activity in the Denver area in 1858 and 1859. But despite the tales of the find in 1850, Ralston Creek was a disappointment to early prospectors and the site did not last long as a gold camp.

However, the site and other nearby sites lingered on for many years with many occupations, and the name Ralston was used on the sites.

Near the original site of the gold find, RALSTON was a site on an early wagon road into the mountain goldfields. RALSTON STATION was an important stage stop on the busy road from Denver City to Central City. It later became an important station and junction point on the Colorado Division of the Union Pacific. And a Ralston station was shown on other early railroads in the area. Some of Colorado's earliest successful irrigated farming was done in this region, and much farm produce and livestock was shipped from the shipping points called Ralston to markets in Denver and the mountain gold fields.

Coal was mined at Ralston in the early 1870s. What was claimed to be the first rural church in the region was built at Ralston in 1870—at a cost of $1800.

The site of the original gold discovery was at approximately 52nd and Eaton.

CARRIZO SPRINGS

(Baca County)

CARRIZO SPRINGS was probably one of the most improbable mining towns in old Colorado. Who would think a mining town would spring up in far southeastern Colorado, with all the classic characters—the girls, the gamblers, the gunmen,—and all the overblown excitement of the mountain mining towns, brought together in attempts to extract medium-grade copper out of hard rock and ship it hundreds of miles by wagon to be processed.

This was Carrizo Springs in the 1880s—the most isolated mining town in the state.

Prospectors who had apparently lost their way in their search for gold and silver saw a streak of ore in Skull Canyon in 1880. However, it wasn't until 1887 that any serious mining was begun on what was believed to be a "a rich vein of silver," and the Carrizo Springs boom (or nightmare) began.

The townsite of Carrizo Springs was officially recorded in November of 1887. It was named for the creek that ran through the site, and its springs, which were known by Spanish word for "reed grass." The Carrizo Town Company was active in the development and in the incorporation of the community in 1888.

Despite the fact that the ore was found to be lacking in silver, and copper was not as romantic as gold and silver, hundreds—one report said between 2000 and 3000—rushed to the site. Not all of them were interested in mining the ground. The *Lamar Register* said it was a gathering place for "roughs and toughs," and was "one of the wildest towns on the western frontier."

The isolated site was ideal as a gathering place for such characters. The Panhandle regions along the southwestern trails were already well populated by rustlers and other roughs and toughs, many overflowing from BOSTON and the other cowtowns. And the cedar groves and narrow canyons north of town were good for getaways and hiding out.

Many of the most profitable business enterprises were not listed in the directories of the day. But there were some legitimate businesses. The Lamar newspaper said the new La Mesa Hotel was "commodious" and "furnished handsomely." There were two newspapers printed during the short life of the community, *The Carrizo Current* and *The Optic*. There were a couple of

stores and a couple of saloons listed. Some of the "unlisted" businesses operated in and out of tents and more temporary structures.

The cedars north of town were good for building and for fence posts. Some stone was also used in construction. There was expected to be plenty of water available from the creek and the springs.

Although the lack of gold and silver was a disappointment, the early reports of copper compensated: early claims said that the ore when melted down was "half copper."

"Capitalists" from Topeka, Kansas, bought up many of the claims, formed the Carrizo Springs Mining and Location Company and were said to have brought in 150 miners.

Like so many towns of the day, especially those that believed they had more to offer than was the fact, Carrizo Springs lived in anticipation of the railroad. Rumors were rife. A railroad "was on its way," and when it came Carrizo Springs would be a "major mining center."

And as in other towns when the railroad didn't come, that lack was blamed for the early demise of the community. Even good ore is costly to refine when it must

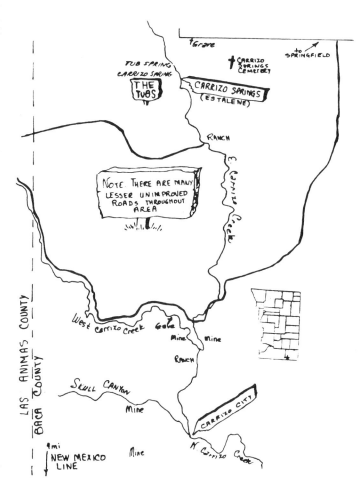

GHOSTS OF THE COLORADO PLAINS

Snapshot of a church group inspecting the entrance of a famous copper mine near Carrizo Springs, summer 1934. (*Photo from Emma Fisher*)

be shipped hundreds of miles to be milled. But the railroad that never came was not the only reason for the early death of Carrizo Springs. There was some good ore here, but it was not as rich as originally promoted, and it was difficult to mine in the hard rock without today's more sophisticated methods.

Some claimed that Carrizo Springs, like Boston in Baca County, dissipated itself to death, that the site attracted too many of the wrong kind of people and they milked the working class dry.

There may be good backing for this view, since another, longer-lasting and more sober community sprung up nearby even before the final death of Carrizo Springs. And even after CARRIZO (or CARRIZO CITY) faded as a mining town, copper mining continued in the region off and on for several decades.

But Carrizo Springs was dead within about two short years. Although some hopeful miners lingered and participated in the activity at nearby Carrizo City, the gamblers, girls and other camp followers were gone. Even most of the buildings were gone, torn down or moved and used for other purposes. Just some weed-covered foundations remained. The site of the once-hopeful community became ranch land. The cowpokes called the site "the tubs" for the big wooden vats left behind by the mining, handy for watering horses and cattle.

CARRIZO (Carrizo City, Carrizo Flats)

(Baca County)

CARRIZO (CARRIZO CITY or CARRIZO FLATS) took over from Carrizo Springs. Much information is confused about the two. It is difficult to separate their history, and few

people tried. The best way to do it is by the time frame and the location. Carrizo began just a short time after Carrizo Springs died, or while it was dying, and at a site about 5½ miles south southwest of the earlier town. Both were in the extreme southwest corner of Baca County, near the Las Animas County line.

Carrizo Springs apparently was enough for the "roughs and toughs," and Carrizo lived a more normal existence. This second Carrizo was more of a company town. The Bear Canyon Copper Company bought up many of the claims in the area. At its peak, in the late 1890s, the company employed as many as 60 or 70 men.

The Lamar Register noted in January of 1900 that Carrizo would soon be giving Lamar a close run "as the liveliest town in southeastern Colorado."

The town was platted—something Carrizo Springs never was. And stone was hauled in to construct "20 sturdy buildings." The *Carrizo Current* was published here. It may have been the same one that was published in Carrizo Springs for a short time also, or perhaps it was another bit of information that was confused by historians. At any rate, the *Current* published notices of an incorporation election to be held on September 15, 1888.

A later newspaper published here was *The Carrizo Weekly Miner*, edited by C. Frost Liggett. There was a hotel here, and a blacksmith; other businesses included a stage with tri-weekly mail delivery from Lamar.

In 1888, when the Boston, Trinidad & Western Railroad was incorporated, it was expected to run through Carrizo from Boston to Trinidad. It never did. Nor did the many other railroads rumored to be built in the ensuing years.

In the plan to divide southeastern Colorado into four counties, Carrizo was considered a "shoo-in" to be the seat of "Carrizo County." But the bubble burst when only one county was formed in 1880 (Baca), with Springfield as its seat.

The old rock school at Carrizo still stands, though it has long been empty. (*Photo from Sarah McKinley*)

There was mining in this region off and on for several decades; since about 1900 much of it has been mixed up with Copper City. All through this time a more stable industry, ranching, centered in the region. Ranching and mining are not always a healthy mixture, but the two lived in apparent harmony here, each possibly too occupied with its own survival in this isolated, arid region to bother about the other.

COPPER CITY and Independence Mine

(Baca County)

As if the history of Carrizo Springs and Carrizo City wasn't obscure and confusing enough, add Copper City to the confusion.

Copper City dates from around 1900 with a new surge of mining in this region. To make things more difficult for modern historians, the few but glowing reports of Copper City do not mention the earlier towns. They were both ghosts—or near ghosts—by this time. But many of the names, such as Skull Canyon, Bear Canyon, etc., were a part of the earlier towns.

The Independence Mine is mentioned more often than Copper City during the next few years, and it was located about two miles from Copper City. *The Denver Times* of March, 1900, in an account of the "new copper excitement" at Copper City, states that the Independence Mine was its major source of ore production.

The news item said there were 200 people at Copper City, a $2000 hotel had been completed in two weeks, there were "several" stores and a saloon, and a post office was applied for. It said that there were tri-weekly stages from Kenton, Oklahoma, and Las Animas, Colorado.

The newspaper story said the town was incorporated by the Gold & Copper Mining and Townsite Company, and that it was located about eight miles north of the New Mexico line and 10 miles from the Las Animas County line. This would put it about midway between Carrizo Springs and Carrizo and a little further east than both of them. It could have been just a rough location by the newspaper. The report mentioned Skull Canyon as a site for mining activity, and that Carrizo Creek was the source of "plenty of good water" for Copper City.

A 1901 item said a 40-ton water matte smelter was to be erected although there is no record that it was built and most reports say the ore was shipped to Pueblo for processing.

Other lodes mentioned in addition to the Independence were the Black Dragon, Pueblo, Blue Boy, Emma O, Silver King, Oregon, Silversite, Flatwood, Old Hickory Bear Canon (cq), Blacksmith. The Old Hickory sold for $12,000 in 1901.

The Independence was located on April 3, 1899. One of the three owners was C. Frost Liggett, Lamar newspaper editor and prominent in the earlier Carrizo towns promotion. Liggett distributed a newspaper in Copper City.

Despite early accounts, the town and most of the mines seemed to have played out by late 1902. There was sporadic activity up until recent years and most of it involved the Independence Mine.

There was a brief, underfinanced spurt of activity in 1916.

In 1923, A.C. Rogers and others worked the Independence, reportedly hauling some ore to Pueblo. Activity ended with the depletion of funds. For several years Rogers, whenever he had a few dollars to spend or when he needed a few dollars, returned to the mine. He lived at the mine off and on for years. He died in Springfield about 1950.

The horizontal tunnel of the Independence in the early 1930s was said to be 1000 feet long and inhabited by thousands of bats.

The Sundust Mining and Milling Corporation was frequently mentioned in the spasmodic operations of the mine over the years, including a little strip mining in the late 1950s. During the early 1970s, former employees gathered for picnics at the site of the Independence Mine.

All the mining was predominantly for copper although there were traces of gold and silver. Oldtimers in the region continue to talk about the possibility of reopening the mining here. They say that no one has found the real "mother lode" yet. Who knows, with prices the way they are today maybe mining will bloom again here.

One wonders where the mining camp will be located and what its name might be.

Some Isolated Coal Towns

Colorado coal is a widespread and never-ending story. It deserves a few volumes by itself. The author had done the next best thing: he has spread it and its ghost towns out over four volumes—one previous book, this book and two to come. Many mountain coal towns were mixed in with the other towns in "Guide to Colorado Ghost Towns and Mining Camps." The bulk of the remaining coal camps will be in upcoming volumes.

A few very historic coal towns on the plains are scattered throughout this book. SOPRIS is with "Dead and Buried Drowned Towns." Two of the most historic coal towns—LUDLOW and HASTINGS—are appropriately with "Tragedy Towns."

One of the author's favorite ghost towns, SERENE, is the last town and last chapter in the book.

The following towns were isolated coal towns found on the plains.

BUICK (Godfrey)

(Elbert County)

One of Colorado's first coal towns was not in coal country at all—it was on the plains. It was unusual in other ways also. It grew up on the railroad line; tracks did not need to be built to it. In fact, the coal was discovered by railroad workers testing ground for laying track for the Kansas Pacific. At a site ten miles northwest of Riverbend (New), in 1870, workers sunk a shaft through what seemed to be a bed of soft, dry coal. Further exploration by engineers determined that a considerable bed of lignite coal lay just beneath the proposed roadbed. It was also determined that the bed was rich enough for extensive mine operations.

Some early reports indicated that the discovery may just have saved the railroad, as there was some discussion of abandoning the line due to lack of easily available coal.

Several stories appeared in the *Central City Register* in 1870 concerning the new coal field. Not all of the stories were encouraging.

A story on September 16 reported that Colonel Staubur, superintendent of the Hazleton Coal Mines (as the mines were called, for a railroad official), said that 160 yards of earth had been removed from the main entrance of the mines and that two entries had been made on the north and one on the south side.

Colonel Stauber said the vein of coal was 7½ feet wide, and "as soon as arrangements for mining have been made, 150 men will be employed and it is expected that they will turn out from 20 to 30 carloads per day."

The same item said that there were four or five families located at the site, others were coming and an application was being made for a post office.

On October 5 the *Register* observed that "Mr. F. J. Stanton, of our city, with a corps of hands, has in the past few days engaged in laying out the town of GOD-FREY, a new town in Douglas County [old Douglas County] on the Kansas Pacific."

The item stated that Dr. Cutts, geologist of Quincy, Illinois, was making an examination of the area, and that the mines inaugurated by the Hazelton Mining Company would be sufficient in themselves to "build up a respectable town."

However, an item on December 11 said that the mines of Godfrey, "from which much was expected have been abandoned on account of a failure to find good coal," and "that the town that was laid out will collapse."

Despite the item, coal was mined here for several years, even in recent years, and the town didn't collapse.

Some coal was used by the railroad, but apparently most of it was used in depots and other buildings and the homes around Godfrey, which remained a railroad stop for decades, primarily as a ranch center.

Coal was mined here as recently as the 1930s. A. J. M. Dolyrimple and Sons reopened the mine in March of 1933. By December of that year they had dug a shaft nearly 100 feet deep and were digging about 50 tons of soft, dry coal per day, employing seven men and one mule. The total workings at the time were some 3000 feet.

The site was later renamed BUICK for a local ranch family whose name was actually spelled Beuck. The name, often shown as BUICK (GODFREY) still appears on some detailed maps and is listed in directories, although there is no population listed today.

McFERRAN (Jimmy Camp) and FRANCEVILLE

(El Paso County)

As early as about 1830 "a little dwarf Irishman" named Jimmy Boyer ("Boyer," according to Mountain Man Jim Beckwith, "Hayes" according to historian Frank Hall, and "Daugherty" according to others), established a snug log house in the form of a fort at a location about ten miles east of present Colorado Springs. He brought many trinkets and knick knacks from the East. Some say he also brought tobacco and liquor. Whatever his wares, he established friendly relations with the Indians and traded what he had for furs.

Once a year he would load up his wagon with furs, return to civilization, sell the furs, buy new provisions and knick knacks, and return to the foot of the moun-

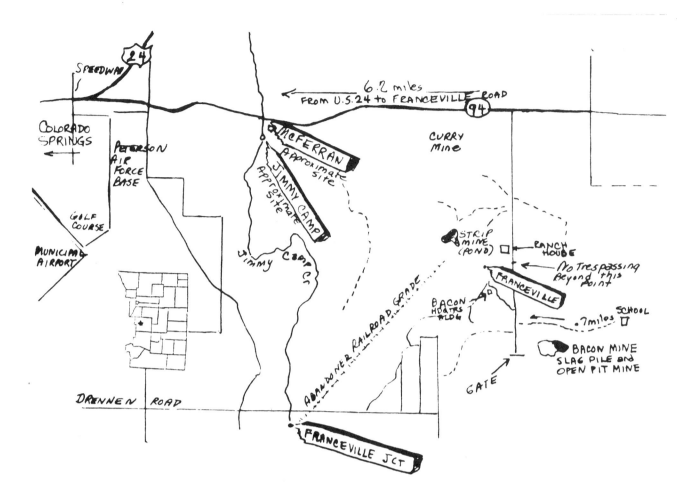

tains. His wagon train would follow a segment of the Cherokee Trail north from the Pueblo area, and his route was called Jimmy Camp Trail, which gave the name to Jimmy Camp Creek.

When he signaled his return by a large bonfire on a nearby hill, the Indians would gather not only to trade with the little Irishman, but also to socialize. They liked Jimmy.

But, alas, Jimmy returned once too often. Shortly after his return one year (believed to be 1833 or 1835), some Mexicans came to his camp, brutally murdered the little Irishman, and carted away the treasures from his camp.

Some of Jimmy's Indian friends led by Beckwith, tracked down the murderers, slit their throats and hung them by their toes from a nearby tree.

The Indians gave Jimmy a proper burial and marked the spot according to Indian custom. The exact burial site was long known to mountain men and was hallowed by the Indians.

Many years later the old stage road between Denver and Pueblo followed much of the Jimmy Camp Trail and established a stage station and tiny ranch center called JIMMY CAMP. In the early 1880s, the Denver & New Orleans railroad built along Jimmy Camp Creek on its

run between Denver and Colorado Springs. An 1882 report said that the new depot will stand on the "very ground" where once was Jimmy's camp.

Early directories and Crofutt reports about JIMMY CAMP and nearby MANITOU JUNCTION told of undeveloped coal fields nearby.

Much of the land around, including the coal fields, was owned by Judge J.H.B. McFerran of Colorado Springs. The good judge had boasted of the coal resources for several years. He did a little mining of it from time to time using hired hands. The coming of the railroad, however, encouraged him to further develop the lands.

In 1884–85, Judge McFerran began development in earnest. He boasted that the lignite coal found here was "superior to any in the country," and that the coal seam was "nearly ten feet thick," and virtually endless.

During 1885 a shaft was dug 150 feet. A plant was constructed at the surface which included engines, a boiler, hoisting and pumping apparatus, screens, other fixtures and outbuildings.

Continuous production began in the fall of 1885 under McFerran. The first couple of months, production was about 50 tons per day, half of the projected capacity. Most of the coal from the mine was taken to

GHOSTS OF THE COLORADO PLAINS

Colorado Springs and used by the Antlers Hotel and other large and small buildings in that city.

In 1886 McFerran sold out to a "syndicate of capitalists," and the mines began to show their full potential. The company constructed a town to accomodate 400 workers, opened new mines and put in some $30,000 in modernizing the mining facilities to produce 1500 tons per day. The Rock Island Railroad also built a five-mile spur from Manitou Junction. The town had a hotel, a large boarding house, and several cottages for workers and families. The post office was called MCFERRAN.

At full capacity, the railroad still could not haul out enough high quality lignite coal to serve the estimated 200 towns on the line.

Within the next few years, another hotel was added, more boarding houses and cottages, all operated by the company. There were company stores and a couple of "well conducted" schools.

FRANCEVILLE, located four to five miles southeast of McFerran, had much the same history. It was located on land owned by Matt France of Colorado Springs. The coal deposits were known for many years before the Denver & New Orleans Railroad built through in 1882. It was believed at the time that the coal seams here were part of "immense coal beds" that extended from the southern part of the county northward almost to Denver.

The Denver & New Orleans built a spur from its main line to the coal mines at Franceville, a distance of about five miles. The mines here were producing up to 20 carloads a day for several months by the time the mines at McFerran began large-scale production. In fact, it was about the same time McFerran started, in July of 1885, that the mine at Franceville cut back sharply due to a cave-in, forcing suspension of work.

At the time, however, a new incline was being developed and a new company was being organized to "produce a better quantity and quality of coal."

In late 1885 a coal vein was opened just north of Franceville, known as the El Paso Banks, and a "complete plant of machinery was placed in position."

By 1889 and '90 the company was mining about 400 tons of coal a day, of "excellent quality and popular in Colorado." The annual report in 1889 stated that there was "quite a little village" at the site.

McFerran and Franceville continued to produce coal for several years, neither apparently reaching their projected potential although the coal was of good quality and there was plenty here. The railroad line changed ownership, eventually becoming part of the Colorado & Southern system in 1898. The coal towns of McFerran and Franceville had maintained a low profile from the beginning, and their passing was barely noticed.

Major new development began in the old Franceville mining district in late 1979 and '80. The operator is Randall and Blake, Inc., a Littleton-based contractor.

The last remnant of Franceville was the schoolhouse for that former coal town. It has since been moved at least twice and seen many different uses.

The property was leased by Capstan Mine Company of Golden, the mine to be known as the BACON MINE.

Development will cover about 170 acres (12 acres at a time), and is expected to produce a peak capacity of up to 40,000 tons of lower-grade sub-bituminous coal a month.

The primary market is the Canon City Power & Light Company, with sufficient production to supply the city of Colorado Springs with its needs.

Officials claim there are enough reserves on the adjacent property to keep the company at full capacity for another 20 years.

SCRANTON *and the Colorado Eastern Railway*

(Adams County)

If one were seeking for the most unlikely operation in Colorado history there would be no need to look any further than Scranton and the Colorado Eastern Railway.

Scranton was an improbable coal camp a short distance east of Denver that, for a very short time, produced coal of such inferior quality that the lumps crumbled into coal dust and slack during the jarring 14-mile ride to Denver and the smelter was said to have mixed it with straw to ignite it.

Yet the coal mine had its own little railroad. The little railroad lasted much longer than the coal mine, although it never ran anywhere else. In fact, it made the 16.3-mile run from the Denver Union Station to Scran-

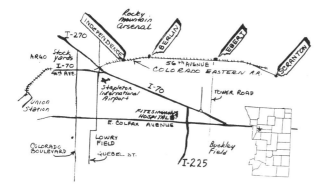

ton every day, six days a week for nearly 30 years. After it stopped hauling coal, it carried nothing but a few passengers and goods—very few. It lost money each year it remained in operation. Most of that time it had a three-man staff, each man doubling in all phases of the operation. The company spent $32,000 it couldn't afford to build a mile of standard-guage track it never used. It carried a bicycle on the engine tender as an "emergency vehicle"—and it was used frequently.

The little railroad bucked heads with the giant railroads, and usually won. But it was finally put out of business by an individual property owner who didn't want it running near his property.

That was Scranton and the Colorado Eastern Railway. A detailed account of the railroad and what little is remembered about Scranton is told by Charles S. Ryland in a booklet for the Rocky Mountain Railroad Club called "The Colorado Eastern."

The company was incorporated on January 16, 1886, as the Denver Railroad and Land Company. From the beginning the railroad had grandiose plans to extend its line to Sand Creek in eastern Colorado and further, to Kansas and possibly beyond.

The tracks were laid from the Denver Union Station to the site of Scranton, 16.3 miles away, between July and November of 1886. The lightweight 18- and 21-pound narrow-gauge rails added to the rickety character of the little railroad.

On January 14, 1887, the company was reorganized as the Denver Railroad Land and Coal Company, and the name of the railroad became The Colorado Eastern. The tracks went through the stockyards area in Denver, following today's 56th Ave. into the plains and paralleling today's I-70 to Scranton.

The company purchased engine No. 6 and most of its other rolling stock from the Denver & Rio Grande. The engine, known familiarly to railroaders as "The Ute" and in neighborhoods of northeast Denver and environs as "The Scranton," had been built by the Baldwin people in 1871, and came with a four-wheel tender.

For a short time the company had another locomotive to relieve the Ute. In the first two or three years the company had the two engines, two passenger cars, two

baggage cars, three other utility cars and 99 coal cars, attesting to the hope the company had for its coal mine at Scranton.

By 1890, the company had but nine coal cars, which it soon disposed of—attesting to the quality of its coal operations.

Actually, extensive coal operations lasted only about two years. About the only good thing to say about the coal was that it was near the surface and easy to mine. Much of the lumps broke apart on mining; much of the rest of it became dust or slack on the way to the Grant Smelter. Another trademark of the little railroad was the dust it spewed on its merry way to the smelter. For a short time, the company attempted to hold down the dust by covering the coal cars with canvas tarps. That didn't work. However, the company soon adopted the only sure way of ending the coal dust pollution problem: they stopped mining coal.*

But that didn't stop the little railroad. Through its 29 years of operation, it continued to harbor plans to extend the railroad to other more promising pastures.

One of its many schemes during its early years was colonization along the line. Some maps at the time show five stations along the short line to Scranton. They were INDEPENDENCE, BERLIN, JOHNSTOWN, ELBERT and SCRANTON. Two of the towns, Independence and Berlin, were actually laid out and promoted, but the promotion did not convince anyone. Berlin actually had a couple of lonesome takers and was listed in a couple of Business Directories between 1887 and the early 1890s.

Scranton was not much more prominent than Berlin. A couple of careless directories between 1887 and 1890 showed the population as 25. It was listed as 10 in 1890 when much of the activity ended here. The only times it was mentioned after that was as a terminus to the Colorado Eastern.

The only station the Colorado Eastern had was the Denver Union Station—which it shared. However, it did have an engine house at about East 39th Ave. and Wewatta Street.

One of the many grandiose schemes company officials had over the years was to make the tracks both narrow and standard gauge, in order to make its operations more flexible. A mile of standard gauge track was laid at a cost of $32,000—another costly plan that went nowhere.

The little railroad continued to run six days a week to Scranton, although there was nothing at Scranton worth running to. The company existed on a minimum of freight business and passengers, many of whom flagged the train down as it churned through ROSE HILL and other one-time Denver neighborhoods. When the

---

* According to Colorado Bureau of Mines figures, the Scranton Mine produced 11,000 tons in 1886, 16,000 in 1887, then sharply dropped in production until 1900, its final year, when it produced a mere 40 tons. Total production for the Scranton Mine was 35,781 tons.

The little engines of the Colorado Eastern Railroad became a familiar sight chugging through east Denver neighborhoods and suburbs. (*Courtesy Amon Carter Museum, Fort Worth, Texas*)

The photo above shows a group about to set out on a dove-hunting expedition on the Colorado Eastern.

At left, a photograph which appeared in the *Denver Times*, August 23, 1915, with a story of the railroad's demise. Engine #6 is shown being shipped off to the Arkansas Valley Smelter between Leadville and Malta. Behind the engine is the only remaining passenger car of the railway. (*Photos courtesy Denver Public Library, Western History Department*)

coal mining ended rabbits returned to the plains, and frequently rabbit-hunting parties would take the train to the end of the line on weekends. During other times over a year the line would have another small spate of business, but never anything to convert the ledger books from red to black ink.

An almost daily bit of excitement caused by the little railroad was its meeting or near-meeting with Denver Tramway cars as the rail lines crossed Denver tramway tracks at 48th and Race Street on the Riverside Cemetery line and at 47th and Humboldt. Charles Ryland said that although there were "several collisions" the tram was overturned only once as a result.

In 1913 the "combination car" was destroyed by fire. It was replaced by an odd creation made by company employees, which added to the personality of the odd little railroad. It was similar to the "Galloping Geese" of some other narrow-gauge mountain railroads in Colorado: an automobile engine was converted into a locomotive.

The Colorado Eastern "Galloping Goose" was a four-wheel passenger car with a flat roof, several windows on all four sides and a platform on both ends. The author and others have searched for a photograph of the car with little luck to date.

To add to its many other problems, Colorado Eastern owners spent much of their time in court sparring with such railroad giants as the Union Pacific and the Burlington over some right-of-way dispute or other. The Colorado Eastern usually either won the case or fought the railroad giants to a standstill.

Burlington and Union Pacific seemed somewhat paranoid in their attitude toward the Colorado Eastern. The reason being, the primary reason the Colorado Eastern owners had for sustaining its losing operation all those years, was that they owned some of the most valuable property in Denver. The railroad's right-of-way was the "most valuable" asset the railroad had.

If the Union Pacific or Burlington couldn't acquire the property, they worried that some other major competing line would take it over.

This apparently was also uppermost in the minds of officials of the Colorado Eastern. If they couldn't expand their operations into more lucrative fields, at least they might be able to sell the right-of-way for a nice profit. It never happened.

Although the little railroad successfully battled the giant railroads to a standstill, a single little property owner brought it to its knees.

A man building a hotel at 47th and Lafayette Street filed suit against the Colorado Eastern to enjoin it from building some needed track near the hotel. The railroad was enjoined on June 7, 1915. It ceased operations two months later—39 years after it started and 39 years without turning a profit. The company had existed a full 50 years, the last 20 years "on paper." The corporation was dissolved on May 22, 1944.

Virtually all traces of the town of Scranton and the little railroad have been covered over or erased except in the memories of oldtimers. Robert Ormes attempted to locate Scranton and the railroad line while "Tracking Ghost Railroads in Colorado." He said the railroad line would parallel east 56th Avenue. Any trace of Scranton, which is now on private property and through three gates, is gone. "The only evidence even of coal was a little pile a badger had brought up out of his hole."

Considering the quality of the coal, the little pile has no doubt blown away by now.

CHAPTER XIV

MULTI-TALENT TOWNS

As you might have noted, many towns worth their salt had more than one purpose in life. Some of the cities and towns of today survived the changes and continued to be useful, whatever the occupation or occupations of their citizens.

It was something like the "survival of the fittest," but not exactly. There were far too many towns—along the railroad track, in a mining area, in a farm region. It wasn't necessary to have several close together when one would do. In some towns there were multiple occupations, so when one job became obsolete there were other things to do and the town lived on. Towns with a single purpose died when that purpose was passé.

But countless towns that survived several changes, often major, very purposefully and usually profitably later passed from the scene, either abruptly through a fickle whim of fate, or simply fading over the years.

Note that most of the towns discussed in this book had more than one *raison d'etre*. The following towns survived changes, or never had one dominant occupation for its lifetime.

MALACHITE

(Huerfano County)

Tom Sharp was the father of MALACHITE. He settled here in 1870 and built his trading post and several other buildings near his post (see SHARP'S PLACE, "By the Side of the Road").

In addition to his well-stocked trading post along a fairly busy road over the mountains, early travelers were attracted by some pieces of copper float found in the area.

Sharp helped stimulate the early interest in gold and copper here. But not much gold in paying quantities was found, and although there was much loose copper, no large vein was ever discovered.

However, some were attracted to the place and built cabins near those constructed by Tom Sharp. And cop-

per provided the community with its name. Malachite is a type of copper, known for its greenish color, which is used in making jewelry.

Even before the mining in Malachite and the roadside business generated by Tom Sharp's trading post there had been some ranching in the region, mostly by early Spanish-American settlers. Sheep were their primary livestock.

Sharp was a cattle and horse rancher. He hated sheep as much as most other cattle ranchers. He brought in mules—which also hated sheep—to help keep his Buzzard's Roost Ranch clear of pests. Cattle became more dominant in the region and the grazing lands were more clearly delineated after Sharp and many of his neighbors settled here.

Another important early settler in this region was Charles or "Captain" Deus. In fact, he is usually credited with encouraging Tom Sharp to settle here. Deus served in the Union Army during the Civil War and some of that time fought Indians in Colorado, primarily in the San Luis Valley. He was discharged a captain and shortly thereafter settled in the valley.

In addition to the two-story, ten-room adobe home he constructed, he built the first flour mill. He also built a small stamp mill to process the copper found here and nearby.

Thanks to Tom Sharp and Captain Deus, Malachite flourished during the 1870s and 1880s, being the second most important community in the region, second to Badito.

During the 1880s the Huerfano Mining and Milling Company had brought up many of the claims and was the major mining interest in the region. The mining district here was the only one in Huerfano County, outside of the La Veta district.

Copper mining was sporadic over the next few years. There was a little mining as late as 1910 and 1915.

Other mountain passes were improved and Mosca Pass and the branches of Sangre de Christo Pass that trailed through Malachite fell into disuse.

Malachite's longtime and most steady occupation was as a ranching center, cattle and sheep, although some didn't admit to the latter.

The residence above, photographed July 16, 1897, was that of Captain Deus, an early settler who is said to have encouraged Tom Sharp, "father of Malachite," to settle in the area. (*Courtesy Amon Carter Museum, Fort Worth, Texas*)

The combination Southern Baptist Church and school at Malachite remains in good condition but is used for storage today. The crossroads store at right closed its doors for good many years ago.

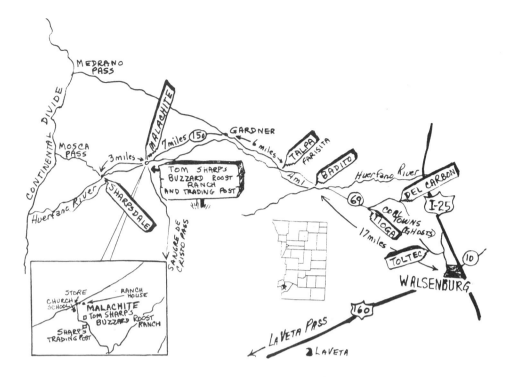

Captain Deus was a pillar of the community. When he prospered, Malachite prospered. Deus returned to his native Missouri in 1902, and died there two years later.

Today, two ranches cover the ground that once was the town of Malachite. There are only a couple of reminders of the town's busy past: the boarded-up crossroads store and the combination school and Baptist Church, with its bell tower and playgrounds. It remains in good condition because it is surrounded by a fence.

TALPA (Fort Talpa, Farisita, Huerfano Canon, Huerfano Crossing)

(Huerfano County)

A close neighbor of Badito—less than five miles further northwest—had several names, several occupations and was almost as historic as Badito although never as large.

It started around 1864 as HUERFANO CANON or HUERFANO CROSSING. It was located at the eastern terminus of Sangre de Cristo Pass at a crossing of the Huerfano River near the mouth of Big Turkey Creek.

Directories during the 1870s and early '80s tell of it being a sheep and cattle center, with some farming. There were two general stores and a post office much

of the time. Also listed was a "teacher." The population never topped 100.

There were other "Huerfanos" in Pueblo and Huerfano Counties. However, this one was no longer heard from after the 1880s.

TALPA came into being on or a short distance east of the site with the discovery of tin in the early '90s. It was also called FORT TALPA, so named, it is said, for the Old Spanish Fort built nearby in 1819 by the Spanish to guard against encroachment on Spanish territory by the Anglos. The poorly armed adobe fort had only lasted a few months when it was attacked "by a band of 100 men dressed as Indians." Six Spanish defenders were killed and the fort was abandoned.

Talpa means "abcess" in Spanish. It may have had something to do with an abcess in the canon, or there may have been a tongue in cheek reason for the name.

By 1900 the population of the district was 300. There was a Catholic Church, a Presbyterian Church, a school and a school board. A resident priest here was one of Colorado's most famous, the Reverend Gabriel Ussell. President of the school board was William Harms, who also ran a general store, was county commissioner and postmaster. There were other businesses in addition to the "tin mines."

Early in the century the population had dropped to 150, half of what it was in 1900. There was also some concern by the post office department about the confusion with Talpa, New Mexico. So the last name of the fading community was FARISITA, named by the postmaster, John Farris, for his daughter (Farisita means "Little Farris").

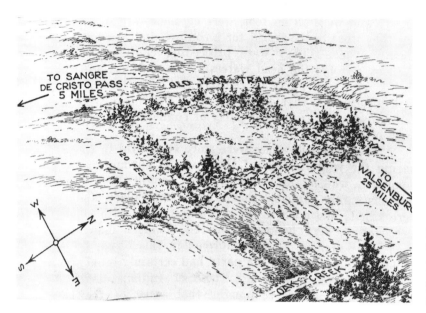

Ruins of the Old Spanish Fort, as sketched by noted historian LeRoy Hafen for *Colorado Magazine*, May, 1937. The fort was built in 1819 to guard against encroachment on Spanish land, a short distance from later Talpa. (*Colorado Historical Society*)

Mule Shoe Curve on Lump Mountain near Ojo was considered quite an engineering feat in its day. (*Pueblo Library District*)

OJO (Ojo Springs, Abata Canon)

(Huerfano County)

There were many descriptions of where Ojo was, many colorful ones. Most of them were in Crofutt's 1885 Gripsack Guide: "Ojo is in a narrow canon, the upper portion of which is called Abata Canon. Up this canon the cars run about three miles to the 'Mule-Shoe,' and then, turning, run around on the side of 'Dump Mountain,' in plain view of the station."

The first railroad (narrow gauge) into the mountains was built over Veta Pass, over Dump Mountain. It was considered a bit of engineering magic, including the steepest grades and sharpest curves up until that time. The "Mule Shoe Curve" used the centrifugal force principle to make the steep rise, and there were many jokes at the time about the railroad crossing over itself and the engineer shaking hands with the conductor in the caboose on the sharp curve.

The D&RG reached the top of the pass in the summer of 1877, and Ojo was made a station at about that time. Crofutt reports in both his 1881 and 1885 Guides that there was a "rich copper mine" nearby, and that there was a report that a smelting furnace was "about to be erected" in the narrow canon. If the smelting furnace was built it was not listed in subsequent years.

Ojo remained a farm center and a station on the railroad until 1899, when the narrow-gauge line was abandoned and the D&RG built a standard gauge about eight miles to the south.

The site was not heard from again until about 1915, when it came back strong as a coal camp. The 1915 directory said that the population was 300. There was a new post office, and the Alliance Coal Company and the Cisnew and South Arkansas Coal Company were the major companies here. Ojo has remained in the directories almost to this day, although its coal activity died several years ago. It was a ranch center.

In 1940, a sudden fire destroyed a store, filling station, café and residence at Ojo. Only a water pipe from the famous springs was available to fight the oil-fed blaze. However, as an indication of how little remained in Ojo and how old the buildings were, the damage to the town was listed at only $3000.

It is interesting that the origin of the town's name played a role in one of its final dramas. Ojo is Spanish for "spring," so the sometime name of OJO SPRINGS was a redundancy.

OVERTON and the Fountain Lake Hotel

(Pueblo County)

Perhaps few areas in Colorado had the wide variety of occupations of OVERTON and its neighborhood a short distance north of Pueblo. Hardly any trace of its many pasts are visible today. It is for the better, perhaps, because much of the activity was ugly, depressing and not very profitable. Much ado about nothing. Today, Pueblo is slowly inching northward and may soon completely cover the entire area.

Richens "Uncle Dick" Wootton (see WOOTTON, Chapter III) lived one of the more frustrating of his many lives here in the 1860s. In 1862, Wootton planted quite a bit of grain along Fountain Creek, and settled down, planning to become a gentleman farmer. Two years later a flood sent an 18-foot wall of water down Fountain Creek, killing nine settlers and washing out most of the farmland along the creek. Then hail destroyed the rest of Wootton's crops. He had had enough of farming by that time and went on to ranching and road building.

In the next few years more settlers came, planted grains and started orchards. One of the largest and most progressive land-owners was Joseph Benesche, who had emigrated from Bohemia in the early 1860s. Country schoolhouses were built for the farm children: Wood Valley, Eden and Dawkins (later Pinon) schools. The Denver & New Orleans Railroad laid tracks along Fountain Creek.

In the late 1880s Pueblo promoter W.H. "Coin" Harvey thought rapidly-growing Pueblo needed a super country-club type resort hotel. So he built the awesome FOUNTAIN LAKE HOTEL about three miles north of Pueblo. The plush hotel had a magnificent view of the mountains. Elaborate landscaping was begun on the 20-some

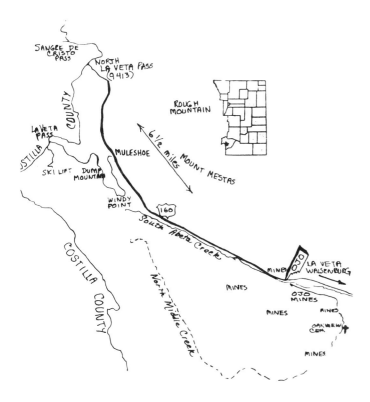

The Fountain Lake Hotel never saw success despite elaborate construction and the high expectations of its promoter, "Coin" Harvey. (*Pueblo Library District*)

The Rocky Mountain Oil Company operation at Overton was not such a pretty sight, but at one time it was fairly extensive—before being squeezed out by oil giants. (*Pueblo Library District*)

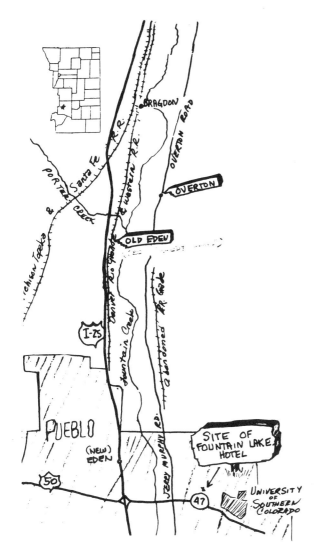

acres surrounding the hotel, focusing on a small man-made lake fed by water from Fountain Creek. A country-club style subdivision was platted around the resort.

Alas, no plots were sold in the subdivision and hardly anybody took advantage of the highly publicized attractions of the Fountain Lake Hotel.

The resort opened and closed within one year.

The next fantastic-but-futile chapter took place in the early 1890s. The Rocky Mountain Oil Company began construction, in 1891, of a giant refinery. RMO had wells in the Florence oil fields (the first oil fields west of the Mississippi and the second in the nation). There were a couple of refineries in the Florence fields, and the end product was shipped in tank cars back east by a long and costly railroad route. RMO believed that the Denver & New Orleans Railroad could cut expenses by shipping its oil to the Gulf ports, for further shipment via tankers.

A special feature of the RMO refinery was a 30-mile pipeline from the Florence wells to the refinery. It is said that some Denverites offered a half million dollars

toward constructing a pipeline to Denver from the refinery. It was much talked about, but never built.

During 1892 the refinery and the pipeline went into full operation. By the end of the year some 200 men were employed at the refinery. Everything looked most hopeful.

The Pueblo Board of Trade reported that the annual amount of eight million gallons each of kerosene and lubricating oils was shipped from the refinery in RMO's own tank cars. Paraffin wax and other side products were being shipped or stockpiled for shipment.

In 1893 a trolley was built from East Pueblo to the refinery. It was to run for many years, long after the refinery closed down, to fill a franchise agreement.

By 1893, however, RMO was already deeply in debt. A major cause of the refinery's final demise was a price war or "squeeze play" inaugurated by the oil giant, Standard Oil Company. RMO was squeezed out of the oil picture during 1894 and 1895 and the refinery was closed. The Central Trust Company of New York foreclosed a short time later.

Adding to the misery, there was another flood in 1894 that played havoc with many low-lying facilities and railroad track. It also washed out much farmland and orchard trees.

Back in the early 1890s, encouraged by the bright prospect offered by the RMO refinery, several Pueblo business leaders organized the Z. V. Trine Investment Company to plat a new city adjacent to the refinery. The new subdivision was named OVERTON for Pueblo Realtor Andrew J. Overton, secretary of the Trine organization. Trine sold 60 acres of its land to RMO: a large superintendent's house and many homes and other facilities were constructed around the refinery.

In 1892, when the refinery was still promising and the town of Overton was planned and a-building, the Fountain Lake Hotel came back to life. In April of 1892, the Pueblo Country Club was formed by Mahlon Thatcher, Alva Adams, J. B. Orman, O.H.P. Baxter and others. Some $10,000 was collected within a short time to prepare the impressive hotel for use and for the improvement of the grounds.

But the exciting prospect was little more than that. The second life of the resort hotel lasted no longer than the original one. Much of the blame was put on the Panic of 1893.

One far different type of enterprise that also began in the late 1890s was more successful. But it was still somewhat depressing. It was the establishment of the County Poor Farm.

Earlier the Pueblo County "Pest House" had been established about two miles north of Pueblo for the isolation of patients with contagious diseases. The foundation of the pest house had been badly damaged by the flood of 1894.

In 1898, 250 acres adjacent to the southwest refinery area was selected for the poor farm. A large two-story building was erected. It had dormitories on the second floor and a large dining room and kitchen on the first floor. Several other buildings, including cottages, were built on the grounds.

Crops were planted, and an orchard. There was also a modern dairy barn.

The idea behind the poor farm was to take persons off welfare and enable them to earn their keep, not only to save the county money but to help a man regain his independence and self-respect. The concept proved successful enough that the poor farm was soon relocated in larger facilities.

The old Poor Farm buildings were remodeled into private residences.

About 1903, the Overton schoolhouse burned down, and classes were held in a boarding house until a new school was built, further north.

In 1906, the 60-acre refinery site was leased and later sold to the Trojan Safety Powder Company of Allentown, Pennsylvania. The refinery equipment had earlier been taken to Florence, but most of the buildings remained, including the huge smokestack. The Colorado & Southern had abandoned its trackage between Colorado Springs and Pueblo in 1898, but with the coming of the powder company, the tracks between Pueblo and the site were repaired and used again.

The powder company operated irregularly until it was finally closed down for good in 1910.

From about that period on the buildings and other remnants of all the activity began deteriorating because of scavengers, vandals and the weather. More flooding in 1914 and 1918, and particularly the disastrous flood of 1921 caused tremendous damage to everything along the Fountain.

While all the to-do was going on with refineries, resort hotels and other construction, the fields throughout the region were planted and replanted with grains, corn, and other farm produce, and orchards were started again, berries of every nature flourished. Many Italian families moved into the region after the turn of the century. The fields were lush and colorful. The floods eventually washed out much of this, leaving the wide sandy channel seen today. Another flood in 1935 did more dirty work.

The Fountain Lake Hotel was used for various things over the years. Once in a rare while it was opened for special parties and dances. For awhile it was used as a sanitarium for tuberculars. Most of the time it was empty. It was considered a place for youngsters to explore—a "haunted house," and a challenge to vandals. Some claim it was an illegal speakeasy and storage place for "bathtub gin" during prohibition. It finally burned to the ground in 1930.

OVERTON, once the fastest-growing "city" in the area, has all but disappeared. Even the thick clusters of pinons and cedars on the low hills above the valley have disappeared, cut for firewood and other purposes.

Despite the grandiose schemes and projects in the past, the entire region is barren except for a scattered remnant among the weeds or fields to tell of the past.

But the region may live again. Pueblo is on its way.

CHAPTER XV

PLAYGROUNDS ON THE PLAINS

Colorado is famous for its many ski areas and mountain resorts. However, there were some colorful resorts on the plains and at the foot of the Rockies.

BARR LAKE (Barr City, Platte Summit)

(Adams County)

BARR LAKE is a state park today and one of Colorado's better bird and wildlife habitats. For a site that was nothing more than a buffalo wallow just 100 years ago that's quite impressive; but it's quite a come-down from all the extravagant hopes people have had for it over the decades.

When the Burlington (CB&Q) Railroad pushed through here in the early 1880s this section of marshland was a gathering place for birds and other wildlife, and a good place to round up the cattle that grazed on the surrounding prairie.

Rails were laid out of Denver to meet the rails being extended from Kansas. The Burlington had a little "Golden Spike" ceremony of its own on this site, which was called PLATTE SUMMIT at the time.

On May 14, 1882, farmers and ranchers in the region had already begun plans for turning this natural depression into a small reservoir for irrigation purposes. The Burlington Ditch and Reservoir Company was formed in 1884, and the Burlington Ditch was constructed in 1886 with a headgate on the South Platte River near Riverside Cemetery.

The railroad people and other developers saw an ideal resort opportunity here, and the original Oasis Reservoir was renamed Barr Lake for an engineer on the railroad. In 1887, the Barr City Land Company was formed. One of its incorporators was Henry H. Tammen, colorful co-editor of *The Denver Post.*

A model resort town was laid out the same year and a hotel built alongside the lake. There were weekend excursions from Denver for the purpose of selling lots.

The town grew rapidly. Many homes were constructed, and the railroad built an attractive station. A modern creamery was erected, and high quality milk was shipped each day to Denver. Soon the community had a school, a church, a grange hall—many of the new buildings constructed from bricks made in the community's own brickyard. Perhaps the town's most substantial home, a three-story house on the lake, was built in 1889 of stone, brought from the Platte Canon near Deckers by a Swiss bookbinder named Emil Bruderlin.

In 1889 also *The Barr City Gazette* began publication. However, the editors of the paper were soon lured away by nearby Brighton.

The fledgling resort community, like so many other non-essential enterprises, was hard-hit by the Panic of 1893. It languished until 1896, when the "Oasis Outing Club" was formed. The club leased the lake and the hotel, primarily for weekend excursions and many special events during the summer months. Fish and casting clubs from throughout the state gathered here for "Fish Day."

In 1903, the Burlington Ditch Company filed application to enlarge the lake. Soon after, the Denver Reservoir Irrigation Company was formed, acquired all rights to the ditch and reservoir, and built a new dam over the old one, increasing the capacity of the lake fourfold. The rebuilt canal was named the O'Brian Canal, and the new reservoir was called Barr Lake.

During the early years of this century there were a number of elaborate schemes involving Barr Lake and the surrounding area. One involved an extensive Dutch colonization plan.* Another would mean the development of an European-type spa, complete with an electric railway from Denver. The most elaborate involved a network of resorts, colonization, and extensive irrigation.

Despite a highly glowing forecast in the 1909 *Denver Republican,* predicting that the Denver Reservoir Irrigation Project would irrigate 25,000 acres and increase the local population by 25,000 within five years, this and all the other schemes and plans did not get very far.

---

* Some Dutch families from Chicago did settle for a few months at a site north of Barr Lake. The site is still called TONVILLE on railroad maps, named for George J. Ton, colony promoter.

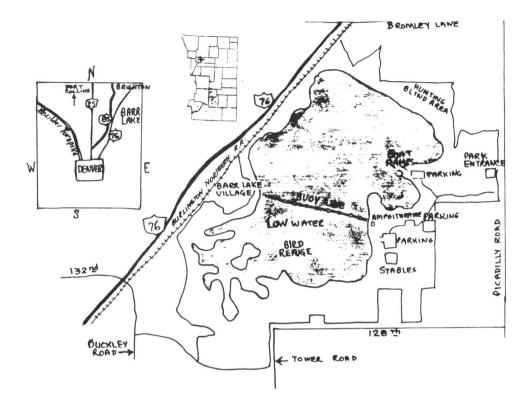

In 1913, the once prosperous creamery closed down. A short time later the local grange, the community's pride and joy since its opening in 1902, closed down.

The site was still prominent enough during World War I to be guarded against possible sabotage. A squad of soldiers was stationed at the lake during the war.

Other plans and schemes popped up from time to time, right up to the present—none promising enough to encourage the Burlington Railroad to reopen the station which it had closed in 1931.

The end of the railroad era seemed to be the death knell for Barr Lake. Denver made the end more inglorious for a while. The headgate of the O'Brian Canal was situated just downstream from the Denver Union Stockyards and Denver Sewage Treatment Plant. The aroma and physical pollution of those activities was transferred to Barr Lake by the canal. It not only chased away most of the remaining people, but the birds and wildlife as well, until the construction of the Metropolitan Sewage Treatment Plant in 1965, and the flood of that same year which flushed out the canal and lake.

Plans continued to pop up now and again, but the most feasible of all emerged within the last few years: a state park. The lake, with nearly 2,000 surface acres, became a state property in 1975, and was opened to the public in 1977.

Named as manager of the park was Carolyn Armstrong, the first woman park ranger in Colorado history.

There remain some buildings around the lake to recall the high aspirations people have had for the site over the years. The birds have been more reliable as residents, and Barr Lake remains of the best bird estuaries in Colorado.*

ELDORADO SPRINGS (Moffat Lakes)

(Boulder County)

ELDORADO SPRINGS is not a ghost. But it has undergone a distinct personality change from the days when its hot springs pool was known around the world, when nine or more packed trolleys a day unloaded or exploded with fun-seekers from Denver, and when the resort at the foot of the Rockies was electric with all manner of things to do.

The new personality involves the fairly new and rapidly growing sport of rock or mountain climbing. South Boulder Canyon, immediately above the old resort eight miles south of Boulder, is considered one of the top

---

* At last visit, it was found that weeds and mosquitos also thrive here. There are good roads and visitor facilities, but, according to one state official, no additional parkland areas are planned, making Barr Lake better picnic grounds for mosquitos and birds than people. The Colorado Park Department owns and maintains the land and facilities around the lake, the Farmers Reservoir and Irrigation Company owns the water.

climbing centers in the nation,* with an estimated 400 different ascents ranging from a "beginners walk-up" to some of the most difficult climbs in the world.

The canyon, now a state park, is filled most weekends with every level of climber, and there are also mobs of people below—watching and photographing the action. Today, the activity in the canyon often overshadows the life in the resort below; but even though the resort doesn't command the widespread fame it once had, the springs are still flowing and the new interest in climbing has spurred new activity below. Its future is secure as long as the hot springs continue to flow and fill the pool.

Like most mineral springs throughout the west, the springs of Eldorado were long known to Indians, and were part of their legend. Indian tribes and bands of wandering nomads camped here over the centuries, and fought for the springs when necessary. White men knew about the springs from the time of early settlement in the 1860s. However, it took many years and many interesting experiments before its "true calling" was discovered.

One early venture included a spiritualist, who proclaimed the miracle contents of the mineral waters and promised all manner of eternal health and salvation for those annointed—for a price, of course. Attempts to bottle the waters and ship them to troubled people worldwide did not progress far. Nor did later attempts to turn the site into a mining bonanza; prospect holes and scars left from quarrying and gravel mining can still be seen. Somewhat more successful was early lumbering. A sawmill once stood on the approximate site of today's mineral pool.

There were some early attempts to exploit the resort potential of the site, but for one reason or another these attempts didn't get far until 1904, when L. C. Stockton and W. A. Garner organized the Moffat Lakes Resort Company. The following year Frank D. Fowler joined the organization and soon assumed leadership, and the Fowler family has been involved in the operation of the resort ever since. Frank's son, J. "Jack" Fowler, helped his father build and develop the resort, and Jack and his wife, Mabel, have operated the resort since the 1920s. Semi-retired today, the couple still lives in Eldorado Springs in a house made from the stones excavated from the site of the mineral pool. Their son now runs the business, leasing out the pool and other facilities.

Frank Fowler's stepson (Jack Fowler's stepbrother) was a fellow named Gene Fowler, who became a legendary Denver newspaperman ("Timberline"), and later a writer and bon vivant in New York and Hollywood, friend and biographer of such notables as John

Barrymore (*Goodnight, Sweet Prince*), W. C. Fields, and others.

Gene was ten years older than Jack and lived with his grandmother in Denver during most of the period when the resort was being built. Jack and Frank Fowler did much of the work themselves. And it was backbreaking work, much of it—including excavating and hauling away huge boulders to clear the springs and collect the radium waters into a giant swimming pool. They also built the first cabins.

In 1905, a spur railroad line reached Eldorado Springs from Marshall, a coal town about five miles away. In 1908, the Denver & Interurban Railroad, with overhead lines running from Denver, reached Eldorado Springs via Boulder.

The D&I scheduled eight or nine runs a day during the summer months, with extra trains or cars on special holidays and for special parties. One source said as many as 18 or 20 trains a day made the roundtrip from Denver. The huge wooden cars of The D&I were a common sight for years as they raced through the countryside. The cars, which were 55 feet long and weighed 125,000 pounds each, were painted green.

In addition to the giant mineral springs pool (120 by 50 feet), there were large indoor and outdoor dance pavilions, a roller skating rink, picnic and camping grounds, gardens, shops and other tourist facilities. In 1908, the first parcels of land were sold for private cabin development.

Prices varied over the years. Original admission was 25 cents, but during the halcyon days the charge was 50 cents for admission to the park, $1.25 for pool privileges, and $2.25 for overnight camping. Round-trip fare from Denver, which included admission, was $1.25 Sundays and $1.50 weekdays.

The top bands of the day played here, including Glenn Miller, who got his start in Colorado.

Other notables who visited the Springs were Buffalo Bill Cody, Damon Runyan, Jack Dempsey, Mary Pickford, Douglas Fairbanks—and there were many famous and near-famous friends of Gene Fowler, who returned frequently over the years.

In 1916, a young Army lieutenant and his bride spent their honeymoon in a cabin here. He would become Supreme Commander of Allied Forces during World War II and President of the United States. But Dwight David Eisenhower and his bride, Mamie Doud of Denver, maintained a low profile in 1916.

The resort didn't close down during the winter. Its brochures boasted "swimming every day of the year" in its outside or inside pool. There was also ice skating and other winter sports, including sleigh riding.

Hiking was long an attraction here, long before Sir Edmund Hillary and others made mountain climbing the popular sport it is today—and there were hiking trails to Weeping Rock, Harmon Falls, Deadman's Cave and Castle Rock Cliffs.

A special but wearing thrill was the "famous scenic

---

* Some local professional rock climbers claim Eldorado Springs ranks among the top three climb centers in the country, along with Yosemite Valley in California and Schwangunks ("The Gunks") in New York State.

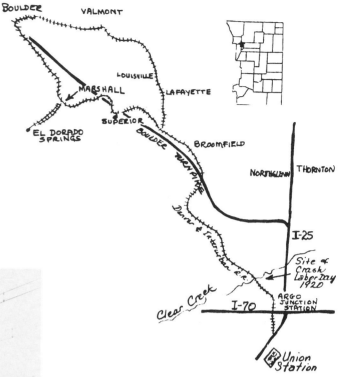

The Denver & Interurban Railroad was called the Kite Line because its route was shaped like a kite with a long tail. Below, D&I cars at the station in Louisville, Colorado, about 1912, when these cars were bringing thousands of revelers to the resort at Eldorado Springs. A head-on crash on Labor Day, 1920, just north of Denver, was the beginning of the end for the railway.

No date is given for the view at right of Eldorado Springs, but the automobiles are vintage 1920s. Today, mountain climbing is what makes this one of the state's most popular resorts.

Photos from Denver Public Library, Western History Department

Ivy Baldwin's tightrope crossing of Eldorado Canyon was called the greatest tightrope feat in the world, and Ivy, the greatest tightrope artist. Above, an early crossing, and at right, Ivy makes his 86th and final crossing on his 82nd birthday, July 31, 1948. (*Denver Public Library, Western History Department*)

The pavilion at Eldorado Springs was once full of activity.

At right, a scene of the flood that almost destroyed the resort in early September 1938. Much of the swimming pool and adjoining building was undermined or swept away. But the damage was repaired and the resort back in business the following year. (*Denver Public Library, Western History Department*)

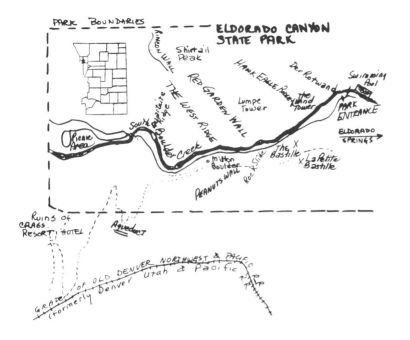

Eldorado Canyon is a climber's paradise, with everything from easy beginners' climbs to ascents with names such as Blind Faith, Last Rite, Terminal Odyssey, C'est La Vie and C'est La Morte, Schizophrenia, Neurosis, Psychosis, and The Naked Edge. For the non-climber, the canyon offers breathtaking mountainscapes.

1,350-foot CRAZY WALK to the top of POINT OBSERVA-TION . . ." where one could see a hundred miles of both plains and snow range. Along the almost-vertical route the hiker could admire another feature of the canyon: "Confetti Rock" with its bright red, yellow, blue and green spots. According to early brochures it was the highest colored rock in the West, outside of the Grand Canyon.

Another popular hike was up and along the winding tracks of the Denver, Utah & Pacific Railroad, the only railway that went beyond Eldorado Springs into the mountains. The objective of this hike was usually Crags, a onetime grand resort that perched perilously on the final lookout onto the plains before the railroad snaked its way into the mountains. (The Crags Resort burned down many years ago.)

Where today many spectators gather at the base of the canyon to watch the expert climbers high above, for many years thousands lifted their eyes for an even more spectacular sight: Ivy Baldwin, "the greatest tight rope walker in the history of the world." His spectacular feats were celebrated around the world. Also known in the Denver area for his balloon ascensions from Elitch Gardens, Baldwin was a mainstay over the years at Eldorado Springs. At least once a year he walked the wire across the highest pinnacles at the entrance of South Boulder Canyon, nearly 600 feet above the crowd. He made his final trip across the canyon, probably the 86th, in 1948 on his 82nd birthday.*

The last regular interurban train reached Eldorado Springs in 1926. The railway was a victim of the automobile, and had other problems.†The tracks were torn up a few years later.

But Eldorado Springs survived, and added a parking lot for automobiles. A flood in 1938 caused much dam-

age to the resort, but repairs were made immediately. Then a fire in 1939 burned down the resort hotel and destroyed many of the records.

Despite the travel restrictions brought on by World War II, the resort remained popular during the war years. It became quite a student rendezvous following the war. For a few years it was turned into a private club and was closed to the public.

The resort underwent a major facelifting in the early 1960s, at a time when it was enjoying a peak of year-round holiday activity. An overflow crowd of some 500 attended the 1961 Christmas party and it was full for other holiday celebrations the following year.

The rock-climbing potential of the canyon developed during the 1950s. The wide variety of climbs and the great challenge of the most difficult ones has caused the reputation of Eldorado Springs to spread. The most difficult routes, such as Redguard and the Naked Edge, were mastered only in recent years, and then by the top experts. There have been many climbing accidents, and some deaths in recent years, generally by those who think they are expert those who take chances, and who climb alone.

The growing number of accidents and the crowds of sightseers, with accompanying pollution and vandalism, increased the tension between the permanent residents of Eldorado Springs and the visitors. There were attempts to screen off the canyon or limit the tourists by charging admission.

Much of the problem was solved in 1975 when Jack Fowler, then 79, sold 200 acres of his property, which included the canyon entrance, to the State of Colorado. The park to be developed there is expected to contain 3,000 acres of colorful canyon lands.

Eldorado Springs has changed in character considerably in recent years, but so has our way of life. Eldorado Springs has survived where other early Colorado resorts have not because it had more to offer and the ingredients to adapt.

* The number of crossings has been reported as up to 200, depending upon the source. One source said that Baldwin made his 99th crossing as a special favor to Gene Fowler, who idolized Baldwin and witnessed several of his feats. However, 86 was the number publicized in the newspapers at his last crossing. The distance across the Canyon has also varied with reports, from 550 to 785 feet. Baldwin died in 1953.

†The D & I never fully recovered from a crash that occurred on the line on Labor Day, September 6, 1920. It was the only major accident on the line, but it was devastating. A special train loaded with tourists bound for Eldorado Springs had just left the station at Globeville when it rounded a curve and crashed headlong into another train full of passengers from Boulder and Louisville, bound for a day of picnicking, etc. in Denver. The inbound train was speeding because it was late, and, although the outbound train was only two minutes out of the Globeville station, it had achieved full speed. A total of 13 persons were killed and more than 100 injured. Nearly half of the victims were from Louisville. Only one crewman was killed, as the others jumped when they saw a crash was inevitable. None of the passengers, many standing in the aisles, knew what hit them. Blame was placed on the crew of the special train. The conductor was new on this train, but the schedule was available and the crew had been warned to wait on a side track at Globeville until the other train passed.

HIGHLAND LAKE (Highlandlake)
(Boulder County)

The little lake about eight miles northeast of Longmont, one mile north and one mile east of Mead, started attracting visitors in the 1870s, if not earlier. It became a ritual in the late 1870s for Longmontites to drive their buggies to the lake, particularly on weekends, to camp and fish and picnic. Someone named the lake Highland Lake, and the little cottage community that grew up there was also called HIGHLAND LAKE.

It wasn't all fun and games at the lake, although that was its major role. Fresh milk, eggs and chicken soon became a trademark and the pride of the community.

And the local community didn't feel right in continuing their fun and frolicking through the Sabbath. In

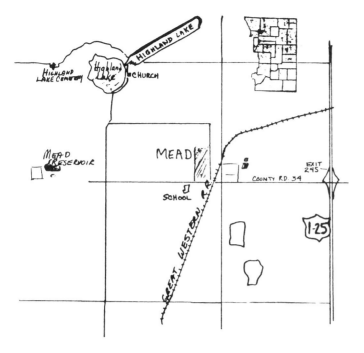

November 1880 the citizens held a meeting and resolved to hold regular church services. The congregation was organized in January of 1881 with a membership of 20. By 1884, when Highland Lake hosted the Denver Association of Congregational Churches, the congregation had grown to 56.

The Sunday meetings were held in different homes each week. After the meetings, potluck dinners were usually held, with other events following.

In 1894, the church obtained the services of a female

The well-kept church at Highland Lake stands alone most of the year. Neighbors and former residents have raised enough money to replace broken panels in the large stained glass windows in the front of the church, now covered by shutters.

pastor, Mary G. Bumstead of Roxbury, Mass. Two years latter, sufficient money had been raised to build the church, and the cornerstone was laid in May of 1896. The building was completed by the end of the year and the first services were held in it on January 3, 1897. The stained glass window was a "gift of the Y.M.C.A. of Naugatuck, Conn."

Of course, the church wasn't everything at Highland Lake, but it was the center of activity and the community's pride and joy, along with the fresh milk, eggs and chickens. Other farm products were shipped. There was a school and a year-round population of 200.

A crippling blow befell Highland Lake in the early years of this century. The Great Western Sugar Company built a railroad spur nearby to pick up sugar beets along the line. The spur missed Highland Lake by a mile or two. At the closest point on the track, a station was established and the town that grew around it was named MEAD, for an important family in the area, one member of which was one of the founders of the Highland Lake church.

Many Highland Lake citizens moved to the new community. After all, they would still be close to their lake, and they could in addition enjoy all the benefits and conveniences of living in a railroad town.

It became more and more difficult to raise money for the pastor's wages and other church expenses. Services became irregular, particularly during the off-season months. The last regular service was held at the little church in 1920.

But local citizens have continued to maintain the church, now the only building remaining in the one-time resort community, outside of a few houses around the lake. The church was opened for weddings and funerals and other special occasions over the years.

In recent years, an annual reunion is held at the church on the second Sunday of June, sponsored by the United Methodists of Mead. Oldtimers and their children get together again. After services there is a potluck dinner and other events, just like in the good old days.

QUEEN BEACH
(Kiowa County)

One of Colorado's most elaborately planned resorts was out on the Plains in "Dust Bowl country." Located about 15 miles due north of Lamar, just north of the Prowers County line, QUEEN BEACH or QUEEN'S BEACH was the first incorporated town in Kiowa County. It was on the east side of Queen Reservoir, one of a series of lakes created here to help irrigate the surrounding farm land.

The elegant resort was platted by the Ball Land Engineering and Development Company of Lamar. It contained 50 square blocks, the most expensive of which fronted the lake on Queen Beach Avenue. In addition to a large bathing beach, the plat contained tennis

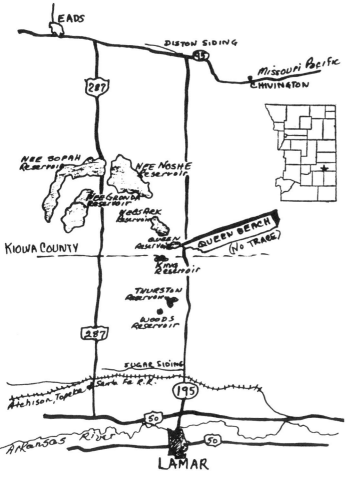

courts, a ball park, sanitarium and a large park. Much of it was built.

The resort was incorporated on September 22, 1910, with no less than 34 electors. There was a post office here. The mayor operated the popular saloon on the beach.

World War I put a damper on the activities at the resort, and business was worsened by the drought and farm depression that began in the 1920s. The Dust Bowl era, when many of the reservoirs on the plains were drained or virtually dried up, sealed the coffin.

No trace remains of the elaborate resort that was born at the wrong time, and local people have no memory of it, though the reservoirs that survived are still popular stopping places for fishermen and Canadian geese.

ROXBOROUGH PARK (Persse [Perisse] and Percy Park)

(Douglas County)

In 1820 Major Long made a short side trip on his southward trek along the foot of the mountains where he discovered ". . . a range of naked and almost perpendicular rocks, visible at a distance of several miles and resembling a vast wall parallel to the base of the mountain . . . with interesting views of singular color and formation, the whole scenery truly picturesque and romantic."

It was the white man's first view of the wonderland at the foot of the majestic Colorado mountains. It would be another 150 years or so before the site would become available for all to enjoy as ROXBOROUGH STATE PARK.

The unique and colorful rock formations, some reaching 200 feet into the sky, are an extension of the formations seen at Red Rocks Park and have been likened to the Garden of the Gods. But the treasures were locked up for decades and might have been destroyed or eternally locked away but for the failure of a commercial venture to turn the entire area into private homes.

Indians over the centuries knew and appreciated the awesome region and, no doubt, attached legend to it. Early settlers viewed the idyllic backdrop as little more than a unique but limiting barrier to good ranch land.

It is said to have been named Roxborough by Edward Griffith, who believed the land was much like that near his birthplace in Middlewich, England.

The Helmers family acquired much of the property in 1872 for ranching, and their descendants lived on the land for the next century.

It wasn't until the 1890s and early 1900s that the scenic and resort possibilities were first exploited.

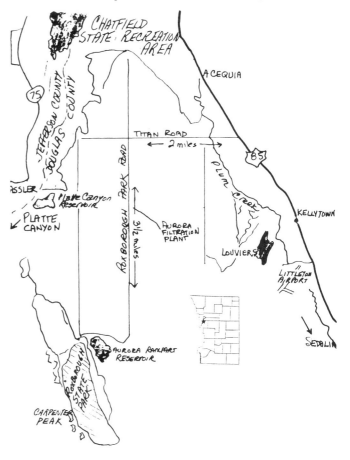

Littleton Historical Museum, Littleton, Colorado   *Colorado Historical Society*

Above, two historic photos of Roxborough Park, the one at left by William H. Jackson, and the other taken in 1910 by Edwin A. Bemis, longtime Colorado newspaper editor and political figure.

At left, a Bureau of Reclamation overview of Roxborough Park before modern development began.

Today, the area immediately surrounding the rock formations has been developed into a park which is surrounded by residential areas. Meandering in and around the rock formations is Arrowhead, one of Colorado's most colorful and difficult golf courses.

Henry S. Persse (often shown as Perisse) acquired a large parcel of the land and began developing it as a resort for Denver society. It was called PERSSE PARK, or sometimes PERCY PARK, but little known outside of the wealthy families who would gather here for outings on weekends and holidays. Persse built a lodge, barn and stables to accomodate the visitors.

It was about this time that the far-sighted John Brisben Walker first promoted the idea of a "ring of parks" around Denver, which would include Red Rocks Park, Roxborough and Mount Falcon above Morrison where he built his castle—the ruins of which are now on park land—and began construction of another castle which he attempted to promote as the "Western White House."

Although Walker has been called "The Father of Denver Mountain Parks," few listened to him at the time and it would be a few years before Denver would put any money into the idea.

Denver's Mayor Speer was one of the few who listened to Walker. He was also a visionary, and Denver citizens owe much of the city's landscaped parks and parkways to his vision. He joined Walker in promoting the Mountain Park system as well. He was instrumental in the eventual acquisition of Red Rocks, but could not stir enough interest to raise the $6000 he needed to acquire the Roxborough area in 1915.

In 1925 an area more than twice the present park area was offered to the city for $23,000. The city fell just $2000 short and the region remained in private ownership. In the 1950s and '60s, the Colorado Park Association, a citizens group, and other groups and individuals attempted to spur the state legislature to acquire the land. They were not successful. But in 1970 a private land development corporation bought 3200 acres of the site for the purpose of building modern homes. And then attempted to sell the scenic formations around the development area to the state for twice what it paid for the land. Fortunately (except for the development corporation), the corporation went bankrupt.

In 1975, the legislature appropriated $1 million to purchase 500 acres of the land. The state purchased another 256 acres for $706,000. Plans call for adding another 300 acres for an overview area. In the fall of 1978, ROXBOROUGH STATE PARK became a reality. Thus far it has cost $1,614,000 in state and federal funds to buy just a portion of what would have cost $23,000 fifty years ago.*

* Acquisitions by the Colorado Park Department in 1983 and 1984 have increased the size of the park by more than one half, from 769 acres to 1,163 acres. Total purchase price for the new land was $943,000, of which almost one-third of the funds came from the Colorado lottery. The acquisitions, primarily at the southern end of the park, will greatly help preserve the wildlife habitat in the park, which has been designated a national natural landmark. Park officials hope to complete acquisition of all land for the park by 1987. Special guided tours of the park began in 1984.

The fragile nature of the park area requires that it be developed slowly and carefully. Originally there were only ranger-guided tours of the site at appointed times and for groups. Eventually there will be nature and hiking trails, all within specified areas. The planned parking lot will have spaces for only 100 vehicles at one time.

Meanwhile, scientists are having a field day. Anthropologists and archeologists are tracing the human and animal life of the region through the ages. Artifacts indicate that human life dates back some 7000 years. A barely traceable ruin of a rock shelter further indicates that ancient man lived here. Other scientists are further cataloging the flora and fauna.

Roxborough will be a state treasure in many ways.

STRONTIA SPRINGS (Deansbury, Deane, Deanes, Newberry)
(Jefferson County)

The resort potential of this site was realized shortly after the first train of the Denver, South Park & Pacific chugged through Platte Canyon in 1874. In the late 1870s DEANSBURY (also called DEANE, DEANES)* of Platte Canyon, gained popularity. There was something here for everyone.

* Early railroad mileage charts showed Platte Canyon as 20.4 miles from Denver Union Station, Strontia Springs as 26.8 miles, and South Platte, at the western mouth of the canyon, as 29.4 miles.

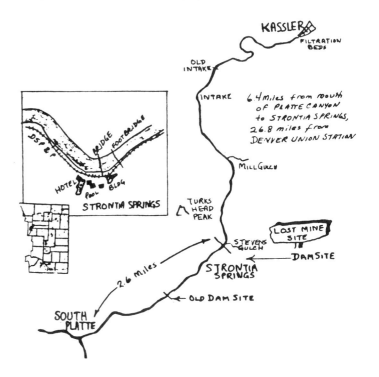

This photo of the resort hotel at Strontia Springs in Platte Canyon after the devastating flood of 1900 shows the flood waters and twisted railroad tracks. (*Denver Water Department*)

It was popular as a daytime resort and as a vacation spot for overnight visitors. During the summer season the resort hotel (from 1884 to 1905) was generally packed, with a capacity of more than 100 during its heyday. At the same time, during the height of the season the railroad might bring 200 to 300 persons here in the morning. The visitors would spend the day fishing, hiking through colorful and interesting Platte Canyon, mountain climbing, rock hunting, flower picking, or just picnicking. Then the train would pick them up at night exhausted, but often loaded down with trout, wildflowers, rocks, and blisters to show for their day.

After a few years, the resort facilities were allowed to run down, and visitors dropped off.

The site made a big recovery during the early years of this century, when a Denver mortician built a lavish resort hotel and restored some of the old facilities. Wealthy Denverites also built homes here, some for summer use and a few for year-round living. The new name was STRONTIA SPRINGS, to promote the nearby mineral springs.

A newspaper, *The Platte Canyon Fly*, was published irregularly between 1912 and 1916.

The hotel was closed about 1920, and the railroad stopped making regular stops here. The railroad stopped running through the canyon altogether in 1937.

In the years since, hikers, bird-watchers and nature-lovers in general have hiked the unique canyon. There was much effort expended to make the canyon an historic landmark and nature trail—all for naught.

The Strontia Springs Dam, built by the Denver Water Board to supply additional water for Denver, was closed on April 21, 1984, and the canyon was opened up to the damsite for the first time since 1978. The dam towers 243 feet above the riverbed and will form a 1.7-mile-long reservoir. Water from the reservoir goes through a 3.4-mile tunnel through the mountains to the Foothills Water Treatment Plant. A ten-mile trail was built around the south side of the reservoir during construction.

The waters will flood the site of STRONTIA SPRINGS. It will not cover the site of one of Colorado's lost gold mines on Stevens Gulch near the foot of the dam. According to legend, the gold was known to Indians who used it in making jewelry. The gold source has been found and lost again several times since. One party that was said to have a map of the mine was killed en route to the site, presumably by Indians. In 1911, a Denver man found some gold samples in Stevens Gulch, off Platte Canyon. When he returned shortly thereafter, he did not find the gold source. He did see a rabbit disappear behind some bushes, however, and thinking about it afterwards, he believed the rabbit may have lived in the old gold diggings.*

---

* See "The Rabbit Hole Tunnel," in *Treasure Tales of the Rockies,* by Perry Eberhart.

CHAPTER XVI

SIN SUBURBS

Agents of the oldest profession braved the frontier in gallant numbers long before their more pious sisters. They were needed and they were there. When more and more of the sisters came, the early birds were shunted into special neighborhoods or even special communities.

Mining camps were not the only settlements where men greatly outnumbered women. So the first women wed many men. All but the most religious colonies had their women, and even those had some women a decent but short distance away.

In many cases the early respectable female types led the campaign to segregate or exile the shady ladies. Sometimes it was the menfolk who led the fight—to impress the ladies or make some point or another.

In many areas on the plains, a roadhouse served several small towns. Or the roadhouse, sometimes disguised, was in the town itself.

Some settlements even fenced off a section of the towns or built a compound to demark "no ladies land."

ARRIBA was one town that segregated all its illegal activities behind a fence. The "sin section" of town was called FRONTIER or FRONTIER CITY.

Steamboat Springs was not the only western town to name its red-light suburb BROOKLYN, located across the river from the mountain town. BROOKLYN was a popular name for red-light districts in the west.

Whatever the name, such districts were a fact of life in the Old West. The larger cities had larger districts or suburbs to fill this purpose. Denver had a large in-city red-light district as well as two or more suburbs to serve the population.

PETERSBURG
(Arapahoe County)

PETERSBURG had an innocent beginning. There was farming along the Platte as early as the 1860s. Peter Magnes came from Illinois around 1859 with many another gold-seeker. Magnes tried his luck in the gold fields for a few months before settling on rich farmland south of Denver City. He platted a farm center along the railroad about the same time he built the Harvest Queen Flour Mill in 1874. At that time Petersburg was located about eight miles south of Denver.

The Harvest Queen mill was never a success, and it burned to the ground in 1883. But by that time Petersburg was considered a "thriving suburban town." It was even considered for county seat. It was first known as a farm center, but it had already begun to cultivate a much more exciting reputation.

Center of this reputation that would last for many decades was a large roadside inn. The original two-story log building was constructed in 1879 of sturdy material and without the use of nails. For the next 60 years the building would have many different names— The Wayside Inn, Petersburg Inn, Dick's Corner, etc.— and many owners.

It achieved its widest reputation under the ownership of "Pap" Wyman. Pap came down out of the gold fields in 1889 and remodeled the Inn, turning it into a three-story brick building with 17 rooms. Pap Wyman soon had a widespread reputation for hospitality. His well-stocked saloon and fine eatery drew many of Denver's finest.

Petersburg achieved its full glory during the "Gay '90s." Wyman's was only one of a half dozen roadhouses in a row. Petersburg was popular with the racing crowd. The run from Denver to Petersburg was a popular one for bicyclists. Gambling was rife and there were "ladies" available for a price. They even had some prize fights in the town. Several shootings and at least one duel resulted from the activity here.

Most of the trouble began around the turn of the century. During much of 1902 there were almost regular battles on the weekends between soldiers from nearby Fort Logan and bar patrons. At one time two ranch hands and William Blain, manager of Hotel Peters, were "beaten into insensibility" by a gang of soldiers. There was also a running feud between soldiers and workers at the local cotton mill.

Some blame Petersburg's growing reputation for its losing to Littleton in the battle for county seat in 1903.

During the early 1900s, through 1912, there was almost constant friction between the police and the taverns. From 1908 through 1910, the Petersburg Inn was closed frequently for gambling, prostitution and other infractions. After traipsing through the courts and paying fines the roadhouse would open again, only to be closed a short time later.

In late May of 1909, four masked gunmen invaded the crowded Petersburg Inn and robbed the patrons of

This log house, built about 1860, was probably one of the first homes in what became Petersburg, one of Denver's "sin suburbs." (*Denver Public Library, Western History Department*)

Saloon and blacksmith shop on Santa Fe Drive in Petersburg, around 1896-97. Both were owned by blacksmith Henry J. Wehrly, shown here with his son Raymond. (*Littleton Historical Museum, Littleton Colorado*)

their jewels and money to the tune of $4000, while another $8000 in jewelry and cash was overlooked. The daring robbery took place during a fancy dinner party of "wealthy Denverites."

The fatal blow hit Petersburg in 1916—Prohibition. During the next few years there were frequent attempts at gambling, prostitution and illegal rum-running in the area, but it was never again like the free-wheeling days of the past. Business and the buildings at Petersburg deteriorated.

The area has since become part of Sheridan. The Petersburg depot became the Englewood station. In 1939, the famed old Petersburg Inn, by then a roadside store and gas station, was razed to widen the highway. The building would have been located at about 3500 South Santa Fe Drive today. Perhaps one day someone will gather together all the adventures that corner had to tell and make an exciting book of it.

RAMONA
(El Paso County)

When General Palmer created Colorado Springs he stipulated that there would be no boozing and sinning in his beautiful new city. So the burden for boozing and sinning fell on the shoulders of "OLDTOWN" or COLORADO CITY for much of the next few years, except when the city fathers and their loving spouses felt the "pangs" now and again and banned sinning from Colorado City as well.

When that happened Manitou Springs and other nearby spas didn't mind it at all. It increased their business.

In 1906, when the "decent folk" swept Colorado City clean of all its bordellos and other sin centers, the "gang" moved just north of Colorado City. It was a

This fanciful building, originally the Petersburg Inn, changed appearances and uses many times over the years. (*Courtesy Amon Carter Museum, Fort Worth, Texas*)

scattered, shanty-type operation for a while, nothing substantial enough to shoot at by local officials.

The "neighborhood" had developed sufficiently by 1913 that there was talk about incorporation. It seemed by newspaper accounts that the more aghast the "decent folk" were about the idea the more determined the "liquor interests" and others were to incorporate. The new town was named for the Indian heroine in Helen Hunt Jackson's famous book, *Ramona*.

Some of the choice words of opposition at the time included this from the May 23, 1913, issue of the *Colorado City Iris*:

There is no secret that the purpose of the starting of the new town is to have that town given over wholly to the perpetuation of the liquor traffic and all its attendant evils. . . .

Incorporation papers were filed in July, 1913. Despite all manner of opposition, the incorporation was approved and Ramona opened with a flourish, according to the November 21 issue of the *Colorado City Independent*:

Ramona, the new booze annex to Colorado City opened Monday Night in a blaze of glory, and according to the papers, "carriages met the cars at Fourth Street to carry patrons."

But were the carriages on hand to haul them home—after the festivities ended?

After incorporation Ramona was harrassed almost continually by the newspapers and by county officials. There was an attempt to withhold water from the new suburb. There were frequent raids and many arrests and fines levied. It took annexation and Prohibition to fell the feisty little neighborhood.

The passing of Ramona was marked by the January 6, 1916, edition of the *Independent*:

CREPE ADORNS RAMONA

No more will the musicians sit before the piano at Ramona and tickle the ivories, while men line up before the bar and keep time with the clink of glasses. No more will Colorado City officials be required to spend most of their time at the corner of Fourth and Colorado Avenue to act as a steering committee to pass the booze soaked hides, on down the line to Colorado Springs.

The oasis has vanished from the desert and the thirsty souls must go to greener pastures or be satisfied with H_2O.

Crepe was tied on the doors up there last Friday Night, and Ramona passed into lost cities of the country.

Now the people up there can settle down to peace and quiet, can boost and boom that location as a beautiful residence site, a place for homes, where scenery and beauty are before the eyes at all times, for this location commands the best view of the mountains to be had in the entire district.

Colorado City can fix up the beautiful little park again and our people can go up there with the knowledge that they will not be disturbed.

Ramona should be a part of the city and it likely will in time, for the people of this town are going to take an interest in the welfare of her people that they never took before. They are going to paint their houses, beautify the lawns, the parkings and the streets with flowers, to make a garden spot here that people will delight to see and Ramona will fall into line and do the same.

Perhaps you do not know it but there are a lot of new faces in this town, people are coming here because this city is and has been clean, and because it will be a good place to raise a family and to build a home.

Of course, the Ramona neighborhood is not nearly as exciting or newsworthy as it used to be, but, I guess, there are trade-offs for progress, too.

There is no hint of Ramona's unsavory past today. The historic little neighborhood was bounded, generally, on the south by St. Vrain Avenue, on the north by Cache La Poudre Street, the west a half block west of 26th Street and on the east by 23rd Street.

CHAPTER XVII

UNIQUE TOWNS

A handful of Colorado towns don't fit any mold or category. Their unique purpose made them historic. Books could be written about them and their purpose. Here are brief profiles.

AMACHE

(Prowers County)

One World War II site in Colorado does not commemorate a proud moment in the state's history.

In the hysteria that followed the Japanese attack on Pearl Harbor on December 7, 1941, many next-door neighbors and long-time friends suddenly became fearsome enemies. To some people all persons of Japanese heritage, whether American citizens or not, were potential traitors. The popular logic of the day was "once Japanese, always Japanese," and if it came down to a choice a "Jap" would stick to his ancestral allegiance and turn his back on the United States.

This thinking was fostered and festered by some political leaders and newspaper columnists. The most prominent of the latter was Walter Lippmann, who recommended that "the civil rights of minority citizens could be set aside for national security."

The feeling was particularly strong in California, where rumors of imminent invasion were constant and where the majority of Japanese Americans (Nisei) lived. Of the 127,000 persons of Japanese ancestry in the United States, 113,000 lived on the West Coast, 94,000 in California.

In February of 1942, President Roosevelt signed Executive Order 9066, authorizing the Army to remove all persons of Japanese ancestry from the West Coast. The Army's decision was to move them into inland concentration camps called War Relocation Centers.

Perhaps much to his credit, but also much to the consternation of many of his political backers, Governor Ralph Carr said the Japanese Americans would be welcome in Colorado.

In 1942 the War Relocation Authority acquired 8000

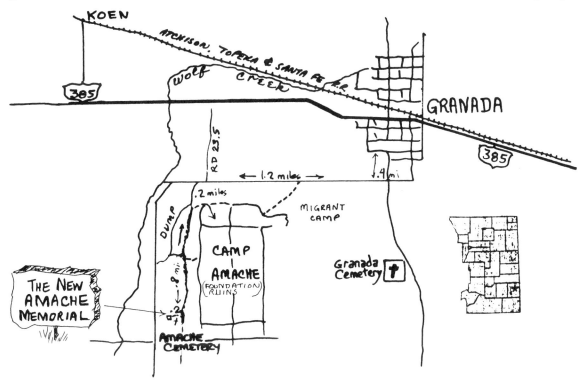

Building of the Japanese-American relocation center at Amache in southeastern Colorado, begun in the fall of 1942, was completed very quickly, as shown by the photograph below, taken a few months later. (*Holly Publishing Inc.*)

In February, 1943, Captain William S. Fairchild tells residents of the Amache center that men 18 to 38 can volunteer in a special combat unit, and other men and women can do defense work. Some 2000 Nisei volunteers served as the "eyes and ears" of American forces in the Pacific, saving thousands of lives. (*Denver Public Library, Western History Department*)

Japanese-American soldiers home on furlough visit the Arts and Crafts Festival at Amache, March 1943, with their girlfriends. (*Denver Public Library, Western History Department*)

The marker at right, erected at the site of the former relocation camp in memory of the Amache volunteers, was dedicated September 3, 1983. (*Photo courtesy Art Moriya*)

acres of land (eventually 11,000 acres) in extreme southeast Colorado, a short distance southeast of Granada.

Army contractors built the camp the way they would build a military base. The first trainload of residents arrived in August of 1942. They were provided with tools and scrap wood with which they fashioned their own furniture and other necessities of life.

It is interesting (perhaps ironic) that the camp was given the name AMACHE. Amache was an Indian princess, the daughter of Chief One Eye, who was killed in the Sand Creek Massacre (a short distance north of this site) by Colorado Volunteers in 1864. She had married John Prowers, one of the earliest successful men in southern Colorado and the man for whom Prowers County, the county in which Amache was located, was named (see BOGGSVILLE).

The contrasting feelings of the time were also interesting. Two thirds of the camp residents were of school age. Grade school classes were held in the barracks. A high school was built. When an outside contractor was hired to build schools at the camp, the WRA was criticized for "wasting money" and for "coddling" the "enemy." Some wondered why a school was needed in the first place.

There was seeming paranoia in the action of the city council of nearby Lamar. When the camp residents' farms thrived, the residents were used on many of the neighboring farms to help save the crops, desperately needed for the war effort. Nonetheless, the Lamar City Council passed an ordinance making it illegal to "sell alcoholic beverages to a person of Japanese ancestry."

Life in Amache was a classic study in contrasts as well.

Coming from California, the dry-land farming of southeastern Colorado—"dustbowl" country—was completely foreign to residents of Amache. But they learned quickly and were most industrious. They not only became successful dry-land farmers, on cropland cultivated to provide for the evacuees' needs, but they experimented with new and different crops.

And although they had been packed up and delivered into a new and difficult situation, and the forced communal living put heavy strain on the family units, they maintained their many American traditions and aided every way possible in the war effort.

Boy Scouts and other organizations met regularly. In addition to elementary, high school and college courses taught, adult education classes were organized to help a great many grownups broaden their skills and knowledge, particularly their language skills. Independence Day, Thanksgiving, Christmas and other holidays became important events, most helpful in breaking up the monotony of camp life. War bonds were purchased and reusable materials were collected for the war effort. Camp residents elected their own officials and published a mimeographed newspaper.

Toward the end of the war, Japanese-Americans were allowed to volunteer for the armed services.* Many fought valiantly in the European theater. Thousands of Nisei served in the Pacific Theater as linguists, translators, etc., with General McArthur's intelligence section. They are credited with saving tens of thousands of lives.

At its peak, Amache was home to nearly 10,000 persons, making it the tenth largest city in Colorado.

The camp was abandoned on October 15, 1945. The land and most of the buildings were sold. Within a year Amache was a ghost town; today there are a few foundations, a tiny cemetery and an impressive memorial monument at the site.

Many of the residents returned to California. Fortunately for Colorado about 2000 remained in the state, contributing in every field of endeavor including farming.

AMITY (Fort Amity)
(Prowers County)

AMITY was a great and noble experiment, an experiment that worked to some extent and was a model for similar experiments elsewhere. It was a Salvation Army experiment.

The Salvation Army was created in England in 1865 by Methodist Minister William Booth, who made himself a General of the new movement. The General spent much of his adult life in and around some of the worst slums in England. He saw poverty degrading and wasteful, and, for the most part, unnecessary. Charity perpetuated poverty. It was worthwhile in emergency and hopeless cases, but most destitute families were merely victims of the system, and prolonged charity eroded their dignity and will to work. Most of them could be salvaged and become useful and prideful human beings again.

He instilled his thinking in his daughter, Emma Booth–Tucker, whom General Booth named consul to America. Her husband, Frederick St. George Booth–

---

* One of the best-kept secrets of World War II was the use of some 6000 Japanese-Americans as "the eyes and ears" of the Allied forces fighting the Japanese in the Pacific. President Truman called them "our human secret weapon." The Nisei, all volunteers, translated captured Japanese documents, maps, battle plans, orders, diaries, letters and publications. They interrogated Japanese prisoners, intercepted enemy communications, and made propaganda broadcasts themselves. There were countless stories of individual heroism and many Nisei received medals for bravery, some posthumously, as many were killed by Allied troops who mistook them for the enemy. Colonel Sidney Mashbir, commander of the Nisei intelligence service, reported that "thousands of American lives were preserved by these courageous men." General Douglas MacArthur's chief of staff for intelligence, General Charles Willoughby, said the Nisei in the Military Intelligence Service "shortened the war against Japan by two years."

Tucker retired from the British army to join the cause as a commander. The Booth–Tuckers set sail for America to practice their beliefs.

Among their most far-reaching activities was the establishment of model communities where men beaten down by life could work, produce and regain their dignity and pride.

Sites were selected in California and Ohio as well as in extreme southeastern Colorado, on the Arkansas River a short distance from the Kansas border. The project was advertised, and applications soon began to pour in.

The first families were selected from a long list of applicants for the Colorado experiment. The first thirty families arrived in April of 1898 , primarily from Chicago, Illinois, and Iowa. Only married men of good character were accepted. They represented every skill and trade. Leader of the first group was Col. Thomas Holland.

This wasn't a charity project. Arrangements were made in great detail. Money, travel and everything that was needed to get started was paid for (borrowed) from the Salvation Army. Each family was given ten acres and the tools, seeds and equipment needed to get started. But everything was noted in the log. Money was lent to each family at a 6 percent interest. Loans were to be paid back in ten to fourteen years.

The families lived in shanties and lean-tos the first year until their homes were built. Most were built of stone that the families quarried themselves from a nearby hill, the site of the later cemetery.

Community buildings and projects were built by the settlers. For all community work, the settlers were paid two dollars a day; half of that could go toward expenses and the other half was applied to the loan.

The major project the first year was the construction of the Amity irrigation ditch. Holland hired A. J. Davy to supervise the construction. The system, also called the Buffalo Canal, became a model of many irrigation systems to follow. Some people came all the way from England to study it.

Livestock was shipped in from Chicago and St. Louis, and the families raised cattle, hogs and chickens. Families drew lots for animals. Virtually all of the families

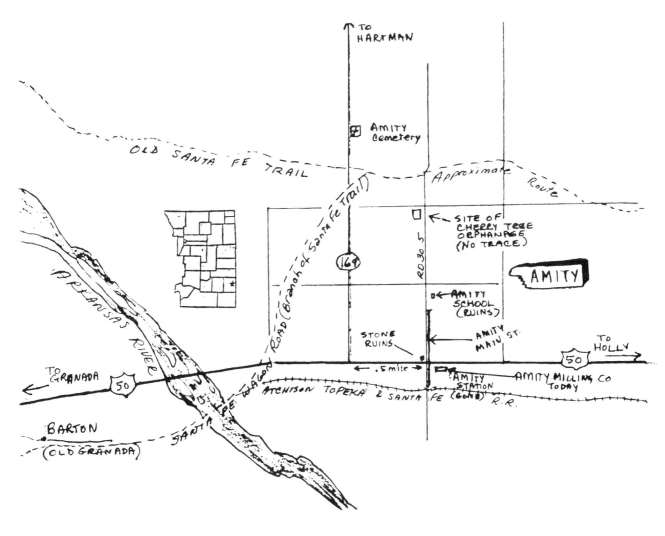

had a vegetable garden large enough to fill their needs, and these were tended by the women and children.

The first year about 80 acres were planted in cantaloupes; all were killed by frost. However, cantaloupes were raised successfully in the years to follow, as were other crops. Within a couple of years, Amity was a major shipper of sugar beets along the railroad.

It was soon evident that ten acres would not be sufficient for most families. Soon the Salvation Army leased an additional ten acres to the first settlers, then the land was added to the original acreage.

The Salvation Army had originally purchased between 600 to 1000 acres for the project, at $25 per acre. It was sold to the colonists for $35 to $40 an acre. Shortly after the turn of the century the value of the land had risen to $100 to $200 an acre. Eventually, some of the colonists would be tending as much as 40 acres.

The year 1902 was a big year for the colony.

A most hopeful sign of success of the project came when the first family had discharged its total debt to the Salvation Army, $900. The family had arrived in 1899 and was now cultivating twenty acres, living in a neat stone house, and raising livestock and chickens.

That year the Salvation Army also made a major addition to the colony. The Cherry Tree Home was built at a cost of $20,000. This orphanage would eventually hold up to sixty children (some said 250), many

delinquents, and most from the Chicago area. There was a staff of eight and the youngsters helped keep the grounds well tended.

In 1905, when an official of the Salvation Army came from England to inspect the colony, he was greatly encouraged by what he found.

There were two schools in the district, two churches—one Methodist (which eventually moved to Holly). There were more than 25 commercial enterprises in the community, including a broom factory and a hotel. A printing shop, run by O. A. Brakeman, published not only religious and inspirational "how-to" tracts but also the weekly *Amity Optimist*. There was a bank, The State Bank of Amity established in 1902, in which most of the families had savings. There were no saloons in Amity. There were 50 families, 600 population, and, the report said, "all the families are contented."

In March of 1905 the Salvation Army added a tuberculosis sanitarium to the colony. Reports said it cared for as many as 100 "workingmen suffering" from TB.

But things began to happen to Amity after 1905.

Much of the crop land was in the flood plains. It was marshy during wet years. The water table was close to the surface. There was seepage from above. Silt filled the irrigation system at times. Other times it was buried. Alkali surfaced in the fields. The Salvation Army

Main Street, Amity. Only the stone foundations of the wagon shop (at right in photo at left) and the dirt road remain today, just north of U.S. Highway 50. At the far end of the street was the railroad station. At right, some other Main Street businesses, and below, wagons lined up waiting to unload the sugar beet crop onto railroad cars. (*Holly Publishing Company*)

The Cherry Tree Home for orphans was established by the Salvation Army at Amity in 1899. Below, dinnertime at the home. (*Colorado Historical Society*)

Produce was shipped from the depot at Amity, and visitors from across the U.S. and abroad stopped here to visit the novel Salvation Army colony. (*Holly Publishing Company*)

The Amity schoolhouse. Only a few fallen timbers remain today. (*Holly Publishing Company*)

spent an estimated $60,000 (this would be about $400,000 today) in an attempt to drain the fields. It had little effect.

A flood that hit the troubled colony on November 18, 1908, washed away much of the colony along the river and left additional silt in the fields.

But that was only an aftermath of a telling blow from which the colony could not recover.

On July 9, 1908, the State Bank of Amity was robbed of all the savings of the settlers by Kid Wilson and Henry Starr, the husband of famed Belle Starr. The money was never recovered and Kid Wilson escaped. Starr was apprehended a short time later and returned to Lamar to stand trial. He was found guilty and sentenced to four to seven years in the state penitentiary at Canon City. (After his release, he returned to Holly and became a bartender and was later shot to death.)

Many mark the beginning of the end of Amity at 1906 and 1907 and the final demise at around 1908. Families did begin to leave around 1906. If they chose to do so, they could carry on at the Salvation Army camp in California. The orphans at Cherry Tree Home were transferred to California. And J. S. McMurtry or McMurty of Holly began buying up acreage at Amity as it was abandoned.

But Amity was not abandoned suddenly. Some attempted to carry on. The 1910 and later Colorado Business Directories said that the area offered "splendid openings for investors and home seekers." The 1911 and 1912 gazeteers still listed Amity with 300 population.

The region became dry farming territory on much of the surrounding land. Later conservation methods helped restore the land to good productivity.

The remains of Amity were lost over the years. The flood of 1921 washed away many buildings. Others were torn down or moved to be used for other purposes. Of course, vandals did their dirty work. But there continued to be much farming activity here, some carried out by Amity settlers or their heirs. The post office was not discontinued until 1937. But the town has been completely deserted since 1957. The little cemetery nearby carries headstones of many women and children who died in the typhoid epidemic of 1902, and other epidemics that followed.

If one looks closely today, one can still find many reminders of the noble experiment, a good idea but a bad time and location.

DEARFIELD and CHAPELTON

(Morgan County)

One of Colorado's unique ghost towns was an all Black farm community named DEARFIELD, located 25 miles west of Fort Morgan on U.S. Highway 34.

The community wasn't so rare in its day. There were similar communities in most western states, and one, Nicodemus, Kansas, has survived. In fact, it has been restored in recent years as an historic site.

In Colorado there were plans for several Black farm settlements during the 1870s, 1880s, and 1890s, in such widespread areas as near Pueblo, Cortez, and Craig in northwest Colorado. There was a short-lived colony in southeastern Colorado, according to some reports, and Dearfield itself had a suburb, called CHAPELTON, just south of Dearfield, that existed for a short period.

All of the communities were inspired by a book by Booker T. Washington called *Up From Slavery*, that reflected the Negro disillusionment with white, urban America and urged Black families to return to the land to make their way on their own with their hands.

Perhaps it was best expressed by an unnamed incorporator of Dearfield, who was quoted in the June 8, 1909 edition of *The Denver Post*:

We realize that the Negro has little or no chance in competition with the white race in the ordinary pursuits of city life. We want our people to get back to the land, where they naturally belong, and to work out their own salvation from the land up.

The Colorado guiding force in the establishment, development and fair success of Dearfield was Oliver T. Jackson, who was worth a book by himself. He was one of Colorado's more colorful and powerful characters. He was a messenger and aide to several Colorado governors, both Democratic and Republican. He was highly respected and had many friends in high places in Colorado and on the national scene. He was called a "kingmaker" in some of his biographies. A descendant of slaves, he was born in Oxford, Ohio, in 1862. He came to Colorado in 1887 and was a waiter and caterer to save enough money to start his own small farming operations in 1894. A reason he gave for ending his farming efforts was that he was unable to get qualified help, either white or black.

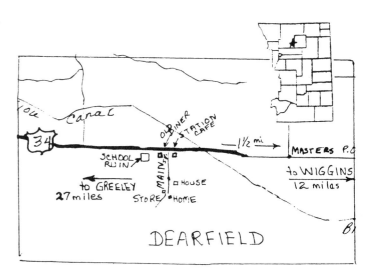

Oliver Jackson, founder of Dearfield, in 1915.
(*Colorado Historical Society*)

In the early years of this century, he was an assistant of Governor John Shafroth, who not only gave Jackson his blessings in establishing a colony but assisted him in selecting land in Weld County and completing the necessary paperwork. The project was incorporated in 1909, with Jackson and other leading Blacks among the incorporators. Most of 1910 was spent in making plans and preparing the groundwork for actual settlement. The community name reflected their hope for the project, "Dear-fields."

Seven families moved onto the land in the spring and early summer of 1911. Men, women and children worked side by side to build homes and clear the land, although there were only three teams of horses among them. They were able, that first year, to put by some of their own vegetables to help them through the coming winter.

The coming winter was particularly severe. Not only was food scarce, but fuel was difficult to come by. Three of the community's six horses died and the remaining three were so weakened that they were unable to haul lumber the three or four miles from the Platte River Valley. The Dearfield family members, young and old, male and female, were forced to trudge the distance, often through deep snow, to bring back the necessary fuel.

Despite the extremely difficult beginning the families stuck it out, and were joined by more settlers in 1912. Although the growth was not as spectacular as the early growth of Nicodemus in neighboring Kansas, the development of Dearfield was solid and sure. Jackson and the community leaders were dedicated to make the

project work and they built a strong foundation, based not only on hard work but on learning the latest farming techniques, such as conservation and land use.

During the early years of the community, Jackson wrote:

> The Negro settlers of [Dearfield] are above average in intelligence and are a studious class. . . . They take daily newspapers, farm journals and many technical publications. They study the agricultural reports of the various experimental stations and colleges and are proceeding with their farms along scientific lines.
>
> Their crops . . . consist of corn, oats, barley, alfalfa, hay, potatoes, Mexican beans, sugar beets, squash, pumpkins, watermelons, cantaloups, strawberries. . . . They also raise hogs, turkeys, geese, ducks and chickens, and are getting quite a start along dairy lines.

Within a few short years they were able to cultivate crops over and above their own needs and shipped some produce, primarily to Denver, hauling it to the railroad at Masters, along the Platte.

The growing number of settlers not only built sturdy homes, according to a town plan, but built commercial buildings, a school and a church. It was a Union Presbyterian Church, but used by all denominations. And there was time for fun and social events.

The church was used for meetings, as was a large barn, which was also the site of many dances and socials, including many community sings. On good days there were many outdoor get-togethers and picnics, hunting and fishing parties. Often, families and friends from Denver would journey up to join in the activities.

Many of the young people left during World War I, either to join the armed forces or to work in plants in the city. But food was in much demand for the war effort and Dearfield produced, and prospered in the process.

However, few of the young people returned to Dearfield after the war, like young people of all races who found life more prosperous and exciting in the city.

And like so many other farm communities in Colorado and elsewhere, the fields strained by wartime production became more susceptible to the drought that hit the plains in the years following World War I.

Dearfield was far from being a ghost town, however. In fact, Jackson believed that the community offered great opportunities for the future. In a pamphlet published shortly after the war, entitled "Will you help build the town of Dearfield?" and sent to wealthy Blacks throughout the country, Jackson said:

> The town of Dearfield has laid a solid foundation for the building of the wealthiest settlement of Colored People in the U.S. The foundation has stood the test of ten years now, and all we need is your support to complete the proof of our being capable of becoming self-supporting and self-governing. . . .
>
> The opportunity is now open and necessary in the town of

Mrs. Minerva Jackson at Dearfield. (*Colorado Historical Society*)

Seen from U.S. 34, Dearfield has a few ruins remaining. Not long ago this entire expanse was covered with homes and buildings. Two of the last buildings: the general store on what was Main Street (below) and a lunch room which can be seen along Highway 34.

Dearfield for a tourist hotel of about 50 rooms, as Dearfield is an ideal health resort, and is conveniently located for Denver automobile parties (72 miles), picnics and society excursions.

The pamphlet said several profitable opportunities existed for a man with a little capital. In addition to the hotel, the pamphlet said the community needed:

A general store carrying groceries, dry goods and hardware.

A contracting carpenter who could conduct a lumber and fuel yard.

A doctor who could also operate a drug store.

A good blacksmith.

A truck line.

"And the greatest opportunity for a collective benefit is a money center, either in the way of a bank or a cooperative loan center."

Although little investment money came as a result of the pamphlet, the little community carried on. In fact, *The Weld County News* reported in 1921:

Today, through all the vicissitudes of the years, the colony has grown until there are nearly 700 people there, all independent and earning a living and more. The lands which were practically nothing when the colony was established are now worth in the aggregate of probably $750,000 with the improvements which the colored farmers have added. Their livestock and poultry are valued at not less than $200,000, and their annual production is in the neighborhood of $125,000.

The article said the community was law-abiding according to county records and had a school and two churches, built, run and patronized "wholly by the colored people" of Dearfield.

"Dearfield offers opportunities to the young colored men and women of the country who are earnest and industrious. It is no place for the idler, for non-irrigated farming entails hard work and indomitable courage."

The newspaper said that Dearfield "ranks high among the 14 of its kind in the United States today."

Jackson, who spent more and more time at Dearfield, worked feverishly to build the community, then to maintain what it had left, then to keep it from dying. For despite his efforts Dearfield dwindled, as did hundreds of other once-thriving farm communities during the 1920s and 1930s. Along with drought and other problems, money was almost impossible to come by. Crops failed. More and more families moved away.

By 1940, the population was listed at only 12.

In 1943, Jennie Jackson, Oliver Jackson's niece, moved to Dearfield to care for her ailing uncle.

She recalled that she was "shocked at what had happened to Dearfield. I had visited it before the Depression, and Dearfield then was lively and growing. People were writing their folks to come out and settle, and there were always visitors at Uncle Oliver's. It was nothing in those days for the governor or other distinguished officials to drop in. Everyone believed in Dearfield.

"In 1943, everything was different. Almost all the people had gone. The houses were tumbled down, and weeds were growing in the streets. Uncle Oliver and one or two others were all that was left in the whole town."

A short time later, Jackson was forced to move to Denver to be near medical assistance and continual health care. He later was moved to Greeley. He died at the Weld County General Hospital on February 18, 1949.

His niece stayed on in Dearfield. In 1946, there was an attempt to sell the townsite, 240 acres in all, including the remaining buildings and a café and garage along the highway.

Despite the "reasonable terms" offered for the townsite, there were no takers. When Oliver Jackson died, the land was inherited by Jennie. She operated the small grocery—café—gas station along the highway until 1953, when she became the last Negro to leave Dearfield. She went to live with friends in Greeley and died in the early 1970s in a Greeley nursing home.

Today, a Conoco sign along the highway marks the site of the once-bustling community. A small grocery and sometime—café still operates along with the gas station. There were (in 1980) three or four other buildings still standing. Two were still being lived in. The colorful false-fronted little grocery store stands in ruins along what was once Main Street. And the large foundation near the highway was once the school.

No one would realize from the ruins that this was once a thriving community of nearly 1000 persons, one that even had a suburb. It was called CHAPLETOWN or CHAPELTON. During Dearfield's heyday, Chapelton appeared to be on its way toward being a "twin city" to Dearfield. But it only lasted a few short years and nothing remains of the site today.

CHAPTER XVIII

VERY SPECIAL PLACES

Ghost-towning offers many rewards. One of the richest is to discover very special places, sites that have brought wealth of meaning for the author: new discovery, deep personal appeal, or a rich personal relationship between author and place. Each ghost town is a gem unto itself, but the following spots are very special, for one reason or another, to the author.

BOGGSVILLE
(Bent County)

BOGGSVILLE was never an incorporated city. In fact, it was never really a town as we have known and studied them in this book. Whatever it was, it was certainly the most historic site in southeastern Colorado, if not all the southern part of the state.

It was the site of the first school in southern Colorado, one the first in the state. It had the first post office in the region. Called the "cradle of the cattle industry" in southern Colorado, it also led in farming innovations. A couple of the largest, most gracious homes in Colorado were here; the famous visited and stayed. It was the first county seat of Bent County. And although it didn't have a "cast of thousands," the few who peopled its stage were the most colorful and powerful of the region and of the time. It was the final home of Kit Carson. But there were others, many of them related through marriage.

The leading character and first settler of the site was Thomas O. Boggs—little known today, but a giant at that time. He was the great-grandson of Daniel Boone and son of the fifth governor of Missouri. During the Mexican War (1846–48), he was a courier, carrying many important messages between Santa Fe and "the States." He was a scout and a guide. He was also a freighter for a time, and brought many trains of goods and supplies to Bent's Fort along the Arkansas, not far from the later site of Boggsville.

This was some of the fame that came to Boggs. Much of his fortune came through his marriage to the 13- or 14-year-old stepdaughter of Charles Bent, first governor of New Mexico Territory. In 1865 Mrs. Boggs, Rumaldo Luna Boggs, who was also a niece of Kit Carson's wife, was given title to 2040 acres of the famous Vigil and St. Vrain Land Grant in southern Colorado.

Boggs had run some cattle in the area for Lucien Maxwell, and Maxwell was said to have encouraged Boggs to settle on the land and develop it.

Boggs journeyed to the site in 1865 (some sources say he began coming here around 1860) and began building his home. He left New Mexico the following year (1866) to live here.

He didn't build the usual "settlers cabin." It was a large structure of Spanish architecture, 50 by 70 feet. It had ten large rooms and four large fireplaces. Boggs raised sheep, goats and cattle.

He was joined the following year by another king-sized character, John W. Prowers. Prowers had married Amache, an Indian princess and only daughter of Cheyenne Indian Chief One Eye, who was killed at Sand Creek. Survivors of the Indian victims of Sand Creek were offered 160 acres in the region. Prowers purchased many plots of the land from the Indians, who were unused to the farming life.

If anyone thought more larger-than-life thoughts than Thomas Boggs, it was John Prowers. We remember Prowers today because there is a Colorado county named for him, but little else. He was only 28 or 29 when he came to Boggsville in 1867, but within the next few years he would be perhaps the most noted man in

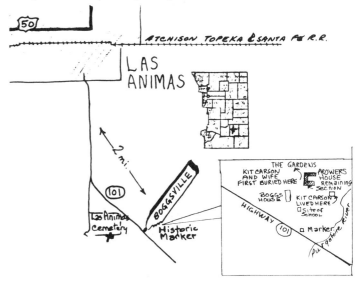

210

Thomas Oliver Boggs, first settler of Boggs-ville, in early and later years. (*Denver Public Library, Western History Department*)

Thomas Boggs' house (*right*)—occupied for more than a hundred years, until the last family moved out in the 1970s.

Below both ends of the remaining section of John Prowers house at Boggsville. Originally there were three sections similar to this one, built around an open court. Kit Carson and his Indian wife were buried behind this house before being moved to Taos, New Mexico.

all of southern Colorado, certainly one of the richest, with the most land and among the largest herds of cattle.

The first hint of his tall thoughts and high ambition was in the construction of his home. He didn't emulate Boggs' home, he bettered it in a big way.

A short distance north of Boggs' home he began construction of a large two-story, adobe home in three equal sections, surrounding a large court facing west. The sections were 20 by 55 feet, and contained 24 large rooms.

It had to be large, because in the next few years it would be the home of a large family, guest house or hotel for some of the more important people of the day, a store, school, stage station, county offices and much else.

Prowers' sister came to Boggsville the same year. She was married to John S. Hough, another awesome figure, particularly in his buckskin outfit, beaded and fringed Indian style, a gift of his good friend Kit Carson. Hough brought with him a large train of supplies to stock a general store to serve a wide area. The Houghs brought an air of culture and refinement to the region. Mrs. Hough was pretty and talented, and for a while she was the only white woman in the community.

Hough would become a leading business figure for the region also. In addition to his other enterprises, he would later join with the Thatcher brothers of Pueblo to found the Bent County Bank in Las Animas.

In the last days of 1867, Kit Carson and his family moved to Boggsville. Despite his fame, despite the fact that he had recently been honored in the nation's capital, he was a tragic figure. His wife, a Spanish member of the proud Jaramillo family, was near death. Kit's health was also broken, and he was broken in spirit. His wife died April 27, 1868. A little over two weeks later, Kit was taken to the hospital at nearby Fort Lyon, where he could receive constant care from his friend Dr. Tilston. It was too late. On May 23, 1868, less than a month after his wife died, Kit passed away.

He and his wife were buried in "The Gardens" behind Prowers' large house. A short time later they were buried in Taos, in New Mexico according to their wishes. Thomas Boggs was executor of Kit's will. He also took in the Carsons' seven children and raised them as his own.

Some other early members of the community that remained for varying lengths of time were L. A. Allen, an early business partner of Boggs; Charles Rite, brother-in-law of Tom Boggs and a highly educated man; Col. A.G. Boone (another descendant of Daniel), an Indian agent and namer of nearby Boone; William Bowman, an early newspaper editor in the region; Charles Goodnight, famed trail boss, father of the Goodnight and Goodnight–Loving Cattle Trails, and cattleman of note himself; Eli Shoemaker, rancher, freighter and politician; Robert Bent, son of William Bent, and many more.

One colorful character that happened upon the scene in 1871 was P. G. Scott. An educated man, Scott was hired by Prowers to teach here; some say it was the second school in the state. Classes were first held in Prowers' home, until a building was completed near Boggs' home.

Scott's first class consisted of two white youngsters; four half-breed Mexicans (Carson children); three half-breed Indians and one Black child.

Boggs began his irrigation project in 1866, the year he arrived. He and others expanded on it over the years, and Boggsville became very productive. Boggs also brought in hundreds of head of cattle the first year. In the years to follow, he and Prowers would greatly expand on their herds. Boggsville had a ready market for just about all it produced the first years, at nearby Fort Lyon. It wasn't long before Boggsville became a major supplier for beef, some of the best in the West. In addition to the cattle, Boggs was perhaps the first large sheep-rancher in the region. In 1875, he was said to have more than 15,000 sheep.

During 1867 and 1868, there were many Indian scares. Indians believed to be Cheyenne raided Boggsville in September of 1868 and killed or stole several head of livestock. Soldiers of Ft. Lyon gave chase. They caught and killed four of the raiders but the rest got away. Two soldiers were killed.

When Bent County was carved out of Pueblo County in 1870 Boggsville became the first county seat, Prowers the first county officer. He ran the county from his home. Boggs was the first sheriff, and he represented Bent County in the Territory Legislature the following year.

Boggs and Prowers planned to plat and build a modern city at Boggsville. But when the Santa Fe Railroad came through the region, along the Arkansas a couple of miles north of Boggsville, and then Las Animas became a boom city, they gave up their plans. Prowers built offices and stores in the new city. Las Animas became county seat of Bent County in 1872. Las Animas grew rapidly, and Boggsville merely became a few lavish homes amid plush farm and cattleland.

Prowers died in 1884 at the age of 46.

Thomas Boggs eventually moved to Springer, New Mexico, and became Territorial Governor. He died in 1894.

Most of the homes and buildings in Boggsville are gone, some moved elsewhere. Many of the remaining buildings were washed away or destroyed by the flood of 1921, including the last ruins of Kit Carson's home. It had been located near the river, directly across from the Boggs' house.

Only one of the three sections of the Prowers' house remain standing. It is rapidly deteriorating but is still impressive, and can give a visitor a good idea of how large and colorful the original structure was.

For the first time in 100 years, the Boggs' house stands empty; the Kerr family moved out during the mid-1970s after living in it almost 25 years. It is also rapidly deteriorating. The Kerr children have won essay contests writing about their historic home. Several years ago the owner of the house, a Denver woman, offered the house to the State Historical Society, for a reasonable price, but the Society could not afford it, plus the needed repairs and the upkeep.

Undoubtedly the remaining structures at Boggsville will be gone and a very important part of Colorado history will be marked only by a stone monument beside State Highway 101, two miles south of Las Animas.

COMANCHE CROSSING

(Arapahoe County)

The most famous painting of Western railroading is the one that shows the Golden Spike being driven with a lot of hullabaloo and ceremonies at Promontory Point, Utah. The painting is supposed to depict the first linking of a transcontinental railroad. The date was May 10, 1869.

Despite the art work, the people of Strasburg say it isn't so, but that the first real linkage of railroads from coast to coast took place just east of their community at a site once named COMANCHE CROSSING.

It seems that the "big event" portrayed at Promontory Point neglected to take into consideration "the missing link": the Union Pacific did not have a railroad crossing of the Missouri River at that time. Until they did open up that bridge on March 22, 1872, passengers and freight had to be ferried across the wide Missouri.

But the Kansas Pacific had finished a bridge across the Missouri at Kansas City on July 3, 1869. So when the final spike was driven at Comanche Crossing on August 15, 1870, it gave the Kansas Pacific direct linkage to the West one year and a half before the Promontory Point event.

There were ceremonies at the Colorado spike-driving but no painter was around to record the historic event.

It took some struggling before the event could take place at all.

Railroad bridges had been established across the Mississippi at Rock Island, Illinois, in 1856, and at

Drawing from Frank Leslie's *Illustrated Newspaper,* June 3, 1871. Buffalo were killed to clear the tracks and to feed construction crews—and buffalo shoot excursions were a form of entertainment. (*Denver Public Library, Western History Department*)

Kansas Pacific work forces laying track into eastern Colorado are shown here in October 1867, 300 miles west of the Missouri River.

This crossing of the tracks over the Republican River in Kansas was one of the final links in making the Kansas Pacific Railroad the first transcontinental route, an accomplishment celebrated at Comanche Crossing in Colorado on July 3, 1869.

Photos courtesy Denver Public Library, Western History Department

Quincy, Illinois, in 1868. After crossing the Missouri at Kansas City, the Kansas Pacific plodded its way westward. It had difficulty raising money, accumulating railroad ties and finding good, dependable workers.

Things spurred forward when General Palmer took over. Track-laying began again on January 1, 1870, and a month later it was eight miles into Colorado.

With all the other difficulties, the Indians were on the warpath, especially hostile to the coming of the Iron Horse. On May 13, 1870, Indians struck at several points along the construction line, killing 11 workers, wounding 19 more and driving off several hundred head of cattle. There were many other reports, some overlapping and some just rumors of other attacks. Construction sites became armed camps, with guards on alert at all times. Armed men also rode with many of the wagons bringing ties to construction sites.

Despite the Indian threats, an almost steady stream of wagons pulled by oxen brought ties from the Pineries to the construction sites. Palmer advertised for 500 wagon teams to bring the ties, offering top prices. It is said that at least that many wagons participated in the frantic push to complete the railroad. Workers were brought from all points. Advertisements ran in Eastern papers as well as in the region. Estimates of up to a quarter of a million ties, piled high at mills in the Pineries, eventually found their place along the track.

Crews worked toward the meeting from both ends, east and west. As the meeting date grew closer, elaborate plans were made. To spur the workers on, a barrel of whiskey was set in place at Comanche Crossing. The grand meeting was finally scheduled for August 15. The work crews couldn't be late, and the whiskey was an enticement.

It is said that 10½ miles of track was laid that final day, more track than had been laid in any one day anywhere. It is also said the crew coming from the east got to the barrel of whiskey first, but kept on working to meet the oncoming western crew.

But even the grand celebration left much to be desired. The officials were there to make speeches, the tired, cheering work crews were there getting drunk, but the guest of honor—the golden spike—didn't make it. The spike, contributed by Georgetown mining, was en route in plenty of time. But the messengers got drunk in Golden along the way, missed the stage in Denver, and didn't arrive until the next day. In place of the golden spike, a regular spike decorated with tinsel was used. The proper golden spike is now on display at the Colorado Heritage Center in Denver.

The 100th anniversary celebration, in 1970, was far bigger and better than the original, although there was no barrel of whiskey on hand. Top local and state officials gave their speeches to the nearly 1000 railroad and history buffs on hand. Governor Love dressed in Western garb and U. S. Representative Don Brotzman led off the speech-making. Youngsters staged a mock Indian raid. A pony express rider attended—100 years late. And jets from the Colorado and Kansas National Guard flew overhead in precision.

Local people of the Historical Society, led by Mrs. Emma Mitchell, are maintaining the site, now just east of STRASBURG, as an historical park, with a railroad museum and other historical buildings and equipment.

With their dedication, the site and its historical significance should continue to grow to national attention as it deserves.

And maybe a painting of the driving of a regular spike with tinsel on it will become a famous painting of the Western movement.

"Unholy" Historic Jumping JULESBERG
(Sedgwick County)

There is a tiny corner of Colorado that has seen more action, more history, than most of the rest of the state put together. This tiny triangle of history enters Colorado with the South Platte River from Nebraska in the extreme northeast corner of the state. It barely travels ten miles into Colorado when it meets Lodgepole Creek coming in from the north, and much of the history trails out of Colorado again.

The very first Colorado history began here, and it is still going on.

Ancient Indian tribes, the first in what is now Colorado—the Folsom man, Clovis and Yuma points, dating back more than 10,000 years—had some of their more permanent sites in northeastern Colorado. They and their predecessors, some of them at least, no doubt entered the region via Lodgepole Creek, as did centuries of Indians to follow. The weather, the hunting conditions, and other elements caused the northern Indians to enter Colorado via Lodgepole and poach on the hunting grounds of Colorado's Plains Indians, primarily the Arapahoe and the Cheyenne. And the Arapahoe and the Cheyenne would go north and return the favor when the situation prompted it.

There is a most convenient lookout along the Lodgepole, which permitted one tribe to see the other tribe coming from a long distance, and to plan an ambush. It also allowed the red man to see white men coming, and to plan the attack, or to scatter if the approaching party wore uniforms. From here they could see the endless wagon trains overrun their land. They preyed upon some of them, but it did not stop the wagons. The smoke signals can still be seen if one looks carefully.

The first white men came through here. At first one or two at a time, then more. The Mallet Brothers passed this way in 1739. Twenty years earlier, Villasur ventured up from New Spain (New Mexico) through eastern Colorado and out along the Platte. The mountain men, trappers and traders came by, and traveled back to

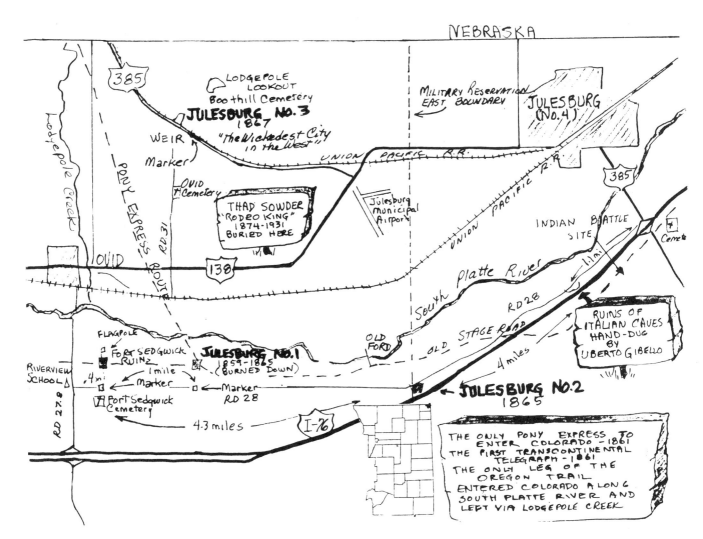

civilization to sell their furs. Major Stephen Long and his party came down the Platte in 1820, across what he called "the great American desert," and first saw the awesome, impenetrable mountains—although his botanist, Dr. James, climbed Pikes Peak, something Zeb Pike couldn't do. Dr. James was also the first man to see and name the tender little columbine, Colorado's state flower.

Some twenty years after Major Long called the mountains invincible, another soldier, John C. Fremont, "the Great Pathfinder," came down the Platte. He climbed many mountains, and discovered people could go through, over and around them.

More and more people began to come. It was inevitable that one of them would eventually find some of the precious metals of which Colorado abounds. Then came the deluge, an endless stream of wagons, horses, wheelbarrows, and many came on foot. When enough of them took root, the "modern" conveniences came. The first stagecoaches into Colorado rattled down the Platte. The Pony Express, brave men on fast horses, could carry messages from St. Louis to California in a week. The only Pony Express to enter Colorado en-

tered via the Platte until it came to Lodgepole and went out again. A couple of years later, in 1861, the Pony Express became surplus when the first transcontinental telegraph system was completed. The first transcontinental telegraph line cut through only a small corner of Colorado, along the Platte and out along the Lodgepole. This, by the way, was also the only branch of the famous Oregon Trail that cut into Colorado. (The telegraph wasn't extended into Denver City until 1863.) Branches of the Bozeman and Texas–Montana cattle trails went through here.

And while all of this history was passing by, an important part of it stayed on in this tiny triangle of Colorado. The problem was that the key town in this triangle was not very stable—and it moved around, too. Historic Julesburg had unsavory reputations, and a lot of bad things happened to them. Everything is plural when you talk about Julesburg because there were so many of them.

Julesburg Number One

One of the first permanent settlers in this area was a controversial Frenchman named Jules Beni. He estab-

Courtesy Laura Gilpin Collection, Amon Carter Museum, Fort Worth, Texas.

Julesburg Number One lasted only one month before it was burned to the ground on February 7, 1865. A depiction of "The Burning of Julesburg by Indians" (below) was painted in 1915 by N. Wade.

Colorado Historical Society

lished a trading post during the 1850s at a popular Indian crossing near the junction of the Platte and the Lodgepole. It was a struggling enterprise until the wagon trains started coming in 1859. Then the Overland Stage was created. Jules Trading Post became the first and most important station in Colorado. Beni became station master.

Other buildings rose around the stage-station-trading-post. There was a blacksmith, large stable, saloon, pool hall, large boarding house, warehouse and some others—twelve or thirteen altogether. The little community became known as Julesburg for Beni.

But things were not all that kosher in Julesburg. Seemingly unnecessary delays occurred on the stage lines. There were some stage and wagon robberies, suspiciously close to the station. Some of the culprits were dressed as Indians. The rumor spread that Beni himself was "singling out" stages and wagons to rob, and that the perpetrators were colleagues of his.

The situation could have gone on indefinitely had not the branch manager of the stage line been one Joseph Slade, a stern businessman to say the least, who is better known in history as "Black Jack" Slade. When Slade discovered the breakdown in the otherwise smooth-working system he set out straightaway to Julesburg and fired Beni.

Beni retaliated by waiting in ambush for Slade and shooting him up and down, enough to kill a platoon of soldiers.

However, they say Black Jack was too mean to die (at this time). He survived and tracked down Beni somewhere along the line and shot him down. Before he did so (some say after), he kept his promise and cut off (with a black whip, some stories say) Beni's ears. They say he nailed one ear to a corral, as a warning to future highwaymen, and carried around the other one as a momento watch fob.

Slade was a most efficient branch manager. Mark Twain, who passed through here going west, said Slade was the "meanest man he had ever seen" and "more feared than the almighty" in this part of the country. The vicious part of Slade's character surfaced more strongly when he drank, and he drank a lot. It caused his downfall a short time later (see VIRGINIA DALE).

In an attempt to smooth over the sordid reputation Julesburg had developed, Ben Holliday, who ran the Overland Stage, renamed the town OVERLAND CITY. But JULESBURG was already too well known, and so the popular name remained.

The growing animosity between the Plains Indians and white invaders, the growing frequency of raids along the Platte River Trail by the Indians, prompted the army, in 1864, to establish a military fort near Julesburg. The installation was originally called CAMP RANKIN, the JULESBURG POST or FORT JULESBURG, and finally, FORT SEDGWICK, after General John Sedgwick, who had been killed on May 9, 1864, at Spottsylvania.

An all-out war was started by one Col. John Chiving-ton on November 29, 1864, when he led a body of Colorado volunteers on a surprise early-morning raid of a village of Arapahoes and Cheyennes at Sand Creek in east-central Colorado. Hundreds (estimates range from 200 to 700) of men, women and children were killed in the attack.

A few days later the Indians held a massive war parley on the eastern plains of Colorado. Other tribes were invited, including the Sioux. From there the Indians set out to destroy everything along the Platte River Trail, to cut off Denver City completely and leave it vulnerable for annihilation.

The first surprise attack was on Julesburg and Fort Sedgwick on January 7, 1865. Most Julesburg citizens were able to take refuge at the Fort. The town was plundered and heavily damaged, while repeated attacks on the fort resulted in the deaths of 15 soldiers, one third of the meagre troops on hand to defend it.

Immediately thereafter General Mitchell organized a scouting party to pursue the attackers. Hampered by extreme cold, he was unable to overtake the Indians and returned to Fort McPherson, Kansas, to plan his strategy. On January 28, 1865, he began a campaign to burn the prairies south of the Platte and smoke the Indians out. The tribes were driven northward, burning, pillaging and killing everything and everyone in their path.

On February 2, 1865, a thousand Cheyenne, Arapahoe and Sioux braves attacked Fort Sedgwick and Julesburg for the second time. Fortunately, Julesburg citizens again received sufficient notice to dash to Fort Sedgwick for protection.

The Indians made short work of the abandoned town. They gathered up everything of any value, rounded up the livestock and burned the town to the ground.

One of the most classic rides to safety in Western history occurred during the Indian raid. Captain N. J. O'Brien and Lt. Eugene Ware and a small body of troops were returning to Fort Sedgwick, accompanying two stages, after an expedition along the Republican River. Arriving at the top of a promontory overlooking the fort, they saw the scene below. Deciding there was nothing else to do, the small party made a wild dash through the Indians to the fort and arrived unscathed, as the guns of the fort concentrated on opening the path to the fort.

The Indians were repeatedly repelled by the heavy artillery at the fort. As dark approached (Indians seldom attack at night), the Indians retired across the river from the fort for a riotous "victory" celebration. They ignited a giant bonfire made up of the telegraph poles from along the Platte trail, they bar-b-qued the cattle they had rounded up, and they whooped it up with the Taos lightning "rescued" from Julesburg, now in ashes.

All during the night, the soldiers and the civilians watched the wild celebration from the fort, and expected an all-out siege come morning.

This photo is dated "1873 or 1877 Julesburg," which would be Julesburg Number Three, "The Wickedest City in the West" railhead and construction site for the Union Pacific. (*Courtesy Amon Carter Museum, Fort Worth, Texas*)

The depot of the fourth and final Julesburg is no longer used for passenger travel but has become an interesting museum.

Below, monuments at First Julesburg and a marker for Third.

But the dawn's early light was a surprise. The Indians had silently stolen off during the night. The reason would soon be apparent. Indian scouts had apparently reported the approach of fresh troops from Kansas.

Although they would still have been greatly outnumbered, the troops and Julesburg survivors had been spared. But Julesburg #1 was no more.

JULESBURG Number Two

This was the shortest-lived and dullest of the many Julesburgs.

After Number One had been destroyed, its residents moved into Fort Sedgwick. The fort was enlarged and became instrumental in protecting and reopening the Platte River Trail into Denver. The Julesburg Post Office was transferred to the fort and renamed FORT SEDGWICK.

The second Julesburg was built three to four miles east of Number One, still south of the river, and just outside the eastern boundary of the Fort Sedgwick Military Reservation, so liquor could be sold. (The soldiers were the best customers.) It was an active stage station and filed as a townsite in then Weld County. Wells Fargo took over the stage line in 1866.

Captain Nicholas J. O'Brien, the hero of the dash to the fort during the seige of Julesburg, retired from the Army, opened a store in Julesburg and became its first mayor.

In June of 1867, the Union Pacific established a railhead construction site north of the river. Julesburg businessmen and residents, accustomed to moving by now, lost little time in pulling up their roots and planting them again in the new city.

JULESBURG Number Three

The third Julesburg made up many times for the dullness of its predecessor. As with all other railroad construction towns, the first weeks and months of Julesburg Number Three was on the wild side—the wildest little pocket in Colorado. In fact, it was dubbed "The Wickedest City in the West."

The town was born in violence. The Indians fought relentlessly to stop or stall the westward invasion of the "Iron Horse." The work gangs, under Generals Grenville Dodge and Jack Casement, were protected by U. S. troops all along the route, including troops from Ft. Sedgwick under General Potter.

Railroad construction men were the wildest of the many wild men on the frontier. And they attracted many another to fill their needs—the gamblers, the painted ladies, the con men.

The Omaha Daily Herald, July 10, 1867, told the story:

JULESBURG—Where two weeks ago a desolate prairie, now are four squares of houses, 150 scattered houses, and about the same number of tents. It has every trade and occupation rep-

resented. Has got 120 grog shops, several gambling halls, and a few dens of vice.

Its population is about 3,000. The principal amusements are getting tight, fighting and occasionally shooting each other down for pasttime.

For the past few days, the first of its existence, the city was ruled by extempore vigilantes, who amused themselves by the exercise of the cowhide halter and revolver.

The Mayor, N. P. Cook, is only five days' resident of the city, and none of the city council have been there over 10 days.

The next day *The Herald* reported:

JULESBURG—Seven Mexicans, five soldiers, eight bull-whackers, four loafers and two half-breeds got into a big bone and sinew muss evening before last off Pacific Street. They fought well and hard for about an hour and then quit almost even, upon condition that the worst whipped should treat the crowd.

Among the many characters who enhanced the reputation of Julesburg Number Three were "Black Snake" Lachut, who terrorized the immediate environment with his deadly swift and accurate whip and Gypsy, who foretold the future, also with deadly accuracy (some wonder if her predictions of death were more a signal for a "hit" rather than a prediction). There was also the stage driver, "Terrible Jake," who acquired his reputation by bringing his stage through hell and high water. They say, and he claimed, that there were many a dead Indian and highwayman along the route to prove it.

Alas, the day came, in November 1867—and none too soon—that the railhead moved on toward Cheyenne. Some remnants of the rowdiness remained awhile, but almost overnight Julesburg Number Three settled back into being an industrious, fairly respectable town.

Julesburg remained a hardy frontier town, but it had work to do. It was a busy railroad center, the nearest railroad stop to rapidly growing Denver. An almost continuous parade of stages and supply wagons picked up people, mail, supplies and equipment at the railroad and rumbled on to Denver over the Platte River Trail. Julesburg was also the commercial center for a wide area.

Large and small bodies of troops passed through Julesburg for the next few months, generally before or after skirmishes with marauding bands of Indians. In 1869 troops from Ft. Sedgwick returned after a valiant and successful battle with a superior band of Indians under Tall Bull at Summit Springs, a few miles southwest of Julesburg. The troops were members of the Fifth Cavalry and Pawnee Scouts, under General E. A. Carr. The Scout was William F. Cody, better known as Buffalo Bill. Buffalo Bill was not new to Julesburg. It was said he was signed up at Julesburg Number One for the Pony Express. As a scout he passed through many times. He also was here often to bring in the hundreds of Plains buffalo he killed to feed the railroad work crews. It is also said that the last performance of his world-famous Wild West Show was in Julesburg, before the famed showman returned to Denver where the show was attached for debts.

Tall Bull was killed and his braves were soundly defeated at Summit Springs. It was the last major battle on the Colorado eastern plains, and for all intents and purposes it marked the end of the "Indian problem" in northeastern Colorado.

In 1871 Fort Sedgwick was declared surplus, and closed its gates for the last time.

It wasn't until 1881 that the Union Pacific finally completed a line from its main east-west track to Denver. The junction point was located a few miles east of Julesburg Number Three. It would obviously be the site of the principal city in the region. The railroad wanted to call it DENVER JUNCTION. But it wasn't long before the businessmen, workers and just plain folk at Julesburg Number Three had moved bag and baggage to the new site. After all, it had happened before. And, even though all the name Julesburg honored a rather controversial character, the overwhelming majority of the new "city" insisted on retaining the name.

The site of old Julesburg Number 3 was virtually empty. Among the few who stayed was the Weir family. James Weir had been the first station agent here. His son ran a grocery, and Edna Weir was the first postmistress of the new town of WEIR or WEIR SIDING, on the site of Julesburg Number 3.

Of more import, JULESBURG had found a home. One it could live with.

Danger Ahead by Frederic Remington

CHAPTER XIX

TROUBLE IN SERENE

SERENE (Columbine Mine)
(Weld County)

SERENE is no more. A black mountain of slag and some cement foundations, hidden by the weeds, are all that is left of this town. During 1972 and 1973 the few remaining buildings of Serene were systematically torn down for salvage. Serene joined the hundreds of other Colorado ghost towns that are only memories.

Serene, however, was much more historic than most, which makes its unheralded death all the more inglorious. Add to this that hardly any Coloradans have ever heard of Serene. Serene and its "day of infamy" aren't found in any history books. In fact, even the owners of the Rocky Mountain Fuel Company, contacted when the ruins were being torn down, didn't know the story of Serene—though the company had owned the property then.

"Then" was the fall of 1927.

The year 1927 was an interesting one in many ways. It was a banner year for sports. Heavyweight Champion Gene Tunney won a rematch with Jack Dempsey, the "Manassa [Colorado] Mauler," and proved that he was a great champion in what was billed as "The Fight of the Century." Babe Ruth hit 60 homers, but lost to teammate Lou Gehrig the Most Valuable Player award as the Bronx Bombers won four straight from the Pittsburgh Pirates in the World Series.

Closer to home, a young football player, Earl "Dutch" Clark, a "one man gang" for Colorado College, became Colorado's first All American.

Elsewhere, another young man flew out of nowhere into immortality. His name was Charles Augustus Lindbergh, and he became the first person to fly non-stop between the New and the Old World.

But 1927 wasn't all fun and games.

An ugly mood roamed the land. The nation was in the throes of one of its periodic witch hunts, which were in this century "Red Scares." The mood was slightly relieved and the nation felt a bit safer from witches, for a while at least, when on August 23, 1927, a shoemaker named Nicola Sacco and a fish-peddler named Barto-

lomeo Vanzetti were put to death in Charlestown, Massachusetts. The official crime of which they had been found guilty was murder and robbery, although they claimed their innocence until their death, and another man had admitted the crime. Their unofficial crimes were that they were "foreigners" and that they were anarchists, or so implied the prosecution.

In Colorado during 1927, unions were once again in disrepute. Any individual and organization that said out loud or even implied that this was not the best of all possible worlds was an "anarchist," a "Bolshevik" or worse.

The Ludlow Massacre thirteen years before (see LUDLOW) had won the union some sympathy and recognition. But the "Rockefeller Plan," a company union,

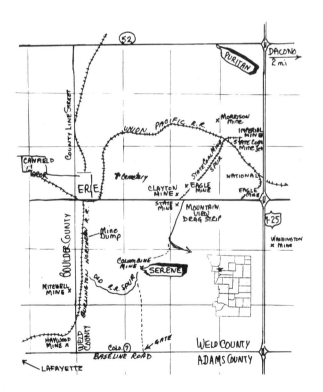

Serene was a typical dingy coal town in the 1920s.

In the photo above, the house of the Columbine Mine superintendent is at extreme right. At left is the water tower where a machine gun was mounted during the 1927 strike to protect the main gate, at the end of "Death Alley."

At right, a view of the wash house shows part of the tipple at right and the water tower in the background.

In the photo below, looking up at Serene from beyond the rail lines, men are lining up at the mine offices.

Photographs from Denver Public Library, Western History Department

greatly diluted the United Mine Workers strength. There had been many timid and short-lived strikes since Ludlow, but inept and conciliatory union leadership gained no ground for the miners.

A recession in the early 1920s caused most mine owners, led by the CF&I, largest mineowner in the state, to reduce wages, some to as low as $5 a day, although the so-called "Jacksonville Scale"—$7.75 per day minimum—had been approved years before. The 8-hour day had been approved even before the Ludlow strike, but it was very seldom enforced. Safety measures were little if any better than they had been years before.

In 1927 the miners needed a friend, a strong friend. The UMW couldn't or wouldn't help them. The company union was designed to keep them in line, not to help them.

The Wobblies emerged as the friend in need, seeing this as a golden opportunity—perhaps their last—to regain stature in Colorado. The Wobblies' official name was International Workers of the World. The IWW was born during the early years of this century to unite the blue-collared workers of the world and to better their conditions. With such leaders as Eugene Debs and "Big Bill" Haywood (well known in Colorado), the IWW spread quickly to most industries, including mining, throughout the nation and abroad.

Its militant activities and its spread at the time the Marxist philosophy was rising around the world led many to equate Wobblyism with marxism. The bosses and the mine-owners encouraged this belief, and eventually were able to discredit the IWW. But while it was here, it made its presence known and it helped father other longer-lasting and effective movements. While it lasted its fortunes and influence rose and fell with the situation at hand.

The situation seemed ripe in Colorado in 1927. The Wobblies surfaced, with the aid of outside leaders, particularly from the West Coast, as the spokesman for the coal miners of Colorado.

One technical mistake the Wobblies were blamed for is that they didn't follow proper procedure. One result of the Ludlow strike had been the creation of the Colorado Labor Commission. The Commission gave workers, all workers not just miners, an instrument to present any and all grievances. The Commission in those days was far from what it was meant to be, but its purpose was to hear complaints and investigate them for a 30-day "cooling off" period before the workers could strike or employers could lock them out.

The IWW did not lodge a formal complaint. This is a most interesting critique of IWW tactics, since the mine-owners, the governor and virtually all other state officials did not recognize the IWW as a bargaining agent for the miners or anyone else. They didn't recognize them at all.

The Wobblies attempted to force an audience with mine-owners and officials throughout the state. No one would listen to them. Instead they were called "outlaws," "reds," "outside agitators" and other things. Governor "Billy" Adams and most newspapers throughout the state agreed.

Finally, Wobbly leaders set October 8 as their last day of talking and their first day of striking.

Governor Adams declared immediately that the strike would be illegal and would not be tolerated.

On October 8 several miners in the Boulder area made good the Wobbly threat, walking off their jobs in coal mines around Lafayette, Louisville and Superior. The strike quickly spread to coal mines throughout the state.

Although the strike was statewide, and although many of the Wobbly leaders (local and imported) were headquartered amid the countless mines in the Walsenburg–Trinidad area, a major focal point of the strike soon became the Columbine Mine. The mine was located in a small coal camp, about five miles northeast of Lafayette, with the ironic name of Serene. (Nobody seems to know why it was named that.)

The mine-owners themselves were largely responsible for the Columbine Mine being singled out by the strikers. They let it be known in no uncertain terms that they would not be bullied, that they would keep the mine open at all costs.

And the Columbine Mine itself made it a good target for the strikers.

Although the Columbine was one of the larger coal mines in the region, the town of Serene was smaller (the population in 1927 was 1100) and more isolated than most. Serene was more easily cut off from the outside world and from outside workers. And, despite its name, dingy little Serene epitomized the conditions the miners were striking against.

Each day a growing number of striking miners would make the rounds, picketing the other nearby mines—the Morrison, Imperial, the Puritan, the State—then the bulk of them would gather around Serene, mill about most of the day, occasionally hurling epithets and threatening gestures at non-striking workers and at guards within the fortress of Serene.

Serene was an armed fortress now. Shortly after the strike began, a barbed wire wall was set up around the entire town, with two gates. One gate was on the hill overlooking the mine town and just a few feet from the superintendent's house. This was at the end of a block-long narrow road with barbed wire walls on both sides. This enclosed road was called "no man's land."

The other gate was at the lower end of town, at the end of Main Street. Most of the activity during the strike was at the upper gate, although both gates were blocked several times.

A giant searchlight was set on the tipple (a large skeletal contraption that loads coal cars by "tipping" the shuttle of coal from the mine), and it swept the area continuously during the hours of darkness. Armed

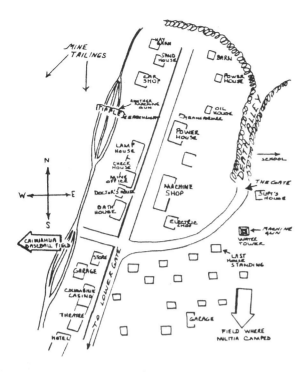

Town Plat of Serene

guards patrolled Serene 24 hours a day. At first they were hired company guards (or "goons" in the vernacular of strikers), then local deputies, then. . . .

Strike activity in other areas of the state helped fire the tension at Serene.

On October 17, Walsenburg businessmen raided the IWW headquarters, burned all the records and told Wobbly leaders to get out of town.

October headlines in the *Boulder Daily Camera* said the Walsenburg jail held 60 picketers—"twenty of them chattering women."

A coal shortage was developing in the Boulder area and elsewhere in the state.

On November 4 Governor Adams, in his almost daily appeal to "decent" miners to get back to work, said all IWW leaders throughout the state would be arrested on sight.

The same day the growing tension at the Columbine Mine made the headlines as pickets stopped and "had words" with non-striking miners working at the mine. Eight local deputies were on duty at Serene.

Monday morning (November 7) dawned to find several hundred picketers choking the roads into Serene. And, newspapers said, there was "vicious intimidation" of all miners who attempted to get through. Only one "Missourian" made it through, by drawing his gun and threatening to shoot his way if necessary. The Columbine closed down.

It reopened the following day, but with only half of the regular work force, the 125 or so non-striking miners living within the confines of Serene. Headlines said the picketing was "near violent" and the intimidation of workers was increasing.

On November 8 picketers blocked the roads to Serene with 150 to 200 autos. Weld County Sheriff Ben Robinson and his deputies, with drawn guns, broke the blockade by escorting non-striking miners through the pickets. Two picketers were arrested.

Nonetheless, picketers broke through the gates of Serene, led by what the newspapers described as a "screaming amazon." The woman urged the men to charge and destroy the tipple despite the threatening guns of the guards. The invaders hesitated and finally withdrew.

Many women paraded and picketed at the side of their striking husbands. Two or three were always at the forefront at Serene. It is doubtful that the "amazon" was Mrs. Beranek, unless the newspapers mistook zeal and energy for size. Mrs. Beranek was a small woman, although she had borne seventeen children and claimed to be the head of the "largest family in Boulder County." She was a fixture in the front line of the picketers, vigorously waving the American flag.

For the first time National Guard airplanes were used to scout strikers' activity on the ground.

There was a growing number of stories of working miners being beaten on their way home, or of "joyriding" strikers taking "pot shots" at non-strikers and their homes. Strikers claimed similar offenses against them and their families, but these stories seldom made their way into the newspapers.

Many of the daily stories concerning Serene and the Columbine mentioned or implied the foreign character of the strikers. A story on November 9 said deputies saw only two "Americans" among the hundreds of strikers. Almost all of the rest were Bulgarians, Mexicans, Greeks and Italians, "many of them incapable of conversing in the English language."

On November 9, Sheriff Robert Blum of Boulder County and four of his deputies were sworn in as "state officers" to give them more authority to freely participate in the guard activities of the Columbine Mine in Weld County.

The work force at the Columbine continued to fluctuate, depending upon how many workers were able to get through the pickets and how much of the resident work force was not intimidated by the gathering strikers. Anywhere from 500 to 1200 strikers and their families would gather around Serene each day, threatening to crash the gates.

They made good their threats on November 12 when between 500 and 600 strikers ignored the pleas of the state police and the deputies, stormed the upper gate and paraded through town, led by a drummer and Mrs. Beranek waving her flag.

Trouble in Serene   225

On November 14, six officers were attacked and beaten when they attempted to arrest the strike leaders. The Columbine closed down again.

As a result of the incidents of the preceding days, Governor Adams warned the strikers that the guards were given orders to shoot if the premises were invaded again. To demonstrate the seriousness of the order, two machine guns were placed at strategic points in Serene. One was mounted halfway up the water tower directly facing the upper gate, the other on the tipple below the gate and near the searchlight.

But even the machine guns did not seem to deter the strikers. They almost crashed the gates on November 16, but cooler heads prevailed.

On Saturday, November 19, an estimated 1200 strikers were turned back from the gates of Serene by the loud, desperate pleas (and threats) of Sheriff Robinson.

On Sunday, more than 1000 strikers and members of their families held a rally in Barker Park. Among the speakers was a Mrs. Robinson, who had been jailed in Walsenburg and who told the crowd not to be intimidated by the machine guns. She knew "from experience" that the guards would never use them. Other speakers were "Duke," a high IWW official from Seattle, and Adam Bell of Lafayette, the top Wobbly leaders in the Boulder region. They and other speakers said such fiery things as "the time is ripe" or "it's now or never" or "we can not allow this situation to continue."

Louis Sherf, chief of the State Law Enforcement Squad, was acting "on a tip," according to newspapers, when he called out every available man to be at Serene on Monday morning. It is said that there were 21 men on duty that morning.

Before dawn on Monday, November 21 (a miner's day began at 5:30, and a striker's day at 5:30 or earlier), a large force of strikers picketed the Morrison Mine, the Puritan and then the State Mine, and began their march to Serene, a little more than a mile away. By the time they reached the long-fenced road of No Man's Land, an estimated 500 to 600 had gathered.

Several stories evolved from the confusion of the next few minutes.

One popular version passed on by some oldtimers is that Mrs. Beranek, alone, first walked down the long, lonely alley to the gate, with her flag in her hand. As she approached the gate, a guard moved forward to greet her on the other side, his rifle ready. Mrs. Beranek asked if she could come in and march through Serene. The guard told her "No" and ordered her to return to the others. Thereupon, this version goes, Mrs. Beranek promptly began to climb the gate. Before she reached the top, the guard struck her on the head with his rifle butt, and she fell unconscious at the foot of the gate, the American flag in the dirt beside her.

Then, and only then, did the other strikers surge forward . . . not to storm the gate, they claimed, but to retrieve Mrs. Beranek and her American flag.

This is a popular version with some oldtimers. Some swear by it. With all the emotion and hatred of the time, one could possibly accept the most supercharged version as the truth. This story has all the ingredients of a union legend.

The guards' version—the one most generally reported in the newspapers—was that IWW leader and "trouble maker" Adam Bell came forward alone. Shots were fired over his head to warn him. Bell called to the others to move forward, that the shots were only blanks. Then, with the others close behind, he acted out the little drama attributed by others to Mrs. Beranek.

Some others, who reflect more calmly on the past, think it was more of a unified charge down the alley. Mrs. Beranek, with her flag, and Adam Bell were probably at the forefront. They usually were.

There is also confusion regarding what happened during the long seconds immediately preceding the firing, and the firing itself. Even newspaper accounts varied.

Some stated that the oncoming strikers threw all matter of rocks and debris at the guards, and that the guards fired several shots over their heads and shouted many warnings. One account said that there was even "hand-to-hand" combat before the shots were fired, and that when "forced to fire," the guards did not use machine guns but rifles.

The first two actions, the rock throwing and the warning shots, were possible, although some recall bitterly that there were no warning shots. No guards were killed and their reported injuries seemed minor, especially when one considers the violence of the strikers and how much they outnumbered the guards. And how about the gate?

The newspapers even pointed up the controversy about the machine-gun fire, a couple of news stories going so far as to say "strikers claim" machine guns were used. The general consensus of the strikers was that at least one machine gun—the one facing the upper gate—was fired.

Jim Fillas remembers that morning well. Jim, former maitre d' of the Denver Press Club, was 14 at the time and living in Lafayette. His father, who was a miner at the Columbine, was on strike but not at the Columbine that morning. Jim and his young friends would follow the strikers wherever they went, hoping to cadge a sandwich the womenfolk prepared for the strikers. That morning Fillas and a friend were walking toward Serene and were less than a mile away when they heard the gunfire break the dark silence. He heard it and swears it was machine-gun fire: "you can certainly tell the difference between machine-gun fire and rifle fire."

The only thing everyone agreed upon was that it was all over within seconds.

After the dust and the din had cleared, several strikers, including two women (Mrs. Beranek was not one of them), lay on the ground at the gate of Serene at the

Miss Josephine Roche in the 1930s, when she was Assistant Secretary of the Treasury under FDR. As a director of the Rocky Mountain Fuel Company, owner of the Columbine Mine, she opposed using force against the strikers in 1927, and was later instrumental in bringing about improved conditions at the mine. (*Denver Public Library Western History Department*)

Above, the tipple of the Columbine mine (*Denver Public Library*); *at right*, the house in Lafayette where Mrs. Beranek, who paraded daily with the strikers at the coal camps, lived with her seventeen children.

Below, skeletal remains of the Morrison Mine tipple.

end of what would be known long after as "Death Alley." Some 60 persons were wounded, 24 seriously enough to be taken to nearby hospitals, mostly Longmont. The seriously wounded included one woman dressed in miner's overalls. She hovered between life and death for days, but did survive.

Three men died at the scene or within minutes of the shooting. Two more died within the next 48 hours. Mike Ridovich fought for his life until November 29, when he became the sixth victim.

Reaction to the "incident" was widespread and varied.

Governor Adams acted immediately. He angrily blamed the striking miners for the bloodshed, declared martial law and called out the State Militia.

A "war parley" was held at noon the same day at the high school athletic field in nearby Erie, and hundreds of striking miners attended. The mood was almost unanimous for gaining revenge, taking over the Columbine and "stringing up" the murderers. Ironically, further tragedy was averted when "Duke," the IWW leader from Seattle who had only the day before urged direct action, now very persuasively talked the strikers out of their disastrous course.

A mass funeral was held for four of the victims in Lafayette a couple of days later. The cemetery was far too small to accomodate the hundreds of miners and their families who attended. The overflow jammed the entire community, and the slow procession past the graves lasted all day.

There were demonstrations all over the country. On November 26, 160 of New York's finest had their hands full containing some 300 persons gathered in Union Square to protest the "Colorado Murderers."

Articles concerning the action appeared in newspapers throughout the country, including the *New York Times*, and magazines such as the *American Mercury*, *Nation*, *Literary Digest* and others.

Another highly significant result of the shootings in Serene was the emergence into international prominence of Josephine Roche. Prior to 1927 Miss Roche had already had a colorful career as Denver's first policewoman—in the city's Red Light District—and as a probation officer for the controversial Judge Ben Lindsey (whose most controversial recommendation was "trial marriages"). During World War I she was stationed in England as a special agent for the Belgian Relief Committee, and later organized the European relief committees in the U.S. under President Hoover. President Woodrow Wilson named her to the directorship of the Foreign Language Information Service. She was also an outspoken leader against child labor, particularly among migrant workers.

She returned to Colorado in the 1920s to be near her father, who was in failing health. Her father just happened to be the president of the Rocky Mountain Fuel Company. When he died in 1927 Miss Roche inherited his stock in the company, then the second largest coal company in Colorado, and became a member of its three-man board.

Her father had been very conservative and strongly anti-union. The other two members of the board were also conservative.

According to a popular story of the time they found out how the new member felt when, hours after the November 21 shootings, she stormed the gates of Serene, took the guns from the guards, and threw them down the mine shaft, declaring there would be no more violence on Rocky Mountain Fuel Company property as long as she was alive.*

Some of the great emotion of the day was manifest in some timely though not necessarily deathless poetry.

As the Wobblies told it:

It was a sad November morning
And the sun began to shine
When a bloody struggle took place
At the gates of Columbine.

Peaceful miners with their families
Marching with our flag that waved
Were met by Company machine guns
That's the game they played.

They murdered the men and women
They did the things the Kaiser did
They used machine guns, bombs and rifles
They opened fire from places hid.

It's the first time in our history
That our flag was shot down
It was carried by a miner
Who laid dead upon the ground.

Governor Adams gave the order
That the state police be sent
For protection to the mine scabs
Who were working for a cent.

All the world cried out in agony,
"Get that Scherf and all his gang
They're the leaders of this tragedy
They are guilty, they must hang."

Those who run the Columbine condemn them
For what happened to our people
They took hands in placing the guns
Which were fired from the tipple.

All the world now is a witness
And will write it down on history's page
That assassins murdered those poor miners
For fighting for a living wage.

---

* This story is told by Jerry Armstrong, current president of Rocky Mountain Fuel Company, who knew Miss Roche well.

The Columbine and Ludlow massacres
Have made the weak and dead arise.
In this great I.W.W.
The whole world will organize.

For the slaying of our members
Who were innocent and peaceful
We shall make this union stronger
Through the world forever grateful.

The State Police retaliated in kind:

It was a sad November morning
And the sun began to shine
When the Wobblies all went crazy
At the gates of Columbine.

Crazy Wobblies and their families
Marching with their Wobblie flag
They were met by well meant warnings
And the game we played was fair.

Only when the Wobblies resisted
Did we open fire on them
And then with rifles and pistols only
And none of us were hid.

We did not drive by in a Ford coupe
And shoot at you and yours,
Yet you holler about fairness
But you're just a bunch of liars.

All the world now is a witness
And will write it down in verse
How the dumb and foolish Wobblies
Committed suicide and called a hearse.

The militia called to Serene was primarily from Fort Collins, Loveland, Boulder and Denver. Many of the guardsmen were very young and many were students. In fact, newspapers often referred to them as "student soldiers." This is a militia sergeant's advice to a rookie on the slag pile:

A dull grey sky above you
A darker earth below you
A whistling wind that sighs and moans
And gives back a sigh so low.

What's that that creeps below in the weeds?
What's that in the sky above?
Why do you jump at the slightest sound,
And cock your rifle at the coo of dove:

The slightest sound will make you shiver
And make your blood run cold.
Why do you hang so close to your rifle?
A soldier on guard should be bold.

You say you expect a fight tonight?
Well what of it you should care
You say you're afraid you might be shot?
Well what's the use of throwing a scare.

Don't worry kid, you'll come through,
And don't be afraid to fight.
You're just a rookie, now, old son,
But keep your nerve, and now "good nite."

There were no budding Shakespeares at Serene, but the feeling was there.

The militia was camped at Serene for three or four weeks, making regular patrols by truck to other "hot spots" in Boulder and Weld Counties. Later they camped at Louisville and Frederick and divided up the patrols. From time to time small squads would remain at certain mines until a threatening situation eased.

There were several minor incidents and many tense situations that could easily have exploded into another "Ludlow Massacre," or worse. Fortunately, it never happened. During the few weeks the militia remained on the scene the mines regained their full work force. It was no secret that known IWW leaders were "blackballed" in Colorado mining camps after that. The "last gasp" of the Wobblies in Colorado ended.

The last of the militia was relieved of active duty on April 6, 1925, and returned to their homes.*

Although the strike had done the miners' lot little good, if any, eventually there was a radical change in labor–management relationships. The change was due solely to Miss Josephine Roche.

Even before that fateful day in November of 1927, she was influential enough to hire liberal lawyer Merle Vincent as company manager. When the strike was imminent, Vincent had ordered the gates of Serene to be left open, and there was to be no shooting although the mine be destroyed. The order was disregarded by mine superintendent Ted Peart, with the support of majority board members D. C. Burns and Horace

---

* The military view of the "insurrection," as the November 21 shooting was called, and the story of the occupation of the Boulder-Weld fields by the Militia, are told in "History of Military Organizations in Colorado," (pp. 246–48), a 1935 thesis by Maj. John H. Nankivell. Copies are found in many local libraries.

Most of the "Serene Story" is contained in reports by Col. P. P. Newlon, Adjutant General of Colorado and in charge of the occupying troops, to "His Excellency" (Governor Adams). He reported that Company F, 157th Infantry of Boulder, and Company H of Fort Collins were relieved within a few days since they were composed "of practically all college men."

One report said that "once again the presence of troops had the usual pacifying effect and at no time during the tour of active duty was it found necessary to resort to extreme measures to enforce peace. The 45th Tank Company was a potent factor in maintaining tranquility in the disaffected area, and the grim, but silent threat of the tanks had a decidedly quiescent effect on the turbulent elements. The company was relieved from active duty on Feburary 8, 1928, and returned to its home station, Denver, on the same date."

Bennett. Peart worked with the state police *to break up the strike and crush the strikers, deepening the emotion of the time.

Because of her actions following the shootings, Miss Roche was declared incompetent by Burns and Bennett, who attempted to have her removed from the board. They didn't know her very well. Due to the strike and for other reasons, Rocky Mountain Fuel Company, like most other Colorado coal companies, was in financial straits. Instead of being dumped by the board, Miss Roche, through some very complex manipulations and with support and money from—of all people—President John L. Lewis of the United Mine workers, was able to gain majority stock in the fuel company.

Through company reorganization the Rocky Mountain Fuel Company came up with, no doubt, the most unlikely partnership in the long history of management–labor relationships. Miss Roche became company president, believed to be the first woman ever to become president of a giant corporation. "Elected" as her vice president was John Lawson, longtime head of the Colorado UMW during and before and after the Coalfield War of 1913–14.†

In just a short period as vice president, Lawson was able to do more for Colorado coal miners than in all his long frustrating years as union leader. He wrote the new union contract, a major landmark in union contracts up to that time and as progressive as the best Eastern contract. The principle of the contract was spelled out: ". . . the men employed are as much an essential factor in the industry as the capital investment in it, and have independent rights in the determination of working and living conditions. . . ."

Rocky Mountain Fuel Company, the second largest coal producer in Colorado behind the CF&I, was the first company to sign a UMW contract, and was the first union shop in the state. The contract provided the highest wages, adhered strictly to the eight-hour day, provided a worker's platform for grievances, insured correction of unsafe conditions and practices.

The contract attracted the best workers, and not only greatly improved their working and living conditions but enhanced company production and efficiency. Production increased nearly 30 percent, and the company was able to weather cutbacks and financial setbacks that hit other companies hard. All this didn't ingratiate Miss Roche with the other companies, particularly since the vast inroads made in the Rocky Mountains by the UMW

greatly enhanced the spread of unionism among miners throughout Colorado.

One wonders what the history of coal mining in Colorado would be if Josephine Roche had been born earlier and had been active during the early years of this century, say before Ludlow. But even her powerful force could not have combated the effects of the Depression of the 1930s and the increasing losses in the coal fields as America turned to other sources of fuel.

The nature of the battle she faced is demonstrated by the fact that the national union was behind her and lent the company money. Miss Roche herself worked without salary much of the time. And the miners invested money when they could and volunteered work to keep the company going.

But the times were against it.

In 1932, she was forced to lower wages, as did the rest of the industry. Through the 1930s there were ups and downs, but in general a recession in coal mining. Production decreased almost steadily. Wages were forced to stay low. Unemployment grew in coal mining as elsewhere. Miss Roche even drew criticism from another liberal who would soon be her boss, President Roosevelt, who questioned her attempts to maintain higher wages when everyone else was asked to "tighten their belts." But Eleanor Roosevelt praised Miss Roche in one of her columns, when she told of her battle against hardship during seasonal layoffs by donating land on coal properties for gardening and farming by miners' families.

It was during the 1930s that Miss Roche turned again to politics in an effort to battle the growing depression.

She worked long hours for the Senate candidate Edward P. Costigan, called Colorado's "Fighting Progressive." Costigan was elected. In 1934, Miss Roche herself ran against moderate Democrat Ed Johnson for the party's nomination to U.S. Senate. It was a vigorous campaign, but she narrowly lost.

Only days after the general election President Roosevelt appointed her Assistant Secretary of the Treasury, the second woman ever to receive such a high post. She was placed in charge of the National Health Service. President Roosevelt named her director of the newly-created National Youth Administration in 1935.

She resigned in September of 1937 and returned to Colorado and the Rocky Mountain Fuel Company, in an attempt to keep the failing company afloat. She received a loan from the Reconstruction Finance Company. It only delayed the inevitable. One by one the Rocky Mountain Fuel Company mines in Colorado closed. The Columbine Mine was the last one to close; Miss Roche was obliged to file for bankruptcy in 1944.

In 1947 she became an assistant to John L. Lewis. The following year she was put in charge of the UMW pension fund. She divided her time during the next few years between union activities and the dormant Rocky Mountain Fuel Company, until she resigned in 1971

---

* Primarily through lawyer Vincent, countless charges were brought against the state police, and the American Civil Liberties Union (ACLU) asked for an inquiry into "the brutality and lawlessness of the state police."

† The powerful story of John Lawson and the Coalfield War is told in the Colorado classic *Up from the Depths*, by Barron Beshoar.

because of failing health. She remained in Washington, D. C., and acted as a consultant to Presidents and government and union officials. She died July 29, 1976, at the age of 80.

Serene and the Columbine Mine were already forgotten in history. It had been opened in 1914 on what promised to be an almost endless seam of coal. After the bitterness of the 1927 strike, and largely due to the efforts of Josephine Roche, the town and the mine blossomed for a few short years. A new shaft was open. The population of Serene topped 2000, and a new suburb called CHIHUAHUA was built across the tracks, west of Serene. The baseball field was here, and the Serene–Chihuahua baseball team was one of the best in the region. The Columbine Casino was one of the busiest saloons around.

The town was already well on its way to being a ghost town when the mine closed. The school closed. The baseball field was covered by weeds. The railroad track was abandoned and the tracks were pulled up.

Many of the homes and buildings were already empty. The population was down to 200 in 1950. The residents worked in Erie or Lafayette, if they had a job. Most of the other homes and buildings were abandoned during the 1950s, and the "ghost town killers" moved in: time, weather and vandals. Target shooters whose cars carry such righteous bumper stickers as "The West Wasn't Won With a Registered Gun" are shooting up the last vestiges of the Old West, and they thoroughly shot up the last few buildings of Serene. Bricks, wiring and "ghost town wood" had been taken from some other buildings, hastening their demise. During 1971 and 1972 the Rocky Mountain Fuel Company tore down the few remaining buildings for salvage. As a company official explained, if they didn't tear down the buildings "the vandals will." He said some local teenagers had held a rock concert a year or two before, and "there went two buildings."

At least we can be assured that Serene had some music—although too late.

Today the foundations are obscured by weeds. Most prominent among the ruins are the cement bases that once held the tipple. They are down by the mountainous slagpile. On the last visit, the gate post was still standing at the end of what once was "Death Alley" and near what once was the superintendent's house.

Much of Serene's life was drudging and troublesome. It also had many happy and historic times.

May she rest in peace.

Epilog: Returning to Serene

To the author who has chased ghost towns throughout the West most of his adult life, Serene was not just another ghost town—it was "family."

Ghost-towners get their leads to a new ghost town from countless sources: old maps, books, directories, friends, fellow ghost-towners, complete strangers, etc. I was "put on" to Serene by "Pappy." Pappy was my stepfather, Carl Howard Haberl.

When Governor "Billy" Adams called out the National Guard the day after the shooting at Serene, a sergeant in Loveland Troop C, a budding reporter named Fred G. Eberhart (who just happened to have left at home, among other things, a three-year-old son with a name very similar to mine) was called. Also called was a sergeant from the Denver company, the above mentioned Carl Howard Haberl. (Another Denver "student soldier" during this period was William "Uncle Bill" Shay, a lifelong friend of Pappy's and his adopted family, longtime curator of Fort Laramie, Wyoming, and one of the top experts of Western military history.)

Although Pappy was a member of the Denver Troop B, he had been working in the mines in Cripple Creek at the time, was sympathetic with the miners' cause, and had strong misgivings about being called for this sort of action.

At Serene and during the other activities in those trying days at the end of 1927, he met and became fast friends with Sgt. Eberhart. Later he would meet Mrs. Eberhart (whose *nom de plume* was Eve Bennett), and ten years later Pappy married her and took on the horrendous responsibility of helping her raise six live-wire children.

It was only because I was involved in seeking out ghost towns elsewhere that I didn't look into Serene years ago. Once I did, I became totally absorbed, not only because of its family relationship, but because of its unique name and its well-hidden but significant past.

I was disappointed that Pappy didn't seem to share my excitement as he returned to Serene with me after all those years. Although he has lived in the Denver–Boulder area all of his life, he never deemed it necessary to revisit the "historic town" nearby. The weather on our return helped further dampen his enthusiasm. Although it was the spring of 1971, it was cold and blustery. The wind went through a person.

The chilling wind helped take him back those 44 years since he was last there. The student soldiers camped in an open field just south of Serene. It was a particularly cold winter and the knifelike wind swept the field constantly. He said the wind "cut through everything you wore, and you wore everything you had."

That wasn't the only reason Pappy remembers Serene as the "Hell Hole of Creation." He remembers the water was terrible and the food was worse. The guardsmen devoted a large part of their time and energy to the rituals of dysentery and diarrhea. The facilities to attend these epidemic conditions were not the most alluring.

All in all, one may understand why Pappy was not

THE FINAL DESTRUCTION

Serene in the early 1970s was slowly turning to rubble. The house where the superintendent used to live was still standing (*left*) in 1971, but two years later it is in ruins (*opposite*). The former wash house and bath house were in the last stages of destruction by the elements.

OF AN HISTORIC
COLORADO TOWN

In 1973, what's left standing is shown above and at right. At left, "Pappy" in 1971, pointing to where Main Street was.

The gatepost and part of Serene's historic gate remain today, just a few feet from the ruins of the Superintendent's house and at the end of what was called Death Alley.

overly excited about returning to Serene. It didn't evoke fond memories.

There was some disappointment also, on my part, in the difficulty Pappy had in orienting himself after we arrived in what little was left in Serene. But, thinking about it, that could be understandable also. After all, it had been 44 years, and when Pappy was last here, as an "outsider," Serene was a "big city" with scores of buildings. Now there were only six ruins left.

And Pappy remembered that much of the town's activities revolved around Main Street and the railroad tracks about a block west of Main Street. No trace remained of either.

Slowly Pappy got his bearings. He remembered the superintendent's house, although it was surrounded by other houses and buildings then, and has since been painted a different color, and has greatly deteriorated. It was the "infamous" gate that helped him remember that. Down below there was also the large foundation and cement footings where the tipple used to be. Ruins of buildings running south from the tipple included the latch building, still in fair shape, and the mine office, in complete ruins. Next to that had been the doctor's office, now completely gone. Next, and easiest to remember, was the bath house, on the corner. It was still in pretty good shape then and still showed 250 locker

spaces. These ruins were completely dismantled and trucked away in 1972 and 1973.

Pappy remembered that Main Street extended south from the bath house.

Across from the bath house at the beginning of Main Street was the gas station and garage, then a food and merchandise store, the casino, a 13-room hotel and a carriage house. Prohibition was still in force in 1927. Pappy recalled that there was plenty of "bathtub booze" available, but the Casino had not been built yet. (Bob Brown, fellow ghost-towner and collector of such things, has seen a token worth five cents in trade at the Columbine Casino in Serene.)

Jim Fillas also recalls a second hotel in Serene, about a block east of Main Street and operated by a Chinese family.

The author has returned many times to witness the systematic destruction of another Colorado ghost town. Pappy never thought it necessary to return again. He did his duty—back in 1927, and again to his step-son in 1971. He had no great affinity for Serene.*

Now, there is nothing to go back to.

---

* Pappy died July 12, 1979. His longtime friend, William "Bill" Shay died a short time later.

ACKNOWLEDGMENTS

A very special thanks to five people.

First, Sandy, my wife-typist-editor-critic-artist-map-maker and fellow explorer. During college, while gathering and publishing a book of college songs, I said with youthful bravado: "I started this collection alone, but eventually I found someone who became instrumental in the compilation and who was a wizard with the typewriter — so I married her. I hope to continue writing books so that we will not be wed in vain." Some six (or ten) books, four children, eight grandchildren and 36 years later, we are still looking for answers but are more relaxed in the pursuit.

Next, thanks to my dear sister, Mrs. Pat Blosser. She did virtually all the final typing, retyping and typing again for the book, and, by her inherent nature and to compensate for her brother's failings, also functioned as severe critic, editor and much-needed grammarian and master speller.

A great many people read parts and/or chapters of the manuscript, but three experts suffered through the entire thing word by word, making countless valuable recommendations, suggestions and corrections. I am sincerely humbled by their interest and assistance. They are Francis Rizzari, lifelong friend and one of Colorado's premier ghost-towners; Eleanor Gehres, head of the invaluable Western History Department of the Denver Public Library; and Tom Noel, Director of The Colorado Studies Center at the University of Colorado in Denver, and author of highly successful books about Denver and the West (*Denver: Rocky Mountain Gold,* and *Denver's Larimer Street,* to mention a couple).

Despite their careful and dedicated scrutiny, there are bound to be errors in a book of this kind. This cannot be blamed on my expert readers. The blame rests with the author, who apologizes and requests the readers' help in weeding them out.

I hesitate to mention more names because I know I will leave out a bunch of them, including the countless friendly and helpful people in the small towns and along the roads throughout eastern Colorado who answered questions and pointed directions.

Some took more time to be helpful, including (in no particular order) Jim Filis, Bette Peters, Bill Hosokawa, Willard Louden, Tom and Thelma Roberts, Bob McQuarie, Larry Steele, Ann Matlack, Pat and Buck Jones, Valentine Coppa, Stan and Kelly Weston, Bill O'Rourke, Inez Hunt, Albert Foos, Arthur Ortega, Art Mariyo, Harry Chrisman, George O'Malley, Jim Davis, Sue Ann Nieniman, Britt Storey, Jim and Mary Lou Egan, Ed Smith, Doc and Nedra Jenkins, Jack and Mabel Fowler, Ed Reutz, Mary Jensen, Patrick Echman, Hal Haney, Al Knight, Greg Chancellor, Virginia Bushman, and Frances Melrose.

We can't forget the many people at city, state and Federal agencies, including many libraries and museums, the Colorado Parks Department, Bureau of Mines, U.S. Bureau of Reclamation, Geological Service, Conservation Service, Bureau of Outdoor Recreation and others.

As for photographs, I would have liked to have reproduced many more previously unseen photos from family albums and other hidden treasure troves. I will continue to dig, and hope that this book will spur more people to dust off their photographic jewels and share them before the faces and places are lost forever.

Besides the private sources, I had a great deal of institutional assistance in amassing photographs, most of them previously unpublished or rare. Many thanks to Augie Mastrogiuseppe and Kathy Swan of the Western History Department, Denver Public Library; Diane Rabson of the State Historical Society; Linda Bushman of the Littleton Historical Museum; Joan Dodds and Noreen Stringfellow of the Pueblo Public Library; Carol Roark and Marni Sandweiss of the Amon Carter Museum of Fort Worth, Texas; Shirley Coe, Phyllis Hamilton, Bob Pauline and Jim Todd of the Bureau of Reclamation; Fred Pottorf of the Holly Publishing Company; Glen Aultman of Aultman Studios, Trinidad; and Bev Carlson, Jackie Conner, Ron Money and Bill Wissinger of Adams County.

SOURCES

Most of the mapping was based on the maps of the U.S. Geological Service, which seem to get better and more detailed all the time. It is particularly heartening to see the Service pay attention to and chart more historical sites and trace the historic trails. The USGS had started a wonderful series of historical maps for various regions of Colorado. I hope they continue. Another map that was most helpful was the Rocky Mountain Railroad Club Hotchkiss Historical Railroad Map of Colorado, republished in 1963.

Scholars have criticized me in the past for not listing, in order, every one of my sources, and *ibid*ing and *op cit*ing my readers to death. I apologize. I'm not built that way. I even tried it once and I found that the *ibids* and *op cits* were taking all the fun and excitement out of the chase. However, in the hope of uncurling some of the raised eyebrows I have included more and more of my sources in the text as part of the normal flow of the writing. I especially tried to do this where there might possibly be some question regarding the point at hand. As in the past, if there was some dispute over a fact, I tried to point up both sides rather than leave it out altogether —a holding action until we can get closer to the truth, if ever.

Time and space can be saved by not listing every newspaper, article and book used in tracking down the material, and the dates and pages thereof. Suffice it to say that all the usual sources listed in previous books were used as well as the hundreds of useful books published since. In addition to the extensive use made of past editions of *The Denver Post, Rocky Mountain News*, and *Pueblo Chieftain and Star Journal*, virtually every past and present newspaper on the Colorado Plains was referred to, as I checked out the microfilm sources cataloged in the indexes of the Denver Public Library and Colorado Historical Society. I cited many of these sources in the text, as well as the book sources used in special areas.

Of course, there were several sources that were most valuable, and essential to any study of this sort. I am often asked, "Where do you start?" The most logical start, it would seem, is with the most comprehensive "Ghost Town Card File," in the Historical Society library. These cards list private interviews and other materials collected by the Works Progress Administration (WPA) during the 1930s. Beautiful! From there, the logical progression is to the microfilm of the file cards gathered over the decades (along with many other things of great value to Colorado) by the late James Grafton Rogers, former State Historian. These microfilms are also at the State Historical Society. From there one branches out to the many card indexes and business directories; "[George] Crofutt's Grip-Sack Guide of Colorado," the 1885 edition of which was recently reprinted by Francis Rizzari, Richard Ronzio and the late Charles S. Ryland (Johnson Publishing, Boulder); *Colorado* Magazine, printed by the Colorado Historical Society; The Yearbooks published until recent years by the Denver Posse of Westerners; the wonderful T.F. Dawson Notebooks, also at the SHS; Ralph C. Taylor's longtime column, "Colorful Colorado," which appeared weekly in the *Pueblo Star-Journal and Sunday Chieftain*, and his books, particularly *Colorado, South of the Border*; Harry E. Chrisman's books and the many wonderful railroad books; *The First Hundred Years*, by the late Robert L. Perkin; and *Colorado's Century of Cities*, by Don and Jean Griswold.

Regional or county histories, many spurred by the Colorado Centennial celebration in 1976, were good reading and useful. Some of these were: *Action on the Plains*, published by the Yuma County Historical Society; the many "Western Yesterdays" by Forest Crossen; the three volumes of *Over Hill and Vale*, by the late Harold Marion Dunning; *Our Side of the Mountain*, by Emma Michell (Comanche Crossing Historical Society); and the books and articles of Janet Le Compt.

Index of Towns

General Index

Page numbers in italics indicate photographs.

Runyon, Damon   183
Rush Creek   133
Russell Gulch   162
Russell, William Green   161, 162
Russell(ville) Gulch   161, 162
Russians   144
Russian thistle   144
Rustlers   82
Ruth, Babe   222
Ruxton, George Frederick   18
Ryland, Charles S.   170
Ryssby (Smaland), Sweden   100
Ryssby Church   98-102, *101*

Sacco, Nicola   222
Sage, Rufus   22
St. Charles (San Carlos) River   2, 69, 73
St. Joseph Church and Cemetery   72
St. Josephs, Mo.   14
St. Louis   13, 69, 73, 74, 82, 115, 141, 201, 216
St. Vrain Cemetery (near Huerfano)   72
St. Vrain, Ceran   70, 71
St. Vrain County   118
St. Vrain Ditch Co.   119
St. Vrain, Golden City and Colorado Wagon Road   28, 119
St. Vrain River   22, 98, 118
Salvation Army   200-206
Sand Creek   11, 13, 54, 131, 170
Sand Creek Massacre   11, 13, *113*, 131, 132, 200, 210, 218
Sandeen, Rev. L. J.   102
Sangre de Cristo Mountains   1, 38, 44
Sangre de Cristo Pass   39, 44, 173, 175
San Luis Valley   1, 44, 173
Santa Fe, N.M.   20, 25, 74, 78, 210
Santa Fe Railroad (AT&SF RR)   20, 38, 62, 67, 92, 94, 110, 132, 133, 137, 212
Santa Fe Stage   5, 8
Santa Fe Trail   8, 20, 21, 22, 24, 36, 62, 69, 86, 92, 114
Sargent, Marvin   42
Schilling, T. C.   42
Schilling Tea Co.   42
Schramm, Dr. Raimon Herron Von   122, *123*, 124
Schramm, Mary   124
Schwangunks (The Gunks), New York   183
Scott City, Kansas   1
Scott County State Park, Kansas   1
Scott, David E.   127
Scottish   82
Scott, P. (or D.) G.   212
"Screaming Amazon"   225
Seattle, Washington   226
Sedalia, Colo.   136
Sedalia, Missouri   136
Sedgwick County   215

Sedgwick, Gen. John   218
Seibert, Colo.   127
Seldon (fireman)   106
Serafina (Autobees)   69fn
Serene-Chihuahua Baseball Team   231
Shannon grain elevator   54
Sharp, Tom   38-40, *39, 40*, 173, *174*
Shay, William "Uncle Bill"   231, 234fn
Sherf, Louis   226, 228
Shenandoah, Va.   73
Sheridan, Colo.   25, 195
Sheridan, Gen. Phil   124
Sheridan Town Co.   124
"Shian Pass" (Cheyenne Pass)   119
Shirk, Irene   49
Shrafroth, Gov. John   207
Shoemaker, Eli   212
"Shoot 'em Up Days"   115
"Shot Gun Wedding"   53
Silsby, Dr.   85
Silva, Jesus   *36*
Silver King Mine   166
Silver Moon Hotel   107
Silver Site Mine   166
Silvis, J. B.   *90*
Simon, Magdalena   109
Simpson, George   69, 73, 76
Sinclair, Upton   149, 154
Sioux Indians   112, 218
Skull Canyon   164, 166
Slade, Joseph "Black Jack"   14-16, *15*, 218
Slade, Virginia Dale   14
Smaland, Sweden   100
Smith and Cluny   54
Smith, A. B.   128
Smith Canyon   82
Smith, Cornelius   88
Smith, James H.   141
Smoky Hill Trail   5-9, 13, 34, 36, 94, 105, 106, 109, 116, 161
"Smoky Hill Trail" by Dr. Margaret Long   11, 14, 34, 36, 116
Smoot, Ira   67
Smythe, Pete   29, 29fn
Snowshoe Itinerant   25
Sodbusters   83
"Sodom and Gomorrah of the Plains   96
Sopris Cemetery   140
Sopris, Gen. Elbridge B.   138
Sopris High School   138
Sopris Mine   138
South America   77
South Boulder Canyon   182, 187
South Boulder Creek   115
South Dakota   144
Southern Overland Mail   20
South Pacific   146
South Park   29, 118
South Platte Canyon   191
South Platte Ditch   12, 13, 65

South Platte River   9, 24, 25, 135, 162, 181, 215
South Platte Valley   65
Southwestern Colony   120
Spain   115
Spanish   1, 115, 175
Spanish-American War   122
Spanish Peaks   114
Sparrow, Joe   93-94
Speer, Mayor Robert W.   191
Sporleder, Louis D.   114
Spotsylvania   218
Sprague, Sara (or Arah)   23
Springer, New Mexico   212
Springfield, Colo.   60, 88, 89, 90, 128, *128*, 165, 166
Squaw Hill   47
Squawman   9
Squirrel Creek   50
Standard Oil Co.   179
Stanley, Clyde   55
Stanton, F. J.   167
Starkville, Colo.   156
Starr, Belle   206
Starr, Henry   206
Starvation Trail   5, 5fn
State Bank of Amity   202, 206
State Law Enforcement Squad   225, 226
State Mine   224, 226
Staubur, Col.   167
Steamboat Springs, Colo.   193
Steele, R. W.   28, 29
Sterling, Colo.   10, 11, 13, 55, 65, 115
Sterling Ditch   115
Sterling, Illinois   115
Sterling Overland Park   10
Stevens Gulch (Platte Canyon)   192
Stevens, Howard   146
Stewart, L. B.   *26*
"Stock Exchange"   122
Stockton, L. C.   183
Stockyards (Denver Union)   170
Stone Age Fair   49, *49*
Stonington Journal, The   92
Stonington Sentinel, The   92
Story, Veryl   147
Strasburg, Colo.   14, 106, 213
Stratton, Colo.   128
Strode, Stephen S.   127
Stromquist, Pastor Luther   102
"Student Soldiers"   229, 231, 229fn
Suaso, Marie de la Cruz, (Doyle)   73, 76, *75*
Summit Springs   220, 221
Sun Dance   131
Sundust Mining & Milling Co.   166
Sunnyslope School   53
Sunrise Saloon   89
Superior, Colo.   224
Swallows Cemetery   133
"Sweat House"   73
Sweden   98, 100, 102
Swedish Lutheran Church   48